CONTEMPORARY SOCIETY: TRIBAL STUDIES

Edited by

DEEPAK KUMAR BEHERA
and
GEORG PFEFFER

VOLUME ONE	—	STRUCTURE AND PROCESS
VOLUME TWO	—	DEVELOPMENTAL ISSUES, TRANSITION AND CHANGE
VOLUME THREE	—	SOCIAL CONCERN
VOLUME FOUR	—	SOCIAL REALITIES
VOLUME FIVE	—	THE CONCEPT OF TRIBAL SOCIETY
VOLUME SIX	—	TRIBAL SITUATION IN INDIA
VOLUME SEVEN	—	IDENTITY, INTERVENTION AND IDEOLOGY IN TRIBAL INDIA AND BEYOND
VOLUME EIGHT	—	STRUCTURE AND EXCHANGE IN TRIBAL INDIA AND BEYOND

The Editors

George Pfeffer is Professor and Head of the Institute of Ethnology, Free University of Berlin (Germany).

Deepak Kumar Behera is Professor and Head of the Department of Anthropology, Sambalpur University, Sambalpur, Orissa (India).

CONTEMPORARY SOCIETY.

VOLUME EIGHT
STRUCTURE AND EXCHANGE IN
TRIBAL INDIA AND BEYOND

CONTEMPORARY SOCIETY: TRIBAL STUDIES

VOLUME EIGHT

STRUCTURE AND EXCHANGE IN TRIBAL INDIA AND BEYOND

Edited by

GEORG PFEFFER
Freie Universität Berlin
Institut für Ethnologie
Drosselweg 1–3
D-14195 Berlin
Germany

DEEPAK KUMAR BEHERA
Department of Anthropology
Sambalpur University
Sambalpur–768 019
Orissa
India

CONCEPT PUBLISHING COMPANY, NEW DELHI-110 059

Associate Editor Dr. Nibedita Nath and Dr. Rashmi Pramanik

ISBN-13: 978-81-7022-640-6 (Series) ISBN-10: 81-7022-640-6 (Series)
ISBN-13: 978-81-8069-623-7 (Vol. VIII) ISBN-10: 81-8069-623-5 (Vol. VIII)

First Published 2009

Published and Printed by

Concept Publishing Company
Regd. Office:
A/15-16, Commercial Block, Mohan Garden
New Delhi-110059 (India)
Phones : 25351460, 25351794, *Fax* : 091-11-25357109
Email: publishing@conceptpub.com,
website: www.conceptpub.com

Editorial Office:
H-13, Bali Nagar, New Delhi-110 015, India.

Cataloging in Publication Data--*Courtesy:* **D.K. Agencies (P) Ltd. <docinfo@dkagencies.com>**

Contemporary society : tribal studies / edited by Deepak Kumar Behera, Georg Pfeffer.
v. 8 cm.
Contributed articles.
Includes bibliographical references and index.
Contents: v. 8. Structure and exchange in tribal India and beyond.
ISBN 13: 9788170226406 (set) ISBN 10: 8170226406 (set)
ISBN 13 9788180696237 (v. 8) ISBN 10: 8180696235 (v. 8)

1. Tribes--India. 2. India--Scheduled tribes. 3. Ethnology --India. 4. India--Social conditions. I. Behera, Deepak Kumar, 1956-- II. Pfeffer, Georg, 1943-

DDC 307.772 095 4 21

ACKNOWLEDGEMENTS

We are grateful to all the contributors to the volume. The academic generosity of the contributors has enabled us to complete this volume successfully. We would like to thank German Research Council, Anthropological Survey of India and Indian Council of Social Science Research for providing us financial support to organize the International Conference "Tribal Society in India and Beyond," at the Department of Anthropology, Sambalpur University. The volume would not have seen the light of the day without the conference. We also thank all others who helped us directly or indirectly for bringing the volume to its present shape. Last but not the least, we are thankful to Concept Publishing Company, New Delhi for publishing this volume.

GEORG PFEFFER
DEEPAK KUMAR BEHERA

CONTENTS

SECTION IV
DESCENT PATTERNS: MIDDLE AND NORTH EAST INDIA

SECTION V
ADMINISTRATIVE "TRIBES" OR ANTHROPOLOGICAL TYPES

STRUCTURE AND EXCHANGE IN TRIBAL INDIA AND BEYOND: An Introduction

GEORG PFEFFER and DEEPAK KUMAR BEHERA

The term "tribe" as such is devoid of any evaluative content, although those who have applied it, whether pejoratively or in praise, may have added value judgements. Thus it is well known that Tacitus, writing in the first century AD, did not really compose a descriptive account of the German Tribes beyond the borders of the Roman Empire but stressed the allegedly tribal purity and equality in contrast to Caesarean autocracy. He simply expressed his nostalgia for the Roman Republic of the past[1]. Similarly Ibn Khaldun (1332–1406), writing on the *assabiya*, *i.e.* the spirit of collective solidarity among the pure and poor nomadic tribesmen of the desert, described the moral alternative to the sluggish and selfish Arab townsmen[2].

Such ideological colouring of the designation "tribe" is obvious in innumerable publications, but *not* a given quality of its etymological content. Being derived from Latin *tribus*, the word was originally a simple reference to "one-third of the people", or to one of the three, supposedly basic, segments distinguishing the people in the Italian region Latium, *i.e.* *Ramnes* (Latins), *Tities* (Sabines), and *Luceres* (Etruscans)[3]. A simple quantitative partition is the only semantic content of a term that was later impregnated with a variety of qualitative connotations. The tribal or segmentary kind of society became the very focus of the new anthropological discipline in the 19th and 20th century. In his classic text on *Tribesmen*, Marshall D. Sahlins[4] characterized the cultural formation as "at once structurally decentralized and functionally generalized" (1968: viii). Sahlins also elaborated on the recent tribal history as follows:

> "Modern civilization knows no borders: those curious peoples beyond the pale have been drawn into the main sphere....Once discovered, they were rapidly colonized, baptized, and culturally traumatized—'acculturated'—is the technical term. And now, having bit deeply into native custom, civilization allows itself the luxury of an intellectual digestion: the primitives are largely anthropologized." (1968: 1)

With the independence of most African nations in the 1960s, however, the term "tribe" was mostly discarded for reasons of the ideological kind. The originally neutral word had been enriched with far-reaching value-ideas and then removed without successor because such distinctive connotations were said to belong to an obsolete era of colonialism and/or romanticism. Morton H. Fried[5], however, offered analytical reasons when pleading against the concept. "(V)aguely defined and grossly overlapping populations" should not be provided "with the minimal organization required for their manipulation" (1975: iii). For Fried, the tribe, was a "secondary" phenomenon.

> "While some of its manifestations go back five millennia or more to the appearance of the earliest states, the major locus of tribal formation has been in the period of European colonialism and imperialism" (*ibid.* 10).

The concept of "tribe" was too vague for him. Fried, unlike the Boasians, needed neatly cut societal boundaries for the units of his theory of politico-economic evolution. Later the "textualist" Clifford[6] (1988: 191; 321) based his somewhat different arguments against the term upon this earlier rejection by the "materialist" Fried. Both authors seemed to focus their attention upon the particularly tragic situation of tribes in North America, just as popular and non-anthropological fashions of "the west" were employed to strengthen academic positions. Like almost all other representatives of theoretical anthropology, Fried and Clifford appeared to be totally unaware of the situation in South Asia.

In India the Constitution reserves certain privileges for some 84 million[7] members of the *Scheduled Tribes (ST)*, a bureaucratic category. These have been the favourite subject of Indian anthropological research over the past century, but, to our knowledge, none of the authors have distinguished the administrative from the anthropological category, as applied elsewhere in the world and as is applicable to many other units of the Indian population who have "missed" the *ST* status for a variety of reasons. Thus the self-conscious terminological scruples of many "western" anthropologists have in no way affected the self-understood Indian classification of "tribals", as the standard topic of anthropology. Whereas tribal formations in North-western Europe were dissolved by the highly effective "kinship policy" of the Roman Church[8] more than a thousand years ago, tribal people of India may themselves be anthropologists or, as was the case at the end of the last century, Speaker of the Union Parliament (*Lok Sabha*). In the light of such equivocal conceptions, the present volume will debate and perhaps clarify some ambiguities of the theoretical, historical and ethnographic kind. Non-Indians will be confronted with "tribes" as a contemporary and regular feature of India and Indian participants with overseas' controversies on the very existence of tribes so that established positions may be questioned.

The present volume begins with a comparative essay by Paula Rubel and Abraham Rosman who, during the past decades, have distinguished themselves by major researches on Mongol Society, on the well-known *potlatch* of the Amerindians settled on the North American north-west coast and on the peoples of Highland, New Guinea. The authors now develop an evolutionary proposition of societal structures, *i.e.* systematic patterns of ideas on society, that are being articulated through public demonstrations of systematic exchanges. Their comparative examples also contrast the famous Trobriand Islanders and the Yanömami of Venezuela with Indian Caste concepts and European or Japanese versions of feudalism.

This cross-cultural comparison of formal patterns of exchange on a global basis is followed by two detailed ethnographic cases, or two local examples, of such social structures. Tina Otten demonstrates how a grand fertility ritual, largely organised and executed by women, annually ties acephalous indigenous communities of the Koraput plateau in southern Orissa to the Micro-king of the region in a demonstration of an explicit "flower-friend" type of allegiance that can hardly be interpreted as an administrative measure. In the other ethnographic case Roland Hardenberg elaborates how the Kond *re-create* their society in the grand buffalo sacrifice. Until the middle of the nineteenth century, this used to be a human sacrifice and numerous colonial and post-colonial historians and anthropologists have dwelt upon the exceptional occurrence in a sensationalist manner but not as a Maussian total social fact. All base their reports on the same sources of about 150 years ago. Hardenberg is the first ethnographer to experience the sacrifice as a participant observer for more than a dozen times, to describe its total, lengthy and complex arrangement and to elucidate the – unchanged – cultural logic of the Kond structure of exchange.

The subsequent contributions offer original research on the central sociological issue of affinity. Chris Gregory, after extended fieldwork in the Bastar District of Chhattisgarh, introduces a perspective of affinal exchanges based neither upon ego-centric nor upon socio-centric reckoning but, as he calls it, on an "us-centric" classification thus explaining what used to be called "dual organisation" in the old literature. Uwe Skoda follows up elaborating on a kind of marriage preference he himself has recorded during his longterm participant observation in the Kuchinda Subdivision of north-western Orissa. This so-called "sister's husband's sister marriage" is closely connected with preferences found all over tribal middle India and known as "marriages in alternating generations".

The next section of the book, offering original ethnography once again, introduces the constitutions of two Indian societies as wholes. Both Peter Berger and Roland Hardenberg have lived in mud huts of tribal villages for more than a year, learnt the languages of their hosts and participated in their work and in their rituals to understand the indigenous concept of the societal whole as is integrated in a greater Indian environment and as is constituted by a limited number of totemic clans and lower order territorial and descent categories. The order of descent, so their indirect message, must not be confounded with textbook examples of African societies, since the relational patterns of the Indian Tribes follows a logic of an entirely different kind, even though the house, the local descent group, the village and the concepts of a tribal territory also make up a series of inclusive wholes.

As a striking contrast to these Orissan constitutions, Piet Erasmus, on the other hand, emphasizes the identity of the South African Koranna as individuals and *only* as individuals. Notions of a tribal past are traced through individual genealogies and detailed histories of events as experienced by individuals. The idea of a greater whole is ultimately discarded in general, as is illustrated by the specific case, whereas the unit called "tribe" may be seen as a construction of interested individuals within the contemporary socio-political setup. The obvious discrepancy between Erasmus' approach and the participant observation of Berger and Hardenberg, leading to quite contrary results, is well-suited to contrast the effects of two different courses of history: on the one hand, the Kond and the Gadaba of tribal India have been by and large left alone as long as memory lasts, or experienced gradual and mostly indirect interferences by the agencies of Indian states. On the other hand, the Koranna—perhaps more than all the other indigenous Khoikhoin people of southern Africa — suffered under European conquest and subjugation, being displaced from their land in the 18th century and being forced to labour under slave-like conditions on farms of the white Afrikaners. The agencies of Indian states were never really out to over-power and enslave the tribes on their peripheries, or to influence their holistic religion, whereas the European settlers forced Khoikhoin families to work for them and to convert to the foreign religion thus promoting their individualisation. Some individuals bound together by family ties could, as described by Erasmus, escape from this subjugation and lead an unsettled existence in the Orange Free State involving changing confrontations with whites and Bantu speaking peoples.

As Alan Barnard's recent work on the Khoisan *Hunters and Herders* (1992) demonstrated at length, the ethnography of the indigenous peoples of southern Africa largely amounts to a reconstruction of the intricate structures and exchanges of past centuries, since the traumatic military interventions by German[9] and other European forces of conquest have undone most of the indigenous constitutions. No other region of the world has probably witnessed such an amount of intensive and competent ethno-historical inquiries as southern Africa has containing brilliant reconstructions of past patterns of societal exchanges. At the same time, such an abundance of excellent anthropological literature on the Khoisan goes together with their presently observed structural poverty, or their loss of societies in a structural sense as a consequence of European interventions. Many accounts, like that of Erasmus in the present volume, relate individual histories because not much more than individual fates has been left for the Khoranna and others, whereas the proponents of a non-individualistic caste society in India simply ignored structures and exchanges of indigenous groups and ideas in their tribal periphery.

In the fourth section of this book, tribal groups and institutions are introduced in traditional style, relating to the somewhat loosely organized Sora of Andhra Pradesh, as described by the Sora expert M. Suryanarayan, and the complex segmentation of Naga society, as witnessed by M.K. Das since many years. Whereas the Sora, renowned as ritualists since long in anthropological textbooks, lack institutions and, as Suryanarayan elaborates, do not even name their local descent groups, the large Naga villages, formerly endogamous, contain action and reference groups on several segmentary levels according to named pedigree. Added to these two detailed ethnographic accounts of a single Tribal unit, as observed over decades, is G. Pfeffer's general attempt to chart out the structural and ideological commonalities of all tribes in western Orissa, as a contrast to the traditional order of castes on the coast, and to offer certain institutional details of five different inner Orissan culture areas for comparison.

The question whether a tribe is to represent a certain stage in cultural evolution or a certain type of society—or both at the same time—will be raised indirectly in the sixth section of the volume. After Pfeffer's short review of the scheme of cultural evolution, other authors introduce accounts on peoples who may be *Scheduled Tribes* in the administrative sense of the Indian Union but not tribal societies in the anthropological sense. Ulrich Demmer contrasts his work among the highly structured tribal Koya in the extreme south of Orissa with the societal "flux" of Jenu Kurumba in the Ghat Forests in the three southern most Indian states, *i.e.* the largest Indian gatherer-hunter community where he recalls his seven years of fieldwork. V. Gangadhar also provides a vivid picture of the contemporary Chenchus as gatherer-hunters in the mountainous Eastern Ghats of Andhra Pradesh. Both the Jenu Kurumba and the Chenchus are well aware of cultivation and animal husbandry but refuse to practice either in the context of wage labour or as independent cultivators. This is the plain technological difference when compared to the tribal economy. At the same time it is obvious that the complexity of societal structures or "necessary relations", as elaborated in the tribal societies of the world, are lacking among the Jenu Kurumba and the Chenchus. None of the grand rituals of exchanges has ever been known, whereas sharing is the standard pattern of sociality. The two "societies in flux"—like several others in contemporary India – neatly represent the model of Sahlins' *Original Affluent Society* (1974), though significantly Indian sociology has hardly taken notice of them.

An entirely different—and structurally refined—autonomous society, the Yerukala of Andhra Pradesh, is presented by S. Narahari in the same section. Like the gypsies living in most countries between India and Portugal (and the Europeanised countries of America), these Indian brush and basket-makers or traditional salt-traders (along with a good number of related Yerukala) must be qualified as *guest tribes* in the language of Max Weber (1956: 949), *i.e.* excluded from commensality and ritual or other social interaction but involved with urban and rural Indians by occupying certain economic niches. The British colonial Government had criminalized many of these migrant tribes of India, arresting them in special colonies since the 1860s, whereas in independent India they are free to move and have even been involved in governmental "protective discrimination", though—significantly—the anthropological public has largely ignored them. They stand in contrast to the standard picture of a tribal society in the sense that they are neither tied to a fixed territory nor to specific routes of migration which, as those of migrant sheep and cattle owners, isolate them from the settled population. Yerukala and other *guest tribes*, though highly segregated, live in close proximity to their hosts. Because of this spatial nearness, or being part of everyday urban life, they remain inconspicuous. S.N. Ratha in his paper argues that there is a great deal of confusion in conceptualizing tribal society in India. Despite this the term *Scheduled Tribe* is unlikely to become obsolete in administrative jargon in Indian socio-political dynamics in any predictable future.

In the final chapter of the volume, Georg Pfeffer debates the tribal issue as such, *i.e.* the question, whether anthropologists may reasonably speak of tribal societies or classify societal types as such when facing the fact that everywhere traditions are being "invented" and the old economic order is being transformed. Probably the majority of the disciplines have entirely abandoned their key term of the past century, and in most contemporary anthropological publications, the holistic approach as such, and especially the social significance of the Tribe as a model, is non-existent or dead. By relating to numerous examples beyond India in neighbouring countries and on other continents, Pfeffer, in analogy to certain procedures of a middle Indian tribal village, continues to meet the undead dead.

NOTES

1. *See* Dorminger, Georg (1964) in his introduction to Tacitus' *Germania*. Munich, Goldmann.
2. *See* Ibn Khaldun 1958. *The Muqaddimah*. 3 Vols. translated by Franz Rosenthal.
3. *See* Langenscheidts Taschenwörterbuch 1963. *Lateinisch-Deutsch*. Berlin, Langenscheidt p. 532.
4. *See* Sahlins, Marshall D. 1968. *Tribesmen*. Englewood Cliffs: Prentice Hall. Foundations of Modern Anthropology Series.
5. *See* Fried, Morton H. 1975. *The Notion of Tribe*. Menlo Park: Cummings.
6. *See* Clifford, James 1988. *The Predicament of Culture. Twentieth-Century Ethnography, Literature, and Art*. Cambridge Mass: Harvard University Press.
7. *See Census of India 2001* as reported in *The Hindu* of 11th July 2004. This is 8.2 % of the Indian population.
8. *See* Goody, Jack 1983. *The Development of the Family and Marriage in Europe*. Cambridge: CUP.
9. Between 1904 and 1907 the German colonial army conducted a war of ethnocide against the Herero and the Khoisan Nama peoples of today's Namibia.

REFERENCES

Barnard, Alan. 1992. *Hunters and Herders of Southern Africa. A Comparative Ethnography of the Khoisan Peoples*. Cambridge: Cambridge University Press.

Census of India 2001. quoted in *The Hindu* of 11th July 2004.

Clifford, James. 1988. *The Predicament of Culture. Twentieth-Century Ethnography, Literature, and Art.* Cambridge Mass: Harvard University Press.

Dorminger, Georg 1964. *Tacitus' Germania.* Munich: Goldmann.

Fried, Morton H. 1975. *The Notion of Tribe.* Menlo Park: Cummings.

Goody, Jack. 1983. *The Development of the Family and Marriage in Europe.* Cambridge: Cambridge University Press.

Ibn, Khaldun. 1981. *The Muqaddimah.* 3 Vols. translated by Franz Rosenthal. Princeton: Princeton University Press.

Langenscheidts, Taschenwörterbuch. 1963. *Lateinisch-Deutsch.* Berlin: Langenscheidt.

Sahlins, Marshall D. 1968. *Tribesmen.* Englewood Cliffs: Prentice Hall.

____. 1974. "The Original Affluent Society," (pp.1-40) *in* Marshall D. Sahlins (ed.), *Stone Age Economics.* London: Tavistock.

Weber, Max 1956. *Wirtschaft und Gesellschaft.* Tübingen. J.C.B. Mohr (Paul Siebeck).

SECTION I

GIVING AND RECIPROCATING

ONE

STRUCTURE AND EXCHANGE: An Overview

PAULA G. RUBEL and ABRAHAM ROSMAN

Earlier in the history of anthropological theorizing, the term social structure was used to talk about a narrowly defined subject which was primarily the realm of kinship. Our own approach to what we call structure has been much broader. The potlatch ceremony on the North-west Coast, as ceremonial exchange, for example was all-inclusive in that it embodied not only kinship, but also economics, politics, religion, theatre, performance and all the arts. In our earlier work, we demonstrated the way in which the potlatch distributions, as well as the ceremonial aspects of the potlatch, followed the alignment of the social structure. These ceremonies are what Mauss long ago characterized as total social phenomena. Later, Levi-Strauss, in his monumental article "Social Structure" elaborated on this approach and also pointed out that social structure extended far beyond kinship (1953). In each of the areas we have examined over the years, in North America, Oceania and Asia, we have looked not only at the way in which ceremonial exchanges were inclusive, but also, more importantly at the way in which they mirrored the social structure.

Our research on social structure and exchange has always been comparative. This is in contrast to the position of the postmodernists who have until recently dominated anthropological discourse in many parts of the world. The relativistic position that they advocate can be seen, for example in the last major work of the American anthropologist, David Schneider. In that analysis, he called into question the conclusions and generalizations which he had reached in his analysis of Yap Society many years before (1984). The basis for his change in perspective was that he felt he had too quickly assumed that Yap Society was matrilineal. He now thought that they had a much more complicated and unique kinship system. He no longer felt that the concept of matrilineality, to which Schneider himself had made a major contribution, was suitable to describe Yap social structure. This represented a repudiation of one of the central tenets of anthropology, that is, the assumption that concepts could be developed which could be applied cross-culturally.

One of the major advances in anthropology during the course of its long history was the development of an analytical framework. This consisted of a series of concepts which could be used to illuminate cultural similarities and differences in different parts of the world. However, one must recognize that when one uses concepts like matrilineality, one is making a series of generalizations which moves the analysis beyond each unique feature of individual behaviour to successively higher more general analytical levels. This procedure reveals commonalities which have enabled anthropologists to make useful generalizations. Eggan's method of controlled comparison, developed many years ago to analyze American Indian Societies of the South-west demonstrates this type of generalization and conceptual usage (1954). In our own work, we have relied on the use of cross-cultural concepts such as avunculocality, father's sister's daughter marriage, Crow kinship terminology and matrilineality.

One of the early criticisms of structuralism was that it did not deal with history, that is, changes which occur diachronically through time. One of the important themes of this paper is to show that structures may remain the same through time. Ceremonial exchange is object specific up to a point, but over time, though, substitutions of goods may occur. Among the Mae Enga of the western highlands of New Guinea, the third stage of the *te* ceremonial distribution had involved only cooked pork but in the 1970s, cow and goat meat began to be substituted for pork, and money substituted for pigs, while the structure of the *te* remained the same. On the North-west Coast before contact, the Kwakiutl potlatch distribution had involved elk skins, but in the 19th century after the beginning of the fur trade with the Hudson Bay Company, Hudson Bay blankets began to be substituted for skins. By the time Boas and Swanton did fieldwork, at the potlatches which they observed piles of Hudson Bay Blankets as well as sewing machines were being distributed. However, structures may be transformed through time, but do not disappear. In the last century, the Tlingit had a four part exchange structure whereas, as we shall see later, they now have a moiety structure, itself weakened by marriages within the same moiety. Many of the societies we have examined have undergone enormous changes over the past century as a consequence of contact with the Western World, Christianization, modernization, and most recently globalization. For some of these societies, like those of the North-west Coast, the relationship between ceremonial exchange and social structure could be more easily discerned a hundred years ago. However, as a consequence of the effects of the forces enumerated above, the social structure, the concomitant pattern of exchanges, and large scale ceremonials like potlatches have been greatly transformed. In the modern context, features relating to the political economy are important, while the kinship, religious and symbolic functions are no longer important. Ceremonial exchanges, like the potlatch among the Tlingit, and the *te* among the Enga are now being used by individuals to gain prestige and expand their political power on a local and national level. The exchange structure has been altered as a consequence of the decline in importance of the kinship structure with which it was articulated. The examples we will discuss below also represent a continuum with differing degrees of incorporation into larger political entities, as well as a shift from kinship based structures to ethnic groups. It is important to consider to what degree the generalizations which characterized these societies as they operated a hundred years ago still hold. Many people on the North-west Coast hold potlatches today, but the structure of the potlatch as well as the social structure have, in the main, been radically altered. In contrast, for many of the societies of Melanesia, and elsewhere, ceremonial exchange continues to be significant and still, for the most part, reenacts the lines of the social structure.

In India, generally speaking, people characterized as tribal people still hold ceremonial exchanges which follow the lines of the social structure, as for example, demonstrated by the articles of Hardenberg, Otten and Surynarayan in this volume. The term Tribe used to refer to such groups still has an official meaning in India, though it was a term first used by the British in the Indian Census in 1872. It continues to be used today by the Indian Government, and has multiple meanings, for example, as a referent for an administrative unit. In most instances it was not used as a self referent since the languages of the groups referred to as Tribes did not have an equivalent term. In America, the term was used by both the American Government, the American Public and as a technical term by American anthropologists until several decades ago. At that point, Fried pointed out that the term did not have an indigenous equivalent in the languages of the groups for which it was being used and that it had been imposed by the American Government and later used in their work by American anthropologists (1975). However, the term still has an official meaning for the United States Government, more specifically for the *Bureau of Indian Affairs* and the *Bureau of American Ethnology*. Indigenous groups must demonstrate that they constitute a tribe, in terms of the Government definition, in order to secure the benefits from the government which accrue to "Tribes". The courts are the arena within which such decisions are made when cases are brought by groups wishing to be designated as Tribes. As a consequence of this official usage, American Indian groups themselves now use the term tribe as well. In many parts of South-east Asia, such as Myanmar and Thailand, hill people like the Karen and Kachin, are referred to as tribes to contrast them with the civilizations of the valleys and lowlands, *i.e.* Burmese/Myanmar. In general, with the development of civilization and its consequent detribalization, elaborate social structures and large-scale ceremonial exchanges disappear or are radically transformed.

In the study of any exchange system, one must pay attention to the meanings of the things exchanged. The things distributed at ceremonial exchanges are clues to the nature of the social structural relationship of exchangers. For example, among the patrilineal Arapesh, whom Mead studied long ago, a man gave pearl-shell rings to affines including mothers' brothers at rites de passage such as scarification of a girl at adolescence, boys' initiation, and funerals. In contrast, men gave yams competitively to their unrelated exchange partners, their *buanyin*, the amount of which had to be equalled or bettered in the next exchange. Pearl-shell rings signified peace and affines, and yams meant exchange partners and competitive exchange. Raw and cooked also frequently have different meanings. Cooked food given at a feast may mean commensality but it may also mean "poison". In the Indian Caste System, food prepared by one caste was polluting to a member of a higher caste. Among the Trobrianders, *urigubu*, which was given to sister's husband, after every harvest always involved raw yams called *taytu*, while *sagali*, the funerary distributions, always involved cooked *taytu*. The *sagali* distribution which also involved banana leaf skirts made by women, was a long term return for *urigubu*. The *buritila'ulo,* exchange between chiefs involves only long hairy yams, called *kuvi,* not yams called *taytu.*

Linguistic theory provides interesting parallels to the meanings of the things exchanged and the relationship between exchangers. Objects exchanged in different ceremonies are contrastive and therefore are structurally identical to phonemes. An example is the pearl-shell/yam contrast of the Arapesh. Like the phonemes of a language, the items being exchanged and their meanings are contrastive with one another. On the other hand, object substitution within an object class in a ceremony, such as the substitution of Hudson Bay Blankets for elk skins resembles the way in which allophones constitute members of the same larger class.

In our view, an approach which combines a focus on structure and exchange can illuminate the evolution or progression between societies based on kinship, and civilizations which have feudal or caste structures. This will involve the building of structural models which utilize a limited number of variables. The least complex model is the egalitarian structure exemplified by the Yanomamo, as well as societies in India, and in other parts of the world. Many of the societies in this category have Dravidian or Iroquois kinship terminology. There is usually a preference for bilateral cross-cousin marriage and sister exchange, or a more complex form of this marriage rule. Ceremonial and other types of exchanges are across the dual division, and it is typically exchange of like for like. This equalitarian structure can evolve into more complex structural forms, still based on kinship, like the Australian Section Systems.

Equalitarian societies may evolve into societies still organized by kinship, but with flexible or fixed rank. Within this category are societies with potlatches, large scale ceremonial distributions, which are the means by which rank is manifested or determined. Societies such as these, with the same pattern of structure and ceremonial exchange, were to be found in different ecological settings, such as the North-west Coast, South-east Asia, and Oceania. We will describe how they operated at an earlier time, using classic ethnographies, and show how they have been transformed through time, but as a consequence of different historical circumstances, operate differently today.

The societies of the North American North-west Coast have flexible ranking of groups. The rank of groups is based upon giving large ceremonial distributions, potlatches. These are competitive, in that the return in the future is obligatory and must be equivalent to what had been received in the past. Rank was manifested in a hierarchy of "names", seating arrangements at a potlatch, and in the amount one receives. The social structure of these societies varied. Some traced descent matrilineally and had exogamous matrilineal clans, and others had kin groups based on cognatic descent traced through both mother's line and father's line. Guests at potlatches were always affinally related to the hosts. The form of the social structure determined the occasions and frequency of potlatching. Guests given "gifts" at potlatches served as witnesses to claims to rank and to mythical rights to privileges, crests and names. By the late nineteenth century, anthropologists had already recognized that societies on the North-west Coast varied in their social structure. Anthropologists like Benedict and Barnett saw the potlatch as a single unitary phenomenon throughout the area. They did not recognize that the potlatch varied in relation to the variations in the social structure.

The Tlingit, described by Swanton in 1905, had already become involved in the Canadian Canning Industry (1908). This was reflected in that they were already giving Hudson Bay Blankets at potlatch distributions. At this time, Tlingit Society was divided into two exogamous matrilineal moieties, Raven and Wolf, each containing many lineages related to one another by matrilineal descent. The lineages and their leaders were ranked within each moiety. Members of matrilineages lived avunculocally in large wooden houses which contained several families. The families and the places they occupied were also ranked with respect to one another. There was a preference for marriage with Father's Sister's Daughter resulting in a four part structure. Each matrilineage had two other matrilineages in the opposite moiety with which they intermarried, both giving and receiving women in alternate generations from each of these two matrilineages. (*See* Diagram 1 and Rosman and Rubel, 1971). The Tlingit had Crow kinship terminology, which is an integral part of this type of structure. This social structure continued to operate in much the same form as earlier.

For the Tlingit there was only one important occasion for a potlatch, and that was the death of a chief, and the assumption to chiefly position of his successor, one of his sister's son. It was also the event at which younger members of the chief's lineage received new names. Seating at a Tlingit potlatch was ordered in such a way as to separate the host and the two groups of guests from the opposite moiety, who were members of the two lineages with which the host group intermarried, affines of the deceased chief on one side, and affines of the new chief, on the opposite side. The affines of the deceased chief from the opposite moiety provided funerary services for the deceased chief, and erected a totem pole in his honour. The affines of the new chief built a new house for him. The distribution at the potlatch was in return for these services. The host lineage was seated at the back of the house, opposite the entrance. There was no competition between host and guests. They were in opposite moieties which were equal in rank and did not compete. Instead, the two groups of affines did compete in song contests at this potlatch. This competition did not affect the ranking of these groups.

The Tlingit can be compared with other societies on the North-west Coast who also potlatched, shared much the same ecological setting but had different social structures and a different potlatch system. The Kwakiutl had a cognatic social structure which included ranked kin groups or *numayns,* and Tribes. One could be a member of mother's or father's descent group or both. This resulted in a system of overlapping kin groups. The Kwakiutl potlatch system differed from that of the Tlingit in that the frequency and occasions for potlatch varied, as did their function. The Tlingit had one major potlatch which honored the deceased and affirmed succession. Among the Kwakiutl there were many occasions for potlatching when names which belonged to *numayns* were bestowed. *Numayns* competed for individuals by giving them names at potlatches they hosted. Through the lifetime of an individual, particularly one of a chiefly family, he or she received names of increasingly important rank at potlatches held to mark his or her various rites de passage. Among the Kwakiutl, competition took the form of claiming higher and higher rank. Shaming one's rival in a different tribe or *numaym* was one of the methods used. This often involved the destruction of property. There was competition within *numayms,* between *numayms*, and between tribes and their chiefs. These rankings were manifested at potlatches in terms of where individuals were seated by the host *numaym.* Tlingit competition was different.

On the other hand, two societies, in different ecological settings in different parts of the world may have the same type of social structure and exchange structure. Like the Tlingit, the Trobrianders, who live in the Massim area of Papua New Guinea, also had matrilineal descent groups, Crow kinship terminology, and father's sister's daughter marriage. That is, Trobriand men were supposed to marry the person whom they call *tabu*. This marriage rule applied primarily to chiefs, but nevertheless could generate a structure of relationships between clans or *dala* (Rubel and Rosman 1970). The matrilineal descent groups or clans were internally ranked and hierarchically ordered. The first sister's son who was able to amass enough goods to hold a *sagali* or mortuary feast for his maternal uncle, the chief who had died, would become chief. The affines of the deceased chief performed mortuary service for him, and the *sagali* distribution recompensed them for this. The pregnancy of the sister of the chief was also the occasion for a *sagali*. Her pregnancy was important to perpetuate the matrilineage. The father's lineage of the new chief and his sister performed a series of services during her pregnancy. The father's sister of the pregnant woman wove a cloak for her and performed magic to protect her. The pregnancy *sagali* was in exchange for these services.

The father's lineage of the chief and his sister gave this new chief his principal wife and was paying him *urigubu*. The chief has several wives and his brothers-in-law compete to give the largest amounts of *urigubu*. The *sagali* payment at the pregnancy ritual for his sister is a reversal for that *urigubu* payment, just as the mortuary *sagali* was a reversal of an earlier *urigubu* payment. At a Tlingit potlatch, the two sets of affines are recompensed at the same time, one, the affines of the deceased chief for mortuary services which honour him, the other, the affines of the new chief, for honouring the chief's matrilineage by building his house. The Trobriand *sagali* is identical to the structure of Father's Sister's Daughter Marriage. Among the Trobrianders, the two clans that intermarry with the host clan are guests at two separate *sagali*, funerary and pregnancy, whereas at the Tlingit potlatch these two groups are present at the same time.

The Trobrianders had other non-kin structures of exchange besides the potlatch-type *sagali*. *Kayasa*, the harvest exchange between villages, involved the ordinary subsistence yams, *taytu*. In Malinowski's time, cricket had been newly introduced, was competitive, and was played between villages. He describes how a dispute between contending factions in two villages over who had won the game was settled by the holding of a *kayasa* in which the leaders of the factions contributed the most to the harvest used in the ceremony. The yield from both villages was given to the chief (Malinowski, 1935: 212–214). As cricket became ritualized and transformed, it became less of a sport and more of a ritual and the hosts were always the winners.

The Trobrianders carry out another non-kin structure of exchange, *kula*, which is structurally different from *sagali*. Chiefs and sometimes wealthy commoners have *kula* partners on other islands which are different culturally and linguistically. The goods exchanged were two kinds of shell valuables, red shell necklaces which moved clockwise from partner to partner and white armshells which moved counter-clockwise. Those who were to receive valuables undertook voyages to the giver's island. To receive armshells, Trobrianders sailed clockwise to Kitava, and to receive red shell necklaces they sailed counter-clockwise to Dobu. The structure of this exchange is identical to the structure of matrilateral cross-cousin marriage. Among the Kachin, who had this marriage structure, each Kachin lineage had its wife givers and wife takers. In the same manner, Trobriand men had shell necklace givers and shell necklace takers. This is quite different from the structure of *sagali,* which is in accord with Father's Sister's Daughter Marriage and which reversed direction in the next generation. The *kula* structure of assymetrical exchange in the Massim area links together ranked societies like the Trobrianders with unranked societies like Dobu. Leach proposed that the structure of *kula* exchange be examined, rather than the question of why *kula* is found in the Massim, which he felt was unanswerable (1983). In a volume devoted entirely to *kula,* no one had examined or analyzed the structure of *kula* exchange. Leach considered the *kula* to be an example of assymetrical exchange contrasting it with reciprocal exchange, the exchange of like for like. The Trobrianders conceive of the armshells as female and the necklaces as male, and when they "meet" (and are exchanged) in the *kula*, they view this as a marriage[1].

The structures we have identified for the Tlingit and the Trobrianders have changed over the more than one hundred years since these societies were described. The forces for change which we have been mentioned above have transformed these structures of exchange and their relationship to the social structures to a greater or lesser extent. For the Tlingit living in Sitka today, the social structure as well as the potlatch system has been greatly changed. Russian Orthodox elders speak Tlingit and tend to be more traditional than middle-aged and younger Tlingit who do not know the language. Since Protestant missionaries were vehemently against the potlatch, Tlingit Protestants tend to be less enthusiastic about potlatching. However, because potlatching has become one of the elements of Tlingit ethnic identity, its frequency has increased. The earlier matrilineal system of lineage, clan and moiety has been undermined by the transformation from avunculocal to nuclear family residence. The marriage pattern has been completely transformed. Moiety exogamy is often breached and personal preference determines whom one will marry. The four part structure generated by Father's Sister's Daughter Marriage has collapsed into a two part moiety structure. The inheritance rule has been violated in that many sons, who fish commercially with their fathers, inherit their father's boats rather than the sister's son, the traditional heir. There are conflicts nowadays over collectively owned property like houses and crest objects which belong to matrilineages and matriclans. Such crest objects have become valuable to museums and collectors. According to Kan, "elders are torn between the desire to help their own nuclear family by selling the artifacts, and the traditional rule which demands that these objects be bequeathed to their direct matrilineal descendants with whom they may no longer have strong ties..."(1989: 410-411). Potlatch performances now include English summaries of what is said and sung in Tlingit, for the benefit of Tlingit who speak only English. But elders are not in favour of this since translation does not convey the metaphoric meanings contained in the speeches in Tlingit. These also include Tlingit kinship terminology, whose translation into English is very problematic.

For Trobrianders today, the structures of *sagali, kayasa* and *kula* appear to be continuing. The changes which have taken place are primarily changes or substitutions in the categories of goods exchanged or changes in strategy. As Weiner noted in the 1980s, despite more than a century of Trobriand contact with pearlers, whalers, beche-de-mer traders, gold prospectors, labour recruiters, Christian missionaries, the Colonial Government and Papua New Guinea national administrators there has not been "...major significant changes in the basic structural features of the exchange system" (1980: 276). Jolly points out that gender relations among the Trobrianders have changed since Malinowski's time. However, since Malinowski focused primarily on the role of men in the *sagali,* the importance and significance of women's role during the period of his research is not clear, hence the exact nature of the changes is unclear. Male and female roles during that early period and continuing today, are distinctly different and complementary. But women's distributions of banana skirts have become much more important. As Jolly notes, "Exchanges of women's wealth have assumed an inflated and novel significance since Malinowski's time—not only securing the regeneration of Trobriand persons but insuring the perpetuity of Trobriand culture in the face of competing values...defending Trobriand traditions and the value of women against both monetary and male values...not unselfish persistences but self-conscious resistances to modernity and monetary values (Jolly, 1992: 38). Maintenance of tradition is seen as a symbol of resistance and a way of supporting the continuation of Trobriand identity. This is similar to the continuation of the Tlingit potlatch described above, which is a way of maintaining Tlingit identity.

Kayasa exchange, in recent times, has come to be held in conjunction with a ritualized cricket game. However, modern *kayasa* competition is associated with the competition between political movements. In the cricket game, which is no longer competitive as it was in Malinowski's time, they utilize elements of clothing and movements formerly associated with warfare, as illustrated in the film "Trobriand Cricket". A recent description of *kayasa* on the island Kaileuna, just West of Kiriwina, presents it as a competition between men of a village to see who can grow the most yams (Schiefenhovel and Bell-Krannhals, 1996). The *kayasa* organizer uses this as a means of increasing his prestige. Chiefdomship, still present, is a matter of ascribed status (Schiefenhovel and Bell-Krannhals, 1996: 249). The *kayasa* associated with cricket matches is presented as an inter-village competition in the film. Prestige accrues to the organizer of the cricket match. Though the game itself does not involve competition, the *kayasa* of which it is a part does.

The Trobrianders are economically integrated with the outside world, more now than in the past. European goods and cash are controlled by men and considered male wealth. In the 1970s, it was the sale of carvings made by men to tourists which brought cash into the Trobriand economy. When tourism declined, male migrant work and remittances became more important as a source of cash. This differential engagement of men and women in the cash economy was countered by women's exchange of banana-leaf bundles and goods, indigenous and foreign. This is the way in which indigenous exchange is now articulated with commodity exchange.

Over the past decade, the results of ethnographic field research with the Trobrianders, as well as ethno-historic research have lead to the conclusion that the *kula* as it operated in Malinowski's time was a product of pacification brought about by the colonial administration. Modernization of the *kula* has meant that power boats have taken the place of outrigger canoes. This is an example of substitution of one element for another in the *kula*, equivalent to the substitution of Hudson Bay Blankets for elk skins in the potlatch. However, no one writing about the *kula* today has indicated that its structure has been transformed or that the rules have changed.

Today, the Tlingit potlatch operates with a two-part moiety structure rather than the four-part structure which was in operation at the beginning of the twentieth century. Our ethno-historical research has revealed that the earlier structure from which the four part Father Sister's Daughter structure developed was a moiety structure of the type found among the Athapaskan Societies of the interior (Rubel and Rosman, 1983). With regard to the Trobriand four part structure, there is a hint in Malinowski's field notes that the clans in the four part structure were organized in a moiety structure earlier in time (Rosman and Rubel, 1989). However, there is no evidence that today Trobriand structure has collapsed into a two part moiety system like the Tlingit. On the contrary, the *urigubu, sagali, kayasa*, and *kula* exchanges all continue to take place today maintaining the same structures as earlier.

Some societies have permanent rank systems. This latter form was defined by Kirchoff as a "conical clan". In Leach's description of the Kachin, the *gumsa* system is an example of a fixed rank system still encompassed by kinship (Leach, 1954). Kin groups of different rank intermarry with women going in one direction up the hierarchal structure. The ceremonial exchange in which they participate mirrors the kinship structure. His analysis also demonstrated the instability of such a system, in that it could collapse into the egalitarian form, *gumlao,* or be transformed into a feudal system, the Shan system. The latter is no longer based on kinship and has three hereditary classes. In systems with permanent rank, the kinship structure usually disappears at some point. One of the exceptions to this was the system found among many Mongol groups centuries ago. A two part structure of White Bone, the nobility, and Black Bone, the ordinary people, co-existed with an ideology that a single kinship structure encompassed the entire Mongol group.

In some societies, the structure of exchange of goods is separate from the structure of affinal relations. An example of this is to be found among the Apa Tani in North-Eastern India, where Feasts of Merits are completely separate from affinal exchanges (von Fürer-Haimendorf, 1962). These Feasts of Merit involve "competition for social prestige…, an extremely important part of Apa Tani life" (von Fürer-Haimendorf, 1962: 139-140, 89). At the largest Feast of Merit, held at the time of the festival of Morom, the donor must kill at least five or six mithan and then the meat is distributed by the men of his clan to each household in everyone of the seven Apu Tani villages. Dr. Stuart Blackburn, who has recently restudied the Apa Tani, reports that their system of ceremonial exchange remains essentially the same.

The *te* structure of exchange, found among the patrilineal Enga who live in the Western Highlands of Papua New Guinea is also separate from the affinal exchange system, though *te* partnerships do develop from affinal relationships. Unlike ranked societies, the Enga are basically egalitarian. Affinal exchanges begin with betrothal gifts to the bride's family, and end at the death of the children born of that marriage which marks the end of a series of payments from the husband's patrilineage to the patrilineage of the wife. Enga patrilineal clans, occupying contiguous areas, fought with their neighbours but also exchanged women and goods with them. An Enga man will have two groups of *te* partners, one set in clans to the east of his clan, and the second in clans to the west of his clan. He transmits goods that he has received from his eastern partners at their *te* ceremonies to his western partners at the *te* ceremony that his clan hosts. The Enga have a system of delayed exchange in which goods move from one group to the next until they reach the end of the chain, when they must reverse and go down the line in the opposite direction (Rubel and Rosman, 1978). In the first stage, people give valuables such as stone axes, shells, plumes, and small pigs to their partners in one direction. In the second stage, the givers of valuables become receivers of live pigs, which move down the chain as they are distributed at successive *te* distributions held in turn by each clan. At the end of the chain, there is a second reversal when the last receiver of live pigs becomes the first distributor of cooked pork. The distribution of cooked pork completes one cycle of the *te*. It will begin again when initiatory gifts begin to go in the direction opposite to the pork. Delay regarding when the next cycle will begin is an integral part of the system.

Giving and receiving in the *te* exemplifies the ambivalence seen in exchange in general. Clans who were neighbours, though potential enemies to one another, were dependent upon one another to pass on the objects of the *te*. If warfare did break out in the middle of a *te* cycle, the *te* was disrupted. It was in the interest of *te* partners in other clans to make peace between the combatants so that goods could continue to move along the *te* chains. The Enga production system was based upon intensive cultivation of sweet potatoes, used to feed people as well as the large number of pigs in the *te*. The size and number of pigs brought renown to the giver when they were distributed to his exchange partners.

The *te* involved competition for wealth, name and status, and therefore, had political significance. Men lobbied for support by making speeches. Though often the son of a Big Man also became a Big Man, everyman had a chance of becoming a leader. There was no permanent class structure (Mapusia, 1980: 63). Besides modernization and the end of endemic warfare for a time, Mapusia notes that "…Christianity… [and] a wave of Western ideologies poured into our society" (1980: 65). Suppression of warfare was one of the accomplishments of the colonial administration. When Papua New Guinea became a new nation-state in 1975, its underdeveloped army and police system had difficulty in keeping order, and periodic warfare broke out again between clans, this time not with wooden spears but with shotguns. This resulted in the killing of individuals as well as the destruction of gardens, trees, and trade stores.

Europeans, both Government officials and missionaries, Lutheran, Catholic and Seventh Day Adventist, in their efforts to westernize the indigenous population had taken a very negative view of the *te* and hoped that with

Christianization it would disappear. Those men whose leadership was evidenced in the *te* became individuals whom the colonial administration came to rely on to become *luluai* and *tultul*, the indigenous representatives of the colonial government. As was typical, Westerners assumed that, when presented with a "superior" cultural lifestyle, the Enga would automatically adopt it. Missionaries saw the *te* as a "satanic" practice. However, it was the most important cultural institution shaping Enga life. Many Big Men and their followers refused to be converted, even when threatened with being thrown into hell. When Big Men did convert and opted out of the *te*, they lost status and friends. Some of those who did convert to Christianity, continued to be involved in the *te*. However, according to Derkley, "...the last great *tee* in a recognizably traditional form seems to have taken place in 1974" (1997: 134). During 1974, we were doing field research among the Mae Enga, and we observed what seems to have been the last stage of the last great cycle of the *te,* in which halves of pigs were distributed by Big Men to their *te* partners (*see* Rubel and Rosman, 1978, Chapter 11). Even at that time, quarters of cooked cow meat were being distributed along with halves of roast pig.

When "modern politics" came in, the *te* was used more and more frequently as an instrument to gain political support. As Mapusia notes, "During the previous election campaign, many people have used the system as a means of winning votes.... [and as].... an important path to gaining support.... [by] giving out pigs to as many people as possible hoping these people would be his supporters when elections are on" (1980: 63). Educated men, who frequently owned trucks and trade stores, or worked in other ways in the monetary sector outside of Enga territory have become involved in the modern political system and may continue to take part in the *te* ceremony. They have cash which they can use to buy pigs elsewhere. These pigs are given out in the ceremony, or alternatively men may attach cash instead of pigs to stakes and boards. These are given out as gifts or to pay debts. Traditional leaders were still playing leadership roles in 1980 though strongly challenged periodically by the rising younger generation of men who threatened the very existence of traditional leadership. The education of these younger men and their exposure to a wider world enabled them to explain to other Enga the changes which were taking place. Traditional leaders were not able to do this. It was the former who filled the elective offices in the National, Provincial and Local Government Council and Village Courts (Mapusia, 1980: 64). There were a few leaders in those days who were able to have one foot in the traditional arena and the other in the modern, being involved in both modern and *te* politics. In this manner, modern political institutions were grafted onto the local *te*.

Enga who have moved out of their villages to the city to pursue permanent employment in the modern cash economy, and to adopt a western way of life, needed to make decisions as to the degree to which they would continue to be involved in the affairs of their natal villages. Some give up participation in the *te* because it is too expensive, and too difficult. The *te* is seen as the old village way of life to which they can no longer adjust. Others try to maintain a dual way of life going back to the village for short periods of time to participate in the *te,* and attend funerals and singsongs (Mapusia, 1980: 70). To those latter individuals, the urban area is still unfamiliar territory.

With modernization, Western commodities, including cattle and goats, live and cooked have been introduced into *te* distribution along with, and as substitutes for pigs and pork as early as 1974. Cash is used to buy pigs or as a substitute for them. The presence of trucks enabled people and pigs to be moved about more efficiently. As Mapusia concluded in 1980, "Despite new changes and the imposition of negative attitudes by colonial agents the *te* ceremonial exchange has continued to operate" (Mapusia, 1980: 72). Derkley remarks that "There is a remarkable underlying continuity between the 'old' and 'new'.... encapsulated in the remark made by a highly educated Engan about the 1989 provincial elections: 'Now, the elections are our *tee*' " (1997: 130). Older informants see it differently, as one, when asked whether there would be another *te*, told Derkley, "The *tee* is like a great river. Now there are too many little rivers" (1997: 135). But in Enga Province, businessmen and women, and politicians who wish to win office at any political level from local to national, must successfully manipulate a network of exchange relationships built up with the help of his or her clan and other clans over many years. Despite the existence of trade stores, the politics of the clan and the *te* has proven hostile to the development of the individualism required for the true Western-oriented businessman. Clan members still expect to have credit when a fellow clansman sets up in business, making running a business difficult if not impossible. Derkley sees the exchange system known as the *te* as "...the brilliant cultural invention which in precontact times enabled the Enga to enlarge their universe and enrich it with goods, ideas, and relationships which might otherwise not have been available" (1997: 150). The *kula* exchange system would seem to operate in the same fashion.

When kin ties which bind ranked groups together disappear, the result may be a caste system, or a feudal system as in the Kachin Shan example. Both of these forms can be productively examined from the point of view of structure and exchange. There has been disagreement over whether caste constitutes a cultural phenomenon found only in India. According to Max Weber, it is "...a fundamental institution of Hinduism" (Gerth and Mills, 1947: 396). Dumont also suggests that "...Indian caste can be understood only if it is not arbitrarily severed from Indian Culture ...though such understanding is of interest for comparative sociological purposes" (Dumont, 1967:28). The opposite position on caste is that of Edmund Leach, who sees caste as a structural phenomenon also found in Non-Hindu Societies (Leach, 1962). Caste Societies have five distinctive features.

1. Castes are hereditary, and thus caste status is ascribed.
2. Castes are organized hierarchically. This is the political power dimension.
3. Castes are economically specialized and exchange goods and services with other groups.
4. Castes are endogamous.
5. Ideas of purity and pollution which pertain to food and sex also separate castes.

The religious and sacred aspects of caste are very important (Tambiah, 1967: 24-25). In fact, Dumont sees this aspect of caste as primary (1967: 33), while others separate the religious ideas from the economic and political aspects of caste. However, in terms of our emphasis on total social phenomena, religious ideas clearly must be considered part of the system. In contrast to potlatch type societies where kin groups compete against one another, according to caste principles, castes in a caste society do not compete (Leach, 1962: 7). Competition between sub-castes within a caste does occur. Sub-caste members consider themselves to be related through kinship. However, relations between different sub-castes and castes are not defined in kin terms (Leach, 1962: 8). Instead of exchanging women, castes in Indian villages, under the *jajmani* system, exchange economic services and goods without using money. With today's monetary economy, much of this has changed, especially with rural-urban migration. In the cities, money does exchange hands between members of different castes. In India, an ideology of pollution separates caste groups not only sexually, but also in terms of commensality. Potlatch type societies are different in that feasting and eating is important, and seating is a major determinant of rank. At potlatches people eat together, whereas people of different castes hesitate to eat together. The potlatch model is one in which exchange, often competitive, is between exogamous groups who are linked in affinal relationships to one another. In contrast, the caste model is of groups who do not compete with one another, nor are they linked through kinship, since affinal links between groups are not present. Instead, caste groups are economically specialized and exchange goods, services, and money. The differential rank of Indian Castes is fixed. However, status changes have occurred when particular sub-caste groups in India changed cultural characteristics such as food habits and were able to change their position in the sub-caste hierarchy. As Berreman noted, "There are ample instances of "passing", of attempted group mobility, of escape, of resistance and even of caste revolt" (1967: 68).

As we noted above, there is a great debate as to whether caste is a structural phenomenon which can be identified in other societies such as the Near East, Japan, and the American South. Coon identified "the mosaic pattern", which he saw as present in the Middle East and North Africa. Different ethnic groups, who are economically specialized, form a system which resembles a caste system. He notes, "...the people of the Middle East are organized into a complicated social system based on an ethnic division of labour... While occupations tend to be hereditary in the Middle East, no person is under strict obligation to follow his father's trade....while marriages between religious groups, are uncommon. families of the same religion, race, and economic level usually marry freely without reference to specific occupation" (Coon, 1951: 3–5). In the Middle East some religious groups like the Jews tended to be economically specialized. Coon, himself, nevertheless notes that, "The mosaic system is not a caste system" (Coon, 1951: 5). However, there are some structural similarities between this mosaic pattern and the caste system. Another example offered is Japan in which the "...pariah caste [Burakumin] are defined by birth as innately inferior...their villages are separate, intermarriage is extremely difficult and 'passing' occurs very rarely" (De Vos, 1967: 76). The group is primarily endogamous. This separation has remained despite a social revolution, the economic transformation of the society, and the fact that this group, the Burakumin, have been declared "equal" since 1871 (De Vos, 1967: 77). But, De Vos noted, "...the situation is not completely static; there is some evidence that the system may gradually disappear in subsequent generations" (1967: 78). The Korean Paechong were also referred to as "pariahs". They seem to have disappeared after the major upheaval of the Korean War (Passin, 1967: 78).

Myrdal, in 1967, suggested that there was "a caste element in the race-relations between Negroes and Whites in America, because there is an unchanging social line which has not been abandoned even though relations across the line have been changing and are now changing rapidly" (1967: 82). Individuals have noted that historically, even after the demise of slavery, relations in the Southern United States and "…relations between the 'untouchables' and other castes in India are closely similar in operation despite differences in content" (Sinha, 1967: 98). Sinha points out that, "…endogamy, status stratification, the concept of pollution in sexual relations, commensality, residence, and belief in the inheritance of bio-psychological qualities along racial or ethnic lines, are common properties of the two sets of relationships" (1967: 98). Before the civil rights movements in the beginning of the late 1950s, lunch counters and water fountains were segregated to prevent commensality.

However, in all of these instances only portions of the structural model of caste are present, and one could therefore conclude that these do not constitute caste systems as we have defined them. In all of these caste societies, caste groups are not linked in affinal relationships, nor do they have affinal exchange. What kinds of exchanges do characterize these societies? They exchange goods, services, and money. They do not compete with one another, because of the presence of the caste hierarchy. The competition that does occur is within, rather than between castes.

The same type of question has also been asked with regard to feudal systems. Was feudalism a unique historical phenomenon which occurred only in Western Europe during what has been characterized as the "Dark Ages", or did it represent a type of society? Marc Bloch, the famous French historian, a comparativist, took the position that feudalism was indeed a type of society that could be identified at different points in world history, as well as in different parts of the world including China and Japan. He noted that "…as the matrilineal or agnatic clan or even certain types of economic enterprise are found in much the same forms in very different societies, it is by no means impossible that societies different from our own should have passed through a phase closely resembling that which has just been defined" [*i.e.* feudalism] (Bloch, 1961: 446). Feudal societies were characterized by a distinctive type of social structure and a particular type of exchange structure.

Bloch, taking an evolutionary point of view, observed that "feudal ties developed when those of kinship proved inadequate…[or] it was the outcome of the violent dissolution of older societies" (Bloch, 1961: 443). In Europe, the Germanic invasions and barbarian raids caused the breakdown of the Roman Empire as well as the disruption of German kin-based tribal society.

The development of the Carolingian kingdoms after Charlemagne united Germanic speaking populations South of Jutland for a time, but their subsequent weakening was a factor in the development of feudalism in Europe. According to Bloch, the "fundamental" features of European feudalism included , "A subject peasantry; widespread use of the service tenement (*i.e.* the fief) instead of a salary, ...the supremacy of a class of specialized warriors; ties of obedience and protection which bind man to man and, within the warrior class, assume the distinctive form called vassalage; fragmentation of authority—leading inevitably to disorder; and [in addition] ...survival of other forms of association, family and State" (Bloch, 1961: 446).

Edmund Leach also argued for feudalism as an ideal type providing a slightly different picture of the structure of feudalism. He noted "...the distinctive feature of Feudalism is service tenure in land. Lordship over land is ordered in a hierarchy. The actual worker of the land is not paid wages, but pays 'rent' in the form of various kinds of services and/or products in kind to an overlord who in turn holds his lordship in fief to an overlord on similar turns. Characteristically there is no direct link between the king at the summit of the pyramid and the farmer at the bottom" (Leach, 1985: 14). Leach's definition emphasizes hierarchy and not the exchanges.

Under church prohibitions, marriage had been forbidden up to the seventh degree. In 1215, this was changed to the fourth degree (*See* Davis, 1951: 101). This was a marriage system based on a rule which forbade the repetition of marriage alliances between families. Instead, it presented a series of negative rules, which compelled families to enter into new alliances after each marriage. Within the noble class, such marriage "alliances" would support political and military objectives, rather than economic ones. Social groups were endogamous, marriage occurring within, but not between classes. As Bloch notes, "... there was a ban on marriage with a person not of the same class...except with special permission..." (Bloch, 1961: 263).

In the eleventh and twelfth centuries, the military fief, which had been held at the pleasure of the lord, became subject to rules of inheritance. Originally, the fief was granted to the vassal for his lifetime in return for military service (Reynolds, 1996: 18). In the twelfth century, a strict rule of primogeniture was adopted to keep landed estates from being subdivided through partible inheritance. Only the eldest son married and received the fief and title. They tended to make strategic marriages to produce legitimate heirs (Duby, 1977: 74). Younger son might be given recently acquired but distant lands; they might enter the church; or they could find themselves an heiress to marry (Barker 1985: 96; *see* also Bloch, 203-205). As Barker observes, "...a woman's body was constructed to be nothing but the container of this pure procreative blood, awaiting the introduction of seed for the production of male heirs" (1985: 97). Under this system, the status of women declined. Where there were no sons or other close male relatives, in-marrying husbands, sons-in-law, would perform the necessary duties, and subsequently the male descendants of the marriage would inherit the fief (Bloch, 1961: 201).

The exchange structure of feudalism is illustrated in Davis's analysis of the fief of St. Aliquis, in Northern France in the thirteenth century (1220) (Davis, 1951). The feudal hierarchy included hamlets of peasants, who were subject to vassals, beholden to the Baron of the fief, Baron Conon. The Baron, in turn, "paid homâge to the Duke of Burgundy".[2] In exchange for the use of the land, peasants had to give *corvee* labour, and taxes, that is payments in money and kind, depending on the size and yield of their farms (Davis, 1951: 256). When a fief was given to a lord, he did not own the land. In exchange for it, he gave his suzerain military service, money in various emergencies, and other kinds of moral and material assistance (Davis, 1951: 147). Definitively, "...a fief includes enough land to maintain at least one knight and his war horse... The average vassal is required to follow his suzerain for fourty days per year on a summons to an offensive war... [and] greater assistance in a strictly defensive war...", add to the retinue to give prestige to the court, provide ransom money, contribute on the occasion of the lord's daughter's wedding or son's knighthood, and give him hospitality (Davis, 1951: 149-150). At court, "...the lord was required by usage as well as by his acknowledged interest to distribute to his men on these occasions those gifts of horses, arms, and vestments which were at once the guarantee of their fealty and the symbol of their subordination" (Bloch, 1961: 222).

Bloch goes on to discuss aspects of Japanese history which support his argument that feudalism was a type of society rather than a societal form peculiar to Europe alone. He saw a number of features of feudalism present in Japanese history. In the earliest period, kinship groups were important. By the end of the seventh century a Carolingian type structure came into being there, but by the eleventh century, its power waned, coinciding with a reduction of commerce. This marked the beginning of what one might call the feudal period. Though the Emperor continued to be at the top of the feudal structure, it had less connection with the Emperor than did the monarchy in Europe at approximately the same stage. There was a class of professional warriors who were vassals to a lord. For their services to the lord, they received grants of tenements like the fiefs of the West. These warriors lived on the rents of their own tenants—the peasant class (Bloch, 1961: 446; *see* also Critchley, 1978: 64).

Feudal systems, as a type, were always characterized by hierarchy, and were systems of fixed rank with several classes which were endogamous. As a consequence, affinal relations were within these classes. There were gradations, within these classes. Rank was not absolutely fixed, but flexible, and there was opportunity to improve one's position within a class. An advantageous marriage, for example, could better one's position, like marriage to a woman with no brothers, who was an heiress. What exchanges characterized this feudal structure? For the peasant class, labour, money and a portion of what was grown were given to the lord in exchange for use of the land. Within the nobility, the vassal received from his lord the use of lands in exchange for military service; and money for ransom and for the rites de passage of the lord's children. At ceremonial occasions celebrated by the lord for these rites de passage, the vassal might receive clothing, armor, and horses. Since the givers were of higher status, receipt of these gifts demonstrated the lower status of the receivers, and the higher status of the givers. Critchley notes that, "Germanic and other heroic feast giving, as far as is known, was not overtly competitive, although medieval European lords sometimes indulged in a sort of informal potlatching. But it was competitive in another sense, in that a lavish board was one of the things which were essential if the loyalty of a warrior following was to be retained...Feasting is an expression of a very important quality of the warlord-follower relationship, namely, its reciprocity. The lord has obligations towards his followers as well as they towards him" (1978: 43).

In many respects, the feudal system was like the caste system. In both, the ranking of the endogamous classes was fixed. They were economically specialized and exchanged goods and services. However, in the feudal system, commensality between classes was present and there were no ideas that one class could pollute another. Competition was limited to sub-groups within the larger classes. Military service was the preeminent service which the vassal gave his lord. The lord in turn was expected to show generosity. His largesse took the form of feasting, and gifts distributed to his vassals. Both giving and receiving marked the rank of all men from the highest like the Capetian Duke to those in the lowest rank of peasant.

Exchange systems can be maintained and transformed within a modern society like that of the United States. The remnant population of Kalmyk Mongols who came to the United States in 1950, despite the vicissitudes of migrations and wars, exemplifies this (*See* Rubel, 1967). One can trace their history back to the early seventeenth century when their Khan decided to leave Djungaria and travel far to the West to settle in an area West of the Caspian Sea. They were Lamaist Buddhist, although at this early time, some still believed in the efficacy of shamanism. The Russians had not yet extended their empire into this area. There is correspondence with the Russian Tsar which indicates that he gave his permission to the Kalmyks to settle in this area in 1604. As the Russian Empire expanded in the 18th century, some Kalmyk Groups decided to take what proved to be a disastrous trip back to their original home in Djungaria. Those groups which remained were gradually absorbed into the empire's political structure. Most remained nomadic pastoralists keeping horses, sheeps and goats until the beginning of the twentieth century although some moved to the Don region and became sedentary. Kalmyk regiments had fought for the Tsar, so that when the Russian revolution occurred many Kalmyk Groups fled Russia, eventually settling in France, Yugoslavia and elsewhere in Europe. After World War II they ended up in displaced persons camps along with other Kalmyks who had fled the Soviet Union during the German retreat[3].

When they arrived in the United States in 1950 and for some decades after that, the Kalmyks constituted a recognizable and distinct ethnic group speaking both Kalmyk and Russian. Despite enormous changes in cultural content, and the adoption on a broad scale of material cultural traits from the successive cultural milieus with which the group was in contact, they had maintained many basic social structural patterns. The ties which still bound the group together were for the most part kin ties, which were periodically reaffirmed and reinforced by gift exchanges which occurred at various Kalmyk ceremonies. There were several different social contexts within which exchanges of goods took place: two rites de passage—marriage and naming a new baby; non-occurring events like the erection of a new house or the formal visit of a long absent relative; and finally, annual ceremonies such as Tsagan Sar, the Buddhist New Year celebration and various other religious rites like the Fire Sacrifice.

Tsagan Sar is still the most important ceremonial period in the Kalmyk social calendar[4]. On the eve of Tsagan Sar, a religious celebration takes place at the Buddhist Temple when the family arrives with an offering of butter, tea, oranges, nuts, candy and the traditional pieces of fried bread as well as a small monetary gift all of which is placed in front of the temple altar. This, in a sense, constitutes a gift to the gods. After the ceremony, at dawn the family presents white scarves to the priests in order of their rank and the priests hand out candy. Members of the laity also exchange greetings and candy with those who were not close enough to warrant a visit during this month long celebration. An examination of the Pallas account of Kalmyk life in the late eighteenth century reveals many parallels to this celebration. After the family returned home and before the feast, a ceremony was held which involved the husband being presented with vodka by his wife who also gave vodka to the other adults in the household. The husband then made a toast. Vodka was probably a replacement for *kumis*, the alcoholic beverage traditionally made by Mongols. In three generation families, which existed in the nineteen sixties, the daughter-in-law presented vodka to the senior male of the household. After the toasts and the feast, a cycle of ceremonial visits began which would extend for a month. Visits were made by the entire family who would bring pieces of fried dough including one in the shape of a ram's head, and a quart, a fifth or pint of vodka. The closer the kinship relationship, the greater the quantity of food and drink. In a general way, these items were conceived of as an offering signifying the respect the giver had for the receiver. The guests were seated around the table and the woman of the visiting family offered the items, and after opening the Vodka Bottle, a shot glass of Vodka was presented to the senior man of the household being visited. The host opened and served Vodka to the adult visitors and then the women of the household served food. At the end of the visit, the guests were presented with gifts of dress material, a blouse, or a handkerchief to the lady visitors, or a shirt or handkerchief to the male visitors by the woman of the household. The value of the gift presented depended on the closeness of the kin relationship between the parties. Later the family being visited will make a return visit in which the roles are reversed and what is given and received is the same type of item—like for like, but not the very same item. Traditionally and ideally, there was a definite sequence of these formal visits which reflected the patrilineal structure of Kalmyk Mongol Society. Households of husband's parents, father's brothers and then father's sisters and other close patrilineal relatives were visited first. Then visits were made to the households of husband's mother's parents and other close maternal relatives of husband and lastly wife's parents and siblings. Junior relatives first visited relatives senior to them in age or generation, reflecting the importance of seniority in the social structure. Seniors were not obligated to return visits. One particularly important visit was that made by sister's son to visit mother's brother and all those for which the kin term was used since the kinship system was of the Omaha type. Among all Mongols, there was a special relationship between a male ego and his mother's brother. While the Kalmyks were still nomadic pastoralists, sister's son could rustle cattle from mother's brother with impunity[5]. The closeness of the kin relationship was the determinant of the timing of the visit, the size of what was brought, and the size of what was given in return. The Tsagan Sar celebration continued for a month. The more distant the relationship the later the visit.

In the United States, there was great variation in the actual range of relatives available to Kalmyk Families because of the chaotic nature of their movement from the time they left Russia, and their resettlement in America. In many families, relatives on one side were deceased and close relatives on the other side also absent. As a consequence, many accommodations were made to keep or reconstruct the sphere of kin-based social relationships. That which constituted a close relationship was changed. In the absence of close relatives, individuals in more distant relationship and very frequently non-traceable relationship such as members of the same *yasn*, or patrilineal clan, have come to occupy the positions of close relatives. Sometimes blood brotherhood was created between individuals who had no relatives in the United States and henceforth their families interacted in the Tsagan Sar cycle as if they were close relatives. The network of relationships which might have been rent by demographic changes nevertheless persisted in a more generalized form. Third cousins might be referred to as "cousin-sisters". The mended network of kinship which was the social sphere for each family, was re-inforced and re-newed at Tsagan Sar by the exchange of visits and of gifts. The showing of respect was the key concept in the minds of participants, particularly respect to the senior generation. This was reciprocated in the gift given the visitor. The return visit further demonstrated the mutual respect of the participants. If the necessary visits were not made during Tsagan Sar, the individual and the family was said to lack respect. Very frequently social pressure was applied resulting in the visits eventually being made even after the month of Tsagan Sar ended.

Marriage was the most important rite de passage for the Kalmyks. The series of visits and exchanges of goods between the bride's family and the groom's family still took place in the first decades after the Kalmyks arrived in the United States. Many of the same events and exchanges described by Pallas continued to take place. Instead of receiving a yurt, the bride and groom received all the furniture necessary to set up a household.

It is now more than fifty years since the Kalmyks arrived in the United States. The first generation born in the United States is now adult with their own families. Many of them attended college and professional schools and moved outside of the original settlements in New Jersey and Philadelphia. A certain proportion of them married non-Kalmyks, while a few have imported Kalmyk brides from the Kalmyk Autonomous Oblast in Russia. As a consequence, kin ties have become attenuated and ceremonies are no longer as important in Kalmyk life. The Kalmyks have become like other ethnic groups in the United States. Their identity is as Kalmyk-American, and they continue to be Lamaist Buddhist. They still try to visit close relatives on Tsagan Sar but the whole cycle of visits seems to have been curtailed. The Kalmyks, like other ethnic groups, use ceremonies to emphasize their ethnicity. Earlier, we have describes how the Tlingit use the potlatch for this purpose. The Kalmyks have not only retained aspects of their culture but also their Lamaist Buddhist religion, and they use both to declare their Kalmyk identity.

Competition is present in all of the structures we have discussed, but where it is present in the structure varies. In egalitarian societies, competition operates in a "see-saw" manner, sometimes between affines and sometimes not. In potlatch structures of exchange among the Tlingit and Trobrianders, based on affinal relations, competition was between affines. In the *te,* competition occurred between exchange partners who were not affines. When these structures are transformed with the decline of kinship and the disappearance of clanship, if competition is present, it is no longer based on affinal relations. Competition may occur between individuals in the same ethnic group as well as between individuals of different ethnic groups. Large scale ceremonies like the potlatch, *kula, sagali* and the *te,* though reduced in frequency and scope, have not disappeared despite the inroads of modernization and westernization. They remain important because they have taken on new functions and meanings. The structures which these ceremonials encoded earlier, most frequently a structure based on kinship, has usually been transformed. Our examples also represent a continuum of differing degrees of incorporation into larger political entities, and a consequent shift from kinship based structures to ethnic identity and ethnic group formation.

Systems of ceremonial exchange like the potlatch, *sagali, kula,* and *te* had features in common which have enabled them to persist in situations of increasing modernization and Westernization. In the past, they represented ways which individuals and their kin groups used to increase their political importance and power. Today, they are being utilized as vehicles to gain political support by a new generation of leaders who are operating in a transformed political system in which clan organization has either declined or disappeared. The *te* among the Enga is now an important means for aspiring political leaders to gain renown, wider reputations and voting support in their campaigns for local and national political office. The Enga earlier had a segmentary lineage system in which Big Men sought support from their kinsmen. Today, in the contemporary political scene, they seek support from kin as well as from non-kin. The *te* has changed from a great river into many individual streams, as individual leaders mobilize support from their own kin groups, from *te* partners, and others. Trobriand chiefs always acquired increased prestige and greater status by exhibiting the yams they received as tribute through *urigubu* in their yam houses, and by acquiring great *kula* valuables from their *kula* partners. Now when they, and other prominent men gain prestige, they may turn it into political power on a national scale when their political movements demonstrate superiority in competitive *kayasa* and Cricket games. Similarly, the sponsorship of a mortuary potlatch among the Tlingit today demonstrates one's importance and worth, and that of one's kin group within the Tlingit community. Ceremonial exchange always involved competition and was ultimately about power. Today, ceremonial exchange continues because the prestige which accrues from the giving can be transformed into power in a new political arena on the local and national political scene. The appeal now for political support is to "ethnic brothers".

Feudalism in an attenuated version continues only in isolated parts of the world where warlords who exchange hospitality for military service are still present. These warlords compete with one another for followers and for power on the national level. Though laws have been passed in India against caste discrimination, because of the religious sanctions which caste involves, many aspects of the caste system still remain. In the democracy which is India, castes compete for power. On a more inclusive level, the competition for power is between the more inclusive religious groups, Hindus and Muslims.

We have endeavoured to demonstrate the utility and efficacy of an approach which combines a focus on structure with one on exchange. In doing this, we have built models using a limited number of variables. The variables include those associated with structure of marriage including group exogamy, endogamy and hypergamy. Rank and the means by which it is symbolized and degree of competitiveness as it relates to political organization are also variables. Variables relating to exchange include reciprocity in exchanges, occasions for exchange including rites de passage, rules regarding eating, differences between raw and cooked food. Some variables are linked to others. Imbalances in reciprocity may lead to the development of prestige and rank. Commensal feasting is emphasized in potlatch type societies, and rank is signified by the order of receiving food and where individuals are publically seated. In contrast, in caste-type societies, rank is signified by which other caste groups one does not take food from. As a consequence, what began as an examination of degrees of complexity of kinship and marriage structures becomes an investigation into more and more complex forms of political systems, ending with caste and feudal societies.

Societies with an equalitarian social structure, those with flexible or fixed rank, caste societies, feudal societies as well as ethnic groups in today's modern society all still have exchanges, ceremonial and otherwise. We have shown that in each case there is a relationship between the social structure and the structure of exchanges; most of the time they are identical. Further, we have shown how social structures and their concomitant structures of exchange change through time as a consequence of a variety of historical forces. What had been separate societies, in many cases have become ethnic groups. Today, these transformed exchange structures are being used by individuals seeking political power on both the local and national level. In the final analysis, the structural approach need not have been abandoned, but only transformed so that it could deal with history and structural changes.

NOTES

1. The *kula* is a marriage only in a metaphoric sense. There are other metaphoric marriages such as a marriage of a nun to Christ, and what Boas described as the Kwakiutl practice of marriage with another man's foot. This practice was also found among the Bella Coola.
2. In feudal Europe, there was a conceptualization of three great classes—clerks (clerics), knights, and peasants. Ideally, feudalism was a hierarchical system extending up from petty nobles to barons, viscounts, counts, dukes up to the King in Paris. Reynolds remarks that, "Almost all, if not all medieval societies ...were divided by many gradations rather than by a single gulf between nobles and peasants" (1996: 416; also *see* Bloch, 1961: 328).
3. Ethnographic accounts of this group date back to the description of Pallas who visited the Kalmyks in 1776. There are also accounts from the 19th century by Government officials who visited them, which enables one to piece together a diachronic picture of the way in which their focal institutions were transformed.

4. The following description is of ceremonies which took place in the sixties and early seventies. As the Kalmyks spread out from their original settlements, the ceremonies became somewhat attenuated.
5. This is reminiscent of Radcliffe-Brown's description of the role of the mother's brother in patrilineal societies around the world (1952).

REFERENCES

Barker, Phillip. 1985. "The Politics of Primogeniture: Sex, Consciousness and Social Organization in North-Western Europe (900-1250 AD)," (pp.87-104) in Edmund Leach, S.N. Mukherjee and John Ward (eds.), *Feudalism: Comparative Studies*. Sydney: Pathfinder Press.

Berreman, Gerald D. 1967. "Stratification, Pluralism, and Interaction: a Comparative Analysis of Caste", In Anthony de Reuck and Julie Knigh (eds.), *Caste and Race: Comparative Approaches.* London: J & A Churchill Ltd.

Bloch, Marc.1961. *Feudal Society*. Chicago: University of Chicago Press.

Coon, Carleton. 1951. *Caravan: The Story of the Middle-East.* New York: Henry Holt & Co.

Critchley, J.S. 1978: *Feudalism*. London: George Allen & Unwin.

Davis, William Stearns. 1951. *Life on a Medieval Barony: A Picture of a Typical Feudal Community in the Thirteenth Century.* New York: Harper & Row, Publishers.

De Vos, George. 1967. "Psychology of Purity and Pollution as Related to Social Identity and Caste," In Anthony de Reuck and Julie Knight (eds.), *Caste and Race: Comparative Approaches.* London: J & A Churchill Ltd.

Duby, George 1977. *The Chivalrous Society.* London: Edward Arnold.

Dumont, Louis1967. "Caste: A Phenomenon of Social Structure or an Aspect of Indian Culture," In Anthony de Reuck and Julie Knight (eds.), *Caste and Race: Comparative Approaches*. London: J & A Churchill Ltd.

Fried, Morton 1975. *The Notion of Tribe*. Menlo Park, Calif.: Cummings Publishing.

Fürer-Haimendorf, C. Von. 1962. *The Apa Tani and their Neighbours: A Primitive Civilization of the Eastern Himalayas.* London: Routledge and Kegan Hall.

Eggan, Fred. 1954. "Social Anthropology and the Method of Controlled Comparison," *American Anthropologist*, 56: 743-763.

Gerth, H.H. and Mills, C.W. 1947. *From Max Weber: Essays in Sociology.* London. (pp.38-63).

Jolly, Margaret 1992; "Banana Leaf Bundles and Skirts: A Pacific Penelope's Web?" (pp.38-63) in *History and Tradition In Melanesian Anthropology.* Berkeley: University of California Press.

Kan, Serge 1989. "Cohorts, Generations, and Their Culture: The Tlingit Potlatch in the 1980s," *Anthropos*, 84 (4-6).

Leach, Edmund. 1985. "Talking about Feudalism," (pp.6-24) In Edmund Leach, S.N. Mukherjee, and John Ward (eds.), *Feudalism: Comparative Studies*. Sydney: Pathfinder Press.

_____. 1983. "The Kula: An Alternative View," (pp.529-538) in *The Kula: New Perspectives on Massim Exchange.* Cambridge: Cambridge University Press.

____. 1965 (1954). *Political Systems of Highland Burma: A Study of Kachin Social Structure.* Reprint Boston: Beacon Press.

____. 1962. "Introduction: What Should we Mean by Caste?" E.R. Leach (ed.), In *Aspects of Caste In South India, Ceylon and North-west Pakistan.* Cambridge: Cambridge University Press.

Malinowski, Bronislaw. 1965 [1935]. *Coral Gardens and their Magic: Soil-tilling and Agricultural Rites in the Trobriand Islands.* Volume I. Bloomington: Indiana University Press.

Mapusia, Mike. 1980. "The *Tee* Ceremonial Exchange System the Enga Province," *Oral History*, 8 (7): 46-74.

Myrdal, Gunnar 1967. "Discussion," In Anthony de Reuck and Julie Knight (eds.), *Caste and Race: Comparative Approaches.* J & A Churchill Ltd.

Passin, Herbert 1967. "Discussion", In *Caste and Race: Comparative Approaches.* Edited by Anthony de Reuck and Julie Knight. London: J & A Churchill Ltd.

Radcliffe-Brown, A.R. 1952. "The Mother's Brother in South Africa", In *Structure and Function in Primitive Society.* London: Cohen and West.

Reynolds, Susan 1996. *Fiefs and Vassals: The Medieval Evidence Reinterpreted.* Oxford: Clarendon Press.

Rosman, Abraham, and Paula G. Rubel 1971. *Feasting with Mine Enemy: Rank and Exchange among North-west Coast Societies.* New York: Columbia University Press.

____. 1986. "The Evolution of Central North-west Coast Societies," *Journal of Anthropological Research*, 42 (4): 567-572.

____. 1989. "Dual Organization and its Developmental Potential in Two Contrasting Environments," In David Maybury-Lewis and Uri Almagor (eds.). *The Attraction of Opposites: Thought and Society in a Dualistic Mode.* Ann Arbor: The University of Michigan Press.

Rubel, Paula G. 1967. *The Kalmyk Mongols: A Study in Continuity and Change.* Bloomington: Indiana University Publications.

Rubel, Paula G. and Abraham Rosman 1970. "Potlatch and *Sagali*: The Structure of Exchange in Haida and Trobriand Societies," *Transactions of the New York Academy of Sciences,* Series 2, 32, 6.

____. 1978. *Your own Pigs you may not Eat: A Comparative Study of New Guinea Societies.* Chicago: University of Chicago Press.

____. 1983. "The Evolution of Exchange Structures and Ranking: Some North-west Coast and Athapaskan Examples," *Journal of Anthropological Research*, 39 (1): 1-35.

Schiefenhovel, Wulf, and Ingrid Bell-Krannhals. 1996. "Of Harvests and Hierarchy: Securing Staple Food and Social Position in the Trobriand Islands," in Polly Wiessner and Wulf Schiefenhovel (eds.), *Food and the Status Quest: An Interdisciplinary Perspective.* Providence, R.I.: Berghahn Books.

Schneider, David. 1984. *A Critique of the Study of Kinship.* Ann Arbor: University of Michigan Press.

Sinha, Surajit. 1967. "Caste in India: Its Essential Pattern of Socio-Cultural Integration," in Anthony de Reuck and Julie Knight (eds.), *Caste and Race: Comparative Approaches.* London: J & A Churchill Ltd.

Swanton, J.R. 1908. *Social Conditions, Beliefs, and Linguistic Relationship of the Tlingit Indian.* 26th Annual Report of the Bureau of American Ethnology for the years 1904-05. Washington, D.C. Smithsonian Institution.

Tambiah, S.J. 1967. "Discussion," In Anthony de Reuck and Julie Knight (eds.), *Caste and Race: Comparative Approaches.* London: J & A Churchill Ltd.

Weiner, Annette. 1980. "Stability in Banana Leaves: Colonization and Women in Kiriwina, Trobriand Islands," (pp. 270-293). In Mona Etienne and Eleanor Leacock (eds.), *Women and Colonization: Anthropological Perspectives.* New York: Praeger.

TWO

KINGSHIP, TRIBAL SOCIETY AND FERTILITY IN KORAPUT: Different Aspects of the Ritual Bali Jatra

TINA OTTEN

Overview

The recitation of large epics is often accompanied by the conducting of agrarian rituals.[1] This paper aims to give a first account of some of these rituals in the region of Dandakaranya. The region reaches from parts of Bastar in Chhattisgarh towards the Eastern Ghats in Andhra Pradesh and covers the new districts Malkangiri, Koraput and Nowrangpur in Orissa. The Koraput district, on which this article will mainly focus, is situated in the Eastern part of this region. Agrarian rituals, called *Bali Jatra*[2] or the procession[3] of the sand, are a major event for the indigenous population. Similar ceremonial occasions, also called *Bali Jatra,* are celebrated in other districts of the Dandakaranya plateau, especially in the region of Nowrangpur and Bastar, but a comparison between these varieties should be the theme of another paper.[4]

The following article will offer a comparison of the *Bali Jatra* rituals in Koraput, but since the name is widely used in the State of Orissa, I must initially distinguish between the different types of *Bali Jatra*. My present subject should not be associated with the *Bali Yatra* fair in Cuttack, held to celebrate the tradition of the long trading link with the Indonesian island of Bali, being now-a-days a big business fair. Outside of the Cuttack District, the *Bali Jatra* rituals are of a very different type. Conducted as royal communication with the divine and as a healing rite they are both carried out by male specialists over several hours or days. My own research is concerned with *Bali Jatra* as performed by female specialists concentrating on aspects of fertility as well as protection against misfortune, especially illness. The rites often run for several weeks. Apparently such a time span coincides with a geographical and a gender pattern, since the *Bali Jatras* in the north are short and conducted by men, whereas the longer southern type is a woman's ritual.[5]

In the longer southern type of *Bali Jatra* we find facets of all other *Bali Jatra* rituals. Furthermore, different aspects of the ritual take on greater importance depending on which community of Koraput it is performed by. Nevertheless, the main components are always the same and show the interrelatedness of the *Bali Jatras*, even though they may primarily be understood and performed as a fertility rite, a protection against illness, or a royal rite. All *Bali Jatras* follow the same temporal structure, being always performed before a new annual cycle begins. *Bali Jatra* in Koraput are carried out in the wet season, the dry winter season and in the hot season before rituals such as *Dussehra*, *Pus Porbo* and *Chait Porbo.* Before a more detailed treatment, some of the main aspects of *Bali Jatra* in Koraput are introduced.

Bali Jatra is mainly carried out by the community of the Modhyo Mali ("Middle" Gardeners) and Sano Mali ("Junior" Gardeners) who are labelled by the State administration as *Other Backward Class*[6] (*OBC*), but other communities, like Rona[7] and Jodhia[8] perform the ritual as well. *Bali Jatra* is regularly conducted in a cyclical series of festivals. Initially organized in three subsequent years by the landholding community of a village, a new cycle begins after an interval of another two or three years.

Each village has its own festival pattern. The different villages do not celebrate simultaneously, and therefore, their time schedules may vary by a few days. The different time schedules coincide with the horoscope of the village, which is drawn by the village astrologer (*disari*). In deciding on the horoscope of the village he considers its birth time. This birth time is determined by the time the village goddess was installed in the village, what will be indicated in its palm leaf manuscript. He also draws the horoscope for the important ritual specialists, such as the sacrificer (*Pujari*) and the singing-narrator (*Gurumai*).[9] By taking into account their horoscope and the horoscope of the village, he determines a suitable day to start the festival. From the start of the festival until its end, the astrologer hands over control of ritual events to those persons of the village who lead the performance of the *Bali Jatra Festival*. These leaders sing in the narration of the epic. They are called *Bali*

Jatra Gurumai-s in order to distinguish them from the divining *Gurumai*-s, in command of healing powers.

Plate-I: Picture of the interior of a *Bali Jatra* shrine with two *Gurumai*-s, one playing a bow in front of the clay pot symbolising the *Bali* god.

The clay pot represents the Bali god (*Bali mapuru*). Every night, when the singing-narrators, the *Gurumai*-s, proceed with the story of the creation of the world, women gather in the *Bali* shrine (*Bali ghor*) and worship the *Bali* god. They pour a leaf-cup full of husked rice into the clay pot which is then again covered with the winnowing fan by the *Gurumai*-s while they proceed with the recitation. During this recitation the gods and goddesses are believed to enter the shrine through the door or swing down from above on a white thread hanging from the roof to the altar place of the *Bali* shrine. The accompanying music, played by the Dom clients of the cultivators, invites the deities to enter the bodies of the women in order that they may dance. From this point on the women will dance nearly every night.

In the course of the recitation certain important episodes, which have been sung by the *Gurumai*, are enacted by the villagers. These chants convey the creation of the entire world with mythical characters being born throughout the epic. Some of the main figures included the queen *Jema*, her brother *Lalit Raja* and their father's brother *Mahapatra*. Another important figure is *Bhima*, who is in some villages, the elder brother of the siblings, but in others the mother's brother.[10] Throughout the course of the epic, *Jema* will find a bride, called *Devirani Phulseri*, for her brother *Lalit Raja* and subsequently their marriage will be celebrated in grand style and re-enacted by the villagers. The main persons who enact the epic, like *Jema*, *Devirani Phulseri*, *Lalit Raja* and *Bhima*, have been chosen by the *gurumai*-s long ago. They have been chosen in such a way so that the kinship relations in the epic mirror their kinship relations in the village where the performers live. This means the people who play the characters of *Jema* and *Lalit Raja* should be in the village in a sister-brother relation and that the girl who plays the role of *Devirani Phulseri* is in the group of marriage partners to the above mentioned people.

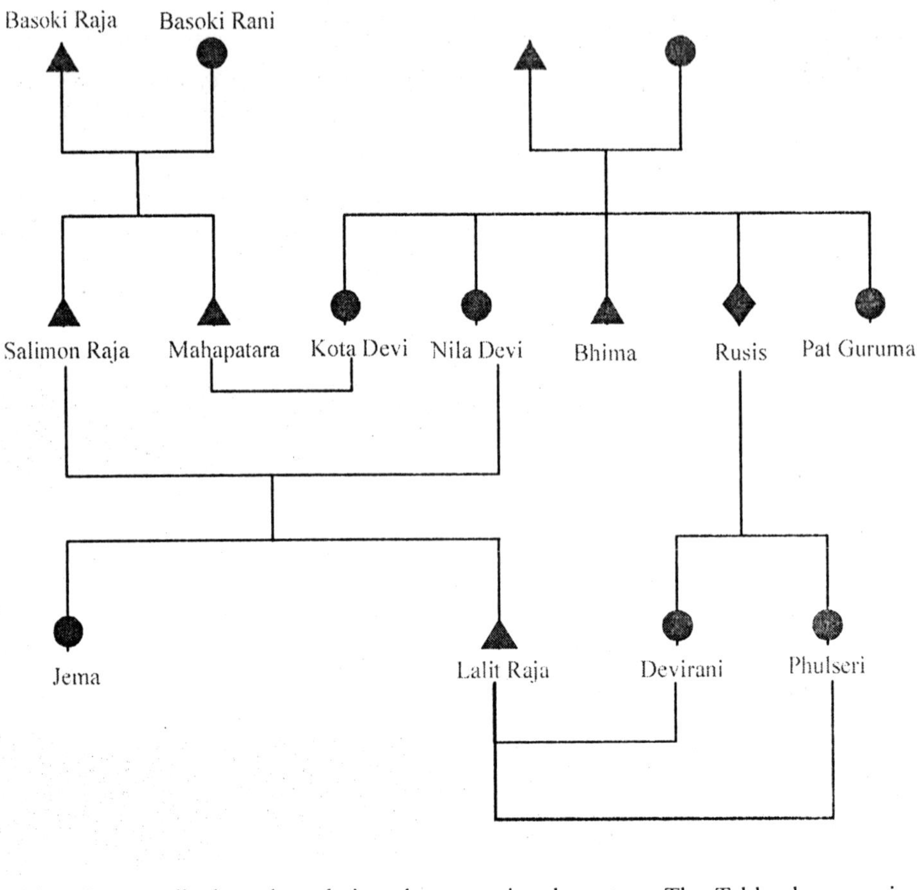

This diagram displays the relations between the characters. The Table shows main characters involved in the play, but not all figures are described in this paper.

Returning now to the synopsis of the epic; in a period of a few days leading upto two weeks after the marriage of *Lalit Raja* and *Devirani Phulseri* the last sequence of rituals start. The starting date is selected in order to ensure that it, as well as the date of the rituals of conclusion, falls auspiciously. From this date onwards, the time schedule is fixed. The *Jatra* will end in ten to twelve days. Rituals of fertility are carried out by the village people while the recitation of the epic continues. From this time onwards, one character of the epic plays a dominant role in these rituals. That is *Bhima*, who is regarded as the god who taught mankind agriculture. The people in the villages could not confirm what kind of agriculture *Bhima* taught mankind exactly, but I found a short note on a *Bali Jatra* myth in a book about the Pengo Language. There, a sequence from the huge epos is recited, the sequence in which *Bhima* asks the deities to allow him to show mankind how to use the plough[11].

In the village, *Bhima* is represented by one man as the main *Bhima* (*mul Bhima*) and several other men who also enact *Bhima*. The rites of fertility of the last ten to twelve days start with a ritual which is called asking for seed (*bion mangba*). In the morning around six o'clock, all men who represent *Bhima* run off to the gardens of the village. Here they pick garden fruits and uproot small trees for instance banana trees. With their "harvest" they return to the village. These agricultural products are to be distributed amongst the *Gurumai*. At around ten o'clock the *Gurumai* will prepare to go to every household in the village to ask for seed (*bion magba*). One of them carries a bamboo basket known as *Jema dala*, neatly decorated with white and red flowers. They are accompanied by the musicians and an old woman, the mother of the Chalan, who belongs to the Dom community, who are the clients of the landholding communities. The procession starts in the colony of the dominant community, in the house of the *Pujari* from where the procession goes to the houses of the *Gurumai* and then to every house in the same manner. It proceeds as follows: by approaching a house the *Gurumai* stand in a row and start singing the song "asking for seed". The *Jema* basket stands on the ground in front of them. While the song continues the female head of the family comes out with a coconut, a small leaf cup of wheat in which sometimes also maize seeds are laid, and a leaf cup full of rice on which a one or two rupee coin is also kept. The rice and wheat is taken care of by the old Dom lady who collects the rice with her basket and wheat with the *Jema* basket, after the *Gurumai* and the head of the house have honoured each other by putting a few grains of rice on each others feet, shoulder and head. Should the house have promised an offering to the gods, and given a coconut along with the seeds, one of the *Gurumai* will break it in front of the house and throw pieces in four directions which is followed by a greeting (*juar*) to and away from it. This is done to ensure fertility and health for the household. Later on the female head of the house carries the *Jema* basket full with wheat by herself to the other neighbouring house. This process continues till every house has given its share. Afterwards the *Gurumai* approach the village goddess *Hundi* and the place of assembly in the village (*Sadar*) in order to offer sweet water (*Pana Pani*) and a song. After completing both the rituals, the *Jema* basket and the basket full of *Orua* rice is taken inside the shrine of *Bali*. The wheat from the *Jema* basket is poured into a winnowing fan because the basket will be used in the next ritual for another purpose. The next step of the ritual, called "sowing of flowers" (*phul bunba*) will be carried out after two or three hours.

For the 'sowing of flowers' ritual the *Gurumai*, the ritual specialist *Pujari*, the *Bhima* and at least one woman from every household go to a pond or brook outside of the village. The *Bhima* takes their place next to the water source. The *Gurumai* and the *Pujari* stand next to them and prepare a make-shift altar. A few wheat grains are placed in a small basket and sweet water is poured into five small leaf cups. At the centre of a drawn diagram (*bana)* we find a white flower with an egg. The *Gurumai* then start singing. Another ritual is performed for the water goddess *Jol Kamini* by the *Pujari* at a place nearby. It also consists of a make-shift altar with a diagram drawn and sweet water placed on it. In addition a white chicken is offered up for sacrifice by the *Pujari*. The *Gurumai* continue singing during the whole ritual. After a while the main Bhima joins them and together they all start collecting sand in their baskets. Bhima puts his sand in a small piece of hollow bamboo (*ada*) and the *Gurumai* in the basket of *Jema* before the women start collecting sand (*bali*) from the surrounding area into their bamboo baskets. The senior *Gurumai* sprinkles puff-rice as a farewell offering and the people walk towards the village. The procession gathers in front of the shrine of Bali with their baskets filled with sand, which they then on a large heap in front of the *Bali* shrine. The sand it is worshipped by the *Gurumai*. After the worship, the baskets are filled again with the sand from the heap and with the seeds, which were collected in the morning and which are now distributed by the main *Bhima* amongst the women. Every woman puts five layers of sand and grains of wheat, rice, maize and beans into her basket. Inside the *Bali* shrine, the *Pujari*, the *Gurumai* and *Bhima* perform the ritual of first of all putting the seeds near the *dunkuli handi*. A diagram is drawn on which coconut and other offerings (*Pana Pani*) are placed. The *Jema* basket is prepared by the *Pujari* and the main *Bhima*. One layer of sand is put in it and then a layer of wheat and maize is sprinkled on top. This is repeated four times making five layers of each in total. Next to the *dunkuli handi*, right at the wall of the house, is the small rectangular arrangement to keep the sand, called *Sona Sorya*. This place is filled with sand and seed in the same way as the *Jema* basket. *Bhima* prepares his small piece of hollow bamboo with sand and wheat. The *Jema* basket will be kept in the house of the most senior *Gurumai*, though in some villages the *Pujari* might host it, and *Bhima* takes the small piece of hollow bamboo home. Outside of the *Bali* shrine, all women who had collected sand are still busy preparing their own little baskets. Each woman puts five layers of soil and seed in their basket. The seeds are grains of rice, maize and beans, but of most value are the grains of wheat. Wheat is difficult to obtain in this area, because the Mali do not cultivate their own and the shops seldom sell it in small quantities.[12] Every woman takes her home to place next to her domestic altar.

In the shrine of *Bali* and in all houses of the village, the seeds are left to sprout under the sand. Everyday they are sprinkled with turmeric water. Everyone eagerly watches the sprouting. People say that it is a bad omen if the seeds fail to germinate, or an indicator of good health and coming fortunes, if the seeds develop abundant scions.

The next five days, the shrine of *Bali* will be closed; no one will gather here at night, no dancing will be performed, like it was performed the last weeks nearly every night. Then, on the evening of the fifth day, the final three days of the festival begin. In the night the main *Bhima* starts painting a mural. He places points on the mural to designate where the gods live. This is accompanied by the music appropriate for each god, which played by the musicians. In the morning of the next day this mural is painted by men and boys of the dominant local lines. The mural shows the following gods: in the enclosed centre of the wall we see gods like the seven sisters (*Sat Bauni*), the seers, *Rusi*, and the king. In the middle is the marriage canopy. Outside the enclosed sphere we find characters that live in the hilly areas and the wilderness such as the teacher of fire (*Agniguru*) and the old Tiger god (*Buda Bag*). My impression is that the place where the gods are drawn shows their place in the sacred geography. We can think of the opposition between culture and nature, symbolised through palace and wilderness (*bana*).[13] While the wall opposite to the entrance shows all the gods involved in the pantheon of Mali culture, the other walls also show people of general interest, like film heroes. Here everybody is invited to paint, while on the wall of the gods only few people are allowed to do so. Not all saints, gods and goddesses painted on the wall by different people are known to all. Not even the *Gurumai* could name all the images[14].

On the two nights that follow now, the dancing in the shrine of *Bali* reaches its climax. All gods are present, and the women dance in trance for hours. The day before the last night of dancing, a few men from the village go to the hills to look for a special kind of thorn bush in order to tie the branches in the form of square seats. The women gather early in the evening in the shrine of *Bali*. Every woman who comes inside pours a leaf-cup full of rice on the mat. The rice slowly develops into a heap which is given later to the *Gurumai*.

The scions at the altar of the shrine have grown now so that they are roughly the size of the palm of ones hand. Next to them leans the bow. The senior *Gurumai* plays it for a short while and then she places it back again. Thereafter all women put a piece of holy thread (*brata*) around their right arms. In front, next to the altar the children gather, most of them girls. A *Gurumai* tells them the story of "seven sisters" and, in a very abridged form, the story of the epic. Meanwhile, men bring representations of their gods, mostly in the form of swords inside the shrine and place them next to the scions. Later on, nearly every family brings rooster and ducks, and black pigeons as sacrifice (*boli*) to the god *Bali*. Like the goddesses, the god *Bali* is thirsty for blood. For vows that were fulfilled by the god against illness and misfortune, people bring what they have promised. They explained to me that if not then the god *Bali* will become hungry and eat them in the course of the year. The women have fasted the whole day, in order to await the gods. The musicians play special tunes, each dedicated to a particular god. They start with tunes of the gods of the dominant group. While listening to the tune, the women of the different local lines get to their feet and start dancing. Once in trance, some of the men prepare seats of thorns. Special seats of thorns are prepared for the main gods and goddesses such as *Lalit*, *Jema*, *Bhima* etc.

but the others can be reused. Swords representing the god of local lines are placed on seats of thorns. Every local line has its sword and seat. People who are in trance sit and stand on it with bare feet. They are not however supposed to bleed nor get injured. It is said that if the gods are displeased then the thorns will hurt. A woman who was hurt by the thorns told everybody that it was not blood, but vermillion, mixed with water. In addition to sitting on the thorns, the main actors of the epic have to stand on small sandals of thorns prepared for them. After long hours of dancing in trance the women get a few hours of rest, before the rituals of the final day begin.

In the morning of the final day, offerings of hens, sheep and goats are made to the village goddess and to the god *Bali*, represented by the clay pot. Thereafter men and boys dance at the village dancing ground accompanied by girls and women who came as guests from other villages and later by girls and women from the village itself. After hours of merrymaking, a short break is announced, before all women and many girls assemble in front of the shrine of *Bali*. All carry their baskets of scions and position them around the village square and in front of the *Bali* shrine. At the same time all paraphernalia is brought out and assembled on the stone platform (*sadar*) where the villagers normally assemble. Final offerings are made to the god *Bali*.

At a time announced by the astrologer some time before the women who have now placed the baskets of scions onto their heads, the *Gurumai-s* who are carrying the *puja* items from the *Bali* shrine, and the whole village proceed to the pond from which they had gathered the sand (*bali*) ten days ago.

These scions are brought to the pond in hundreds of baskets, now coloured yellow with turmeric. Here the *Gurumai* sings the last part of the epic. This part details how the scions are brought to the pond. A final ritual for goddess *Jol Kamini* offers her eggs and hens. Thereafter the husband of the eldest *Gurumai* cuts some scions from the *Jema* basket and distributes them between the *Pujari,* astrologer and the *Gurumai*. All other women then "harvest" the scions from their baskets. The latter become flowers of *bali,* called *bali phul*. These are now exchanged between friends and neighbours. The *Pujari*, astrologer and *Gurumai* exchange the flowers of *bali* which they too have received. In having conducted such a formal exchange, those who had not previously been related will now call themselves "*bali phul*". The bond of friendship as such is also called *bali phul*.

Plate-II: The *Gurumai* leaves the *Bali Jatra* shrine with the *Bali Jatra* pot. In front the *Bhima* act with their swords and in the back a part of the mural is visible which shows the gods involved in the divine play.

Plate-III: Women place the baskets with the scions, called *bali phul* on the village assembly place (*sadar*). In front is the bamboo container (*bhima kada*) with the *bali phul* of *Bhima* and behind is the big basket (*jema dala*).

Plate-IV: Women carry baskets with scions, and the items of the *Bali* shrine to a nearby pond.

Variations of Bali Jatra

The above outline holds true for all *Bali Jatra* I have documented in Koraput. However, the performance of *Bali Jatra* in the Koraput District also offers certain variations of which I could distinguish three main types so far. The most common type is the *Bali Jatra* performed in the cold season before the New Year festival in the month of *Pus* (December-January). Normally the festival lasts for eight weeks, or, in a somewhat abridged form, for a minimum of nine days. Another type of *Bali Jatra* is conducted in the wet season for twelve days in the month of *Osa* (August-September) being called *Osa Bali*. At the former king's court *Osa Bali* had been performed until some decades ago.[15] The third type of *Bali Jatra* carries on for twelve days in the hot season just before the festival of *Chait Porbo* (April). This occasion marks the beginning of the new agricultural cycle and its structure is strikingly similar to a structure found by Gregory in similar agrarian rituals of Bastar[16].

Bali Jatra in the Winter Months before the Beginning of the New Year (Pus Porbo)

The *Bali Jatra* during winter time follow a certain pattern though they can also be conducted for different spans of time. The full version of a cycle will last for eight to nine weeks though a nine days version is also acceptable. Some villages always perform the full version of the festival; others the abridged version. The distinction is mostly based on two criteria: the astrological sign of the village as well as the well-being and prosperity of its different households.

Some villages always perform *Bali Jatra* in an abridged form in case the astrological sign of their village demands that practice, since all villages, like human beings, have their particular horoscope. It is related to the time when the village "was born", that is, when the shrine of the village goddess was established. According to the horoscope (*rasi*), each village has its auspicious day, on which it is advisable to start or terminate a ritual. The abridged form of *Bali Jatra* is named after the day of the week on which it has to end. The final day is binding for the entire life span of the village and is chosen by an astrologer. The name of the *Bali Jatra* will be *Roila bali*, if the final day is always celebrated on Sundays. When *Bali Jatra* ends on Monday it is *somari bali;* when it ends on Tuesday it is *mangala bali* and if ending on Friday, then it is *sukri bali*. No *Bali jatra* ever ends on a Wednesday or Saturday, because these days are connected to the demons *Ketu, Rahu* and *Sani*. The difference between the abridged and the full version of *Bali Jatra* is, as *gurumai*-s told me, insignificant, being just a matter of elaboration. Whereas some villages always perform *Bali Jatra* in an abridged form due to their astrological sign, others decide to perform it in nine days or so because preceding poor harvests disallow major expenses. *Bali Jatra* in its full version is called *jema bali*[17]. The queen *Jema* is a strong character, loved and adored by her family or known as a pampered girl (*ladri toki*) who conducts all kinds of mischief, but who finally accepts the responsibility to continue the local line by selecting a bride for her brother, the king. While *Jema* is the active character throughout the epic, her brother plays passive role. He is called *Lalit Raja* which, in the translation of the village people, means unfit for work. Accordingly, *Jema*, the strong woman, has to get things done. This story of *Jema* is the theme in all *Bali Jatra* epics throughout Koraput district, whether they are conducted in their full length or abridged form.

Bali Jatra in the Hot Season Before the Hunting Festival (Chait Porbo)

Bali Jatra before *Chait Porbo* is rarely celebrated in the Koraput District whereas in the adjacent Nowrangpur District, where it is the high time, it lasts for over ninety days. In this case, the villages confirm their lasting mutual friendship between themselves. *Bali Jatra* in general implies a time of reciprocal exchanges between different villages. The festival *Chait Porbo* which is celebrated directly afterwards, concentrates—on the contrary—on the relations inside a village, whereas *Chait Porbo* finds its visual expression in the fact that the villages paths and streets are closed off with roadblocks.[18]

Bali Jatra in the Rainy Season (Osa Bali)

Osa Bali is performed for twelve days from new moon to full moon in the month of *Osa* (August-September) according to Desia language, which is known as month *bhadrobo* in Oriya. This type of *Bali Jatra* is performed not just in villages but also at the king's court. At the king's palace in Jeypore, *Osa Bali* was celebrated until the reign of Vikrama Dev Brahma VII who died in 1944. The *Bali Jatra* rituals have been discontinued ever since his daughter's son Vikram VIII has suffered from a prolonged illness. Some old servants of the *Ragunath* Temple opposite the old king's palace (*moti mahal*) still remember how they participated in former *Bali Jatra* festivals. In my fieldwork area, many Rona people—formerly the militia of the king of Jeypore—still perform *Osa Bali.* It is followed by the *Dussehra* festival at the full moon in the month of *Dosera* (September-October). At the *Dussehra* festival, the representatives of the tribal villages assemble along with their gods and goddesses at the court of the king to deliver their annual token tribute.

The nine-day-long *Durga Puja,* well known in Orissa and Bengal, and the ritual *Dussehra* which takes place on the tenth day are even celebrated today in Jeypore, with much pomp and circumstance at the former court of the king. In the year 2004 delegations of more than 60 villages and towns came to the palace to which they all brought along their gods symbolised by long sticks (*lathi*) and chariots (*potuar*). The arrival of the *lathi* indicated the subordination and affiliation of their home to Jeypore and even today, without a reigning king, people wait eagerly to learn which particular *lathi* will be brought to Jeypore[19]. During the time of the king's rule the arrival of the gods belonging to the former court of Nandapur and to the kingdom of Jagdalpur (Dantewara) was required to confirm their subordination to the court of Jeypore.

One month before the *Dussehra* festival[20], the *Bali Jatra* was celebrated in Jeypore. Five shrines for the Bali god were erected, one of them in the king's palace, others in the respective sides of the city.[21] Singing-narrators (*Gurumai*) performed the rituals inside of the shrine of *Bali*. All of them were men, being dressed in saris and acted in a feminised way. The eyewitnesses of the *Bali Jatra* performed at the kings court told me, that it was celebrated like the *Bali Jatra* in the villages today: they placed the *Bali* god at the altar (*bedi*) represented by a clay pot, along with a winnowing fan, a bow and an arrow. Through their songs they invited the gods of the country to visit the shrine of

Bali. The *Gurumai* also brought the sand called *bali* from a pond or stream and put the seeds together with sand in the baskets in order to sprout. Those of the neighbourhood gathered their own *bali* seeds in baskets for their *puja* rooms. While the epic was sung by the *Gurumai* the women came to the shrine daily to worship in the manner described above. The last day of *Bali Jatra* was celebrated in grand style: inside of the *Bali* shrines the baskets of scions, called *bali Phul*, were worshipped for a last time before being taken out. Outside, men performed the *nato*, a special kind of drama, based on the stories of the Ramayana.

In those old times, women, men and *Gurumai* went to a pond, most probably in the same way as we see today. At the pond, the scions were taken out of the baskets. The scions were called the "flowers of the sand", the *bali phul*. But in those times, in contrast to today's practice, the *bali phul* were not immediately exchanged between friends and neighbours. First they

Plate-V: The picture shows three men in the 1960 ties, who perform the *nato* at the kings court in Jeypore. All feminine characters are played by men. The person on the left shows Purohit Gopinath Patro (†2005) who described the proceedings of *Osa bali* to the author.

had to be handed over to the king. Therefore, the men proceeded to the *Dussehra* ground.[22] The king sat on an elephant in a golden *palanquin*; his guests next to him on animals with silver *palanquins*. Among the guests, officers and functionaries, martial arts contests were performed, awards like gold or linen clothes being given to the winners. Afterwards, the *Gurumai* handed the first *bali phul* over to the king. The representatives of the villages did so as well before beginning to exchange *bali phul* amongst themselves. The king then proceeded to his palace where he exchanged *bali phul* with his friends and ministers, while the tribal people exchanged the *bali phul* among their friends and neighbours on the *Dussehra* ground.

Conclusion

My impression is that the structure of the different *Bali Jatra* is very similar. We find structural similarities of performance and time frame in all. Five points are significant: (1) All *Bali Jatra* in Koraput are performed at the village level, not by a local line or a single family. (2) *Bali Jatra*, when conducted, are always performed before other festivals begin, which usher in the practices of the agrarian cycle. (3) The contents of the epic vary from village to village, but the main characters are the same in all versions. The general outline of the epic—with slight variations—is also the same. Consequently, it is unlikely to have been very different at the court of Jeypore, forty years ago, where the royal form of *Bali Jatra* was performed. (4) All *Bali Jatra* performers display a bow. However, the bows vary in size and also in the frequency they are employed. (5) Finally, the major point is the display of ritual friendship bonds on the last day. The exchange of the scions, or *bali phul*, publically re-enacts this relationship.

The performance of all *Bali Jatra* in Koraput follows a double performance structure as found in other festivals as well (Flueckiger, 1996). Women of the village worship god *Bali* inside the shrine and their houses and women or feminised men, called "*Gurumai*", sing the *Bali Jatra* epic inside the *Bali* shrine whilst men dance and perform a drama called *nato* outside in front of it. The female role is prominent in all *Bali Jatra*. All action of the villagers follows the pace set by the *Gurumai* with their song and the village astrologer announces only the start and the end of the *Jatra*, the auspicious days. His ritual power is handed over to the *Gurumai*. Fertility as ritually organised by women and related to the products of the land and the authority of the ruler, may be said to be the central messages of the long ritual cycle.

NOTES

1. The recitation of the various forms of the Ramayana epic is often connected with rituals concerning the well-being of gardens, livestock and the farmer's family. For Middle India *see* e.g. Fuchs, 1960; Flueckiger, 1996; Gregory, 2003.
2. I will write the names associated with gods in italics and with a capital letter. Therefore the procession of god *Bali* will be written as *Bali Jatra*. Desia names indicating posts or nouns will be written with italics and small letters, for instance *Gurumai*.
3. *Jatra* has different meanings in Oriya it has the connotation of going and festival, fair and *tirtha jatra* is pilgrimage (Padhi:1163). In Sanskrit it is journey, procession, *see* Böhtlinck and Roth, 1990: 122. Therefore I translate *Jatra* here as procession, since the sand is brought from a brook situated outside into the village and later placed back.
4. My fieldwork was carried out between 2000 to 2005 about a period of 12 months in Koraput and 2005 for three months in Nowrangpur district of Orissa.
5. These topics have been discussed by many papers at the conference in Sambalpur in February 2004 named "*Dialogues with Gods*" and focusing on rituals similar to my research on *Bali Jatra*.
6. The Indian administration differentiates "Other Backward Classes", "Scheduled Tribes" and "Scheduled Castes". Communities of all three types belong to the "Desia" category of Koraput, *i.e.* the indigenous people.
7. Rona have the administrative status of an *Other Backward Class* in Orissa and a *Scheduled Tribe* in Andhra Pradesh. For a more detailed description of Rona *see* Otten 2007b.
8. Jodhia, also known as Jorhia Poroja, are a *Scheduled Tribe*.
9. The process of drawing a horoscope is described in Otten 2007a.
10. The observation of variations of the same epic even in a small area is a quite common feature; *see* (Flueckiger, 1996; Gregory, 2004).
11. Burrow, T. and S. Bhattacharya (1970).
12. Beteille has worked on the cultural differences of the wheat favouring North and the rice favouring South of India (1974).
13. See for a discussion of *vana* and *ksetra see* Sontheimer (1987).
14. This feature is very common in Koraput. It reminds me of polythetic classification. The idea of polythetic classification was introduced into social science by Needham (1975) and used in the Hindu context by Eichinger Ferro-Luzzi (1989).
15. This could be the more general type of the royal New Year ceremony called "*suniya*" which is performed in Puri and Parlakimedi, and which marks the beginning of the new *anka*-year of the king (Berkemer, 1993:132).
16. Gregory 2004:95.
17. I have the full record of the village Lamanda, which is presently being analysed.
18. For a description of *chait porbo see* Otten, 2002.
19. When the villagers arrive in Jeypure, some go to certain families, who have given a vow beforehand to worship their deity and to dress their deity *(lathi)* in new cloth.

20. Information from Purohit Gopinath Patro, who participated at that time in the festivals.
21. Other *bali* houses were erected in Purnagod, Nua Sahi, Dhoba street, Godia street. Where the Bali houses were erected, now the Durga idol is erected. Everyside and community had its own goddess. Each of the five *bali* houses hosted one of the following devis: Durga, Kalika, Dongordei, Bhagaboti and Gongadei.
22. Today Vikram Dev College Ground.

REFERENCES

Appadurai, Arjun, Frank J. Korom and Margaret A. Mills (eds.) 1991. *Gender, Genre, and Power in South Asian Expressive Traditions*. Philadelphia: University of Pennsylvania Press.

Berkemer, Georg. 1993. *Little Kingdoms in Kalinga. Ideologie, Legitimation und Politik Regionaler Eliten.* Stuttgart: Steiner.

Blackburn, Stuart H. 1988. *Singing of Birth and Death: Texts in Performance.* Philadelphia: University of Pennsylvania Press.

Blackburn, Stuart H. and Brenda E. Beck (eds.). 1989. *Oral Epics in India.* Berkeley: University of California Press.

Böhtlinck, Otto and Rudolph Roth. 1990 [1855–1875]. *Sanskrit-Wörterbuch*, in Kaiserliche Akademie der Wissenschaften (ed.) New Print of the St. Petersburg Edition. Delhi: Motilal Banarsidass.

Fuchs, Stephen. 1960. *The Gond and Bhumia of Eastern Mandla.* London: Asia Publishing House.

Flueckiger, Joyce Burkhalter. 1996. *Gender and Genre in the Folklore of Middle India.* Ithaca and London: Cornell University Press.

Gell, Alfred. 1997. "Exalting the King and Obstructing the State. A Political Interpretation of Royal Ritual in Bastar District, Central India," *Journal of the Royal Anthropological Institute,* 3 (3): 433-50.

Gregory, Chris A. 2004. "The Oral Epics of the Women of Dandakaranya Plateau," In Mallebrein, Cornelia; Guzy, Lidia Julianna (eds.), *Facets of Orissan Studies, Journal of Social Sciences*, 8 (2): 93-104. (Special Issue).

Gregory, Chris A. and Harihar Vaishnav. 2003. *Lachmi Jagaar*, Kondagaon: Kaksad Publications.

Mishra, Mahendra Kumar. 2004. "Oral Epics in Kalahandi," *Folklore*, 26: 811-900.

Narayana Rao, Velcheru 1986. "Epics and Ideologies. Six Telugu Folk Epics," (pp. 131-64) In Stuart H. Blackburn and A. K. Ramanujan (eds.), *Another Harmony. New Essays on the Folklore of India*, Berkeley: University of California Press.

Narayana Rao, Velcheru 1991. "A Ramayana of Their own: Women's Oral Tradition in Telugu," (pp. 114-136) In Paula Richman (ed.), *Many Ramayanas: The Diversity of a Narrative Tradition in South Asia*, Berkeley: University of California Press.

Otten, Tina 2002. "Changing Annual Hunting Festival Chaitra Parba. An Outsiders View," *Adivasi*, 40 (1/2): 82-91.

____. 2007a. "Cosmic Time and its Influence on Rona Girls and Women." (pp. 137-156) In Angelika Malinar, (ed.), *Time in India: Concepts and Practices*. Delhi: Manohar.

____. 2007b. "Given by God and Come by Itself. Illness among the Rona." (pp. 173-198) In Georg Pfeffer, (ed.), *Periphery and Centre: Studies in Orissan History, Religion and in Anthropology*. Delhi: Manohar.

Padhi, Baba Baidyanath 2001 [1964]. *Bruhata Oriya Abidhan*. Cuttack: Friends Publishers.

Richman, Paula 1991. "Introduction: The Diversity of the Ramayana Tradition," (pp. 3-21) In Paula Richman, (ed.), *Many Ramayanas. The Diversity of a Narrative Tradition in South Asia*. Berkeley: University of California Press.

THREE

THE BUFFALO SACRIFICE OF THE KOND AND THE CREATION OF SOCIETY

ROLAND HARDENBERG

Introduction[1]

Ritual performances (...) momentarily make manifest what is otherwise a fiction (Leach, 1954: 16).

In a nutshell, this quotation of Edmund Leach captures the essence of the relationship between ritualised action and social structure. Ethnographers of Middle Indian tribal societies are often confronted with the fictional nature of social distinctions: people claim to belong to certain descent and status groups, yet in daily affairs one hardly ever observes corporate groups in action; informants distinguish various sacred and secular offices, titles or ranks, but nobody appears to have any marked authority over others in regular village affairs. The impression of general tribal anarchy partly vanishes, however, when people begin performing rituals. In such ritual contexts, social bondedness and separateness is defined by divisions of work, distributions of meat or cooked food, and distinctions of space.[2] During ritual action, the segmentary character of tribal society becomes visible. This is particularly obvious in so-called feasts of merit (*e.g.*, Birket-Smith, 1967; Jones, 1974; Jacobs, 1990) which are often arranged in a series of ranked ritual events involving ever higher and more encompassing levels of society. The most simple feasts of merit are usually attended by members of the patron's own family or descent group, while the organisers of the largest and most expensive events typically invite the "whole valley" or "all villages".

A central aspect of all these rituals is exchange in the form of gift-giving, distribution and sacrifice. Depending on the context, relations between givers and receivers vary in these exchanges on a scale from proximity to distance—in social and in territorial terms—and may be characterised by various degrees of either co-operation or hostility. Affines are allies but, at the same time, potential enemies, and exchange relations between them create alliances but involve hostility and conflict as well. The most elaborate rituals in tribal middle India often require the participation of both the proximate and the distant—the agnates and the affines—and express themselves as a contest between the two groups. These events can be compared to the potlatch which according to Rubel and Rosman can be seen as "a drama in which are played out the essential elements of Kwakiutl culture and society, while revealing the components of the social structure" (1971: 157).

This paper deals with the grand buffalo sacrifices (*kodru parbu*) performed by Dongria Kond as an offering to their earth goddess.[3] This ritual event manifests the most important social distinctions in Dongria Kond society, marks social boundaries, creates alliances between social groups and takes the form of a drama or contest. Before illustrating these points with ethnographic data, I initially provide a brief introduction of the people and the history of these sacrifices. This is followed by a general overview of the timing, the place, the preparations and the major events of the buffalo sacrifices. In the final section, I present my answers to the question of the type of society these ritual activities generate.

The Dongria Kond[4]

Dongria Kond populate the Niamgiri hills, a mountain range with peaks up to 1600 m. which are part of the Eastern Ghats dividing Orissa into two regions, the coastal plains and the hilly hinterland where most of the tribal people of the Union State live. According to the latest survey (Kanungo, 2004), the Dongria consist of about 8000 people who reside in 112 villages spread throughout the mountains. Although it is illegal, they continue to practice shifting cultivation on the hill slopes, which are still relatively densely covered with forest when compared to the plateau area in south Orissa. Each Dongria village has its own territory clearly demarcated by stones and claimed by a particular clan.[5] The members of this clan are responsible for organising the buffalo sacrifice to the earth goddess who is represented by a stone arrangement in the centre of their village.

In most villages, the Dongria Kond do not reside alone, but together with a smaller community of people referred to as Dombo. In the plains and valleys, members of this community are considered to be Harijan or "untouchables". In the hills, too, they have a lower status than the Dongria whose houses they cannot enter, whose daughters they cannot marry and who will not accept food from them. However, they perform important functions as middlemen and "culture brokers" (Pfeffer, 1997). The Dombo sell a number of products produced by the hillmen to towns people. Furthermore, they buy products in public market places or shops outside the hills in order to sell them again to the Dongria. The Dombo provide their tribal patrons with the animals they require for sacrifices to the gods and ancestors. Dongria pay for these animals in cash, which they obtain from selling their agricultural produce either directly to the townsmen or again through their Dombo interlocutors. Applying an exchange model devised by Bloch & Parry to these transactions, one may say that the Dombo assist the Dongria in converting the "short cycle of exchange", linked to individual competition and reproduction, into the "long-term cycle of exchange" concerned with the collective efforts to uphold the social or cosmic order (Bloch and Parry, 1989).

During my fieldwork in the Rayagada District of Orissa in the years 2001-2003. I observed a total of eleven buffalo sacrifices among the Dongria Kond residing in the Niamgiri hills and their neighbours, the Desia Kond, who populate the valleys. In each case, the sacrifices required weeks, if not months, of preparations, lasted for several days, and were an occasion for extensive feasting and merriment. In the following account, I briefly summarize some aspects of this very complex event, which I have described in more detail elsewhere (Hardenberg, 2005).

Timing

Among the Dongria Kond, the buffalo sacrifice is performed in the months of *Phalgun* or *Chaitra*, *i.e.* between February and April, whereas their neighbours in the valleys, the Desia Kond, usually conduct it one or two months earlier (in *Pausa* or *Magh*). The festival is celebrated by each Dongria village at irregular intervals of roughly ten to twenty years. The main reason for this sacrifice, locally referred to as *kodru parbu* or "buffalo festival", is to fulfil the wishes of the earth goddess. If the goddess wants to be given a sacrifice, she appears before the village shaman in a trance to ask him: "I am giving you rice, millet, and water, but what do you give to me?" The male villagers then sit together and discuss whether they are able to sponsor the festival. They fix a date for the sacrifice which may, however, be postponed for one or more years should the fields fail to produce rich crops. Only when every single household in a village has brought home a rich harvest, do the sponsors begin with the elaborate preparations. Even then, the event may be postponed for another year if, for example, an epidemic befalls the village or one of the important village elders dies.

Another reason given for organising the buffalo festival is the establishment of a new settlement within the village territory. Dongria Kond settlements are usually not very old because people often abandon their village sites when the local earth goddess is believed to be angry and cause death and illnesses among the people or make the crops shrivel and wither in the fields. In such cases, all or some of the residents may decide to desert their houses and either move into an already existing settlement of their clan brothers or, if land is available, set up a new settlement in a village territory that had earlier been abandoned and has lain fallow for many years. In the latter case, they must perform rituals in three consecutive years while beginning to cultivate the hill slopes, with the last event in this series of rituals being the buffalo sacrifice to the earth goddess. This is performed at her representative stone near the place where the new settlement is to be built. Again, the event may be postponed when the harvest has not been abundant or when calamities have caused suffering among the people.

The intervals between two buffalo sacrifices are further influenced by the circulation of sacred objects which are displayed during the festival. These objects, such as brass pots or knives, are collectively owned by a certain number of villages of the same clan and passed on from the villagers who conducted the sacrifice last, to those who will perform it next. The exact number of villages united in such a sacrificial community known as a *muta* varies between three and seventeen villages. In the Niamgiri hills, I recorded thirteen such sacrificial communities belonging to the nine territorial clans[6] of this area.

Place

The main sacrificial events take place at various shrines inside and outside the village sponsoring the festival. Of these shrines, those of the earth goddess and her husband, inside the settlement, become the focus of the most elaborate ritual activities.[7] The earth goddess is represented by a certain number of round, polished stones, as well as some flat, rough ones, collectively referred to as *Jakeri*. Villages usually have more than one *Jakeri* on their territory, which are of two types: some mark places where—either in the past or the present—people built settlements, and others identify certain hillslopes as fields used for shifting cultivation by a particular village.

The *Jakeri* is often addressed as "mother" (*aya*) by the Dongria. Each *Jakeri* represents the earth goddess *per se* and at the same time a particular representation of her within a certain territory. For example, each *Jakeri* has a particular name, and like the land itself is attached to a specific clan worshipping her. From a myth collected about a hundred years ago by Moodaliar (*see* Thurston, 1987 [1909]: 368-71), one derives the idea that each *Jakeri* marks the site where a part of the flesh of the mother of all Kond had been buried. According to this myth, she asked her eldest son to sacrifice her, cut off her flesh, and bury it in the ground to bring firmness and fertility to the soil. The son fulfilled her request and buried her flesh in various different places which he then covered with stones. According to MacPherson, the Kond used to bury the flesh of the human victim at the shrine stones as well as in their fields. Today, the Dongria continue to offer the buffalo flesh obtained at a sacrifice in another village to their own earth goddess by placing it near to her stones before consuming it.

Next to the *Jakeri*, usually only a few meters towards the east, one comes across a flat, crude megalith which may be as small as 20 to 30 cm. or as large as two meters. It stands upright, has a peak, and thus resembles a mountain. The Dongria call this stone *Koteiwali* and address the deity represented by it as their "father". He is considered to be the husband of the *Jakeri* and may be said to represent the male principle in relation to the earth goddess, the female principle. At the place of both divine beings, the sponsors, with the help of a large number of other people, set up shrines in the weeks preceding the actual sacrifice.

Preparations

In the centre of their village, above the stones representing the earth goddess, the sponsors of the sacrifice build a house with one room. They are assisted in their work by people from brother villages who belong to the same sacrificial community. It takes about three to four days to complete the house, but the work is spread over a period of several weeks. Dongria men are responsible for cutting trees, shaping logs and planks, setting up beams and pillars and making bamboo mats to be fixed as walls at all four sides of the house. Women smear the ground with cow dung and plaster the bamboo walls with mud. Once these are dry, they first apply a layer of white paint on the walls before decorating them with triangles and lines of different colours. When ready, the house appears as an image of the goddess herself: the beams of the house represent her breasts, the eastern wall has two holes resembling her eyes, the straw on the roof is likened to hair, and the paintings on the wall sport the same patterns as the shawls worn by young girls and boys on festive occasions.

Towards the east, another shrine is built near the site of the stone representing the husband of the earth. Instead of a house, the villagers construct only a simple wall made of two or three pillars and a bamboo mat plastered with mud. However, like the house of the goddess, the wall for her husband has two holes and is decorated with the same paintings. In between these two shrine sites, the sponsors set up sacrificial stakes. Depending on the number of victims to be offered to the earth goddess, one or more sacrificial poles will be fixed into the ground just in front of the two holes in her house. It is to these poles that the victims are tethered on the night before the actual killing. In front of the wall representing the husband of the earth, another T-shaped stake is set up. During the festival, the heads of chickens sacrificed in the name of different deities are placed on top of this T-shaped stake.

About a week before the three main days of the buffalo sacrifice, men from a number of different villages turn up to assist the sponsors in protecting the sacrificial site. These people are not like the "brothers" from the same sacrificial community as they belong to different clans when compared to that of the sponsors. These helpers are potential affines referred to as *Mudrenga*, a word probably derived from the Oriya term *Mudra* meaning "coin" or "seal", or in its verbal use (*mudriba*) "to close". They are responsible for "closing" off the village and the sacrificial site by constructing bamboo fences around the whole village and around the place where the victim is to be tethered. In addition, they are responsible for protecting the buffalo until the proper time of sacrifice on the Sunday morning.

The exact number of buffaloes to be sacrificed depends upon the number of *Jakeri* or village territories claimed by the sponsors. The victims are purchased outside the Niamgiri hills by a Dombo and sold to the Dongria for a relatively high price. Until the beginning of the festival, the village Dombo takes care of the victims, but from time to time the sponsors lead them on ropes to neighbouring villages to show them to their friends and relatives. In these villages, the buffaloes are taken from house to house, fed with rice, and anointed with oil and turmeric water. The same procedure is repeated in the sponsors' village at the beginning of the three day festival.

The Three Main Days

sukrawar satar line
saniwar desa runda ane
adiwar dine kodru mada ane

These three sentences capture the essence of the three main days of the buffalo sacrifice. The first line states that on the Friday (*Sukrawar*) the umbrella will stand. The word for umbrella, *Satara*, actually refers to one or two long bamboo poles upon which the sponsors attach a brass pot and a small shade made of bamboo or iron. The brass pot circulates within the sacrificial community and is retained by the sponsors until the next village celebrates the buffalo sacrifice. On this Friday, the long bamboo poles are carried to each and every house of the village to be worshipped before they are fixed into place next to the wall representing the husband of the earth goddess. There, the local shamans climb up the poles, become possessed by the male deity and bring him down to the ground for further worship. At the end of the ceremony, chickens and a white ram are sacrificed to the god.

The next line describes the events on the Saturday when the *desa* or "people of the whole country" assemble (*runda*) in the village. While close relatives of the sponsors as well as their ceremonial friends, known as *Tonenga*, will have arrived the day before, young boys and girls from various villages and the representatives of a number of different affinal clans turn up on this Saturday to enjoy the festival. During that night, they meet either in the girls' dormitories or in the woods for sexual encounters. On this day, the rituals focus on two places, firstly the stones representing the deity of the local line (*Kona penu*) and the god of hunting (*Lada penu*) outside the village, and secondly, the wall of the goddess of wealth and prosperity (*sita penu lahi penu*) inside the house.

The third line mentions the most important event on this third and last day of the festival, the killing (*Mada*) of the buffalo (*Kodru*). It should ideally take place early on the Sunday morning when light first appears over the horizon and when all other major rituals have been completed. During this night and some of the previous ones, ritual specialists invoke the earth goddess by sitting in her hut and chanting verses for hours and by offering alcohol, incense and small pigs to her. When these incantations reach their conclusion on the Sunday morning, the main sacrificial specialist takes a knife and pierces it through the one of the holes in the eastern wall of the house. When he touches the victim, tethered to a post in front of the house, this is the sign for the young men to kill the buffalo. The *Mudrenga*, who are expected to protect the buffalo until this time, withdraw and the young affinal men run towards the fence, pull it down, and hack the victim to death with their axes. In most festivals I witnessed however, the sacrificial specialists were not able to complete their rituals because the young men managed to break through the fence and kill the victim in the middle of the night. Once the victim has been killed, someone hurries to cut off its head and carry it inside the hut where, together with a piece of liver and a coin, it is placed in front of the stones. One of the ritual specialists quickly collects some of the buffalo's blood in a bowl or cupped hands and carries it to the earth goddess. This is considered to be the most important gift as the blood signifies the life of the victim.

On this Sunday, pieces of flesh are distributed to the sacrificers who leave the village with gestures of triumph and, when reaching their own villages, place the buffalo meat at the shrine of their own *Jakeri*. Whereas in the past, this meat would be buried near the *Jakeri* and in the fields, it is cooked now-a-days and consumed by the sacrificers. The remainder of the dead animal is divided into different pieces, distributed to some people as a means of marking their status, and finally, on the following day, cooked and consumed by all those who are present.

In the following interpretation of the sacrifice I restrict myself to the question of the type of society generated by these ritual activities. My answer is divided into two parts. In the first, I show how the sacrifice is linked to a particular social organisation, and in the second part I discuss the structural principles that order relations between those involved in the event.

Sacrifice and Social Organisation

The buffalo sacrifice manifests the various levels of Dongria Kond social organisation. Firstly, the sacrifice is intimately connected to the clan system. Each clan is made up of villages and the shrines of the earth goddess. The sponsors buy the victim and organise the sacrifice, but are not allowed to kill the buffalo, a task that must be undertaken by others. The latter rule creates a strong unity between all members of the same clan, even if they never form a corporate group and do not occupy a clearly demarcated, compact territory.

Secondly, the level of segmentation below the clan, the *Muta*, is intimately linked to the performance of the festival. In contrast to other areas populated by Kond, a *Muta* in the Niamgiri hills is not made up of different clans. Instead, it is a sacrificial community of people belonging to the same clan who jointly own certain objects necessary for the performance of the sacrifice. Each *Muta* consists of a certain number of villages whose earth goddesses are linked to the same clan, but the *Muta* as such does not correspond with any discrete area. Rather, it is a unit of cooperation and mutual assistance, since ideally all members of a *Muta* should partake in preparing the sacrificial site and performing the rituals. It is uncertain whether the *Muta* as a sacrificial community has ever been identical with the *Muta* as an administrative unit in the royal organisation for collecting revenue from the tribals. Certain titles used by the Dongria such as *Saanta*, *Bismajhi* or *Naika* may imply this, but additional historical sources are required to make any firm assertions regarding this question.

On the next level down in the social organisation we observe those villages which are relevant for the buffalo sacrifice in a double sense. Firstly, the festival is performed by people who, irrespective of their actual clan affiliation, cooperate on the basis of their common residence. This means that even residents belonging to clans distinct from the sponsoring clan assist in preparing the sacrificial site or organising the feasts. Secondly, each settlement has at least one, if not more village territories (*Padari*) marked by stone arrangements representing the local earth goddess. The buffalo sacrifice is performed for one or all of these territories and the dominant clan claiming rights over these territories has to bear the main costs of the sacrifice.

At the village level, people are differentiated according to their affiliation to distinct local lines, or *Punja*, and houses, or *Ijo*. The word *Punja* is used in a double sense since it refers to a certain status category as well as to a particular local descent group. The titles of these status categories—*Jani, Pujari, Bismajhi, Mondal*—are probably derived from functions exercised by certain specialists during rituals. For example, Nayak, in his book on the Dongria Kond, cites a saying according to which the *Bismajhi* brings the rice, the *Jani* calls the gods, the *Pujari* cooks and the *Mondal* supervises everything (Nayak, 1989: 134). The lowest level of the social organisation, the house, acts as a unit in different phases of the festival, most clearly so when the victim is driven from house to house and bathed in water, anointed with oil and fed with rice by the chief woman of the house. Certain houses have a prominent status as custodians of the sacred objects that either circulate within the *Muta* or remain within the village even after the completion of the sacrifice. The seniority and status of particular houses is further expressed by the custom of placing a leg of the buffalo victim on their roofs.

Creating Society

The buffalo sacrifice creates and maintains relations between villages of the same clan as well as between villages of different clans. The rule that forbids someone to kill the victim of their own earth goddess creates an opposition between clans, in this case between the clan of sacrifiers (the sponsors) and the clans of sacrificers (those who kill the victim). The latter are affines, but not all affines act as sacrificers. Rather, two categories of affines, the *Mudrenga* and the *Tonenga*, should not kill the victim. This can be compared to rules prohibiting marriage. Clan exogamy establishes an opposition between agnatic and affinal clans. However, certain additional rules prohibit the direct repetition of inter-marriage among the Dongria and thus in effect define some people within the affinal category as non-marriageable. The same holds for the buffalo sacrifice. On the one hand, all sponsors are opposed to members of affinal clans by the rule stating that clan members of the sponsors may not kill the buffalo. On the other hand, among the affines, some will join the sponsors rather than act as sacrificers because they are also prohibited from killing the victim. Thus, the organisers of the buffalo sacrifice will be joined in their preparations by villagers from an affinal clan called *Mudrenga*. The latter are the protectors of the sacrificial victim and they may not become involved in the actual killing. In addition to the *Mudrenga*, the *Tonenga*, or ceremonial friends, come as guests to attend the festival. The *Tonenga*, although belonging to an affinal clan category, are not really affines because one is not permitted to intermarry with ceremonial friends. As in the case of the *Mudrenga*, these friendship relations do not simply link individuals but whole communities, for instance five Sikoka with five Wadaka villages. Unlike the *Mudrenga*, the *Tonenga* do not have to perform any function, they are simply very honourable guests who bring gifts such as a buffalo, rice and alcohol with them, and in turn receive gifts from the hosts at the time of their departure. However, both *Mudrenga* and *Tonenga* may not kill the buffalo, and this rule distinguishes them from the other type of affines, the young men, who are not only allowed, but expected, to put the buffalo to death. According to Aparajita, these young affines are collectively referred to as *Padria* (1994: 236), a word I have not encountered in my fieldwork. The Dongria refer to the assembly of these young people in their village as *Desa Rundam Ane* meaning the "people from near and far have assembled". The word *Desa* implies that these are people from various places who are neither agnates nor bound to the sponsors as protectors or ceremonial friends.

The buffalo sacrifice thus brings together members of four types of villages: (1) the *Muta Loku* or "brothers", (2) the *Mudrenga* or "protectors", (3) the *Tonenga* or "friends", and (4) the *Desa Loku* or sacrificers. The distinctions between these different types are made on the basis of the following structural principles: territory, affinity, and rivalry. Firstly, all *Muta* villages are united territorially on the basis of their common clan land and their co-operation in performing the sacrifice to that land, and stand in opposition to, or are demarcated from, other villages whose members worship the earth goddess of another clan territory. Secondly, the *Muta* villages unite with the *Tonenga* because they may not intermarry with one another, although they may marry into other categories of people if this is not ruled out on grounds of clan exogamy. Finally, *Muta*, *Tonenga* and *Mudrenga* villages are united in their opposition to the young visitors from other villages as only the latter are expected to kill the victim. Furthermore, while members of the former three types of villages unite on the basis of mutual assistance and friendship, the latter are real or symbolic rivals. The buffalo sacrifice thus 'creates' Dongria Kond Society by establishing relationships of different values between the various social units that depend on each other for their well-being and the fertility of their land.

NOTES

1. The data presented here were collected in three consecutive years in villages either located in the Niamgiri hills (Dongria Kond) or in the valleys around the small market town Kalyansingpur (Desia Kond). Various sequences of the buffalo sacrifice (*kodru parbu*), including the elaborate preparations, have been observed by myself in eleven different villages in the years 2001 to 2003. For further details *see* my post-doctoral thesis. I am grateful to Kate Sullivan for the final language correction.
2. In a recent monograph on the Gadaba of Koraput District, South Orissa, Berger (2007 *see* also this volume) argues that feeding, feasting and consumption are value acts that actively create social distinctions. He illustrates this point with his very detailed ethnography.
3. For a history of the buffalo sacrifice, which used to be a human sacrifice called *Meria*, *see* Boal (1997) and Padel (2000).
4. For previous studies on the Dongria Kond *see* Nayak (1989) and Jena *et al.* (2002). My own monograph has been submitted in 2005 as post-docthesis ("Habilitation") to the Westphalian Wilhelms University, Muenster (*see* Hardenberg, 2005).
5. For details *see* my other article in this volume.
6. Jakesika, Kadraka, Kruska, Nandruka, Niska, Pusika, Sikoka, Wadaka, and Wengesika.
7. For more details concerning the Dongria Village *see* my second paper in this volume.

REFERENCES

Aparajita, U. 1994. *Culture and Development. Dongrias of Niyamgiri.* (Tribal Studies of India Series T 167) New Delhi: Inter-India Publications.

Berger, P. 2007. *Füttern, Speisen and Verschlingen. Ritual and Gesellschaft im Hochland von Orissa, Indien.* Berlin: LIT Verlag.

Birket-Smith, K. 1967. "Studies in Circumpacific Culture Relations. Potlatch and Feasts of Merit," *Det Kongelige Danske Videnskabernes Selskab Historisk-filosofiske Meddelelser* 42/3.

Bloch, M. & J. Parry. 1989. "Introduction: Money and the Morality of Exchange," (pp. 1-32) in M. Bloch, and J. Parry (eds.), *Money and the Morality of Exchange.* Cambridge: Cambridge University Press.

Boal, B. 1997. *Human Sacrifice and Religious Change. The Kondhs.* New Delhi: Inter-India Publications.

Hardenberg, R. 2005. *Children of the Earth Goddess: Society, Marriage, and Sacrifice in the Highlands of Orissa (India).* Post-doctoral Thesis, Westphalian Wilhelms-University, Muenster, Germany.

Jacobs, J. 1990. *The Nagas. Society, Culture and the Colonial Encounter.* London: Thames and Hudson.

Jena et al. (Jena, M.K., P. Pathi, J. Dash, K. Patnaik and K. Seeland) 2002. *Forest Tribes of Orissa. Lifestyle and Social Conditions of Selected Orissan Tribes. Vol. 1. The Dongaria Kondh* (Man and Forest Series 2). New Delhi: D.K. Printworld.

Jones, S. 1974. *Men of Influence in Nuristan. A Study of Social Control and Dispute Settlement in Waigal Valley, Afghanistan*. London & New York: Seminar Press.

Kanungo, A.K. 2004. Problems in Educating Tribal Children: The Dongria Kondh Experience. *www.anthroglobe.ca/docs/Dongria.pdf* (20.10.2004)

Leach, E.R. 1954. *Political Systems of Highland Burma*. London: Athlone Press.

MacPherson, S.C. 1865. *Memorials of Service in India: From the Correspondence of the late Major Samuel Charteris Macpherson, C.B., Political Agent at Gwalior during the Mutiny, Formerly Employed in the Suppression of Human Sacrifice in Orissa, edited by his brother*. London: John Murray.

Nayak, P.K. 1989. *Blood, Women and Territory. An Analysis of Clan Feuds of the Dongria Konds*. Delhi: Reliance Publishing House.

Padel, F. 2000. *The Sacrifice of a Human Being. British Rule and the Konds of Orissa*. New Delhi: Oxford University Press.

Pfeffer, G. 1997. "The Scheduled Tribes of Middle India as a Unit: Problems of Internal and External Comparison", (pp. 3-27) in. G. Pfeffer and D.K. Behera (eds.), *Contemporary Society: Tribal Studies. Vol. 1: Structure and Process*. New Delhi: Concept Publishers.

Rosman, A. & P. G. Rubel 1971. *Feasting with Mine Enemy. Rank and Exchange among North-West Coast Societies*. New York: Columbia University Press.

Thurston, E. 1987 [1909]. *Castes and Tribes of Southern India* (Volume III-K). New Delhi & Madras: Asian Educational Services (Reprint).

SECTION II

AFFINAL PATTERNS: CATEGORIES AND RULES IN MIDDLE INDIA

FOUR

BROTHERHOOD AND OTHERHOOD IN BASTAR: On the Social Specificity of "Dual Organisation" in Aboriginal India[1]

CHRIS GREGORY

Introduction

This paper will present ethnographic material on the hitherto unreported Halbi kinship system of Bastar District, Chhattisgarh. I will argue that it has the logic of the four section system of the Kariara of Aboriginal Australia but not the same social form. Instead of the socio-centric moiety system of the Kariara, the Halbi system divides kin into "us" (*dadabhai*= brotherhood) and "them" (*saga*= otherhood). This is cross-cut by an "our generation"/"parent's generation" distinction. The semantic value of all kin terms derives from this quadripartite structure and in this sense the Halbi system is logically prior to the Kariara system which requires a 4×2–part structure (four generations and two moieties) to account for semantics of the kin terms. An interesting feature of the Halbi system is that it is semantically identical to the Maria Gond kinship which has a Dravidian lexicon. A logical consequence of this system is the possibility of daughter's marriage. The existence of this system in Bastar raises empirical questions about its geographical distribution and theoretical questions that lie at the heart of debates between Dumont, Trautmann and others about the nature of Indian kinship. It also raises questions about Aboriginal kinship in India and the cultural politics of identity.

The Halbi Kinship System

The Otherhood/Brotherhood Distinction

Halbi is an Indo-Aryan language spoken in the Bastar District, Chhattisgarh. Bastar District lies in the heartland of the Dandakaranya (DNK) plateau, a relatively isolated ecological zone that contains speakers of many languages including Gondi, a Dravidian language. The linguistic divide that runs through the DNK plateau is the basis upon which many observers distinguish tribe from caste in this region: the Gondi-speakers are "tribes" and the Halbi speakers are "castes". However, if we compare the Halbi kinship system with that of the Gondi we find that the only difference is the lexicon; from a semantic point of view they are identical.

The only published account of the kinship system from this area is the brief description of the Maria Gond system provided by Grigson (1938: 236-40, 244-48, 308-9). He was influenced by the prevailing orthodoxy (Russell and Lal, 1969: III, 64) that the clans of the tribes of Central India fitted into a moiety system but found that his examples of "triangular" marriage contradicted this theory. Lévi-Strauss (1969: 394) seized on this point and used it as an example of the existence of a system of generalized exchange in India. However, the Halbi system is an example of neither "restricted" exchange nor "generalized" exchange and this can be seen if we example more closely the nature of the dualism that the early observers noted.

The terms used by the Gonds to capture this dualism is *dadabhai/ akomama.* Grigson (1938: 236) translates *dadabhai* as "brother-clan" and *akomama* as "wife-clan". The term *dadabhai* is a compound consisting of *dada*, which means "elder brother" and *bhai* which means "brother". The term *akomama* is also a compound: *ako* means "mother's father" and *mama* means "mother's brother". The corresponding terms in Halbi are *dadabhai* and *saga*. The semantic value of this distinction is identical to the Gondi case; the difference between *saga* and *akomama* is purely lexical.

The key to grasping the meaning of this distinction is to see it in "us-centric" terms that divides the social universe into "us" and "them" rather than in socio-centric terms as moieties. I gloss this distinction as "brotherhood" *versus* "otherhood". This is a perspective that can be thought of lying between the extremes of an individualistic ego-centric perspective and a god-like socio-centric perspective. Yorke (1979: 98), in his study of kinship among the Raj Gonds of Andhra Pradesh, has correctly noted that "Gond Society works on complex notions of "them" and "us" but the significance of his insight has not been developed.

The brotherhood for the Halbi speakers of Bastar consists of the following three categories of people.

1. Ego's *thoka*. This can be defined as a modified minimal patriline that includes in-marrying women and excludes out-marrying women, *i.e.* *thoka* = ego's patriline + wives – married sisters.

The patriline is minimal in the sense that only known close male relatives are included. Given that lineages typically have a shallow genealogical depth, it usually only includes ego's father and mother, his father's brothers and their wives, and his brothers, their wives, and unmarried sisters and daughters. The unity of this group is ritually affirmed once a year at the time of the *navakhani* (literally "new eating") ritual when the first fruits of the rice harvest are eaten in a communal feast. This is the only occasion in the year when men, women and children all eat together. On every other day of the year men eat before women and children may eat apart from both.

The composition of this group reflects the fact that marriage radically severs a daughter's link with her father's lineage. A married woman is completely absorbed into her husband's lineage. This is a widespread phenomenon that occurs throughout India (Trautmann, 1981: 25-6).

2. Ego's *bas*. This word can be translated as "otem" and it includes all those *thoka* in ego's occupational group who share the same totem. It is, therefore, a modified maximal patriline (or "clan") that includes in-marrying women and excludes out-marrying women. It is maximal in the sense that it includes unrelated lineages. Members of a *bas* are not allowed to enter the kitchen of another member unless they share the same *thoka*. If different *thoka* of a *bas* live in the same village they usually share a temple where the deities of the *bas* are kept and worshipped. These temples are distinct from the temples that each *thoka* keeps its own deities in.

The forgoing distinction between *thoka* and *bas* is best illustrated by considering the words of one of my informants, Jaidev Baghel, whose full name is Jaidev Baghel Gadwa. Gadwa is the occupational group to which he belongs, that of bronze caster. For Jaidev this is a marker of his *adivasi* ("tribal") status and he has vigorously challenged the claims of Government officials for whom it is a marker of his "Scheduled Caste" status. Jaidev argues, on good grounds as we shall see, that the officials who classify him this way have no understanding of Gadwa kinship and culture. The name Baghel literally means "Tigerman" and its tells us that his *bas* (totem) is a tiger *(bagh)*.

> We say a *thoka* is like this: four to five generations above our paternal grandparent's were one. Our ancestors, too, were one. Just like Rameswar Baghel's and our ancestors were one. So Rameswar's *thoka* and our *thoka* is one.…So it is said that if our paternal ancestors were one there was one *thoka*. But Bihari Baghel and us have one clan (*bas*) but his lineage (*thoka*) and our lineage (*thoka*) is different. His paternal ancestors and our paternal ancestors are different. So Bihari Baghel and us are *dadabhai.* For this reason that our surname *(sarnema)* is one. (Jaidev Baghel, 2 October 2001, my translations from the Halbi).

On *dadabhai* and *saga* he had the following to say:

> The difference is like this. Bihari Baghel's family and mine are *dadabhai.* We have the same surname, *i.e.* Baghel and Baghel. But our lineage *(thoka)* is different. And when we say *saga* it includes people like Manoj Sagar. He is a member of the Sagar clan and we are the Baghel clan. Our surnames are different and we are able to intermarry. This is because both clans are different. So, Manoj Sagar belongs to our *saga.* A *saga* relationship is said to be a little distant. It is not a close relationship.

This distinction must be modified slightly to take account of the third component of *dadabahi.*

3. Ego's *sarhu-bhai.* A *sarhu-bhai* is ego's wife's sister's husband. Thus a *sarhu-bhai* is a brother *(bhai)* who may be from the same or a different *bas.* Thus Jaidev's *dadabhai* includes not only the Baghel clans but it may also his *sarhu-bhai* from different *bas* and *thoka.*

The following chart captures the above three points in visual form.

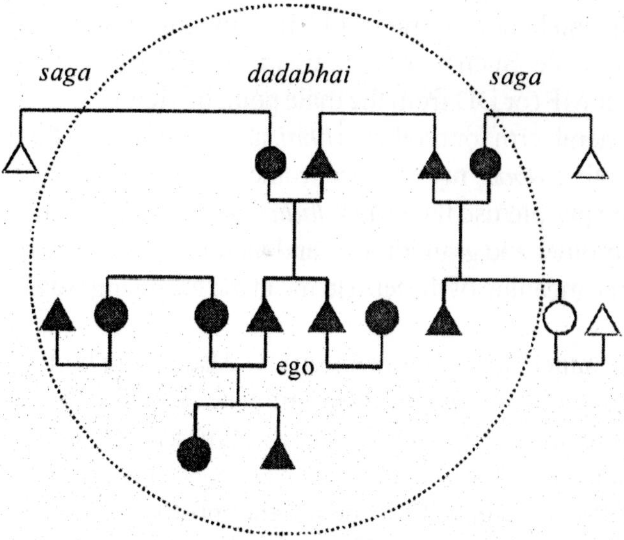

It should be obvious that the form of dualism that underlies the brotherhood/otherhood has nothing in common with the moiety divisions found in Aboriginal Australian kinship systems. However, it has a close affinity with the "cross/parallel" distinction found in South India. Strictly speaking, the cross/parallel opposition makes no distinction between married and unmarried cross siblings but the brotherhood/otherhood opposition does. In this sense the Halbi opposition makes verbally explicit what is implicit in all Indian kinship: the radical severance of a daughter from her father at marriage and her total incorporation into the family of her husband.

The Our-generation/Other-generation Distinction

This vertical distinction between "us" and "them" is crosscut by a horizontal distinction between "our generation" and "other generation". This distinction is not lexically marked in the way that the vertical distinction between *dadabhai* and *saga* is; however, it is possible to elicit the expression *bap/beta, may/beta* (literally father/son, mother/daughter relation) for the 'other' generation and *bhai/bahin* (literally brother/sister) for 'our' generation.

The implication of the generational distinction is to conflate alternate generations: grandparents and grandchildren belong to "our" generation, such that the "parallel" grandparents (FF and MM) are members of the brotherhood (*dadabhai*) and the cross grandparents (FM and MF) are members of the otherhood (*saga*). Thus parallel grandparents are like siblings and cross grandparents are like cross cousins. As cross-cousins are in a joking relationship and hence marriageable, it follows that cross grandparents are also marriageable. Such marriages are rare but I do have a case of a woman marrying her MF (or DD from the male point of view).

The general term for brother is *bhai,* and this defines a field that includes my elder brother, *dada,* my younger brother, *nani bhai* and my father's father, *dada.* Some people use the terms *dada* and *dadi* interchangeable. Sukdai Korram, a mother and grandmother and member of the Weaver community, explained the meaning of the term to me in the following way.

> The father's father is our *dada* (eB). *Dada* is our brother *(dada hamco bhai lage).* We respect everything he says. We honour him. We are fearful in his company. *Dada* regards us as his little sisters. We do not stand freely in front of him. The name of my *dada* is Mangaru. His brother's name is Pilu and another brother's name is Khandu. We touch the feet of *dada.* He touches us on the chin. *Dada* talks nicely to us (Sukdai Korram, 22 February 2001).

The term for mother's mother is *aji* and that for sister *didi.* Mrs. Sukdai Korram gave me the following account of the meaning of *aji,* whom she calls *bai-didi* literally women-sister.

> I call my mother's mother *bai-didi.* I regard *didi* as a sister. We greet her by touching her feet. She greets us by touching our chins and giving us a blessing. We do not joke with her. We regard her as an elder sister. If she tells us not to go somewhere we do not go. When she hits us we do not get upset. It is good when the young respect the word of the elders. My sisters (*i.e.* MM) are two. My real sister's name is Parvati but I do not know her sister's name. *Didi* calls me by name. We do not call her by name. We do not do anything in front of *didi* Like that she is a sister.

The term for mother's father is *aja* and the term of reference for a male cross cousin is *maina bhai* (and *maina bahin* for a female cross cousin). They both occupy the same semantic field called *hansinata,* joking relation. Sukdai Korram defined *aja* as follows:

> We call our mother's father *aja.* He makes jokes with us saying, "You are my wife's sister's". We get angry with him and reply, "Hey old

> man, what is happening, don't you feel embarrassed? You are joking with daughter's daughters". He replies, "You are my daughter's daughters therefore I joke. I will marry you". We pretend to get very angry with him. My *aja's* name was Jhitaka'. He had two brothers. One called Dibi, one whose name I do not know. *Aja* is a joking relation. We touch his feet. He touches our chin.

The term for father's mother, *ai,* also belongs to the semantic field of *hansinata,* joking relation. Consider Sukdai Korram once again.

> We call the father's mother *ai*. *Ai* is a joking relative. *Ai* jokes with us. She will do funny things. My *ai's* name is Dasmi. My *ai* were a group of four sisters. One was called Bhayari. I address my *ai* as '*ai'*. *Ai* addresses me as *noni* or Sukdai. *Ai* gives me much affection. I touch the feet of *ai.* My *ai* touches my chin. She gives blessings. We tickle *ai.* We will make *ai* roar with laughter. We make many jokes. If my daughter Sabita asks my *ai* for money when I am given some, my *ai* will brush her off. *Ai* gives me much affection. Therefore, I will joke with her. Sometimes she will pretend to get angry. When my daughter Sabita was menstruating she jokingly said (to her *ai),* "Give me money otherwise I will touch you". My daughter Sabita sleeps with her *ai.* If, one day, her *ai* does not feed her she will ask again and again.

The Four Semantic Fields of Halbi Kinship Terms

The two cross-cutting distinctions create four semantic fields as follows:

	B OTHERHOOD *(saga)*	A BROTHERHOOD *(dadabhai)*
1 Other Generation	1B cross parenthood *(mama-bubu)* MB, FZ	1A parenthood *(may-bap)* F, M, FB, MZ
2 Our Generation	2B joking relationship *(hansinata)* X-cousins MF, FM	2A siblingship (ego group) *(bhai-bahin)* B, Z, FF, MM,

For ease of exposition I have labelled the vertical division A/B and the horizontal division 1/2 such that the four fields become 1A, 1B, 2A, and 2B. The semantic value of 2A and 2B has already been discussed above. The sibling group, 2A, includes brothers, unmarried sisters, and parallel grandparents. This is the ego group and the semantic values of the other fields only have meaning with respect to this ego group. Each field should be conceived of as containing reciprocal sets. Thus the kin relations in 1A should, strictly speaking, be written as F:S, F:D, M:S, M:D, etc. but as this only serves to complicate the exposition I shall leave it to the reader to fill in these details. The joking relationship field, 2B, defines the people from whom 2A must obtain a spouse. It is taboo for them to obtain spouses from the generation above (or below) them. In this respect, Halbi kinship differs from the Dravidian kinship system of South India where cross cousin marriage is also possible.

The question that now arises concerns the semantic value of the two groups in the senior generation 1A and 1B. The two groups have the general value of "parenthood". Group 1A includes the parallel parents of 2A and the relationship between them is that of respect and familiarity. Members of 2A touch the feet of those of 1A when greeting them and address them by using kin terms; members of 1A reciprocate by touching the chins of those of 2A and address them by name. This behaviour contrasts markedly with that between 1B and 2A. I have glossed 1B as "cross parenthood" for it contains one's MB and FZ but the term "inverted parenthood" best captures the semantic value of this field because the greeting behaviour here is the inverse of what happens between 1A and 2A in the sense that the MB touches the feet of ZS.

The four categories I have distinguished, 1A, 1B, 2A, 2B not only define semantic fields, they are also logical operators that inform the calculation of kinship relationships. The kinship logic of reproduction informing them can be expressed in a Table of the following form which reads: A man from 1A marries a woman from 1B and their children belong to 2A, a man from 1B marries a woman from 1A, and their children belong to 2B, a man from 2A marries a woman from 2B and their children belong to 1A, and a man from 2B marries a woman from 2A and their children belong to 1B.

Father's Group	Mother's Group	Children's Group
1A	1B	2A
1B	1A	2B
2A	2B	1A
2B	2A	1B

If this classificatory logic is applied to the relationships generated over four generations we get the following:

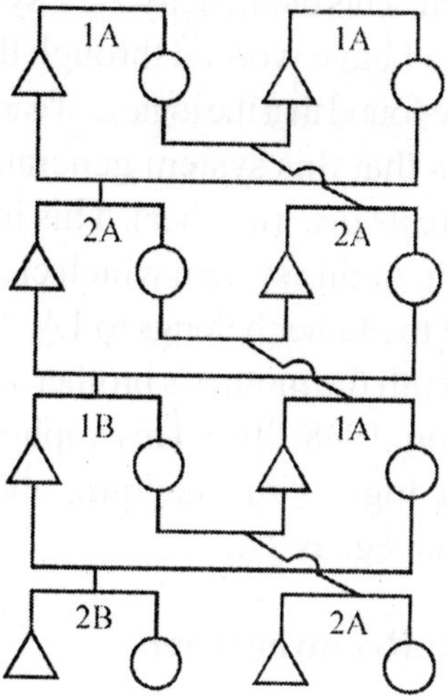

Given the equivalence of alternate generations this chart can be reduced to two generation reproduction model of the following form:

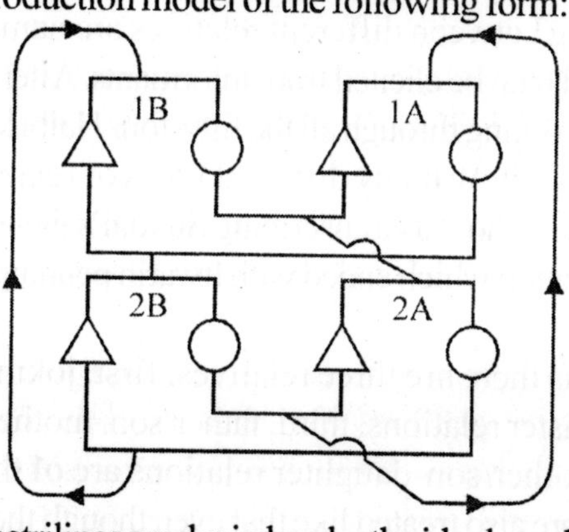

Given the fact that matrilines are denied under the ideology that married women acquire the lineage identity of their husbands, this chart can be reduced to the following:

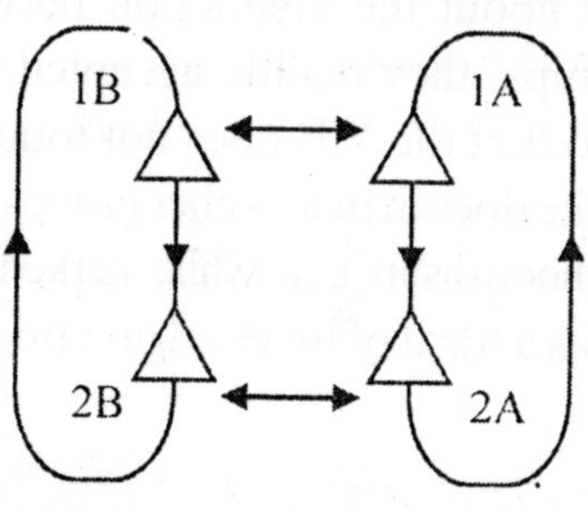

Women's status here is reduced to the horizontal arrows that link men, which reflects the patriarchal notion of Indian kinship as a relationship between men mediated by women. This elementary 2 × 2 system is unique to the Halbi system. I have used it as I have worked through the semantics of kin terms with informants and have found that the logic of it can explain all the paradoxical genealogical equations that this system generates. For example, a father addresses his son's wife as *aya* (mother). This implies that SW = M. This consistent with the logic of this system which classifies both M and SW as belonging to class 2B if the father belongs to 1A. Among the Maria Gond, to take another example, both the mother's brother and the wife's brother's son are called *mama* (Grigson, 1938: 308). This implies that MB = WBS which is also consistent with the logic of the diagrams above because both MB and WBS belong to 1B when ego is 2A.

Halbi Kinship Terms: Reciprocal Sets

This logic of this elementary 2 × 2 system is more of a "generative" model than a "reductionist" one. It generates the four semantic fields within which complex shades of meaning between different relatives are named and defined. The four semantic fields can be elicited from informants. After spending some three days laboriously working through all the fifty-four Halbi kin terms with Sukdai Korram, I asked her how many different types of relations there were. She and Itwarin Baghel, who was transcribing Sukdai's dictation, then got into an animated conversation which ended with Itwarin penning the following:

> Among us there are three relatives: first, joking relations; second, brother/sister relations; third, father/son, mother/daughter relations. These mother/son-daughter relations are of the real womb. Other children are also treated like that even though they are not of the same womb. They are regarded as a little distant.

When I inquired about the distinction between cross and parallel parenthood relationships, they readily accepted that the distinction was meaningful but added that the MB does not touch the feet of ZS in their occupational group as he does in many other groups in Bastar. In other words, the cross/parallel parenthood distinction, while marked lexically, is not universally marked semantically as a form of inverted greeting behaviour between MB and ZS.

It is interesting to note that informants tend to talk in terms of reciprocal sets when discussing their kinship system with me. The kin lexicon can be captured in some fifteen reciprocal sets, all of which belong to one of the four main semantic fields. The following Table captures this.

Semantic field	*Terms of reference*
2A	*dadi* (FF) + *aji* (MM) *nati* (SS ms, DS fs) + *natnin* (SD ms, DD fs)
2B	*aja* (MF) + *ai* (FM) *nati* (DS ms, SS fs) + *natnin* (DD ms, SD fs)
1A	*baba* (F) + *aya* (M) *beta* (S) + *beti* (D)
1A	*bare baba/kaka* (FeB/FyB) + *bare aya/kaki* (FeBW/FyBW) *bhatija* (BS ms) + *bhatiji* (BD ms) + *devar-beta/beti* (HyBS/HyBD)
1A	*bare baba/kaka* (MeZH/MyZH) + *bare aya/nani aya* (MeZ/MyZ) *bhatija* (ZS fs + WZS) + *bhatijin* (ZD fs, WZD)
1B	*bubu* (FZ) + *mama* (FZH) *bhaca* (BS fs, WBS) + *bhaci* (BD fs, WBD)
1B	*mama* (MB) + *bubu* (MBW) *bhaca* (ZS ms, HZS) + *bhaci* (ZD ms, HZD)
1B	*satara* (WF, HF) + *satari* (WM, HM) *janwaii* (DH) + *bohari* (SW)
2A	*dada/nani bhai* (eB/yB) + *didi/ nani bahin* (eZ/yZ) *dada/nani bhai* (eB/yB) + *didi/ nani bahin* (eZ/yZ)
2A	*sarhu bhai* (WZH) *sarhu bhai* (WZH)
2A	*jethani/devarani* (HeBW/HyBW) *jethani/devarani* (HeBW/HyBW)
2B	*maina bhai* (MBS, FZS) + *maina bahin* (MBD, FZD) *maina bhai* (MBS, FZS) + *maina bahin* (MBD, FZD)

Contd....

Semantic field	*Terms of reference*
2B	*munis* (H) *bayle* (W)
2B	*bohu/bohari* (eBW/yBW) *susara/devar* (HeB/HyB) + *sas/nanand* (HeZ/HyZ)
2B	*bhato/janvai* (eZH/yZH) *susara/sara* (WeB/WyB) + *sas/sari* (WeZ/WyZ)

This system of kinship terminology is unique: its defining characteristics are captured by the grandparent/grandchildren terms; its Dravidian characteristics by the parents/children terms; and its Indo-Aryan characteristics by the own generation terms.

The classification of grandparents as cross (2B) or parallel (2A) siblings (*maina bhai/bahin* or *bhi/bahin*) means that, for a female, the mother's father is marriageable, and not the mother's brother as in the Dravidian systems. (Or, from a male perspective, the daughter's daughter is marriageable and not the sister's daughter).

The parents/children terms are semantically identical to that found in Tamil and other Dravidian languages. The terms distinguish between cross and parallel parents which is, of course, a sign of cross-cousin marriage. In this respect they differ from the Indo-Aryan system where a distinction is made between patrilateral and matrilateral parents.

Of interest is the rich lexicon of terms in "our generation". In this respect the Halbi system is Indo-Aryan. The key semantic operator here is a distinction between "elder/younger" (e/y) whose semantic value is "respect/familiarity". The impact of this is to redefine joking relatives at marriage as either "respected joking" (*i.e.* negative joking, avoidance) or "familiar joking" (*i.e.* positive joking, intimacy). Thus the pre-marital joking between a couple now related as HeB/yBW is nullified and turns into an avoidance relation while the pre-marital joking between HyB/eBW is now intensified and often ends in marriage on the death of the elder brother. This redefinition is ritually marked at weddings. At a crucial stage in the three-day ritual, when the bride is to be anointed downwardly with a turmeric and oil mixture, she will sit on the lap of her HeB. This ritual announces to the audience that the joking relation between them is about to end and that, from now on, an avoidance relationship will prevail.

The Kariara System

If we now compare the Halbi system to the Kariara we find that the logic is identical but the semantic values of the logical operators, 1A, 2A, 1B, 2B, is radically different. Among the Kariara, the four logical classifiers are named socio-centric marriage classes called Banaka, Burung, Palyeri, Karimera with the first two comprising one moiety, the second two the other moiety. The rules of reproduction are such that a Banaka man marries a Palyeri women and their children are Burung, a Palyeri man marries a Banaka women and their children are Karimera. The Burung and the Karimera then intermarry to reproduce their parent's groups. The logic of this system of reproduction can be mapped directly onto the formal model above to give the following Table:

Father's group	*Mother's group*	*Children's group*
. 1A Banaka	1B Palyeri	2A Burung
1B Palyeri	1A Banaka	2B Karimera
2A Burung	2B Karimera	1A Banaka
2B Karimera	1B Palyeri	1B Palyeri

This logic is obviously identical to that outlined above for the Halbi case.

In the Kariara system the operators 1A, 2A, 1B and 2B are the basis for a four generation replacement cycle of kinship terms. Thus we find, for example, that the father's father and the son's son are called *maeli*. In formal terms, FF = SS = *maeli*. In the Halbi system, by contrast, the operators are the basis of a two generation cycle of kinship semantics such that, for example, FF = B = *bhai*.

This account of Halbi kinship terminology has implications for the debate between Dumont (1983: 175-91) and Trautmann (1981: 434-37) about the nature of Dravidian kinship and its relationship to the Kariara. It is beyond the scope of this paper to consider this debate here, suffice to say that both Dumont and Trautmann recognized the key importance of grandparent terms, but that only Trautmann foresaw, on the basis Grigson's brief account, that we will "have to rethink the Dravidian terminology in the light of the intriguing case of the Maria Gond" (Trautmann, 1982: 200). However, Trautmann, who draws his theoretical inspiration from historical linguistics, is, perforce, led to overemphasise the Dravidian/Indo-Aryan linguistic divide in his analysis. This prevented him from seeing that the Indo-Aryan Baiga system described by Elwin (1939: 527-29) which he re-analysed (Trautmann, 1982: 137-40) is identical to the Maria Gond case; but, in Trautmann's defence, the quality of anthropological information on kinship terminologies in this area was, to use his expression, "woefully inadequate" (1982: 137) when he wrote his book. It remains that way today but hopefully the material I have presented on the Halbi system goes some way to reversing that situation. I have restricted my analysis to the Halbi case for that is the one I know best; but my researches in North Bastar lead me to believe that the Halbi system is widely distributed throughout this region across the Dravidian and Indo-Aryan language divide. Thusu (1965: 82–91) contains a brief description of the Dravidian-speaking Dhurwa system to the South, Elwin (1939: 178–82, 527–8) a brief description of the Baiga system to the North, and Buradkar (1940) a comprehensive descriptive of a Dravidian-speaking Gond system to the West in the Nagpur region. The semantics of these three systems are identical in every respect to the Halbi system with the lexicon almost identical in the case of the Baiga. Moving westward towards tribal Orissa we find the same theme but with some variations. Tina Otten (personal communication) informs me that daughter's daughter marriage is possible among the people she worked with in Koraput District, Orissa; Pfeffer (1982) noticed the importance of cross-grandparent joking relations and the equivalence of alternate generations in his early synthesis of kinship in tribal Orissa; the new data that I report here is further support for the argument he advances in his most recent synthesis (Pfeffer, 2004). The fact remains, though, that, Tribal Orissa aside, there is dearth of reliable accounts of middle Indian kinship. My hunch is that when this material does become available the Halbi system, and others like it, will cease to be seen as an "intermediate zone" between the Indo-Aryan North and the Dravidian South and come to be seen as "middle Indian" (Aboriginal?) systems in their own right with the Hindi, Tamil and other systems seen as peripheral transformations of it. We will also need a new theoretical language: linguistically derived categories such as "Dravidian" and "Indo-Aryan" are, as Pfeffer (2004: 383) has noted, conceptual barriers to the understanding of the middle Indian systems that straddle this divide.

On the "Tribal Question"

The significant fact about the Halbi System is that it is semantically identical to the Gondi System of North Bastar. So, if kinship is an index of aboriginality, and if the Gonds are tribals (which is the generally accepted view), then the Halbi Speakers are also tribals (which is not the generally accepted view). On the other hand, if one wants to argue that the Halbi Speakers are not tribals then it follows that the Gonds are not tribals either. Dilemmas such as this raise a theoretical question for the academic commentator: what is the anthropological basis upon which a tribe can be distinguished from a caste?

For the Halbi Speakers of Bastar, the question is not an academic question but a political question that lies at the basis of their cultural identity. This is because the terms "tribe" and "caste" are no longer academic concepts but official classifications enshrined in the Indian Constitution. As such, it behoves the anthropologist to treat these terms with great caution because our arguments can have economic and political implications for the people we work with. I find it very disturbing, therefore, that many anthropologists, from Elwinon, are quick to jump to the conclusion that Halbi Speakers in Bastar are "castes" rather than "tribes" on the basis of almost no evidence. Virtually nothing is known about the society and culture of the Halbi Speakers of the DNK plateau and until reliable data is available anthropologists have no right to speak about this vexed political question. For the time being I can report that my research into the kinship system of the Halbi speakers does not contradict their political claims that they are Aborigines; indeed, given that their tetrahedral system is, from a logical point of view, the most elementary system possible (Allen, 1989), their kinship system is not only central in the geographic sense, it is truly primary. A Halbi-centric view of the world, which sees other systems in India as peripheral and derivative, is clearly one that would repay carefully scholarly investigation.

NOTE

1. I am grateful to Nicolas Prevot for helpful comments on an earlier draft of this paper. I am also indebted to the participants of the 2004 Sambalpur conference where I first presented this paper. I am particularly grateful to my discussant, Georg Pfeffer, for his many helpful comments, suggestions, and additional references.

REFERENCES

Allen, N.J. 1989. "The Evolution of Kinship Terminologies," *Lingua*, 77: 173-85.

Buradkar, M.P. 1940. "Kinship Among the Gonds," *Nagpur University Journal*, 6: 1470-80.

Dumont, L. 1983. *Affinity as a Value: Marriage Alliance in South India, with Comparative Essays on Australia.* Chicago: Chicago University Press.

Elwin, V. 1939. *The Baiga.* London: John Murray.

Grigson, W.V. 1938. *The Maria Gonds of Bastar*. Oxford: Oxford University Press.

Lévi-Strauss, C. 1969. *The Elementary Structures of Kinship*. London: Eyre & Spottiswoode.

Pfeffer, G. 1982. *Status and Affinity in Middle India*. Wiesbaden: Franz Steiner.

____. 2004. "Order in Tribal Middle Indian 'Kinship'," *Anthropos*, 99: 381-409.

Russell, R.V. and R.B.H. Lal 1969. *The Tribes and Castes of the Central Provinces of India*.

Thusu, K.N. 1965. *The Dhurwa of Bastar*. Calcutta: Anthropological Survey of India.

Trautmann, T.R. 1981. *Dravidian Kinship*. Cambridge: Cambridge University Press.

Yorke, M. 1979. "Kinship, Marriage and Ideology among the Raj Gonds: A Tribal System in the Context of South India," *Contributions to Indian Sociology*, 13 (1) : 85-116.

FIVE

DELAYED SISTER-EXCHANGE IN MIDDLE INDIA: A Preliminary Sketch of Co-sister-in-law and Granddaughter Marriage Among the Aghriaa and Neighbouring Communities

UWE SKODA

Introduction

A lot has been written about the cross-cousin marriage in India as is practiced in the south and non-existent or almost everywhere ruled out in the north. However, this fairly simple pattern is much more complicated in the transitional zone where features of both systems are combined (Trautmann, 1998 [1979]: 85). The picture of the "frontier zone" is further complicated by a middle Indian, "Mundaic" kinship system that is apparently more limited in its geographical distribution. Presumably, because of its peripheral position, less research has so far been conducted in this zone. During the last 20 years, however, more features of this system—notably the principles of alternation, seniority and symmetry—have been discovered through field research and analysis of empiric data by Pfeffer (1982, 1983, 2004 et al.) as well as through Parkin's (1992, 1998, 2005) comparative approach. This article will contribute to the discussions on Middle Indian kinship by presenting my own data as collected among the Aghriaa, a peasant community of the region. In a second step I will add material collected among neighbouring communities, often classified by the Government as *Scheduled Tribes*, in the north-western part of Orissa, especially in the Sambalpur and the Sundargarh Districts. Finally, I will supplement the material by reviewing the regional ethnographies.

Primarily based on material from this transitional society in the region north of the river Mahanadi, I argue initially that, apart from McDougal's (1963) material on the Juang and scattered hints in the ethnographic literature[1], an important category and form of marriage has been largely neglected by the ethnography: namely marriages with the category *sibling's spouse's sibling* (SbSpSb[2]) and the related *co-sister-in-law*[3]. The neglect—in spite of several hints to the existence of this category and form of marriage—may be explained by a certain bias in favour of other forms of marriage, notably that of the cross cousin. Though it is usually not advisable only to consider elements of a whole, such as a kinship system, in the following I will concentrate on this particular aspect of middle Indian kinship, which I consider to be a form of delayed sister-exchange[4]. While sister-exchange as such, though practised frequently, is officially despised by the upper castes of north India (Parry, 1979; Conzelmann, 1996) and well-established in the South, a separate category SbSpSb is nowhere to be found.

Secondly, I will argue that *co-sister-in-law* marriage is not a kinship feature limited to "tribal" communities such as the Juang. Rather it is shared by all kinds of groups of this "North of the Mahanadi region" or "Northern Mahanadi complex", *i.e.* by tribes, peasants such as the Aghriaa, royals and Brahmins alike. Consequently, I propose a regional or subregional approach here rather than one based on language affinities.

Finally, delayed sister-exchange, as practised by the Aghriaa and their tribal and non-tribal neighbours, may well be combined with granddaughter-marriage as another distinct and important regional feature in middle India—given the by now well known principle of alternation. If considered together in the manner proposed here—as parts of a whole that includes kinship categories as well as joking relationships and the like—it may be easier to understand a common underlying structure in which granddaughters are identified with younger sisters; SbSpSb-marriage may therefore offer a possible path to perpetuate this specific structure over generations or generation-sets.

Taking into consideration the evidence in the literature as is concerning this form of delayed sister-exchange, I will ultimately argue that the category SbSpSb and *co-sister-in-law* marriage appear to be limited to the area north of the river Mahanadi leading into West Bengal and Uttar Pradesh. As Pfeffer (2004: 396) has recently suggested, the river Mahanadi might be a natural boundary demarking cultural variations and my data back this line of thought.

Thus we may now be in a position to acknowledge sub-regional differences in Middle Indian kinship, *i.e.* a northern Mahanadi pattern introduced here which is primarily characterised by the existence of a SbSpSb-category as well as a concurring absence of separate cross-cousin terms. Consequently other structures will appear in southern Middle India, as the data of a Gondi complex indicate, to internal variations within the general Middle Indian kinship system.

McDougal and the Discovery of *Co-sister-in-law* Marriage

Sound ethnographic work on a Middle Indian community, with particular emphasis on kinship and marriage, has been supplied by McDougal's (1963) monograph on the Juang of Keonjhar in northern Orissa. To my knowledge McDougal was the first to document the apparently pivotal category of BWZ / ZHZ as a marriage preference. He states:

> "There are five ... kintypes from which a spouse may be taken: saliray (eBWyZ or eZHyZ), aji (MBD), bokoray (FZD), na (*e.g.*, FMBSD), and bokosini (*e.g.* FFZSD). Saliray, na, and bokosini are to a certain extent structurally equivalent, since the relationships are all based on prior marriages of persons belonging to Ego's generation-set, namely, eB or eZ, FF, and FFZ. The other 2 relationships are traced through persons in the adjacent generation. Saliray is the preferred spouse." (McDougal, 1963: 157)

Accordingly, the Juang prefer to marry a BWZ which implies a repetition of the marriage direction—or accepting a wife from a family that has already given a daughter as in the case of the *mother's brother's daughter* marriage or *wife's younger sister* marriage—but a man's preferred marriage with a *saliray* may also imply a reciprocal exchange, in case this term for the married person must be translated with ZHZ. Thus, the sister-in-law marriage of the Juang—as well as of the Aghriaa as I will illustrate below—indicates the social value of a repetition of intermarriage within the same generation as well as a symmetry of the relation, *i.e.* a lack of status differentiation between wife-takers and wife-givers.

Table 5.1: Pattern of SbSpSb-Marriage

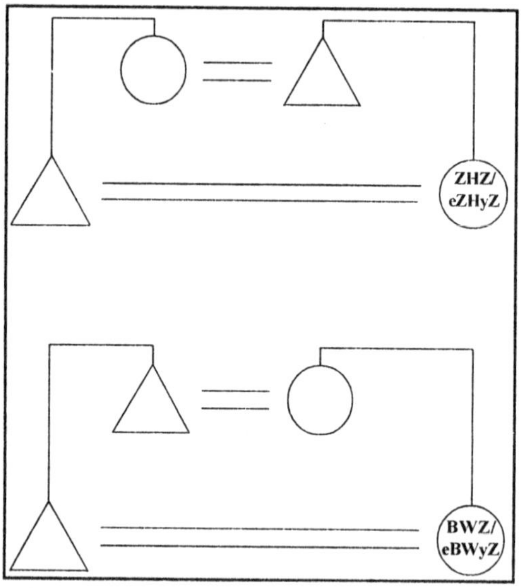

However, McDougal's description is not always consistent. While he documents clearly an equation of alternating generations and places great emphasis on the eZHyZ, the classification, *e.g.* of the yZHyZ seems to have been omitted.[5]

Apart from these questions, the marriage preference as well as the rather conformist practices are crystal clear. Significantly, the category of *saliray*, including eBWyZ, eZHyZ and WyZ, is prescribed and statistically most marriages (54%) are arranged with brides belonging to this category as shown by McDougal's rather small sample (1963: 162). In contrast, only 18 per cent matrilateral and another 6 per cent patrilateral cross-cousin marriages have been arranged among the Juang (*ibid.*). Another 4 per cent of the marriages have taken place between classificatory *grandparents* and grandchildren, while another 18 per cent of all marriages do not conform to the rules, *i.e.* the marriage partners belonging to adjacent generations.[6]

Furthermore, McDougal (1963: 102ff, 133ff) mentions the following joking relationships among the Juang, which often indicate a status as potential marriage partners.

Co-sister-in-law Marriage among the Aghriaa and Neighbouring Communities

The Aghriaa Kinship System

Historically in the second half of the 19th and first half of 20th centuries peasant castes such as the Aghriaa[7], who hosted me during my field research (Skoda,

Table 5.2: Joking-relationships among Juang

WeB / yZH
WyB / eZH
WyZ / eZH
BWyZ, ZHyZ / eZHB, eBWB
SWF / DHF
ChSposPa / ChSposPa
FPa / SS
MF / DD
eB / yB ; eZ / yZ
eBW / HySb
yBW / HeSb

2005), have migrated into a region that was predominantly populated by tribes. The newcomers helped to clear large parts of the forests and became revenue collectors of the "little kings" thus being influential in integrating a tribal population into the emerging structures of the state, or rather of a number of princely states in north-western Orissa.

As an initial surprise, I found the Aghriaa, an apparently immigrated peasant community, sharing many features with the Juang in terms of the kinship system. Since I have elsewhere tried to elaborate on the Aghriaa kinship system in detail (Skoda, 2005), I will highlight only a few significant points here, as related to sister-in-law marriage. I will start with the kinship terminology: Most important is the category *sangaat/ sangi* includes BWZ, ZHZ as female and BWB/ZHB as male relatives—*i.e.* all *siblings' spouse's siblings* (SbSpSb). This category implies a symmetrical system without any distinction into wife-givers and wife-takers. However, there are several other categories for sisters-in-law, *i.e.* from a male perspective: *de.d;saa;s* for WeZ,*;saalii* for WyZ, *bahu* for eBW and *bhaaibaha* for yBW.

Besides, the category*;sa;sur* does not just designate a wife's or a husband's father, as is common in North Indian ("Indo-Aryan") terminologies, but it also includes ZHF (and ZHM = SpM accordingly), which indeed hints at a marriage prescription as provided by the equation MB = FZH = SpF in South Indian ("Dravidian") systems. In contrast to the latter, only a limited cross-parallel separation is found among the Aghriaa in equations such as MeZ = FeBW. Significantly, distinct category for cross-cousins is missing. Among the Aghriaa all cousins fall into the category *sibling* and in this regard the Aghriaa differ from the Juang classification. Thus the terminology does not clearly imply a positive cross-cousin marriage rule.

Yet another difference, in comparison to the Juang, is evident: the Aghriaa have only one category for *grandparents* as reference terms, *i.e. ajaa* and *aaii* for males and females respectively. However, as an address term a *grandfather* can be called *elder brother* (*dadaa*), while a *grandmother* is addressed as *elder sister* (*baai*). Similarly the *grandchildren* are referred to as *naati/naaten*, but may be addressed as *younger brother* (*bhaai*) or *younger sister* (*bahen*). This categorization is hinting at the principle of alternation which is even more clearly formulated in the category (*ba.du/ba.di*) denoting FeB, MeZH, FFF (all *great grandfathers*), yBS etc. and thus running through all odd generations. Thus, in a simplified way, the Aghriaa terminology might be represented by the following diagram:

Table 5.3: Simplified Aghriaa Terminology (Male Categories Only)

<table>
<tr><th>Gen.</th><th colspan="2">Parallel</th><th colspan="2">Cross</th><th colspan="3">Affines</th></tr>
<tr><td>+3/– 3</td><td colspan="7">ba.du</td></tr>
<tr><td rowspan="2">+2/–2
(+4/–4)</td><td colspan="7">dadaa (ajaa)–eB</td></tr>
<tr><td colspan="7">bhaai (naati)–yB</td></tr>
<tr><td rowspan="2">+1/–1</td><td colspan="2">ba.du (FeB, MeZH, yBS (ms), HyBS, WyZS)</td><td rowspan="2">MB,
ZS (m.s.),
BS (f.s.)</td><td rowspan="2">FZH,
DH</td><td colspan="3" rowspan="2">SpF
(SbSpF)</td></tr>
<tr><td>F/FyB
S/eBS (ms.)</td><td>MyZH
WeZS</td></tr>
<tr><td rowspan="2">0</td><td colspan="4">dadaa—eB (BWBe/ZHBe/WeB/WZH)</td><td rowspan="2">SbSpSb, WZH,
WeB/WyB</td><td rowspan="2">ChSpF</td><td>eZH</td></tr>
<tr><td colspan="4">bhaai—yB (BWBy/ZHBy/WyB)</td><td>yZH</td></tr>
</table>

After the discussion of Aghriaa categories, I now turn to their marriage rules:

The Rule of Generation-set Endogamy

In addition to caste endogamy, another rule also restricts marriage to one's own generation. In effect, this implies a form of intra–generational endogamy or an endogamy of generation–sets. Marriage between persons of adjacent generations should be avoided. Persons belonging to the *grandparent's* or *grandchildren's* generation—in fact to any alternating generation—may be married provided they belong to a different clan (*see* below). This rule is quite consistent with the principle of alternation as found in the terminology.

The Rule of Clan Exogamy

As many other castes and tribes, the Aghriaa too are divided into exogamous, patrilineal clans known as *bansa* (*bana*) and *gotra* (*barga*), and marriage within one's own clan is strictly prohibited.

The Rule of Cross-cousin Marriage

The rule of cross-cousin marriage, which, as shown above, should not be confused with a prescription, or categorical imperative, seems to have been widespread previously with a preference for the matrilateral cross-cousin (MBD). Significantly, some Aghriaa claim, that—apart from the *bhanjaa daan*—the biggest gift a *mother's brother* can give to his *sister's son* is *kanyaa daan*, the gift of his daughter. By offering a daughter a *mother's brother* earns not only the common religious merits (*puniya*), but the greatest possible merit—the *maahaapuniya*. Earning this merit is regarded as a way to reach *mukti* or salvation, the ultimate goal of leaving the cycle of birth and rebirth.

Yet marriage with the patrilateral cross-cousin (FZD) is possible as well, though practiced only rarely. Nowadays, the rule of cross-cousin marriage, or any marriage with a close relative for that matter, seems to have lost its general importance due to the increasing occurrence of sickle cell anaemia—a relatively frequent genetic defect. Accordingly, many Aghriaa try to avoid cross-cousin marriages and prefer structurally and spatially rather distant marriages. As a result, I suggest that a process of social change is imminent. Earlier cross-cousin marriage as a rule, or MBD—marriage as a preference, is supplanted by completely new kinship ties. This does not rule out further cross-cousin marriages, but only indicates that they will no longer be taken as preferred as they have been in the past. Cross-cousin marriages are still possible and in no way prohibited in the manner known from North India.

Rules of Avoidance, Respect and Joking

Since Radcliffe–Brown's (1952 [1940]) pioneering work on joking and avoidance, the structural implications of these relationships have been revealed and they have become a part of every analysis on kinship. On the normative level, rules of avoidance and joking do not only determine behaviour and limit the contact between certain relatives, they also, on the one hand, indicate taboos regarding sexual relations, marriage and status differences as far as avoidance is concerned and, on the other hand, possible marital, intimate and sexual relationships in terms of joking.

Avoidance is expressed in the local language as "to give way" (*baa.t chha.daa*). The Aghriaa mentioned several such relations between the following relatives: *e.g.* (1) HeB and yBW (*e.g.* a yBW is expected to be veiled (*u.dhni*) in the presence of her HeB); (2) HMB and ZSW; (3) between WeZ and yZH; (4) *Samdhi* (ChSposPa) and *Samdhen* (ChSposPa). Interestingly enough, these rules of avoidance stand in conflict with the rules of cross-cousin marriage in practice. Considering the second rule—avoidance between HMB and ZSW—and a case of matrilateral cross-cousin marriage, we *see* that the father must avoid his daughter (or an FB his BD) which rather obviously does contradict my own observations.

In contrast to the rules of avoidance, ritualised, public and partly obligatory joking is practiced in various "joking relationships", which may hint at a familiar relationship and imply possible sexual relations or later marriages, *e.g.* in levirate-relations. Correspondingly, among the Aghriaa, relatives with whom one can joke, such as a *husband's younger brother* (a brother-in-law) and a *wife's younger sister* (as a sister-in-law) are allowed to be married, while relatives one must avoid—here the *husband's elder brother* or the *wife's elder sister*—are not matches for a remarriage. A junior-levirate, *i.e.* a marriage with the *husband's younger brother* after the husband's death, seems to have been frequent in former times, although people rarely remember any case. In contrast, no case of senior-levirate-marriage with the *husband's elder brother* after the death of one's husband—was known. However, junior-sororate marriages with the *wife's younger sister*, and—as may be emphasised—not only after the wife's death, are quite possible and indeed practiced (*see* marriage statistics). In contrast, marriage with a *wife's elder sister*—a senior—sororate—is not allowed.

Several such joking relationships characterise the Aghriaa. However, the jokes and the intensity of joking vary. Women are generally expected to joke more mildly or with more reserve. Differences are shown in the following Table:[8]

Table 5.4: Joking Relationships

Joking relation	*Characteristics*
1. salaa and baa.to (WyB and eZH)	Strongest joking (including
2. baa.to and ;saalii (eZH and WyZ)	physical jokes)
3. diar and bahu (HyB and eBW)	
4. sangaat and sangii (BWB and ZHZ)	
5. bahu and nanand (eBW and HyZ)	
6. bha.tuaa–sasur and bhaaibohu (HeZH and WyBW)	
7. nati/naten and ajaa/aaii (ChCh and PaPa—sexual allusions only with *ajaa;sasur*—WFF, WMF)	Mildest joking (limited to verbal jokes)

For the present topic it is significant to note that no joking is practiced between relatives belonging to parent's and children's generation (including the generations of great-grandparents and great-grandchildren). To all persons of the parents' and great grandparents' generation, respect is shown as a rule.

In addition to the aforementioned joking relationships, there are some ritual occasions for joking. In contrast to formal joking relationships, which take place in everyday life, this second type of joking, which I propose to call "contextual joking", is limited to specific situations and contexts. First and foremost it is conducted with persons of one's own generation, for example, between brothers and sisters and between brothers or between sisters in the wider sense. These joking relationships are of central importance during wedding ceremonies and occasionally include persons of the grandparents' or grandchildren's generation, when generation-sets are found to be in action.

Thus, joking is limited to one's own generation-set, *i.e.* an intra-generational joking affair. Joking is also practised between affinal relatives, *i.e.* certain types of brothers-in-law and sisters-in-law and also particularly between *sangaat* and *sangii*. In all cases of joking-relationships, marriage is—as I have shown—possible. However, this does not mean that only persons with whom one can joke are potential marriage partners. There are no formal joking relationships between cross-cousins and yet the ideal of a marriage between them remains.

However, it is important to note that no formalized joking exists between cross-cousins among the Aghriaa and, apparently, among other groups as well. Here cross-cousins keep a social distance, though they are not avoiding each other. A distance, kept between cross-cousins and expressed by non-conversation during adolescence and prior to marriage, contradicts the simple equation between joking relationship and possible marriage partner, as cross-cousins are potential marriage partners with whom one does not joke. Most likely, joking is necessarily related to the existence of these clear-cut categories. As far as cross-cousins among the Aghriaa are concerned, a separate terminological category does not exist, cross-cousins being subsumed as siblings. Thus, inconsistencies between the levels—cross-cousins being preferred marriage partners, though they are not categorically distinguished—may have resulted in a form of social distance other than joking between cross-cousins.

Finally, I consider the marriage practices of the Aghriaa: returning to the first rule and practice of generation-set endogamy I have to elaborate briefly on a former custom among, *i.e.* the symbolic marriages of girls when reaching puberty. In case a suitable groom for a girl had not been found to that date, she was married either to a distant *grandfather*, to an *elder sister's husband* (a brother-in-law), to a turban, or to certain flowers. Leaving aside the last two options, the first two are particularly intriguing, since they demonstrate generation-set endogamy.

To give the daughter into marriage with a distant grandfather or *ajaa*—this marriage was known as *ajaa-bihaa*—was one opportunity to marry a daughter off at an early age. Although close grandfathers (FF, MF) were not eligible, it was possible to marry one's *mother's mother's brother* (MMB) or one's *father's mother's brother* (FMB) and more distant grandfathers. In fact, one had to select a grandfather who belonged to another clan and was already related by marriage.[9] Apart from the grandfathers, an *elder sister's husband* (*baa.to*) was a possible marriage partner as well, indirectly underlining the equation of alternate generations. Typically, the girl was subsequently divorced from her "*grandfather/brother-in-law–cum–husband*" and married to her "proper" husband, whenever a suitable match could be arranged. The girl never stayed in the house of her grandfather as a wife would stay with her husband. For the first marriage with the grandfather, most of the rituals, in particular the anointing with oil and turmeric, the *teila bhi.sek/tel cha.daa* and the circling around the fire were performed. Later, such a husband had to sign the divorce papers. For the second marriage another *teila bhi.sek* was not necessary, but the circling was repeated before the bride was brought to the groom's household. This custom clearly demonstrates the endogamy of "generation-sets". No "uncle" or relative of the father's generation would have been a possible match. The Aghriaa I spoke to agreed that a marriage with a distant grandfather is more acceptable than marrying a distant niece or nephew such as a brother's daughter or a distant uncle or aunt like a father's sister or mother's sister. However, as early as 1921, the *Aghriaa samaaj*—the caste organisation—had begun to prohibit and thus to eradicate this custom—possibly considering it to be degrading[10].

In practise I came across several cases of such symbolic marriages with a *grandfather*, *e.g.* an elderly lady had married her *father's father's younger sister's husband's younger brother* (FFyZHyB). This Aghriaa woman married her classificatory grandfather at the age of four or five (around 1930) before marrying again thirteen years later (around 1943). Another woman remembered that her *father's sister's daughter* had married a distant *grandfather* as well. The groom was her *mother's father's younger brother* (MFyB). However, this custom seems to have been in decline already by the 1930s. One reason might be the caste organisation's attempts to abolish it.

Nevertheless, even without those symbolic marriages, there are still cases of marriages arranged with a distant *grandfather*—although they are rare. In 1996, an Aghriaa woman I met had married her *mother's father's mother's brother's son* (MFMBS). According to my data, 6 out of 373 marriages, including this one, were arranged in this manner, but the figures I suppose were higher previously. Most Aghriaa I spoke with vaguely remembered that some family members were married to a *grandfather* without being able to specify the exact relation.

My own data on the frequency of certain types of marriages are shown in the Table below:

Table 5.5: Statistical Frequency of Marriage Types

Villages	*No.*	*Close*				*Distant*				*Other distant relatives*
		MBD	*FZD*	*sangaat*	*saalii*	*MBD*	*FZD*	*sangaat*	*saalii*	
Munda-loi	49	2			1	4	2	4		5 (1 MyZD, 1 FBD, 1 BD, 1 ZD)[11]
Other villages	324	12		6	5	7	5	7	1	33 (11 FBD, 5 BD, 4 FZ, 1 MyZ, 4 ChD, 6 MZD[12]
Total	373	14		6	6	11	7	11	1	36

In my sample 92 marriages were arranged within one's own circle of relatives, a little less than 25 per cet. The figure excluding the village Mundaloi is a bit above 23 per cent, while the figure for Mundaloi with 35 per cent is significantly higher. As I spent most of my time in Mundaloi, this figure should be more precise, even though the sample—in terms of numbers—is rather limited. However, careful research in the other villages could reveal a higher percentage of marriages among relatives as in Mundaloi[13].

The rules demanding the avoidance of marriage to persons of adjacent generations and of the same clan can be evaded in practice, if the marriage partners are related to each other very distantly. For example, one man married the daughter of a distant, classificatory sister—though this is not the ideal. In my sample, 13 out of 373 marriages (3, 7%) were arranged with a partner from an adjacent generation. None of these marriages involved close relatives.

Apart from matrilateral cross-cousin marriage, the data show two other types of relations occurring frequently in marriage: *sangaat* (ZHZ/BWZ) and *saalii* (WyZ). In addition to matrilateral cross-cousins, marriages have only been arranged with these two categories of close relatives—at least in my sample. In contrast to matrilateral cross-cousins which, as I have tried to show, is not based on categorical prescription, there is a certain preference for these categories, but it is not formulated as a rule in the sense that someone can earn *mahaapuniya* such as a *maamu* (MB) giving his daughter. The category WyZ, I argue, might be considered as a "secondary prescription" in the sense that it presupposes an earlier marriage of ego. Thus, it does not prescribe first marriage. The category ZHZ/BWZ could be considered a categorical imperative for marriage in the sense of Needham (1973), but this category *alone* is not sufficient for a positive marriage rule running through generations, as it prescribes marriage as a repetition of a sibling's marriage—either in the same direction or reversed—but does not indicate whom the first sibling has to marry. Appareantly a logical difference must be noted when compared to a prescription for cross-cousin marriage. I will return to this point later.

However, the above mentioned categorical imperatives imply a diachronic repetition of intermarriage among the Aghriaa, that is, marriage between cross cousins or even, with a gap of a generation, as marriage with a distant *granddaughter* as *naten* (or *grandfathers* as *ajaa*). In all cases of cross-cousin, *sangaat* and *;saalii* marriages, successful marriage relations are repeated, even though the direction may be reversed. Furthermore, the considerable number of marriages conducted with distant relatives such as a man's FBD—always provided she belongs to a different clan—appears to indicate how much affinity is indeed valued—to use Dumont's famous phrase.

The Immediate Tribal Neighbours of the Aghriaa

In the context of my research I did not only observe the Aghriaa practices but also collected comparative data on their neighbours—most of them classified by the Government as *Scheduled Tribes*—in this transitional tribal and caste society. My findings are summarized below:

Table 5.6: Comparison of SbSpSb-categories of "Tribal" Communities Spatially Close to the Aghriaa

Terms of Reference	*Kinship Category*
Oraam	
yaaaar	BWB, ZHB
goyaa/goi	BWZ, ZHZ
Ga.n.d	
sangaat	ZHZ, BWZ
sangi	ZHB, BWB
Mu.n.d.aa	
sangaat	eZHZ, BWZ
sangi	eZHB, BWB
Kandh	
sangaat	ZHZ, BWZ
sangi	ZHB, BWB
Kisaan	
saangha	ZHZ, BWZ
saanghi	BWB, ZHB
Kha.diaa	
eaar	ZHB (ms), BWB (ms)
goi	ZHB (fs), ZHZ, BWZ, BWB (fs)

As a Table documenting the terminologies, this reference to the *ST* does not differ much in regard to the categories for BWZ/ZHZ. Additionally, in all of these terminologies cousins are equated with siblings and we find one category for *grandparents* and another for *grandchildren*. Furthermore, the category *ba.du/ba.di*, though sometimes lexically different, includes the same semantic scope as among the Aghriaa and runs through the generations in the very same way. The only major difference I noted between the Aghriaa and many of their neighbours, such as Ga.n.d, Mu.n.daa, Kandh, Kha.diaa and Kisaan, is the equation MB = FZH (but not = SpF) non-existent among the Aghriaa, but existent among their neighbours.

Returning to the category BWZ/ZHZ, only the Oraam and Kha.diaa differ lexically[14], but apparently not structurally. Marriage with *sangaat/goi (goyaa)* is allowed and practised. Besides, the terminologies do not deviate from the

Aghriaa pattern as far as cross-cousin marriage is concerned. In no community is there a separate category for cross-cousins and marriage with them is not ruled out—only the Oraam and Kha.diaa, as the two christianised local communities, prohibit marriage with first-grade cross-cousins but may marry second grade cousins. Furthermore, to my knowledge, all communities allow marriage with distant *grandparents* and in a few cases, such as among the Ga.n.d and Kisaan, I found several empirical cases.[15] It is also found among many other village neighbours of the Aghriaa such as the Malaar or Tuurii.

Further, in the mixed tribal and caste society of which the Aghriaa are part, the rules of joking and avoidance should not be considered specifically Aghriaa customs, rather they are apparently shared by most communities. According to my enquiries in the village community, tribal groups such as the Gand, Kandh, Kisaan, Mundaa, Malaar but also Christian tribals like the Khadiaa and Oraam all practice a similar pattern of joking and avoidance as described for the Aghriaa, even though some of the details may differ.[16]

Table 5.7: Case 1 of Granddaughter-marriage

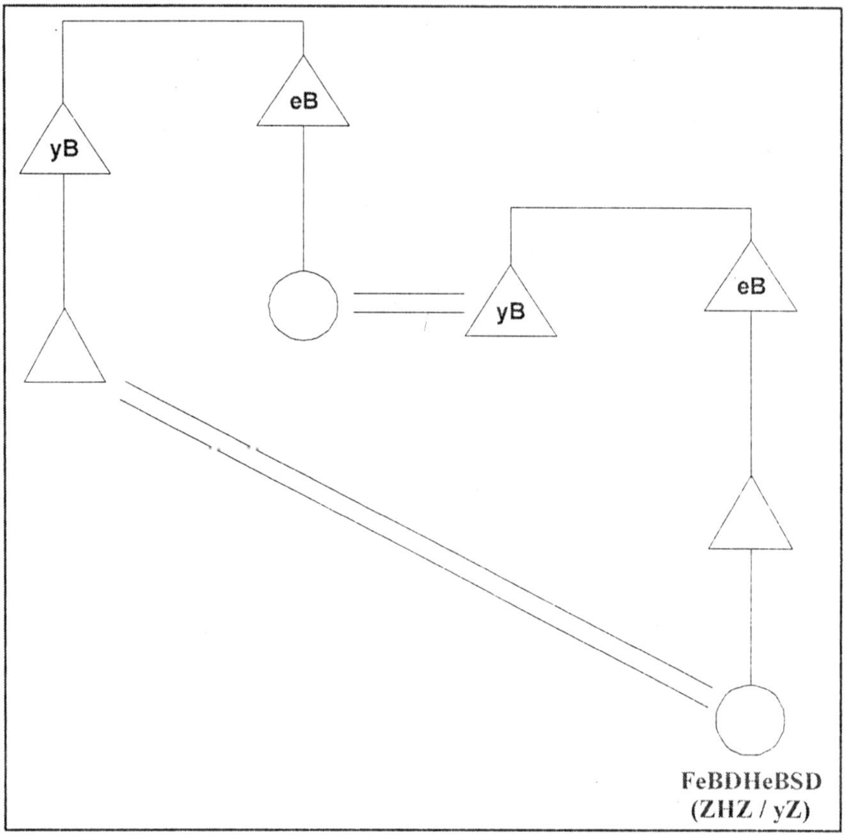

Grand-daughter and Co-sister-in-law Marriage among the Neighbouring Communities

From the above mentioned cases it becomes clear that the rule of BWZ/ZHZ or sister-in-law marriage usually does not occur alone, but in combination with the principle of alternating generations or "generation sets". Furthermore, as I tried to show for the Aghriaa, a prescription SbSpSb alone would be rather incomplete to maintain a structure as it indicates the marriage with a (elder) sibling's relative but does not state whom this sibling would marry. Therefore, I want to argue here that both forms—marrying *co-sisters-in-law* and *grand-daughters*—may not occur in coincidental combination and may also be related in an overarching system. Thus, *grand-daughter*-marriage could be viewed as a part of a delayed sister-in-law marriage or as a sub-type of *co-sister-in-law* marriage, since *grand-daughters* are also viewed as *younger sisters* (and *grandfathers* as *elder brothers*).

In terms of address, but also in forms of joking etc. eB is equated with FF and all grand-fathers and vice versa yB with SS (grand-sons). Similarly for women the rule is eZ = FM/MM etc. Thus, implicitly, the category of *sangaat* or BWZ/ZHZ can be extended to the *grandparents'* and *grand-children's* generations and can be formulated as FFWZ/FMHZ etc. Or, to put it the other way round: following the logic of alternation, *grand-parents'* marriage could be implicitly understood as a distant sister-in-law marriage. Let us look at two concrete cases I came across recently among the Ga.n.d in former Bonai State.

In the first diagram a Zamindar married his FeBDHeBSD. Following the rule that all cousins are considered his siblings, FeBD could be regarded as his eZ. Furthermore, the eZH considers his eBSD as his *grand-daughter* and yZ. Thus, the marriage of FeBDHeBSD could also be understood as a distant eZHyZ marriage. However, in a still wider sense, the FeBDHeBSD could also be seen as a very distant yZ, but not as a cross-cousin. Therefore, we find the case of two families or lines in which a bride is returned after a gap of one generation yet not in the following generation as it would be possible, theoretically, in patrilateral cross-cousin marriage.

In the second case of the family of the Zamindar's bard, a man marries his eBDHeBD. In this case one may view the relation via the eBW as a case of an eBWDHeBD marriage. For the eBW a DHBD is a *grand-daughter* or yZ and the whole marriage could thus be understood as an eBWyZ marriage and as a way of repeating a successful marriage relation.

Table 5.8: Case 2 of Grand-daughter Marriage

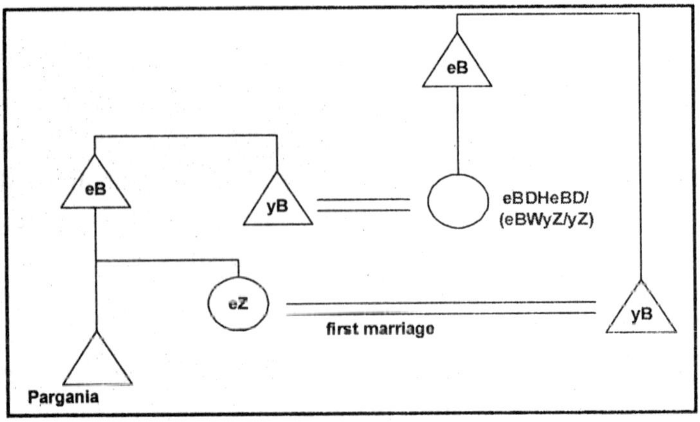

Thus, in summary I want to propose the viewing of *co-sister-in-law* marriage and *grand-parent*-marriage together as elements of one marriage rule.

The Non-tribal Neighbours

Not only neighbours commonly described as "tribal" share the category *sangaat* with the Aghriaa, but also—as I want to argue here—groups not usually known for their "tribalness"[17]. Less than 100 km from my research among the Aghriaa I recently returned to the "little kings", or rgw latters' Rajput caste and the surrounding communities like Brahmins. Though certain differences exist, one finds the same category *sangaat*.

Among the Danuaa Brahmin of Bonai I was informed that *sangaat* designates BWZ/ZHZ, but also BWB and ZHB. Gender is apparently not marked here. In addition to that, the structure is relatively similar to the one found among the Aghriaa. But in terms of rules the Brahmins differ to some extent, *i.e.* cross-cousin marriage is explicitly prohibited, though *sangaat* marriage is allowed and practised. The royal families of Bonai and Bamra use the category *sangaat* in much the same way as Brahmins do, *i.e.* there is no need to distinguish between BWZ or BWB, since all can be referred to as *sangaat*. But if one wishes to differentiate one can designate BWZ and ZHZ as *sangaatani*. As in the case of the Brahmins all cousins are considered to be siblings, but in the case of the royals, cross-cousins are often married repeatedly over generations. Furthermore, my brief enquiries among other peasant communities like the Chasaa have indicated the same pattern. Thus, it becomes apparent that not only "tribal" communities exhibit this trait, but it is rather common in the region north of river Mahanadi.

Other Evidence of Co-sister-in-law Marriage (SbSpSb) in Middle Indian Ethnographies: A Stocktaking

Having started from the Juang and having turned to the Aghriaa and their neighbours, in a final step I would like to scan the ethnographic literature for more evidence of the phenomenon in question here[18]. Data on *co-sister-in-law* marriage in early ethnographies are rather scarce. The anthropological pioneers of the region did not particularly concentrate on kinship; rather they saw it as an aspect of culture and reserved an—often small—chapter of their monographs. If they wrote about kinship and marriage rules at all, most of them were generally preoccupied with cross-cousin marriage that is mentioning whether or not it was practised. Many of them also added kinship terminologies to their ethnographies which, however, did include only the nearest relatives. The well-known ethnographers of the region such as Verrier Elwin, Sir Wilfrid Grigson, or Sarat Chandra Roy do provide kinship terminologies in their books but only to a very limited extent. Accordingly, though terminologies are given by them and by many other authors later (*e.g.* Mukherjea, 1962), these lists of terms are limited to very few relations and nothing is mentioned on—in our western perception—more distant relatives such as ZHZ or BWZ, who are not even specifically named in English. Thus, we simply do not know that much about how they were classified in Middle India. However, in their writings there are certain hints about the importance of these relatives in terms of marriage.

Although one does find only few hints at BWZ/ZHZ marriage, significantly no scarcity of data on joking with BWZ/ZHZ as well as WyZ, HyB and *grand-parents* is observed. To the best of my knowledge joking in Middle India usually implies the possibility of marriage between persons of the related categories and therefore, I include such data here.[19]

Evidence in the Northern Mahanadi Region

For example, for the Paudi Bhuyan of present Northern Orissa, Roy (1935: 143) only indicates the possibility of a BWZ marriage by mentioning that "two brothers may also marry two sisters". However, in his terminology no term for ZHZ/BWZ is listed and the relationship as such is missing in his kinship account.

In his book on the Kharia[20] Roy (1937: 160ff) notes that:

> "When two brothers marry two sisters, the relationship of mother's sister's child and father's brother's child are combined in one and the same person. Exchange marriages by which a brother and a sister are married respectively to a daughter and son of the same father is in vogue among the tribe." (Roy and Roy, 1937: 157) and he goes on: "a Kharia may marry—(i) his wife's younger sister; and (ii) his brother's wife's sister; and a Kharia widow may marry either her deceased husband's younger brother or her sister's husband's brother" (*ibid.*: 160-1).

Furthermore, Roy (1937: 159ff) mentions the following rules among Kharia:

1. A man may joke with his WyZ, WyB, BWZ, BWB and grand-parents
2. A woman may joke with her HyB, HyZ, ZHyB, ZHyZ and grand-parents[21].

Later on Vidyarthi and Upadhyay (1980) indicate the possibility of ZHZ/BWZ marriage among the Kharia, but do not elaborate on the matter. They state:

> "When two real brothers marry two real sisters, there the relationship terms are fixed from the collateral side... Also recorded are cases were a brother and a sister are married respectively to a sister and brother from another family." (Vidyarthi and Upadhyay, 1980: 117)

Pfeffer (2004: 406) also recorded a separate category ZHZ (*donku*) among the Kharia of Jharkhand.

An account on the Santal is offered by Kochar (1970), who mentions similar joking relations as Roy, but they framed slightly differently, in the sense that relative age becomes a decisive factor:

Male speaker	*Female speaker*
1. yBWZ	1. ZHeB
2. eBWZ	2. ZHyB
3. eZHyZ	3. eBWyB

Kochar (1963, 1970) does not provide a full list of terms, but he mentions various terms for the relations: *erwelin kori* (yBWZms, but also HyZ and WyZ?), *sangat* (ZHeBfs), *hili* (eBWZms, but also eBWms/fs), *hopon jawai* (ZHyBfs), without stating any related marriage preference. A joking pattern similar to the Kharia is also known from the Santal (Kochar, 1963: 52 & 1970: 72ff; Mukherjea, 1962 [1939]: 148). The material provided by Kochar proves the existence of a SbSpSb category among Santal in Birbhum District of West Bengal and it would be interesting to know if there is other evidence further eastwards.

Though Roy (1925) does not mention anything about SbSpSb marriage among the Birhor of Chotanagpur, of the Birhor of Hazaribagh (Jharkhand) Williams (1968) notes sister-exchange and particularly BWZ-marriage.[22] He writes:

> Evidence in terms of Ho kinship categories is scarce. Only "*Father's brother's wife's sister*" is marriageable, and in fact is almost inevitably chosen, when available. Although a number of forms of marriage are named and can be described by the Birhor, only one kind commonly occurs; this is sister exchange." (Williams, 1968-130)

Deeney (n.d.: 130) writing on the Ho of the Chaibasa region mentions the category *bala-era* (DHM, SWM, yZHeZ, SWeZ, DHeZ).[23] However, Dhan (1961: 70ff) clearly mentions that marriage with BWZ is frequent in conjunction with the joking relationships among Ho of Saranda (southern Jharkhand).[24]

Bhattacharya (1970: 458) mentions the SbSpSb category as *gui* and *iar* among the Munda.[25] This is confirmed by Sachidananda (1979) who compared three villages and found the category SbSpSb in two of them, in which, however, the terms for the category differed (sometimes *yar, gayee, year*, but also *sangat, sangatin*). An account of the joking with SbSpSb though neither identical with Santal, Kharia etc. nor even fully consistent in itself[26]—exists of the Munda of Chotanagpur (Choudhury, 1977: 66–7).[27]

Some hints on the category in question here can also be found in publications of the *Anthropological Survey of India* such as on the Nagesia (Ekka and Danda, 1984) and on the Kodaku (Singh and Danda, 1986)—both communities in northern Chhattisgarh. In the former case the terms *sangi/eyar* (BWBms/ZHBms), *goi/sanghat* (BWZms/ZHZms/BWBfs/ZHBfs) and *sanghatin* (BWZfs/ZHZfs) are mentioned, while in the latter case *goyi* (female

SbSpSb) and *yar* (male SbSpSb) are used. Again these categories go along with a joking pattern among the Kodaku of Surguja (Singh and Danda, 1986: 57)—a pattern of joking that does not resemble rules known from North or South India. Similar categories are also found among the Korwa of Mirzapur (U.P.), who, however, as stated by Bhandari (1963), have migrated from Palamau (Jharkhand) and Sarguja (probably Surguja—Chhattisgarh) and might possibly be linked to the Kodaku there. Here one finds categories for ZHBms (*yar*) and ZHZms (*jai*), with whom ego can crack jokes as well.[28] The Korwa of Raigarh, however, according to Bahl (1962: 155ff) have not only a category *goi*, translated by Bahl as "a girl in the wife's sister's category, a female friend", but also seem to have separate terms for cross-cousins (MBeS=FzeS).[29]

In his comparative collection of data on communities speaking Mundaic languages Parkin (1992: 128) found additional sources, which were not available to me, mentioning or rather hinting at separate BWZ/ZHZ categories among the Santal, Munda, Asur and Korwa—apart from the already listed authors. Interestingly, the existence of a SbSpSb-category in the empirical cases just mentioned seems to correspond to the absence of separate terms for cross-cousins and very inclusive sibling-terms *e.g.* among the Ho (Deeney *ibid.*), Juang (McDougal), Kharia (Roy and Roy, 1937: 148ff; Pfeffer, 2004)[30], Korwa (Bhandari, 1963: 91), Munda (Sachchidananda, 1979; Choudhury, 1977: 58ff)[31], Nagesia (Ekka and Danda 1984:75-6)[32], Paudi Bhuyan (Roy, 1935: 134ff)[33]. Among the Santal (Kochar, Mukherjea, *ibid.*) no terms for cross-cousins are mentioned either. The categorical absence of cross-cousin terms may or may not go along with a rule/ideal for or against cross-cousin marriage.[34] The absence of a cross-cousin terminology is apparently combined with the presence of separate categories for spouse's parents.[35]

The Absence in the Southern Mahanadi Region

In his monograph on the Baiga, Elwin (1939: 181) describes a specific case of cross-cousin marriage in which the son and daughter of a person named Ketu married respectively and simultaneously the daughter and son of Ketu's sister. The interesting point here is that obviously the cases of cross-cousin marriage—one FZD and one MBD marriage—are at the same time cases of BWZ or ZHZ marriage. Thus, both forms of marriage apparently overlap to some extent, but Elwin clearly concentrates on CCM.

Table 5.9: Case of Baiga-marriage

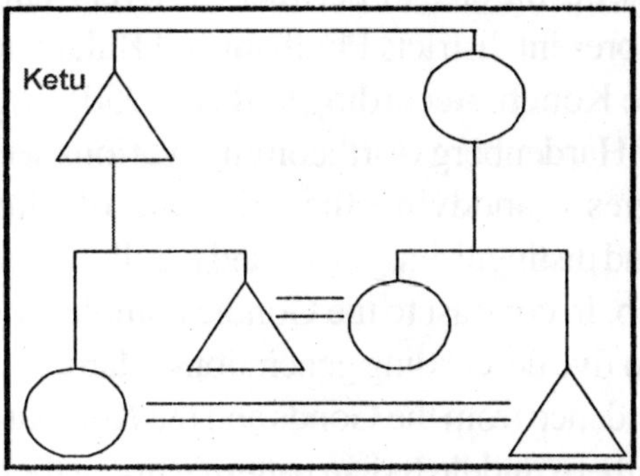

Leaving Elwin aside, there seems to be no specific evidence regarding the categories of ZHZ-BWZ/ZHB-BWB or any such preferences of marriage among the Gond, though it is clear that this form of marriage is permissible among them in Bastar (Grigson, 1991 [1938]: 248) and in Andhra or Adilabad (Fürer-Haimendorf, 1979: 356). The kinship system of various Gond groups is relatively well-documented, but neither Grigson nor Fürer-Haimendorf nor Buradkar (1940) for the Gond of the Nagpur Plains offer any hints on such a category. Thus, it is fairly safe to conclude that this category is absent among Gonds of middle India. Taking the three authors together it seems that among the Gond one finds terms for cross-cousins (Buradkar, 1940: 177; Grigson, 1991 [1938]: 308-9; Fürer-Haimendorf, 1979: 351), which do not exist among the empirical cases presented in the northern region. What is also striking is the distinction among grand-parents and grand-children into cross and parallel—equating MF = DS, SS = FF and yB = SS etc. Simultaneously terms for SpPa are absent and one finds the equation MB= SpF.

Among the communities of Southern Middle India rather closely related to the Gond, such as the Koya in Khamman District of Andhra Pradesh (AP) (Tyler, 1968) or the Dhurwa of Bastar (Thusu, 1968), the picture is apparently very similar. The same is true of the Domb[36] of Visakhapatnam District, AP (Raghava Rao, 1968) in regard to the general pattern outlined.

Apart from that a distinct category SbSpSb appears to be absent in the Koraput region, where Pfeffer (2004: 406-7) collected material, for example, among the Gadaba[37], Bondo (*see* also Elwin, 1950: 275), Parenga and Didayi. These cases do not differ much from the Gonds in the sense that here one finds separate terms for cross-cousins too and may distinguish cross from parallel-grand-parents.

While quite a bit of research on Gond kinship has been done since the early ethnographers and the "Koraput-Complex"[38], which comprised various communities, has been analysed by Pfeffer, less research has been conducted further northwards, *i.e.* the area in-between the river Mahanadi and Koraput/ Bastar, *e.g.* in the present districts Phulbani and Kalahandi. There are only a few sources on the Kondh. According to Ray (1950), Niggemeyer (1964)[39] and most recently Hardenberg (forthcoming) various sections of the Kondh have terminologies embodying the principle of alternation, equating MB=FZH=SpF and distinguishing cross and parallel cousins, but do not have a category SbSpSb. In contrast to the Gondic complex, one finds the feature of classifying up to five descending generations (Hardenberg forthcoming).[40]

Taking the evidence from the Gonds and the Koraput-Complex together, this suggests a southern middle Indian pattern without the category SbSpSb.[41]

Mapping the Ethnographic Evidence

Thus the clearest evidence so far of such a category SbSpSb is found in southern Jharkhand or Chotanagpur, northern Chhattisgarh, particularly surguja, and northern Orissa (*see* the map).[42] The case of the Korwa in Raigarh (Bahl, 1962) near Raigarh on the river Mahanadi with the category *goi* and the existence of cross-cousin terms may suggest the transitional area between these two patterns.

Map 5.1: Middle India

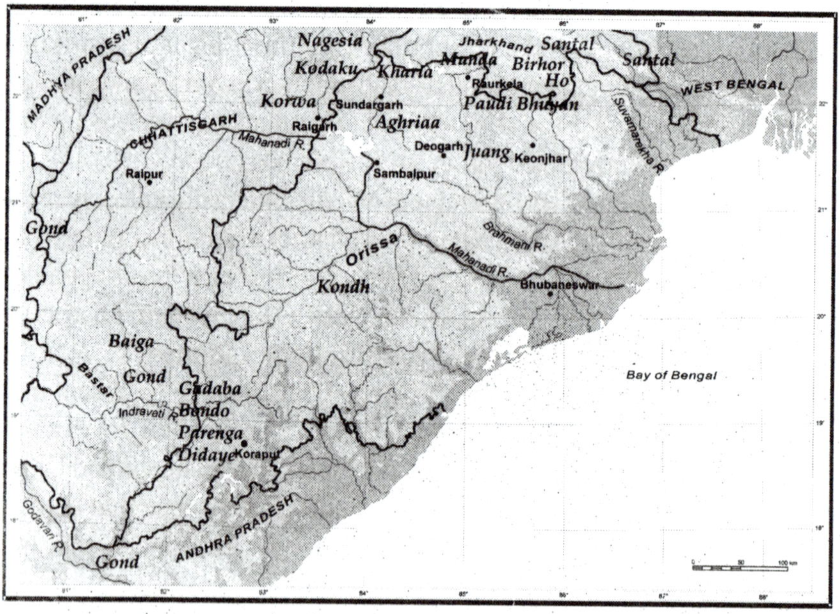

Note: The place of the Community in the map is only for a rough orientation.

Recently Pfeffer (2004) suggested that the Middle Indian kinship categories such as the Juang may have evolved from a four-line-terminology. This might have been the case for the Aghriaa as well and for the northern Mahanadi region in general, though in practice the clarity and unambiguousness of a four-line-model is missing everywhere and empiric cases rather appear as changed, transformed or broken variants of a possible historically precedent proto-Middle Indian kinship system. Given the evidence from the northern and southern Mahanadi region it might also be possible that in the south of Middle India a simple two-line-terminology might have been a starting point of which one now finds variants when compared to the more complicated and elaborate northern variants.[43]

Conclusion

Co-sister-in-law marriage as a terminological prescription is neither "Indo-Aryan" nor "Dravidian", rather it is "Middle Indian" or, more specifically, presents a "northern Mahanadi pattern". The category as such—though not a clear concurring prescription—has been confirmed in my preliminary mapping of the northern Mahanadi region comprising of northern Orissa, northern Chhattisgarh, southern Jharkhand and even West Bengal and Uttar Pradesh and seems indeed to be a major feature. It may be suggested that this region—compared to the south middle Indian area—has been more influenced by the non–prescriptive "Indo-Aryan" systems characterised by negative rules. Therefore, a broken or more open pattern relatively compatible with north Indian standards may have evolved–acceptable even to Brahmins who otherwise despise south Indian structures with their diachronic repetition of marriage (*e.g.* cross-cousin marriage).[44] However, as the Aghriaa case shows, cross-cousin marriage as a preference or even ideal may will be combined with a certain terminological prescription for delayed sister-exchange. Therefore, the Aghriaa case also underlines the necessity of considering the levels of kinship systems separately.

Furthermore, *co-sister-in-law* marriage may be combined with *grand-daughter*-marriage, which may in turn lead to a perpetuation of *co-sister-in-law* marriage within generation-sets. This structure (with some minor variations) is found among peasants like the Aghriaa, among various communities considered to be tribal such as the Gand as well as Rajputs and even Brahmins. Thus, it indicates a common pattern in the northern Mahanadi region. However, bearing in mind the middle Indian empirical evidence in general one could tentatively conclude that within middle Indian kinship there might a significant variation particularly in two respects:

Table 5.10: Tentative Categorisation of Middle Indian Kinship

Northern Mahanadi Pattern	*Southern Mahanadi Pattern (Gondic Complex or/and Koraput Complex)*
SbSpSb category	Absence of SbSpSb Category
Apparent absence of cross-cousin category (in favour of an extended sibling-category)	Widespread presence of cross-cousin terms

So far I have not found empirical evidence to support a co-existence of SbSpSb and cross-cousin categories. Apart from that, there might be another difference in the sense that there is perhaps a stronger tendency for grand-parent-merging in the north as compared to a distinction parallel and cross grand-parents[45], but the material is too scarce to draw conclusions. As indicated there might be more regional variations in the sense that a Gondic complex may differ in certain aspects from a Koraput complex.[46] These indications, for distinct features in the areas north and south of the river Mahanadi, however, should not conceal the common features between both regions—most notably the principle of alternation and the strong emphasis placed on seniority.

Appendix—Terminologies (Terms of Reference)

The Aghriaa Terminology

Terms of Reference	*Relation*
Generation +4	
Paenajaa	all men (FFFF, FMFF etc.)
Paenaaii	all women (MMMM, FMMM etc.)
Generation +3	
ba.du	all men (FFF, FMF, MFF, MMF etc.)
ba.di	all women (MMM, MFM, FFM, FMM etc.)
Generation +2	
ajaa, dadaa	all men (FF, MF etc.)
aaii, aaimaa, baai	all women (MM, FM etc.)
ajaa;sasur	WFF, WMF (possible specification)
aaii;saas	WMM, WFM (possible specification)
Generation +1	
baapaa, buaa	F
Maa	M

contd....

Terms of Reference	*Relation*
babaa, ba.dkaa baapaa	FeB, MeZH, MeZHB, (HBWF)e>F, (HZHF)e>F, (WBWF)e>F, (eSbSpF)
ba.di	FeBW
munubaapaa/saanbaapaa	FyB, MyZH
munumaan/saanmaan	FyBW, MyZ
Kakaa	FyB, BWFyB, (HBWF)y<F, (HZHF)y<F, (WBWF)y<F, (ySbSpF)
Kaaki	FyBW, (ySbSpM)
Phuphu	FZ, FZHZ, MZHZ
Phuphaa	FZH, FZHB
mamaa, maamun (MeB: baramaamo; MyB: sanmaamo)	MB, MBWB, FBWB, MBSWF, MBDHF
maami, maain	MBW
munumaan, maausii (old form: musi–baai)	MyZ, (MBWZ)e>M, MyZHZ, FyBWZ
baramaa, ba.dkaamaa	MeZ, (MBWZ)y<M, FeBW, FeBWZ (eSbSpM)
munubaapaa, mausaa (old form: mausiaa)	MyZH, MyZHB
;sasur	WF, HF, ZHF, SbSpF
;saas	WM, HM, ZHM, SbSpM
babaa;sasur	WFeB, HFeB
kakaa;sasur	WFyB, HFyB
phuphu;saas, boroma;saas	WFZ, HFZ
maamo;sasur	WMB, HMB
maain;saas	WMBW, HMBW
maausi;saas	WMZ, HMZ
Generation 0	
barabhaai, dadaa	eB, (FBS)e, (MBS)e, (FZS)e, (MZS)e, (BWB)e, (HeBWeB)e, (HeBWeB)y, (HeBWyB)e
Majlaabhaai	mB
saanbhaai, bhaai	yB, (FBS)y, (MBS)y, (FZS)y, (MZS)y, eZHB, (BWB)y, (HeBWyB)y
barabahen, baai, naani	eZ, (FBD)e, (MBD)e, (FZD)e, (MZD)e, eZHZ, (HW)e, (ZHZ)e/eZHZ (usage varying), eZHSWM, eZHDHM, (HeBWyZ)e, HeBWeZ
Majlaabahen	mZ
saanbahen, bahen	yZ, (FBD)y, (MBD)y, (FZD)y, (MZD)y, (ZHZ)y/yZHZ (usage varying), (HW)y, (HeBWyZ)y
baa.to	eZH, eZHB (if eZHB much older than ego, if not: sangii), eZHZH, eZHSWF, eZHDHF
Bahenjuien	yZH, yZHB (siehe eZHB), yZHZH
Sangii	BWB, ZHB (old: baa.to/bahenjuien)

contd....

Terms of Reference	*Relation*
Sangaat	ZHZ (m.s.), BWZ (m.s.)
Guiyaan	ZHZ (f.s.), BWZ (f.s.) (old form)
Bahu	eBW, WeBW, BWBW
bhaaibahu, bahariaa	yBW, WyBW
bar, swaamii	H
kaniaan, strii	W
de.d;saas	HeZ, WeZ
bha.tuaa–;sasur	HeZH
Nanand	HyZ
nandiaa (nandiaa–diaar)	HyZH
de.d;sasur	HeB
Diar	HyB
jethen	HeBW
deenren, debaraanii	HyBW
salaa (WeB: ba.d;salaa, WyB: san–;salaa)	WB, DHMyB + SWMyB + (WBWB)y<W as salaa, DHMeB + SWMeB + (WBWB)e>W as ba.d;salaa
saalii	WyZ, WBW, WBWZ
sa.dhu (reziprok)	WZH
samdhi, samudhi	SWF, DHF
Samdhen	SWM, DHM
Generation –1	
ba daa po, bada betaa, ba dkaa be taa	eS
majlaa po, majlaa be taa	mS
saan po, saan be taa, chu te be taa	yS
ba da ji, ba da be tii, ba dkaa be tii	eD
majlaa ji, majlaa be tii	mD
saanji, saan be tii, chu te be tii	yD
baha, baharia (old usage)	SW, yBW
Juen	DH [DHB, BDH (m.s.), HBDH]
Putraa	eBS (m.s.), ZS (f.s.), eZHZS (f.s.), HeBS, SWB, BWBS (f.s.), ZHBS (fs)
Jhiaarii	eBD (m.s.), ZD (f.s.), DHZ, HeBD, eZHZD (f.s.), BWBD (f.s.), ZHBD (f.s.)
Bhatijaa	BS (f.s.), WBS (bei Agh), BWBS (m.s.)
Bhatiji	BD (f.s.), WBD (bei Agh), BWBD (m.s.)
Bhanjaa	ZS (m.s.), BS (f.s.), WBS, HZS, ZHBS (m.s.), ZHZS (m.s.), BWBS (m.s.)
Bhaanjii	ZD (m.s.), BD (f.s.), WBD, HZD, ZHBD (m.s.), ZHZD (m.s.), BWBD (m.s.)
ba du	yBS (m.s.), HyBS, WyZS, BWyZS (m.s.)
ba di	yBD (m.s.), HyBD, WyZD, BWyZD (m.s.)

contd....

Terms of Reference	*Relation*
mausaa po	WeZS, BWeZS (m.s.)
mausi ji	WeZD, BWeZD (m.s.)
putraabaha (baha)	eBSW (m.s.), HeBSW
Putraajuen	eBDH (m.s.), HeBDH
Bhanjaajuen	ZDH (m.s.), HZDH, WBDH, eBDH (f.s.)
bhaanjiibaha (bhaanjii)	ZSW (m.s.), HZSW, WBSW, eBSW (f.s.)
ba dijuen	yBDH (m.s.), HyBDH
ba dibaha	yBSW (m.s.), HyBSW
Generation –2	
Naati	all men (SS, DS, WBSS, HZDS etc.)
naaten	all women (SD, DD, HZDD, WBSD etc.)
Generation –3	
ba du	all men (SSS, SDS, DDS etc.)
ba di	all women (DDD, SSD, DSD etc.)
Generation –4	
naati, ajaa, paenba du	all men (SSSS etc.)
naaten, aai, paenba di	all women (DDDD etc.)

NOTES

1. Some have been listed in Trautmann (1995 [1981]) and Parkin (1992, 1998).
2. Elaborate descriptions of kinship relations can be avoided through appropriate abbreviations, whereby I would stick to the following system as outlined by Trautmann (1995 [1981]: 31):

m.s.	*male speaker*	*f.s.*	*female speaker*	*CC*	*Cross-cousin*
F	Father	M	Mother	Ch	children
B	Brother	Z	Sister	Pa	parents
S	Son	D	Daughter	Sb	sibling
H	Husband	W	Wife	Sp	spouse
e	Elder	y	Younger	os	opposite sex

The relations mentioned above can be combined, to express relationships of second or third degree, for *e.g.* FF (father's father), MB (mother's brother), FZH (father's sister's husband), MyB (mother's younger brother), eZDy (elder sister's daughter, younger than ego) or FBSe (father's brother's son, elder than ego).

3. While thinking about how to name the phenomena of marriage with brother's wife's sister and sister's husband's sister I was reminded of a German kinship-category called *Schwippschwägerin*, hardly used, but nevertheless existent and designating ZHZ, BWZ (but also WBW and thus not identical with the Middle Indian category SbSpSb). In English, I was told by native speakers the sister of one's brother-in-law (ZH) or one's sister-in-law (BW) would be also known as sister-in-law too. However, to distinguish BWZ/ZHZ from close sisters-in-law I prefer to speak of co-sisters-in-law. The term co-sister-in-law was proposed to me during a conference on middle Indian tribal society and I am grateful for this

suggestion. For the difficulties to name the phenomena *see* also Parkin (1998: 256). The term seems to fit, since other sisters-in-law, *i.e.* WyZ and eBW (ms), though they are usually categorically separated, can be married as well and may even be analysed as being subcategories of a more inclusive category "(co-)sister-in-law".

4. In contrast to "straight sister-exchange" – *see e.g.* Muller (1980).
5. The categories aji and bokoray mentioned by McDougal as marriageable in the case of MBD and FZD respectively also include FBD, MZD (elder or younger to ego) as well as Z (also distinguished according to relative age). Therefore, one does not find clear-cut categories for cross-cousins.
6. Recently Parkin (2005) tentatively called into question McDougal's observation— partly based on his on cursory field-research among the Juang and particularly questioned a strong reliance on his material as primary source in relation to the phenomenon of SbSpSb marriage (in contrast to his own earlier writings). However, the data of the Aghriaa I am going to present here seem to confirm McDougal's findings.
7. For technical reasons I have omitted all diacritical marks.
8. Relatives who joke with each other can usually also accept food leftovers from each other, *e.g.* a WyZ could accept the food remains of her eZH or *vice versa*. However, it is disputed whether or not a HyB should accept food from a *bahu* (eBW).
9. The case of the mother's father is not exactly clear in situations if his whole clan was excluded.
10. *See* Aghriaa Samaaj Publications, *e.g.* "Great Convention (Mahaasabhaa) of Laida. Dt. 27.03.1921"; A list of fixed rules for women: rule 27 and 48.
11. Another very distant relative, who could not be specified exactly.
12. Out of these 6 cases: 4 MyZD, 1 MeZD and 1 case is not specified.
13. The research conducted by Dey (1997: 68) documents the frequency of cross-cousin marriages among the Aghriaa in two different regions: a northern region, including parts of the undivided districts Sambalpur and Sundargarh and a Southern region, a part of the undivided Balangir district. In the northern region the frequency of cross-cousin marriages is roughly 10 per cent in a sample of 876 marriages. The higher percentage of marriages with the matrilateral cross-cousin compared to the patrilateral cross-cousin is significant. In the southern region there is only a 5 per cent frequency of cross-cousin marriages, however, here the sample is far more limited in numbers.
14. During my brief encounters with the Birhor (Makriaa) I found the same category *goi* as well.
15. Such a provision has been mentioned by Grigson (1991 [1938]: 245) for the tribal Gond of Bastar too. Grigson (1991 [1938]: 245) notes "A man may not marry his mother-in-law or her co-widow or any woman related to them as a 'sister', or any of his aunts or nieces, even though of an *akomama* or wife-clan." Although there are considerable terminological differences between the Maria Gond and the Aghriaa, the rule seems to be identical-even though there are no brother and wife clans among the Aghriaa. Grigson found, however, only one marriage relationship with a grand-daughter. Also, Choudhury (1977: 67) mentions

the possibility of marriages with grand-parents/grandchildren, even though they rarely occur.

16. According to the preliminary data I collected, Chasaa, Kandh, Ga.n.d, Kha.diaa, Malaar, the Oraam, Tuurii, Kisaan and Mu.n.daa share the same joking patterns as the Aghriaa except for the relationships between eBW/HyZ and HeZH/WyBW. I came across these two relationships among the Aghriaa at a later stage of my research, after an initial survey among other communities had been completed. However, it seems likely that these relationships exist not only among the Aghriaa and Munda, but also among many neighbouring communities.
    I also noticed minor differences, for example, in regard to the joking between grand-parents and grand-children and among the Kisaan only distant grand-parents were proper joking partners—a restriction also found among the Aghriaa. In one case among the Kisaan a joking relationship with ChSpF was mentioned, but I could not confirm this in other cases. As far as avoidance is concerned, all the aforementioned communities practiced the avoidance of HeB/yBW and WeZ/yZH. The Khaiaa stressed the avoidance of (WMBD)e, but it might have been a special variant of the WeZ rule. An avoidance of HMB/ZSW, however, could be confirmed only for the Kandh, Chasaa, Tûrii and Malaar.
17. Some authors like Pfeffer (1982) have, of course, always argued for an analysis of all communities within a certain area as elements of a local culture or a culture complex, thereby considering *e.g.* in Koraput not only *Scheduled Tribes*, but also *Scheduled Castes* as parts of a 'tribal society'.
18. In his comparative analysis of Munda systems Parkin (1992) already collected various sources on and evidence of SbSpSb marriage. His extensive bibliography certainly helped to locate several of the sources I have cited below.
19. However, non-joking does not exclude the possibility of marriage, whereas avoidance usually does.
20. Published together with R.C. Roy. I omit their diacritical marks here.
21. Additionally a man has to avoid WeZ, (WMBD)e and WeB and a woman has to avoid HeB and yZH.
22. Cross-cousin marriage is apparently not practised among the Birhor.
23. Majumdar (1950) does not record anything of that sort.
24. Dhan (1961: 71-2) limits BWZ at one point in the text to eBWZ (not yBWZ), but writes also that marriage with yBWeZ is possible, while yBWyZ is restricted. She also mentions a MBD marriage. Unfortunately no list of kinship terms is offered.
25. However, Bhattacharya does not mention any evidence for any other community or rather language he compares. It is certainly not his main focus.
26. In Roy's data the question remains as to why a differentiation between ZHyB/ZHyZ versus ZHeB/ZHeZ is considered important, when he also mentions that ZHB, as such, is marriageable as well BWZ etc. and as far as marriage is concerned clearly no differentiation is made between elder and younger. The mentioning of two rules of avoidance HeZH/WyBW and HyZH/WeBW seems to be doubtful in Kochar's list and, considering the Aghriaa pattern, only the latter can be a relationship of avoidance.

27. The material and terminologies collected by Icke-Schwalbe (1983) on the Munda and Oraon of Chotanagpur do not offer evidence on a SbSpSb category, but seem to be rather incomplete in the light of other evidence on the Munda mentioned above. However, Icke-Schwalbe confirms the general pattern in certain aspects such as the absence of cross-cousin terms and equations B=PaSbS.
28. Unfortunately Bhandari did not include the classification of BWSb into the otherwise very extensive list of term.
29. The term *samdhi* given by Bahl is a term often used for SWF and DHF, but Bahl does not mentioned if these relations are included into the category as well. Furthermore, Bahl notes a term for FyBS, but not for FeBS nor for MZS.
30. In Roy and Roy's terminology sisters and cousins are equated in terms of address, but can be differentiated by reference.
31. Choudhury mentions very inclusive sibling-categories, but no SbSpSb, but it seems likely he may have overlooked this relatively remote category.
32. Cousins can only be distinguished by composite terms such as *mamera bahin* (MBD). However, *bahin* (Z) seems to be the central category here.
33. The evidence by Roy himself is rather weak. He neither mentions separate terms for cross-cousins (though he mentions cross-cousin marriage) nor a SbSpSb category, though he mentions that two brothers may marry two sisters. However, combined with my own preliminary investigation among Paudi Bhuyan in Bonai I think it is likely that the Paudi Bhuyan fall into this category too.
34. E.g. Hahn (1907: 74) mentions a prohibition of (first?) MBD marriage among the Kol. However, the account is incomplete in various regards. Kochar (1970: 68) mentions the same for the Santal.
35. The terminology of the Juang is slightly ambivalent in the sense that SpF (*kwingkar*) is clearly separate, but SpM (*mami*) suggests a link to *mamu* (MB = FZH), though MBW and FZ fall into the category *sasu*, which in turn is often the category of SpM elsewhere in the region.
36. An exception to the Gond pattern as outlined is the existence of terms for four ascending and six descending generations.
37. For the Ollar Gadaba see also Thusu and Jha (1972).
38. For the term *see* Pfeffer (1982: 29).
39. Niggemeyer's terminology is, however, rather incomplete.
40. Ray (1950: 154) mentions Risley's data collected earlier and hinting at a classification of five ascending generations. The data of Thusu (1977) on the Pengo Poraja may embody the same feature.
41. Quite different from the pattern summarized here for Southern Middle India appears to be the case of the Pengo Porajas of Koraput as described by Thus (1977). Here one finds equations such ays B=S=ZS(fs)=FB(y)S=MB(y)S= children of one's own cross-cousins=SDH=WZS. This appears to resemble Crow-Omaha-systems in the sense of an "inter-generational merging". Further research seems to be required here. However, among the Pengo Poraja a separate SbSpSb category is absent.
42. However, that does not mean that all communities of the northern Mahanadi region must have a category SbSpSb. In some accounts of the regions such as Sarkar (1934) such a category is not mentioned, though it is also not clear, if the account is indeed complete.

43. Pfeffer (1982: 75) argues that the existence of separate terms for FeBD and WZH in Grigson's list of Gond terms indicates a four-line terminology and there might have been later "simplifications" towards a 'Dravidian' order. However, it might have also been the case that the term for WZH is the result of a North Indian influence. Besides, neither Thusu (1968) nor Buradkar (1940) mention separate terms for FeBD. Therefore I would not exclude the possibility of a two-line terminology and transformations of it.
44. This point regarding Brahmins presupposes that at one point of time Brahmins have migrated into the area. While many Brahmins certainly did arrive at a later stage and may have been influenced by earlier settlers, other Brahmins just may have acquired a status of Brahmins in processes of upward mobility and might be relatively more 'indigenous' than other groups.
45. These terms were first suggested to me by Chris Gregory (personal communication).
46. I could not include and evaluate the feature of blocking re-marriage for three or four generations expressed in the terminology by categorizing four to five descending and/or ascending generations. Compare Raghava Rao (1968), Hardenberg (forthcoming).

REFERENCES

Bhal, K.C. 1962. *Korwa Lexicon*. University of Chicago: South Asian Language Programme, November 1962.

Bhandari, J.S. 1963. "Kinship, Marriage and Family among the Korwa of Dudhi (Mirzapur, U.P.)," *Eastern Anthropologist* 16 (2): 79-106.

Bhattacharya, S. 1970. "Kinship Terms in the Munda Languages," *Anthropos*, 65: 444-65.

Choudhury, N.C. 1977. *Munda Social Structure*. Calcutta: KLM Private.

Conzelmann, E. 1996. *Heirat, Gabe, Status: Kaste und Gesellschaft in Mandi*. Berlin: Arabisches Buch.

Dhan, R.O. 1961. "The Hos of Saranda: An Ethnographic Study," *Bulletin of the Bihar Tribal Research Institute,* 3 (1): 37-105.

Dumont, L. 1983 [1966]. "Descent or Intermarriage? A Relational View of Australian Section Systems," (pp.192-214) In: ibid. *Affinity as a Value. Marriage Alliance in South India with Comparative Essays on Australia,* Delhi: Oxford University Press.

Elwin, V. 1939. *The Baiga*. London: Murray.

____. 1950. *Bondo Highlander,* London: Oxford University Press.

Fürer-Haimendorf, C. von 1979. *The Gonds of Andhra Pradesh. Tradition and Change in an Indian Tribe.* New Delhi: Vikas.

Grigson, W. 1991 [1938]. *The Maria Gonds of Bastar*. Delhi: Vanya Prakashan.

Hahn, F. 1907. *Einführung in das Gebiet der Kol-Mission*. Gütersloh: Bertelsmann.

Hardenberg, R. (forthcoming). *The Children of the Earth Goddess*, Post-doctoral Thesis. University of Münster.

Icke-Schwalbe, L. 1983. *Die Munda und Oraon in Chota Nagpur*. Berlin: Akademie Verlag.

Kochar, V. 1963. "Kinship Terms and Usages among the Santals of Bolpur Area, Birbhum," *Bulletin of the Anthropological Survey of India,* 12 (1-2): 47-56.

____. 1970. *Social Organisation among the Santal*. Calcutta: Temple Press.

Majumdar, D.N. 1950. *The Affairs of a Tribe. A Study in Tribal Dynamics.* Lucknow: Universal Publishers.

McDougal, C.W. 1963. *The Social Structure of the Hill Juang*. PhD. Thesis, University of New Mexico.

Mukherjea, C. 1962 [1939]. *The Santal.* Calcutta: AMC.

Muller, J.C. 1980. "Straight Sister-Exchange and the Transition from Elementary to Complex Structures," *American Ethnologist*, 7 (1): 518-29.

Needham, R. 1973. "Prescription," *Oceania*, 42: 166-81.

Niggemeyer, H. 1964. *Kuttia Kond. Dschungel-Bauern in Orissa.* München: Klaus Renner Verlag.

Parry, J. 1979. *Caste and Kinship in Kangra*. New Delhi: Vikas Publishing House.

Parkin, R. 1992. *The Munda of Central India. An Account of their Social Organization.* Delhi.

____. 1998. "Dravidian and Iroquois in South Asia," *In*: M. Godelier, T.R. Trautmann and F.E. Tjon and Sie Fat (eds.), *Transformations of Kinship*. Washington: Smithsonian.

____. 2005. "Tribal Kinship in Central India. A Reply Article," *Anthropos,* 100 (2): 567–70.

Pfeffer, G. 1982. *Status and Affinity in Middle India*. Wiesbaden: Franz Steiner Verlag.

____. "Generation and Marriage in Middle India: the Evolutionary Potential of 'Restricted Exchange," *Contributions to Indian Sociology*, 17: 87-121.

____. 1999. "Gadaba and the Bondo Kinship Vocabularies *versus* Marriage, Descent and Production," In: D.K. Behera and G. Pfeffer, (ed.) *Contemporary Society: Tribal Studies, Vol. 4: Social Realities*. New Delhi: Concept.

____. 2004. "Order in Tribal Middle Indian Kinship," *Anthropos*, 99: 381-409.

Raghava Rao, D.V. 1968. "Domb Kinship Terms," *Man in India*, 48 (2): 115-23.

Ray, G. 1950. "Characteristic Features of Kondh Kinship Terminology," *Eastern Anthropologist*, 3: 151-7.

Roy, S.C. 1925. *The Birhors. A Little Known Jungle Tribe of Chota Nagpur*. Ranchi: The G.E.L. Mission Press.

____. 1935. *The Hill Bhuiyas of Orissa.* Ranchi: Man in India Office.

Roy, S.C. and R.C. Roy. 1937. *The Kharias Ranchi.* Man in India Office (2 vols.).

Sarkar, S. 1972 [1934]. "The Malers of the Rajmahal Hill," *Man in India*, Vol. 14, reprint 1972, Amsterdam: Swets and Zeitlinger N.V., p. 248-70.

Sachchidananda. 1979. *The Changing Munda*. New Delhi: Concept Publishing.

Skoda, U. 2005. *The Aghria: A Peasant Caste on a Tribal Frontier*. New Delhi: Manohar.

Suryanarayan, M. 1999. "Impact of Dravidian Marriage Practices on a Mundari Speaking Soara Kinship Terminology." In: D.K. Behera and G. Pfeffer, (eds.), *Contemporary Society: Tribal Studies. Vol. 4: Social Realities*. New Delhi: Concept.

Thusu, K.N. 1968. *The Dhurwa of Bastar.* Calcutta: Anthropological Survey of India.

____. 1977. *The Pengo Porajas of Koraput*. Calcutta: Anthropological Survey of India.

Thusu, K.N. and M. Jha. 1972; *Ollar Gadaba of Koraput*. Calcutta: Anthropological Survey of India.

Trautmann, T.R. 1998 [1979]. "The Study of Dravidian Kinship," *In*: P. Uberoi, (ed.), *Family, Kinship and Marriage in India*. New Delhi: OUP.

Tyler, S. 1968. "Koya Kinship Terminology: The Relation between Syntactic and Semantic Analysis," *In*: B. Krishnamurty (ed.), *Studies in Indian Linguistics*. Poona: Centre of Advanced Study of Linguistics.

Vidhyarti, L.P. and V.S. Upadhyay. 1980. *The Kharia: Then and Now*. New Delhi: Concept.

Williams, B.J. 1968. "The Birhor of India and Some Comments on Band Organisation," (pp. 126-31) *In*: R.B. Lee and I. DeVore (eds.), *Man the Hunter*. Chicago: Aldine Publishing Company.

SECTION III

THE WHOLE AND THE INDIVIDUAL

SIX

CONCEPTUALIZING AND CREATING SOCIETY IN HIGHLAND ORISSA:
Descent, Territory and Sacrificial Communion

PETER BERGER

Introduction

In the Koraput District of Southern Orissa some 15,000–20,000 (Rajan and Rajan, 2001:9) people calling themselves Gutob or Gadaba live on a plateau about 900 meter above sea level. My colleague Arlo Griffiths, a noted Indologist of Leiden University, is suggesting that "Gutob" might mean "earth creatures" (*see* also Griffiths in press), and, as is often said by the people themselves, the name "Gadaba" may be derived from the Godaveri river, their mythical place of origin. Like their diverse neighbours on the plateau they also consider themselves to be Desia, meaning "people of the land", who all share a dialect of the state language Oriya, whereas on their own, the Gadaba mother tongue is Gutob, a language belonging to the Munda group of the Austro-Asiatic language family.[1] Gadaba subsistence is based on the cultivation of dry rice and finger millet as well as wet rice. The present article intends to show how they conceptualise their society and what kind of activities they perform in order to articulate, maintain and recreate the relationships the society consists of.

Initially the main social units, relationships and categories of Gadaba society are introduced before the focus will shift to ritual performances with special reference to communal blood sacrifices as well as the distribution and consumption of food. When analyzing these rituals it will become apparent that the distinction of opposed levels like value *vs.* action, symbolic *vs.*

instrumental, expression *vs.* performance or, for that matter, conceptualizing *vs.* creating is unsatisfactory, because such an analytic division cannot be derived from ethnographic facts. Worse still, it may be a hindrance in the approach to the understanding of these rituals by the participants themselves. Meaning or value is not external to ritual acts and they are not just a way of doing something but rather a realization of values. For example, the Gadaba refer to *niam* when they talk about the norms of behaviour, their tradition or, in a broader sense, their social order. But this order is never conceived in an abstract manner. It is not a dogma and far from being rigorously fixed. *Niam* realizes itself only through ritual action.

Of course others have felt this analytical discomfort before, particularly the French anthropologists working in the tradition of Marcel Mauss. Dumont (1986: 236, 243) for example criticized the modern tendency to separate being or *facts* from *value* and more recently de Coppet referred to the same problem in his attempt to reintroduce the notion of "re-presentation" in the sense of re-enactment or "to make present a new" (1992: 71). Ritual action for him is a "creative fusion" of "activity, thought and reality" (*ibid.*: 70), or in the words of Kuper summarizing de Copper's ideas: "The characteristic unit of social life is neither individual act nor social value but the re-enactment of values" (Kuper, 1992: 9). After having broadly outlined how the Gadaba conceive their society I will focus on three examples of such re-enactments of value and order which figure on different levels of society: visibly the house, the village and Gadaba society as a whole.

Conceptualizing Society: Brothers and Others

The indigenous conception of society distinguishes different inclusive levels each of which is conceived as an association of "brothers". Such a scheme points towards the value of agnation as "being brothers" with the important implication of a territorial attachment and a sharing of sacrificial food, as we shall *see* later. Apart from the bottom level of the social structure the idea of agnation is not based on descent in a genealogical sense, rather the opposition of like and unlike, of agnatic and affinal segments, or brothers and others is stressed. As will become apparent, the term brother, *bai*, denotes various social units on each of the given levels. I have illustrated the levels of the social structure in Table 6.1. In the left column the different social wholes are ranked according their inclusiveness. In the middle column the related descriptions of these wholes in terms of brotherhood are listed. In the right column 1 mention the constitutive segments of the social wholes. This Table will serve as a guideline to the first part of my paper, as will become clearer in due course of time.

Table 6.1: Associations of "Brothers" on Different Levels of the Social Structure

Social (sub-) Wholes	*Fraternal Association*	*Constitutive Segments*
Desia "people of the land"	*the twelve brothers* *baro bai*	*tribes* *jati, kul*
Gadaba	*elder/younger brother* *boro Gadaba/sano Gadaba*	*ibid.*
Gutob "earth creatures"	*"twelve brothers thirteen seats"* *baro bai tero gadi*	*village-clans* *ga, ungom**
Gangre, Mundagoria, etc. (limited) village-clan	*the four brothers* *cari bai*	*local lines* *kuda*
Sisa, Kirsani, Munduli, Boronaik *kuda*	(*attributional names*)	*local sublines* *kutum*
Garsa Gor, Purnamundia, etc. (unlimited), *kutum*	*"own brothers"* *nijoro bai*	*houses* *gor, dien**

Desia Society

Desia Society is the most inclusive whole that is described as *the twelve brothers* (*baro bai*), each brother representing one tribal community like the Gutob, Ollar, Bonda, Parenga, Dombo and Rona among others. These are conceived as distinct *jati, i.e.* communities or tribes. Stories explain how they originated from one womb in mythical times. These "brothers" are hierarchically ordered by seniority as Pfeffer (1982, 1997) has pointed out and are arranged in pairs according to a general Middle Indian pattern. In this way the Gutob Gadaba are related as seniors to their complementary segment, the junior Ollar Gadaba who speak a Dravidian tongue. Ollar and Gutob Gadaba frequently intermarry, but otherwise affinal exchange between the Desia tribes is uncommon. When in the following I will speak of the Gadaba I shall be referring to the Gutob only.

Gadaba Society: *Twelve Brothers Thirteen Seats*

The Gadaba consider themselves to be a distinct society, a valued whole with a distinguished order or *niam*. Geographically the Gadaba occupy a rather continuous stretch of land, which borders the area of the Parenga to the South, that of the Ollar Gadaba to the East and North, the Joria land to the Northeast and that of the Bonda and Didayi to the Southwest (*see* Map 6.1).

Map. 6.1: Gutob Gadaba Village and the Surrounding Tribal Communities

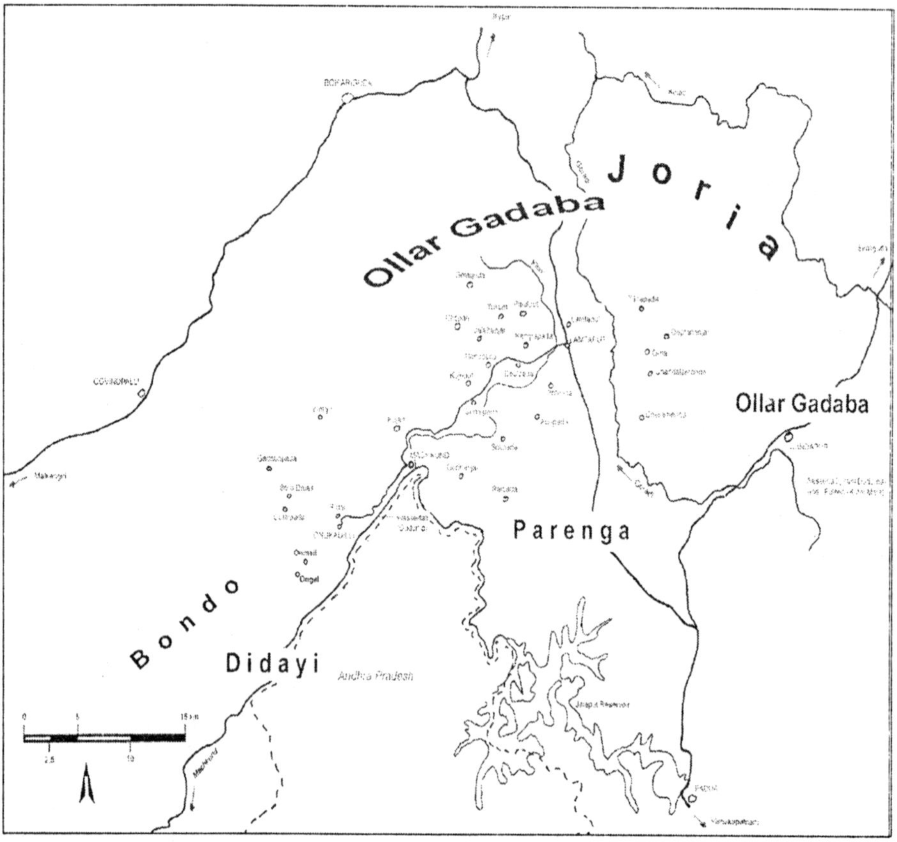

Nevertheless it would be a mistake to conceive a homogeneous Gadaba territory. Other communities like the above mentioned Dombo or Rona are living within the very same area and frequently even in the same villages as the Gadaba. However, the Gadaba are considered as the original inhabitants or *the earth-people* (*matia*) and their neighbours of the other ethnic categories as *the late-comers* (*upria*). The point will be elaborated later.

When the Gutob Gadaba refer to their society as a whole, which they like to do particularly in a ritual context and during invocations of divine beings, they speak of *baro bai tero gadi*, which literally means *twelve brothers thirteen seats*. The twelve agnatic "brothers", in other words, are supplemented here by an additional affinal category. In fact this level is introducing the opposition of agnates (or "brothers") and affines—*bai* and *bondu*—in the local tongue. The social universe, which includes *all* of the Desia tribes, is divided into sociocentric descent categories conceived as both patrilineal and totemic. The indigenous term is *bonso* but they will be called 'totemic clans' in the following. Among the Desia eight such clan-categories are found, but some tribes only employ a part of this set (Pfeffer, 1997; Berger, 2002). While the Bonda distinguish only two such patrilineal categories among themselves, the Gadaba classify themselves according to the following four: *Cobra*, *Tiger*, *Sun* and *Monkey*. All people belonging to the same category regard themselves as agnates and therefore strictly prohibit any mutual intermarriage. The most relevant point in this context is the fact that clan classification cuts *across* the different Desia communities. It is not confined to the Gadaba or any other a single tribe. This is one reason why Pfeffer (1997: 16) calls the whole Desia configuration the Koraput Complex.

As a reference category *the twelve brothers thirteen seats* are quite omnipresent, even though the substantial content of it is far from being clear at all times. The Gadaba inhabitants of the village my hosts informed me that the origin of *the twelve brothers* goes back to a time long ago, when they arrived from the Godaveri river to settle in their present habitat. The men of the *Cobra* clan performed a sacrifice and, for this purpose, cooked the sacrificial food called *tsoru* which, however, was sufficient for only for twelve of them who henceforth were regarded as *the twelve brothers* and eligible to share the same sacrificial food. The remaining *Cobra* people had to associate themselves with other groups. Within the *Tiger* clan the same situation occurred, leaving some out. The *Sun* and *Monkey* people, however, being so few in number, did have sufficient food, it was said. Today, the twelve *Cobra* brothers are actually represented by twelve villages, but in fact all villages only very rarely act as a group. When they do, their affines are incorporated as a separate but complementary category: the thirteenth seat.

Village-clans, *Earth-people* and *the Four Brothers*

On the level just described, the association of *the twelve brothers thirteen seats* consists of villages. For a Gadaba a village is a specific social unit bearing a name of its own. Members of such a village belong to one clan category only, have a strong territorial attachment and form a distinct commensal group. For a better understanding, I distinguish this aspect of the social structure from any empirical village by calling them "village-clan" (Berger, 2007a: 104f).

The village-clans constitute the form that the different clan categories take on the ground. Ideally a village (*ga*, *ungom**) is inhabited only by Gadaba of the same clan-category. We therefore have cobra village-clans that are agnatically related to other such units and related as affines to village-clans of the tiger, sun or monkey category. Empirically, however, most villages are *not* inhabited by members of their village-clan only, since other Gadaba groups have also settled on the same site, just as members of other Desia tribes may be immediate neighbours. This difference between the village-clan and the settlement generally known as village may be exemplified by the village of my fieldwork: Gadaba of the *Cobra* category dominate it and—as village founders—are called *earth-people* (*matia*) who in turn conceive all other groups of their settlement as *late comers* (*upria*). The relation between the *earth-people* and their territorial earth deity is crucial, because their founding ancestors had erected the shrine for the deity at the time of settlement with the subsequent generations acting as sacrificers ever since. The deity is called *hundi* and addressed as "village mother-father" (*ga mata pita*). It is the only collective shrine that is located within the confines of the village. To the opposite of this shrine, a platform made of dozens of flat and upright stone slabs has been erected in the course of time, an abstract representation of all generations of *earth-people* who ever lived on this territory. Such a twin configuration of territorial deity and stone platform is the centre of all Gadaba villages. The specific village of my fieldwork is called Gangreungom in Gutob, which means village of the Gangre. Though some members of this Gangre descent group have been living in other villages since generations, they are still regarded as Gangre at their more recent homes. In other words: membership to a village-clan (like that of the Gangre) is assigned irrespective of the actual place of residence. People remain Gangre wherever they live. Conversely, Gadaba of other village-clans staying in Gangreungom also remain what their forefathers have been. Thus one of the "late-comer" groups in this village are Ollar (or "junior") Gadaba originating from the nearby village of Mundagor. As their "moved in" affines they have stayed with the Gangre since generations and completely forgotten their original mother tongue Ollari, frequenting Gutob in the manner of the dominant *"earth-people"* of the village. For all practical purposes the Ollar Gadaba are undistinguishable from the Gangre and yet they remain unequivocally Mundagoria. The difference of village-clanship is most pronounced in the context of sacrificial communion. Would the Ollar Gadaba of Gangreungom share the sacrificial food of the *earth-people* at the shrine of the earth deity, they would *become* Gangre. Their categorical exclusion, however, lets them retain their Mundagoria status.

So far, the category called village-clan above has not been understood in the literature on Middle Indian Tribal Societies, even though related ethnographic facts have variously been reported (Elwin, 1950: 24f; Fürer-Haimendorf, 1943: 163, fn. 2, 1945: 331; Mohanty, 1973/4: 133; Pfeffer, 1982: 48, 1997: 17, 21, 24; Thusu, 1977: 20-37; Thusu and Jha, 1972: 53f). The particular idea of *territory* among the Gutob Gadaba—which is also most likely to prevail among neighbouring Orissan tribes as the Bonda, the Ollar Gadaba and the Pengo focuses on the village status in a manner that differs markedly from the territorial concept found among the Kond, for example, where villages are located within a much broader and basically homogeneous clan territory (*see* Hardenberg in this volume).

These village-clans, according to the above description, may be mutually related as agnates, if they share the clan category, or as affines if their clan membership differs. However there are in addition specific ways linking them together of which I will only mention one type of relation since it is of particular relevance for the moment. Local groups, such as those village-clans who are sharing the same clan-category, may be permanently related as so-called *tsorubai* or *tsoru*—"brothers". As such, their assignment is the reciprocal cooking and feeding of sacrificial food, or *tsoru,* on different occasions such as marriages, deaths, excommunications or other precarious situations. With such services, the *tsoru*-brothers are said to "restore" the social order, or *niam*. They sacrifice in the name of *the twelve brothers*. Accordingly, within the twelve agnatic village-clans constituting *the twelve brothers*, one of them—such as the above mentioned Gangre—maintains such a particular *tsoru*-brotherhood with any single other village-clan. I will come back to this very important relationship at the end of my paper.

Whenever the members of the village-clan, or the exclusive *earth-people*, assemble in their settlement, they do so under the designation of *the four brothers*, thereby emphasizing the fact that all four segments of the village-clan have come together. The village as a whole is present to make decisions or to sacrifice, even though this "village as a whole" is not the empirical village community of the substantial inhabitants. Any village-clan anywhere—irrespective of the totemic clan category and place of residence—divides into the same four segments known as *Sisa*, *Kirsani*, *Munduli* and *Boronaik*. I follow Pfeffer in calling these units local lines, because the term 'lineage' would wrongly insinuate pedigree and descent, whereas many people known as *Sisa*, *Kirsani* etc.—but belonging to different village-clans—intermarry frequently, being absolutely unaware of any common ancestry. In fact, *locality* is the principle to be emphasized, because the classification of local lines is only meaningful when they are recognized as complementary parts of their specific village-clan; those *Sisa* of different village-clans have nothing in common except the title, being a part of an individual's name (Pfeffer, 1997: 20f).

A village-clan is divided into four fraternal segments or local lines which in turn sub-divide into an unspecified number of local sublines which are called *kutum*. Thus the local line of the *Sisa* in Gangreungom divides into four *kutum*-groups which bear descriptive names, while the Munduli local line consisting of just three houses remains undivided. The sub-divisions of Sisa and Munduli local lines of other village-clans would be quite different in number and designation when compared to those of the Gangre. While the segments on the level of the local line are thus fixed in name and number there is no such homogeneity as far as the next lower level is concerned.

Men of the same local subline or *kutum* conceive each other as *own brothers* (*nijoro bai*) stating that they are born from one womb, literally *one stomach* (*gote pete*). Thus the idea of filiation is found here, although this is not to be confused with biological facts. In a sense this genealogical idea is still classificatory because actual descent often cannot be traced—Gadaba do not care tracing it or pretend to know—and as I could observe, descendants of empirically different fathers and mothers still regard each other as "own" brothers and sisters. Rights to land is allotted within this group of "own brothers" and if a man dies without sons the deceased brothers' sons will take, literally "eat", his land.

The smallest social unit is the house, the living quarters of a man, his wife and unmarried children along with a widowed parent. In collective annual festivals the ritual rhythm oscillates between village and houses, between the whole (the village or *ga matam*) and the constitutive parts of that whole (that is all houses or *gulai ga*).

Creating Society through Sacrificial Communion

Having so far introduced the basic features of the Gadaba social structure the second aspect of the article will demonstrate how society is created through ritual action. The most important way of representing value and society in de Coppet's sense, *i.e.* of symbolizing and at the same time creating relationships, is the sacrificial communion. I have already mentioned the category of sacrificial food or *tsoru* (*go'yang**) standing at the centre of all such processes when I summarized the story of how *the twelve brothers* came into existence, just as the particular relationship of *tsoru*-brothers has been introduced, *i.e.* the reciprocal cooking and feeding obligation of two village-clans. Space does not permit a further elaboration of the general significance of alimentary processes when it comes to the transformation of the Gadaba person in the realm of life-cycle rituals (Berger, 2001, 2007a, b). Instead I will focus on sacrificial communion in the context of some annual rituals, when social relationships are renewed by *tsoru* commensality.

Initially the characteristics of this particular type of food will be shown. *Tsoru* is always part of a blood sacrifice to be eaten, after being offered to the respective deity, by a limited group of people on the spot. It must not be taken away. Along with meat and rice *tsoru* consists of the blood and the liver of the sacrificial animal. Both are closely associated with the essence of life or vitality. All of these ingredients are cooked in a new earthen pot by a "female" agent, not by the male sacrificer. Frequently the head of the animal is prepared as *tsoru*, while the body is prepared as an inferior or "junior" type of food which, being called *lakka**, is complementary to *tsoru*. In other words: food types and the respective groups of eaters hierarchically oppose one another.

The Gadaba do not conceive *tsoru* commensality as an idea of "coded-substances" that would enter the body through ingestion possibly to be transformed and constitute social relatedness. Such an interpretation is commonly suggested for the Hindu context by the scholars following McKim Marriott in the so-called *Chicago School* (Marriott and Inden, 1977) and is also found elsewhere, *e.g.* in Highland New Guinea (Strathern, 1973). However, the process of *tsoru* preparation is implicitly associated with sexual intercourse. For the Gadaba I suggest that it is rather the activity of sacrificing and commensality as such which makes the procedure an effective value-act.

Of the units and relationships so far introduced in the first part of this article some but not all are regularly recreated through *tsoru* commensality. The "junior" Ollar and the "senior" Gutob segments never assemble together as "the Gadaba whole" to share *tsoru*, nor is there any context in which all Desia tribes, Gadaba along with eleven other indigenous peoples of the plateau, participate in sacrificial communion. In former times the Dushera festival of the local King might have been an occasion on which all of his "subjects" are joined in ritual action (*see* Otten in this volume). Bits of evidence suggests that the Dongria Kond (Nayak, 1989: 180f) and the Juang (McDougal, 1963: 364-68) acted in such a manner. However, for the Desia (the indigenous tribes of Koraput) and the former Jeypur or Nandpur petty kingdoms of the region no such data are available (*see* Schnepel, 2002: 255-92). The most inclusive Gadaba unit assembling—though infrequently—as a commensal group is that of *the twelve brothers thirteen seats* who as such represent Gadaba society as a whole. The lower-level wholes to assemble most regularly are that of *the house* and that of *the four brothers*, *i.e.* the village-clan, to be reconstituted through ritual action. An example of the actual proceedings of a village sacrifice as part of an annual festival will illustrate such a major communion as will a brief comment on the *tsoru*-commensality of the house. An outline of a precarious situation will follow, *i.e.* the events necessitating the sacrificial communion of *the twelve brothers thirteen seats*.

The succession of ritual events marks and reproduces hierarchical relationships of seniority, as is manifested in every annual festival when the collective sacrifice of the village precedes that of the individual house. During one of the main Gadaba festivals, lasting for about a month, the first collective sacrifice is performed at a particular shrine *beyond* the village boundaries called *the senior house*. This shrine is considered to be the "elder brother" of the village deity, *i.e.* of the *hundi* situated *within* the village, who receives a sacrifice a week later. On the same day, but after the sacrifice for *hundi*, all householders sacrifice for their individual house gods.

Village Sacrifice at the Senior House

I start with a description of the sacrifice at *the senior house*. All of such collective rituals are led by two village specialists: the village sacrificer and the ritual cook[2]. The two are the first to approach the deity whose shrine is some 600 meters away from the village boundary and is located at the foot of a hill on a mud platform where about 40 people might find a place to sit down and eat. As the preparations proceed, more Gadaba, among them *earth-people* and affines, join the group and around noon the sacrificer and the cook will start invoking the god to be followed by the sacrifice of a cock and a he-goat. After the goat's blood is caught in a leaf plate, its head is immediately placed inside the small shrine, the body being dragged away for some meters. The ritual cook prepares a small quantity of *tsoru*—some rice grains, some blood, a piece of the liver and some meat from the throat—placing it in front of the shrine for the deity to eat. Then the goat's head is removed from the shrine and cooked as *tsoru*.

Meanwhile the Gadaba not belonging to the village-clan, the village-internal affines of *the earth-people*, on a fire at a distance of some meters from the shrine, cook a piece of the goat's neck for themselves and even further away the rest of the animal's body is cut up for the meat to be divided into exactly identical portions. Each householder, irrespective of group membership, receives one of these more than a hundred raw portions to be taken away and cooked on a spot, *i.e.* in the dry fields between shrine and village boundary. Thus, *three* groups are ritually distinguished in the process. Their relationships *re-presented* by sacrificial and commensal activity. The structure of the sacrifice is illustrated by Table 6.2.

Table 6.2: Structure of *tsoru* Commensality at the "Senior House"

Social Categories	*earth-people* or **"four brothers" (cobra)**	*late-comers*	
		Gadaba affines (fish and tiger)	**non-Gadaba**
Alimentary Category	*tsoru* ("senior" *tsoru*)	*lakka'** ("junior" *tsoru*)	*lakka'**
Part of the Animal	*head*	*neck*	*body*
Place of Eating	*at the shrine (near the god)*	*near the shrine/ on the platform*	*far away from shrine*
Sequence	*eat first (after the deity)*	*eat second*	*eat last*

The four brothers or *earth-people* of the village share the *tsoru* cooked from the goat's head consuming it in the immediate vicinity of the shrine. Moreover, of all the three groups they start and finish eating first. Through these *value-acts* they recreate and confirm their privileged relationship to the deity, as well as their senior status with regard to all other groups. In fact, they represent the village. Those Gadaba classified as village-internal affines jointly share the meat of the goat's neck. The food they consume is of the junior *lakka*'* category although it is sometimes euphemistically called "junior" *tsoru* in comparison to the "senior" *tsoru* of *the earth-people*. The affines' intermediate status—that between the *earth people* and the non-Gadaba group—is again expressed and confirmed by the alimental, the spatial and the temporal codes. They eat the neck, *i.e.* the intermediate part between head and body, just as they sit in-between the other groups and start eating after *the earth-people* but before the non-Gadaba. Finally, the last group, the eaters of the goat's body, are these non-Gadaba inhabitants of the village, besides those Gadaba that are not ritually eligible because they are either unmarried or have not fasted beforehand, or both. In the first two sacrificial units all of those household members belonging to the same local line or sub-line cook their meat on the same fire, but on this most junior level of the sacrificial structure considerations of ongoing disputes and friendships enter the arrangement of commensality, aspects quite unthinkable in the realm of *the four brothers*. Given these particularities, the non-Gadaba of a village observe the division into different cooking groups year after year. Individuals tend to change their loyalties only to rejoin their local line on the next occasion after twelve months.

Having finished their sacrificial meal at the shrine, the Gadaba salute the god and join the non-Gadaba groups in the fields outside the village. Jointly all men then enter the village and the particular manner in which they proceed deserves mentioning. The two specialists among *the earth-people*—like sacrificer and cook—along with other dignitaries of *the earth-people*, are taken in on the shoulders by their Gadaba affines and carried across the village boundary to the house of the sacrificer. This simple act, like *tsoru* commensality as such, is equally meaningful and effective. The position of *the earth people's* bodies on the shoulders of their affines expresses and simultaneously recreates the hierarchical relationship between *the four brothers* and the others, that between *earth-people* and *late-comers*.

House Sacrifice

In an annual cycle the relationships between *the earth people*, their gods and the other social groups of the village are regularly re-presented in the manner described. Furthermore, every householder sacrifices twice a year for his house god, a local earth deity of the same kind as the god in the village center though relatively inferior or "junior". His wife cooks the *tsoru* to be eaten by all members of his household. Within the local sub-line, or *kutum*, this *tsoru* may then be shared but apart from these close agnates nobody else is eligible. Only *lakka** food is distributed among other Gadaba households. The recently departed of the household must also be served sacrificial food on the cremation ground though their status is somewhat ambivalent like the one of the *earth peoples*' affines in the context of the just described collective sacrifice. These dead relatives have not left the village and are still lingering around; yet, having joined the "community of the dead" (*duma kul*), they do not belong to the living anymore. While the affines of *the earth-people* might be described as the "included others", the dead are the "excluded own". Both of these ambivalent statuses are re-established in relation to the living *earth-people* by the consumption of *lakka** food.

"Twelve Brothers Thirteen Seats"

My final example returns to the idea of Gadaba society as a whole or *the twelve brothers thirteen seats*. This most valued whole is not, as the one of *the four brothers,* re-created on a regular basis but only in cases of emergency, when *niam* or the social order in general is threatened by severe violations of the social order in general. *Tsoru* then has to be shared among *the twelve brothers* to "restore *niam*" (*niam korbar*) and to re-present Gadaba society as a whole. During the phase of almost two years of field research, I witnessed only one such case. Even then not all of *the twelve brothers*—*i.e.* representatives of the twelve constitutional villages—were present. The following will recall the occasion in brief (*see* Berger, 2007a: 279-83).

A senior person of the Gangre village-clan died as a consequence of having been severely beaten by his own son. During the subsequent death ritual the deceased's spirit did not receive the sacrificial gifts according to the traditional rules: neither a cow nor an oxen had been killed for the sake of the dead elder who, outraged by this gross insult, took possession of his own brother. Moreover, a sacrificial pig, planned for a ritual to heal the shortcoming, proved to be insufficient, since it died on its own during the preparations. People then started considering the case to be very serious. Through the medium of the affected brother the village elder was promised the cattle sacrifice that had been withheld from him until then. As a token, a cow's ear was fed to the spirit via his brother's body—but to no avail, the brother also died. Villagers soon agreed that a sacrifice in the name of *the twelve brothers thirteen seats* should be performed in order to prevent further calamities.

At this point the so-called *tsoru*-brother relationship became important. The Gangre sent notice of their urgent case so that one of their *tsoru-brothers* soon arrived at their village. Together with other Gangre he invoked the elder man's spirit in the name of *the twelve brothers thirteen seats*. An ox was scarified in the name of *the twelve brothers* and a pig in the name of the remaining affinal unit. After the invocation the two sides' activities were kept completely separate. The brothers cooked *tsoru* to be eaten on the spot by those present. Then twelve portions of raw meat were laid down for the twelve villages. When they had to be dedicated to the respective villages by those present, the first seven or eight villages were instantly named, but then people became hesitant being uncertain of the remaining villages. Obviously the ritual was not a frequent affair. After a few minutes the 'right' twelve seemed to have been identified and the meat was put aside, later to be sent to these villages. At a different place the village-internal affines of the Gangre were in charge and shared *tsoru* from the pig's head among themselves. After finishing their meal raw portions of pork were put down for the bride-taking villages of the deceased's local sub-line. Nineteen villages were identified, the number here being obviously unimportant and not generally fixed. At the end of the day the sacrificial communion of *the twelve brothers thirteen seats* had been accomplished and the death rituals for the elder and his brother were later resumed and appropriately completed.

Conclusion

The extended stay in a contemporary Gadaba village revealed how they conceive their social order. In their own perspective, sacrificing and sharing *tsoru* re-creates social relationships on different levels of society. I follow de Coppet in regarding these ritual and alimentary processes as a "creative fusion" (1992: 70) of thought and activity or as value-acts. Among the Gadaba and elsewhere the re-presentations of social relationships include those between different groups of human beings as well as those between the living, the deities and the dead. Their valued social whole to be reconstituted most regularly is that of *the four brothers* or *the earth-people* of a certain village territory. Far from being merely an empirical settlement, a morphological feature, for the Gadaba a village is a value, a central concept of their social universe. It is an association of "brothers"—a sacred quaternary brotherhood—whose existence depends upon their relationship with the earth deity of the particular piece of territory they call *hundi* or "village mother-father". This relationship is re-created when the earth deity shares *tsoru* with the *earth-people* and all other groups are defined in relation to this basic proximity or even unity. But the villages—or rather the village-clans of my terminology—also depend upon external relationships with other such groups to exchange brides and services of *tsoru* preparation and feeding. Every local unit requires *tsoru*-brothers from outside.

Gadaba do not really worry much about the periphery of their society which is embedded in the broader framework of the Koraput Complex. But this does not mean that they have no idea of the whole. When traditional rules have been violated, when *niam* has been bent or even broken, only the authority of the society as a whole—*the twelve brothers thirteen seats*—can be called upon and only through sacrificial communion can the eternal order be re-enacted.

NOTES

1. In this paper all Gutob words will be marked with '*', like *go'yang*, all other indigenous terms will be Desia.
2. The village cook is male, as all other village dignitaries. However, in opposition to the "male" sacrificer he is considered as being the "female" counterpart.

REFERENCES

Berger, P. 2001. "Feeding the Dead: Rituals of Transformation among the Gadaba of Koraput," *Adivasi*, 41: 35–50.

_____. 2002. "The Gadaba and the 'non-ST' Desia of Koraput, Orissa," (pp.57–90) In: G. Pfeffer and D.K. Behera (eds.), *Contemporary Society: Tribal Studies, Vol. 5. The Concept of Tribal Society*. New Delhi: Concept Publishing.

_____. 2007a. *Füttern, Speisen und Verschlingen. Ritual und Gesellschaft im Hochland von Orissa*. Berlin: LIT.

_____. 2007b. "Sacrificial Food, the Person and the Gadaba Ritual System," (pp.199–222) In G. Pfeffer (ed.), *Periphery and Centre. Studies in Orissan History, Religion and Anthropology*. New Delhi, Manohar.

Coppet, D. de 1992. "Comparison, a Universal for Anthropology: From 'Representation' to the Comparison of Hierarchy of Values," (pp.59–74) In A. Kuper (ed.), *Conceptualizing Society*. London: Routledge.

Dumont, L. 1986 [1983]. *Essays on Individualism. Modern Ideology in Anthropological Perspective*. Chicago: University of Chicago Press.

Elwin, V. 1950. *Bondo Highlander*. Bombay: Oxford University Press.

Fürer-Haimendorf, C. von 1943. "Megalithic Ritual among the Gadabas and Bondos of Orissa," *Journal and Proceedings of the Royal Anthropological Society of Bengal*, 9: 149–78.

_____. 1945. "The Reddis' Place among the Tribes of the Eastern Ghats," In C. von Fürer-Haimendorf (ed.), *The Reddis of the Bison Hills*. London: Macmillan & Co.

Griffiths, A. (in press). "Gutob," In G.D.H Anderson (ed.), *The Munda Languages*. Curzon: Routledge.

Kuper, A. 1992. "Introduction," (pp. 14) In A. Kuper (ed.), *Conceptualizing Society*. London: Routledge.

Marriott, M. und R.B. Inden. 1977. "Toward an Ethnosociology of South Asian Caste Systems," (pp.227–238) In K. David (ed.), *The New Wind. Changing Identities in South Asia*. The Hague: Mouton Publishers.

McDougal, C. W. 1963. *The Social Structure of the Hill Juang*. Unpublished Dissertation. The University of New Mexico. Alberqueque.

Mohanty, U. Ch. 1973/4. "Bond-Friendship among the Gadaba," *Man in Society*, 1: 130–55.

Nayak, P.K. 1989. *Blood, Women and Territory. An Analysis of Clan Feuds of the Dongria Kondhs*. New Delhi: Reliance Publishing House.

Pfeffer, G. 1982th. *Status and Affinity in Middle India*. Wiesbaden. Franz Steiner.

____. 1997. "The Scheduled Tribes of Middle India as a Unit: Problems of Internal and External Comparison," (pp.3–27) In G. Pfeffer und D.K. Behera (eds.), *Contemporary Society. Tribal Studies Vol-I: Structure and Process*. New Delhi. Concept Publishing Company.

Rajan, F.H. and J. Rajan. 2001. *Gutob-Gadaba Phonemic Summary*. Lamtaput (Orissa). Asha Kiran Society.

Schnepel, B. 2002. *The Jungle Kings. Ethnohistorical Aspects of Politics and Ritual in Orissa*. New Delhi: Manohar.

Strathern, A. 1973. "Kinship, Descent and Locality: Some New Guinea Examples," (pp. 21–34) In J. Goody (ed.), *The Character of Kinship*. Cambridge: Cambridge University Press.

Thusu, K.N. 1977. *The Pengo Porajas of Koraput. An Ethnographic Survey*. Calcutta: Anthropological Survey of India.

Thusu, K.N. and M. Jha 1972. *Ollar Gadba of Koraput*. Calcutta: Anthropological Survey of India.

SEVEN

VILLAGE RELATIONS: Descent, Sacrifice, and Territory in the Highlands of Orissa

ROLAND HARDENBERG

The Indian Tribal Village in Theoretical Perspective[1]

This article takes up a recent revival in Indian village studies[2] which had been neglected for many decades following the strong critique made against them. The different debates about the Indian village—caste as well as tribal—focused on two major aspects: firstly, the question of the "self-sufficiency" of the village, and secondly, the relevance of territory in contrast to descent as an organising principle of social relations. In *Homo Hierarchicus*, his opus magnum, Dumont (1998 [1966]) made the criticism that since the 19th century, the description and analysis of Indian society had focused predominantly on villages (1998 [1966]): 158-69; *see* Inden, 1990: 131-61). In the third decade of the 19th century, English administrators such as Wilks, Elphinstone or Metcalfe represented the Indian village as a small, self-sufficient and politically autonomous republic, as though India were a "worm whose segments are the villages" (Dumont, 1998 [1966]: 159). In Victorian times, this alleged "communism" of the village community became the central issue in most writings. Karl Marx in particular stressed the economic autarky of the village which he regarded as the main productive unit. Later, Indian nationalists painted a similar idyllic picture of the Indian village, stressing in particular the "democratic" nature of institutions like the *Panchayat*. Indian social anthropologists (*e.g.* Dube, 1955; Mathur, 1959; Srinivas, 1955) continued this trend when they produced various village studies in the 1950s, claiming that the complexity of Indian society could be studied with fieldwork methods focusing on these small village communities: "The village was considered at least as isolable, if not independent of environment" (Dumont, 1998 [1966]: 160).

This picture of the Indian village was soon to become deconstructed. The aspect of dominance, for example, which Srinivas detected in the "dominant caste" (Srinivas, 1955) at the village level, was later discovered at higher levels of the territorial and political order such as the "little region" (Mayer, 1958) or the "little kingdom" (Cohn, 1959). Furthermore, Srinivas and others began to *see* a correspondence between the function of the dominant caste at the village level and the king in the context of larger political—as well as ritual—organisations. The earlier picture of a democratic, homogeneous village community was called further into question by studies providing empirical evidence for fractions and conflicts in Indian villages (*e.g.* Lewis, 1958).

Dumont and Pocock concluded that from a sociological perspective India is not made up of villages (Dumont & Pocock, 1957b: 25) and that the village cannot be regarded as the primary denominator of social organisation: "It is a secondary factor in relation to the fundamental factors of kinship and caste" (Dumont & Pocock, 1957a: 18). Dumont arrived at this conclusion after conducting fieldwork among the Pramalai Kallar of Tamil Nadu, who in his view exhibit no larger units than that of lineage, and whose fundamental organisational principle is kinship, not territory.

In contrast to Dumont's studies in south India, Karve (1994 [1953]) had earlier pointed out the importance of the territorial factor in north India. Her examples included village exogamy in the western and central areas of north India, and the differentiation of Rajputs into western bride takers and eastern bride givers. Karve identified two main trends in north India: firstly, that caste consciousness determines the occurrence of marriages within a group defined in terms of territory and genealogy; and secondly, that village exogamy and negative marriage rules jointly result in members of the affinal category being dispersed over a wide area (Karve, 1994 [1953]: 56). Later studies arrived at a similar conclusion, namely that territory plays a significant role in India's social organisation. Thus, Shalini Randeria (1992) demonstrated that among the so-called untouchable castes in north Gujarat, a number of units exist, being larger than that of lineage, whose organisational principle is territory rather than kinship (1992: 148). In particular, she focused on marriage networks, which in Gujarat, in contrast to other areas in India, are highly structured and embedded into concrete territorial units. Other authors have stressed the territorial connotations of kinship concepts in north India. In contrast to Sylvia Vatuk (1975), who defined the term *dhyane* solely in terms of kinship, William Sax, for example, defined the expression *dhiyani* as "outmarried village daughter" and the more comprehensive term *disa dhiyani* as "she who is given to the directions," that is, married outside the village (Sax, 1991: 37).

In the context of the emerging focus on studies of indigenous concepts, initiated by the so-called Chicago School in the 70s and 80s also at times referred to as the school of ethnosociology (MacKim Marriott & Inden, 1977), various American anthropologists began to recognise the territorial factor as an important principle in the ordering of social relations in north as well as south India. Valentine Daniels, for example, discussed the Tamil categories *ur* and *kiraman* and came to the conclusion that the former relates to a biophysical unity in which village residents "are believed to share in the substance of the soil of that territory" (Daniels, 1984: 63), while the latter is best understood as a political unit for administrative purposes. Melinda Moore in her analysis of marriage (1988) and house-building (1990) among the Nayar of Kerala, could demonstrate that the matrilineage (*taravad*) is considered to be a "house and land-unit" which is symbolically constructed in the wedding rituals (Moore, 1988: 269-70). She further provided evidence that among the Nayar, the qualities ascribed to a house are considered to have an effect on the activities of its residents (1990: 169; 176–9). This idea of a mutual influence of space—in particular the village and house—and person has similarly been shown to exist in north India. William Sax (1991), for example, argued that the many visits a woman pays to her natal home after her marriage demonstrate the importance of space, in particular the village, for the world view of the local people: "Behind these visits lie a set of cultural assumptions, a world-view according to which people and places have powerful mutual effects. Given such a world-view, the biological, social, and moral relationships in a house or a village are not only among the people who live there but between them and the place, house, or village itself; all are parts of complex, biomorales wholes, are related through place" (Sax, 1991: 125).

While the focus in studies of caste society shifted from villages to an examination of descent and the territorial factor in general, studies of middle Indian tribal societies developed in a different, almost opposite way. The importance of descent groups and the territorial factor for tribal social organisation was recognised right from the beginning in the early ethnographies produced for example by Verrier Elwin, Christoph von Fürer-Haimendorf or Wilfried Grigson. Frederik Bailey, in his attempt to distinguish caste from tribe, made territorial segmentation and descent linked to landownership defining factors of the latter type of society (Bailey, 1961: 11).[3] However, the idea that the village and not the territorially defined clan is the major "agent" in the contexts of exchange[4], such as marriage, sacrifice and feasting, was only expressed by later ethnographers.

One of the first to discover the relevance of the village in tribal social organisation was Niggemeyer in his study of the Kuttia Kond of Orissa. He came to the conclusion that the village is the most important territorial unit among these people. In his view, the residential community provides the strongest and most important social bonds in Kuttia Society (Niggemeyer, 1964: 40-1). According to his analysis, this had not always been the case, and he speculates that in the past the clan had been the more important social unit (Niggemeyer, 1964: 48). He mentions two rules of exogamy, first the proscription to marry inside the clan, and second the prohibition to marry inside the village. In his view, the second rule must have been a later invention since he assumes that in the past each village was occupied by one clan only. In this presumed condition, the rule of clan exogamy already implied the rule of village exogamy. Only when members of other clans began residing in the same village did the explicit formulation of a rule of village exogamy became necessary to preserve the old conditions of inter-territorial marriage exchange. Living together turns villagers into "brothers and sisters" who for this reason cannot marry (Niggemeyer, 1964: 48). However, Niggemeyer provides no data to prove this assumed historical change from a genealogical to a territorial definition of clan membership among the Kond.

Not the village itself, but rather relations between villages were the focus of analysis in the work of McDougal among the Juang: "Intermarriage is the chief means by which relations of solidarity are established between different villages, which are highly self-sufficient except with regard to the acquisition of spouses" (McDougal, 1963: 220). In McDougal's view, the village itself is the main unit of affinal exchange. However, from his statistical data it can be inferred that each village is linked by marriage to only a small number of other villages (McDougal, 1963: 169-70), most of which are located within a radius of only four miles and do not include any more than two to three clans.[5]

When anthropologists studying caste society had already abandoned the village as a topic of research, Simeran Gell, after conducting long-term fieldwork among the Muria Gond, came to the conclusion that "among the Muria if not elsewhere in India, the 'village' is quite appropriately considered a fundamental unit for analysis" (Gell, 1992: 65). To her, "the village is the unit of structure which shows the highest elaboration of social rules governing membership, the rights and duties incumbent on village members, and it is only in the light of village framework that kinship and clanship assume their determining influence on social relations, never independently" (Gell, 1992: 67). She sub-stantiates this statement with her rich ethnography. Thus, among the Muria, a person is mainly defined with respect to his village of origin. The village creates a community based on joint living, land ownership and common political as well as ritual actions. The village has a special relationship with the surrounding land (*nel*) and its gods, which receives various gifts or "tribute" when the village community performs sacrifices on various occasions. Although the Muria, in contrast to the Juang and Kuttia Kond, do not prescribe village exogamy, Gell nevertheless comes to the conclusion that marriages are an important factor in the structuring of inter-village relations. To her, the solidarity of the clan depends on these marriage alliances (Gell, 1992: 53) and these, in turn, are said to be determined by locality. On the one hand, relations between clans can only be understood from the perspective of a particular village in which these clans are present; on the other hand, relations between villages become intelligible only when the agnatic and affinal links between clan segments are known.

In his comparative analysis of marriage rules in various middle Indian tribes, Pfeffer (1997) deduces that among all these groups, affinity is closely linked to the localized village community. Like McDougal for the Juang, Niggemeyer for the Kuttia Kond, and Gell for the Muria Gond, Pfeffer asserts that all tribal communities of this region have two basic social categories, one comprising affines, and the other including all non-marriageable people. According to Pfeffer, these categories, like *bai bondhu*, do not apply to individuals but to collectives such as villages and clans (1997: 24). He regards this collective definition of affinity as the major difference between tribal notions of marriage, and those detected by anthropologists in north and south India: "Diachronic affines of the village community permanently reside in a limited number of other settlements. Affinal relations between such villages lend their colour to all other aspects of life" (Pfeffer, 1997: 25).

In his recent work on rituals of the Gadaba tribe of Koraput District (Orissa), Peter Berger (2002, 2007) illustrates the important structural position of the village in the overall social order. According to his analysis, Gadaba Society is built upon three major principles: descent, territory and commensality. These principles are realized most clearly at the village level. For example, Gadaba Society as a whole consists of four totemic descent categories (*bongso*). Every Gadaba belongs to one of these four categories and has to find a spouse from one of the other three. Furthermore, the Gadaba distinguish four local lines (*kuda*) and ideally (but rarely in practice) members of these four *kuda* should be present in each village. Membership in a local line like in a totemic category is based on the idea of common descent, yet *kuda*, unlike *bongso* works as an exogamous category only on the village level. In other words, two Gadaba who reside in different villages but belong to a *kuda* of the same name (*e.g.* Sisa) may marry each other given their *bongso* are different. Peter Berger discovered another, a third descent category at the village level which is neither identical with *bongso* nor with *kuda*. Thus a village may have more than one name and one of these names often denotes a descent category associated with the territory of the village. For this reason, Berger also speaks of "village-clans". As among the Muria Gond (*see* above), the Gadaba identify themselves with their own "village-clan" and even if some migrate to a different place, they are still considered as members or representatives of their original village descent category. For more details *see* Berger's contribution (Ch. 6) to this volume.

The Argument

In this paper I take up two issues which have figured prominently in the above summarized debate about the Indian village. One of the first issues addressed was the question of whether descent or territory is the more important principle within the types of society under study, *i.e.* caste and tribal society. In the context of the latter, I argue here that we should distinguish carefully between three aspects, namely territory, descent, and *residence*. In case of the Dongria Kond, the whole society is divided into named clans, ideally linked to certain territories. Clan affiliation is of importance in two contexts, marriage and sacrifice. Both events are organised at the village level and generate relations between villages. The ideal equivalence of clan and territory finds its manifestation in the "village territory" (*padari*) which is said to belong to only one clan, whose members organise the sacrifice to the earth goddess. The issue of where a particular individual resides has no effect on his clan affiliation. Residence does not alter clan affiliation and thus has no effect on the system of clan categories manifested in "village territories". However, Dongria Kond do migrate and take up uxorilocal residence, and nowhere do we find village settlements (*nayu*) inhabited by members of only one clan category. In these mixed settlements, which are the norm, residence does play a role. People who migrate and take up residence in another village, for example, often try to establish new links with a local descent group of their *own* clan category. Furthermore, common residence creates strong bonds of solidarity, expressed in contexts of weddings, sacrifices and conflicts, when the village community acts as a *collective agent*.

A second issue in the general debate was the deconstruction of the image of the village as a "self-sufficient unit". Various writers emphasised the longstanding inclusion of Indian villages in wider political, social and economical systems. Relations between villages were seen to exist as part of the caste system (*e.g.* Dumont, 1998 [1966]), the little kingdoms (*e.g.* Cohn, 1959) or the wider economic system (*e.g.* Fuller, 1989). In tribal village studies, the lack of autarky of each village has been demonstrated by demonstrations of how each village is included in a network of intermarriages (e.g. McDougal, 1963; Pfeffer, 1997). Adding to these insights, this paper illustrates a further dimension of village interdependency in the context of tribal society. I demonstrate how not only marriages but also *rituals and sacrifices* generate a network of interdependent villages and bring into being what may be called a tribal social system. I argue further that *spatial divisions* in a village itself express the dependency of its residents on various spiritual forces and social actors from outside their settlement.

The two issues dealt with in this paper are actually closely related. They both address the question of "what is a village?", in this case a Dongria village in the Niamgiri Hills of Orissa. In my view, there is no simple answer to this question because we have to take into account the complex social organisation within which the village plays an essential role. The question further leads us to examine how the village as a residential unit, or "settlement" made up of individuals, is valued in relation to the village as a clan-owned territory. Additionally, it should incorporate an elaborate account of the elements a village comprises, the patterns and relations that give order to these elements, and the forces that consistently involve each village in a network of exchanges.

In order to elucidate these points, I first introduce the reader to earlier writings on the Kond before exploring the distinction made by Dongria between *nayu* or settlement and *padari*, the village or village territory. In my interpretation, the former is best understood as the empirical settlement whose residents act as a collective *agent* on certain occasions, while the latter is best viewed as an ideal territorial-cum-descent unit linked to a particular local earth goddess and her cult. Next, I analyse how the layout of a Dongria Kond settlement expresses the dependency of the village on outside forces. On the one hand, I describe the ritual sites in a village where Dongria try to regulate the flow of the forces of gods, dead people and ancestors as they enter and leave the village along the east-west axis. On the other hand, I provide data illustrating the interior male sphere of the village and the opposing outer domain, where women, young girls and Dombo reside, who connect the village with the outside world in terms of marriage and trade. In my conclusion, I ask how the distinction between model and practice helps us to understand the relationship between descent, marriage, territory and the village in Dongria Kond society.

The Kond in Anthropological Writings

In the past, the Kond have figured prominently in anthropological writings as a result of certain social and cultural practices that outraged British colonialists when they first encountered members of this tribe in the 1830s. Accordingly, we find references to the Kond practice of female infanticide in McLennan's (1970 [1865]) grand theory of the evolution of human marriage, and to the famous *meria* or human sacrifice in Frazer's (1968 [1890]) "Golden Bough". These authors drew on sources provided by two British officials, Samuel Charters MacPherson (1863 [1842], 1852, 1865) and John Campbell (1864), who both spent many years in the Kondhmals of India as "Agents for the Suppression of Human Sacrifice and Female Infanticide". Both wrote extensively about their experiences in these remote mountain tracts, where they finally managed to convince the inhabitants to substitute the human victim by a buffalo in their grand sacrifices to the earth goddess (*tari* or *dharni*). The historical background of these events has been analysed in detail by Barbara Boal (1997) and Felix Padel (1995).

Anthropological studies first focused on politico-economical conditions in the frontier area between caste and tribal society in the writings of Frederik Bailey (1957, 1960, 1994), the first scholar to conduct extensive ethnographic fieldwork in this area. Descriptions of various rituals including the *meria* sacrifice were provided by Barabara Boal (1997, 1999), who over a period of twenty years repeatedly lived with the Kond and witnessed their Christianisation. One of the best monographs on Kond culture and society has been produced by the German Hermann Niggemeyer (1964), who in the years 1955-6 spent only seven months among the Kuttia Kond of Phulbani District but nevertheless managed to obtain enough information to give us a comprehensive picture of their social organisation, rituals and myths. In more recent times, two important monographs have been produced by local Indian anthropologists focusing on the Dongria Kond living in the Rayagada District of Orissa. The work by Nayak (1989) deals with the feud system of these people who are renowned for their fierceness and aggressiveness, while the research work of an Indian team (Jena et al., 2002), collaborating with Klaus Seeland, looked in particular at indigenous knowledge systems and forest protection.

Dongria Kond Today

The Dongria Kond populate the Niamgiri hills, a mountain range with peaks up to 1600 m. which are part of the Eastern Ghats and divide Orissa into two regions, the coastal plains, and the hilly hinterland inhabited by the majority of the union state's tribal people. According to the latest survey (Kanungo 2004), the Dongria number about 8000 and reside in 112 villages spread across the mountains. Some of the villages are made up of only three to four houses, while a few of the largest settlements contain up to 60 or 80 houses. In most villages, Dongria Kond do not reside alone but together with a smaller community of people referred to as Dombo. In the plains and valleys, members of this community are considered to be Harijan or "untouchables". In the hills, too, they have a lower status than the Dongria, whose houses they cannot enter, whose daughters they cannot marry and who will not accept food from them, yet their lower status is not conceived of in terms of impurity but rather with reference to other values (*see* Hardenberg, 2005).

Even today, the Niamgiri hills are relatively densely covered by forest that the Dongria Kond cut down from time to time to gain land for shifting cultivation. Although this practice is illegal, no one enforces the law in this relatively remote area. Apart from one proper road linking a town in the foothills with the biggest Dongria village in the southern part of the Niamgiri Hills, there exists only a single bumpy path leading into the north-western area where I conducted my research in the years 2001-3. During that time, the Government spend large amounts of money employing Dongria to build roads between their villages, but work proceeded slowly and the first monsoon destroyed almost all efforts. Contact with the outside world occurs when Dongria visit the small market towns in the foothills on festive occasions, or when they sell their agricultural produce and buy items they themselves cannot produce. From time to time, traders move into the mountains to buy brooms or other items produced by Dongria. In the late 60s a first "mini project", the Dongria Kond Development Agency (DKDA), was established in one part of the Niamgiri Hills and some years later a second one was setup in a less accessible part of the mountains. The officers of this development agency supply cheap rice, kerosene oil, etc. to the Dongria, buy their produce for fixed prices and teach them to use new agricultural techniques. The relatively low impact from outside, the lack of infrastructure and the general hostility of the mountain dwellers towards outsiders may explain why the Dongria Kond, compared to other tribal groups in Orissa, are less assimilated to the Hindu mainstream culture.

Settlement (*nayu*) and Village (*padari*)

Most authors writing about Kond villages begin with the assumption that villages were originally inhabited by only one clan and that members of other clans did not move in until a later stage (*e.g.*, Niggemeyer, 1964: 46; Jena et al., 2002: 48-9). In this assumed original condition there would have existed perfect village exogamy, since all village members shared the same clan title. Only later, when affinal clans began residing in the village would marriage within its boundaries have sporadically occurred. Such a historical explanation is sheer speculation and is not based on any evidence. Dongria themselves speak about their villages as belonging to only one clan when they refer to the village land, while in other contexts they present the village as settlement whose residents co-operate under various circumstances.

A village or *padari,* in its widest sense, refers to one or more territories, each marked by a *jakeri,* or site of the earth goddess, denoting where a residential unit can be built. A village, according to this wider sense, always belongs to a particular clan. Members of this clan usually represent the majority in a settlement (*nayu*), but people of other clans are often present as well. Members of these non-dominant clans belong to the village community, but never to the collective defined by the land. For example, when arranging a marriage, all residents of a village act, independently of their clan, as a group. They jointly capture a girl or bring her to the village, they discuss fines or fights in cases of conflict, and they share the meat and rice cooked at a wedding. Again, when performing a village festival, all houses participate and contribute to the expenses. All are considered as belonging to one "family" (*kutumb*) and the residents of a village as a whole are responsible for each of its members, irrespective of agnation or affinity. However, those who do not belong to the dominant clan, *i.e.* the local affines, often referred to as "sister's sons" (*banaja*) or tenants (*raiti*) have no right to buy the buffalo that is to be sacrificed to the earth goddess and they may not cultivate the soil unless members of the dominant clan share their land with them. As individuals, these local affines can join the village collective, but they can never change the territorial identity defined by the village of their ancestors and expressed in his clan title.

The Dongria village thus has two dimensions, it is a territorial-cum-descent unit in the sense that each *jakeri,* and the territory connected with it, belongs to a particular clan, and it is a residential and co-operative unit in which people from different clans interact as one group. When an individual leaves the village in which his or her clan dominates, he or she joins a new residential unit, but not a new descent-cum-territorial unit. Thus, even if a marriage takes place within a settlement, which happens from time to time, an affinal relationship is established between people belonging to different territorial-cum-descent units as long as the rule of clan exogamy is observed. The relation between *nayu* and *padari* is in my view a good example of what Dumont calls an "encompassment of the contrary", which entails a reversal when shifting from the level of a whole to the level of its parts. On the one hand, the word *padari* is used for the highly valued "whole" of land and people, the "village". On the other hand, the *padari* is also an element of the whole and stands in opposition to *nayu*. *Nayu* refers to the current residential unit of living individuals who co-operate (or quarrel) in the contexts of marriage, sacrifice, feuds, etc. As an element, the *padari* is opposed to this empirical aspect of the village as it is associated with territory and the earth goddess (the land *is* the earth goddess). Since *padari* or "territory" is linked to a particular earth goddess and claimed by dominant local lines who worship her in the buffalo sacrifice (*kodru parbu*), it has a transcendental and descent-based character. The settlement (*nayu*) constantly changes, while the village land (*padari*), through its association with the earth goddess, and with a particular clan, gives permanence to the "village" (*padari*) as a whole. It may also be claimed that collective permanence, defined here in terms of descent and the cult unit, encompasses its opposite, namely the constantly changing settlement and its individual residents.

Structural Layout of Settlements

In attempts to deconstruct the image of the village as a self-sufficient unit, the importance of space as a means to express mutual dependency has often been neglected. It is argued here that the dependency of a Dongria village on the "outside world", i.e. spiritual forces, other villages as well as the market towns in the valley, is clearly expressed in its structural layout. To illustrate this argument, I describe the arrangement of ritual sites and the distinction between inner male and outer female space within a village. This ethnographic data shows that each village is considered to be linked to outside forces which bring life and death, and that rituals are meant to regulate the flow of these forces into and out of the village. Rituals demarcate the site of the village in a framework of divine space, which is ordered along an east-west axis defined by the movement of the sun. While interaction between these forces and the village occurs along an east-west axis, interaction between villages in terms of marriage is ordered by the opposition between the "front side" and the "rear side" of the houses. The front side is the realm of men, who are "permanent" to the village owing to the ideal of virifocal residence, whereas the sphere of women and young girls is located behind the houses. Married women come into the village from outside and young girls leave for other villages at the time of their marriage. All women are thus "intermediaries" and link the men of the village with those in other areas. The same holds for the Dombo, who connect the village with the outside world by way of their trading activities and their function as "culture brokers" (Pfeffer, 1997), and, in the same way as women and young girls, they inhabit the space to the rear of the houses. It may therefore be claimed that the east-west axis defines exchange between the village and spiritual forces, including ancestors and the dead, while the opposition between the front and rear of the houses structures the "exchange" between human beings.

Exchange with Spiritual Forces: East and West

A Dongria village (*nayu*) is ideally made up of two rows (*chahada*) of houses (*ilu*) standing on a relatively flat, slightly inclining slope, near hills which are used for shifting cultivation. The entrances (*dueri*) of the village[6] normally lie towards the Eastern and Western end of both rows of houses, these being the only directions named in their language. The East is referred to by Dongria Kond as *dharmu giri*, the West as *surju giri*, the word *giri* meaning "path" or "way" while *dharmu* and *surju* are two expressions for the sun. The sun is considered to be a man when rising in the east and a woman when setting in the west. Due to certain topographical features, some villages have their entrances facing the south and north, and in such cases it lay be inferred from ritual actions that the south is identified with the east and the north with the west.[7] The dual division of space (and time) into east—including south—and west—including north—provides a meaningful order to the layout of the village as a whole. The significance of this layout derives from rituals that order the relations between the village and the forces which enter the village from the east and the west. The figure below enumerates the various ritual sites (*see* Figure 7.1) beginning from the extreme east of the village and moving across to the extreme west.

Figure 7.1: Ritual Sites of a Dongria Kond Village

WEST AND NORTH (Surju giri)

1. *Mahanenga*	cremation grounds
2. *Yatra kudi*	shrine for various deities
3. *Surju dueri*	western village entrance
4. *Dharni kudi/jakeri*	shrine for earth goddess
5. *Bisimunda*	sacrificial post for earth goddess
6. *Panikimunda*	sacrificial post for her husband
7. *Koteiwali*	stone representing her husband
8. *Palawara*	wall for her husband
9. *Dharmu dueri*	eastern village entrance
10. *Ghata kudi*	shrines for *ghanta parbu*
11. *Bali kudi*	shrine for *bali yatra*

EAST AND SOUTH (*Dharmu giri*)

Taking into account where Dongria perform collective rituals one may distinguish three ritual sites: the east, the centre and the west of the village. Outside the eastern village entrance there are relatively few places of worship.

In some villages one finds a small shrine erected at the time of the *bali yatra*, a village festival in the name of the god of fire (*bera*). The site for the *bali yatra* is usually marked by a posts for animal sacrifices and by a pit for fire-walking. The other permanent place of worship are the "shrines of the house deities" (*ghata kudi*) located outside the eastern entrance of the village. The deities are represented by stones, with each stone being identified with one "house" in the sense that all householders worshipping the same stone claim common ancestry. The number of stones varies according to the size of the village. The "houses" of the village founders usually possess one such stone outside the village, with often two or three houses sharing one stone, while people who migrated to the village at a later stage may still continue to perform the worship at the stone of their local line in their original village. Among the immigrants, only those families who have been well established in the new villages for two to three generations and were able to sponsor the major rituals (*e.g. ghanta parba*) have their own stone.

Most rituals take place in the centre of the village where one finds the stones marking the sites of the earth goddess (*jakeri*) and her husband (*koteiwali*). They are considered to be the "mother" and the "father" of the Dongria, their children. The *jakeri* usually consists of a few flat as well as one or more conical stones in addition to a slab with a grinding stone. Her husband, the *koteiwali*, is usually represented by a single conical megalith standing east of the *jakeri*. Both deities receive the most elaborate worship during the buffalo sacrifice (*kodru parbu*) celebrated by each village in irregular intervals. Depending on when the last buffalo sacrifice was celebrated, the shrine area of the earth goddess may vary in appearance. In a village that has recently organised the buffalo sacrifice, one finds a newly built house of the goddess with decorated walls and a roof thatched with grass or made of tin. Inside the house, the *jakeri* stones are neatly arranged on an earthen platform, usually covered with thick layers of cow dung. Next to this "house of the goddess" (*dharni kudi*) one will find a fenced area with sacrificial posts to which the buffaloes were tied in the night of the sacrifice. Near the megalith representing the husband of the goddess stands a single decorated wall (*palawara*) and t-shaped sacrificial pole (*panikimunda*).

If ten or more years have past since the villagers celebrated the last buffalo sacrifice, one will normally find only the rotten remains of the house and of the sacrificial posts. The stones of the earth goddess and her husband are usually covered with dust and nobody pays any attention to them, except at the time of village festivals (*parbu* or *yatra*). Then the shamans of the village assemble at the stones of the earth goddess and call the deities from the east to this place. The shamans offer their "body" to the deities so that they can talk, dance and consume the food and drinks offered to them. At the end of the festival, the deities are sent out of the village. For this purpose, the shamans possessed by the deities, their assistants and some villagers who carry the ritual paraphernalia and the sacrificial animals leave the village in the western direction. The purpose of this procession is to "throw away" (*tuchpoli*) the deities and ancestors, in other words, to lead them out of the village to a place called *yatra kudi* where people bid them farewell with some final offerings.

The *yatra kudi* in the west of the villages is one of the most important sites of worship. It usually consists of four pillars and a few beams covered with branches and leaves on festive occasions. It is considered to be the place of the goddess of small pox, *aji budi*, who is believed to be the female ruler (*thakurani*) of the settlement. The *yatra kudi* also serves as a watch-post, keeping away evil influences that may come from the westerly direction and afflict the village. After inviting gods and ancestors to the centre of the village for worship, the villagers will "accompany" them out of the village to the *yatra kudi* where they are served food and alcohol. Then the gods and ancestors are sent away and asked not to cause any harm to the villagers. Further towards the west of the village, one comes across the cremation grounds of both the Dongria and the Dombo, often located at opposite sides of the path. A cremation ground is referred to as *mahanenga* literally meaning "(place of) ancestors".

What are the main ideas linked to this layout of sacred sites in the village? The earth goddess and her husband as "mother" and "father" of the Dongria are permanent to the village while the other spiritual forces pass through it, normally from east to west. The Dongria consider the east to be the direction where the sun god is born and the west the place where he dies each evening. Correspondingly, rituals pertaining to "life" and "wealth", such as bringing the harvest or a bride into the village, are performed in the east, while all ceremonies linked to "death" take place in the west. The places of the recently deceased, like the houses of the Dombo[8], are located in this western region, while the shrines of the local lines founded by their ancestors are in the east. Evil forces are expected to come from the westerly direction and for this reason the *yatra kudi* guards this entrance to the village, whereas gods and benevolent ancestors arrive from the east and leave the village in the west. Finally, the gender opposition appears to correspond with the distinction between east and west since the sun is considered to be a man when rising in the morning and a women when setting in the evening. Correspondingly, this structure is further reinforced by that fact that the "father" of the Dongria, the *koteiwali*, always stands to the east of their "mother", the *jakeri*.

Figure 7.2: Ideal Layout; East and West of a Dangria Village

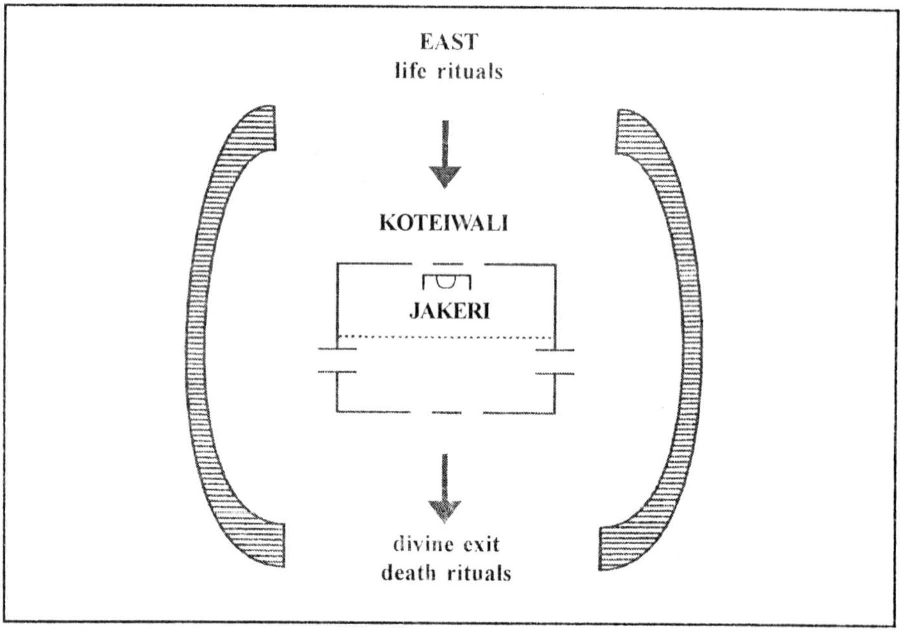

The village as a whole appears to have the same structure as the house (*ijo, ilu*) of the Dongria. A Dongria house usually consists of three rooms, a central room (*ijo*) with the hearth where the parents sleep and small children sleep at night, a front room (*duki*) for boys and male visitors and a back room (*dapa*) used by young girls and female visitors and by the women of the house during their menstruation. A village similarly seems to have a tripartite structure: the centre with the shrines of the "mother" and "father" of the Dongria, and two rows of house which correspond to the front and back room of a Dongria house. In other words, the Dongria as "children" of the Earth thus take up the same spatial position in relation to the "house of the goddess" as the young male and female adolescence in relation to their parents. Another striking symmetry becomes apparent when we take into account cooking practices. The hearth (*holu*) of a house is always located in the central room and it is here that the mother cooks the food for her family or for the guests on festive occasions. Similarly, the house of the goddess turns into a place where food is cooked on the occasion of the buffalo sacrifice.[9] For performing the sacrifice the villagers preserve an old iron hearth (*holu*), a pot (*daka*) and a spoon (*hetu*) which are taken to the house of the goddess shortly before the sacrifice. On this hearth, the ritual specialist prepare the sacred food that is then distributed first to the descendants of the village founders and later to the whole village community.

Figure 7.3: Ideal Layout of a Dongria House

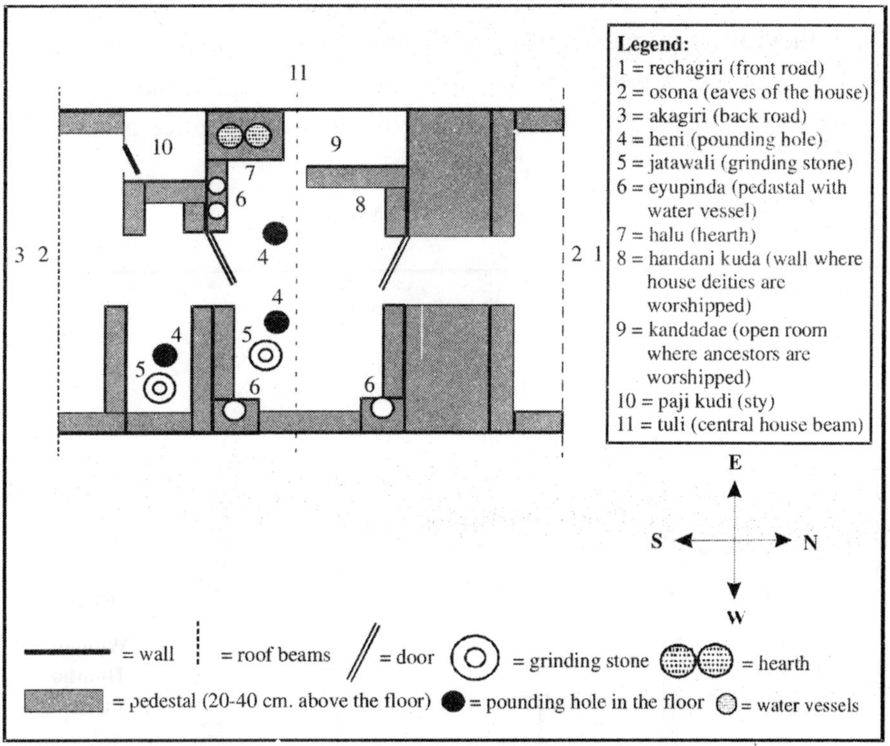

In my interpretation, then, the village is itself a "house" and its inhabitants a family consisting of mother earth (*jakeri*), her husband (*koteiwali*), and her children (the villagers). It corresponds with this interpretation that the village community as a whole is referred to as *kutumb*, a word meaning "family" in Oriya. The village as a house has two entrances, the east and the west, and rituals are meant to control the flow of spiritual forces through the "house" by asking the life forces to come from the west and by sending away potentially destructive forces to the west.

Exchange with Humans: Front and Rear

In addition to the opposition between the east and the west, one comes across the opposition between the "front road" (*rechagiri*) and the "back road" (*akagiri*). The space behind or to the rear of the houses is mostly associated with Dombo and with unmarried youth. Dombo are not permanent members of a village since they normally change villages quite often during their life. As traders, their profession demands a certain mobility and as they are normally landless, they have no reason to remain in a certain place for generations. In a way, they always remain "outsiders". The same holds true for the young girls of the village, who normally leave their native home upon marrying. Before marriage, their places in their native village are the dance grounds and

Figure 7.4: Ideal Layout; Front and Rear of the Village

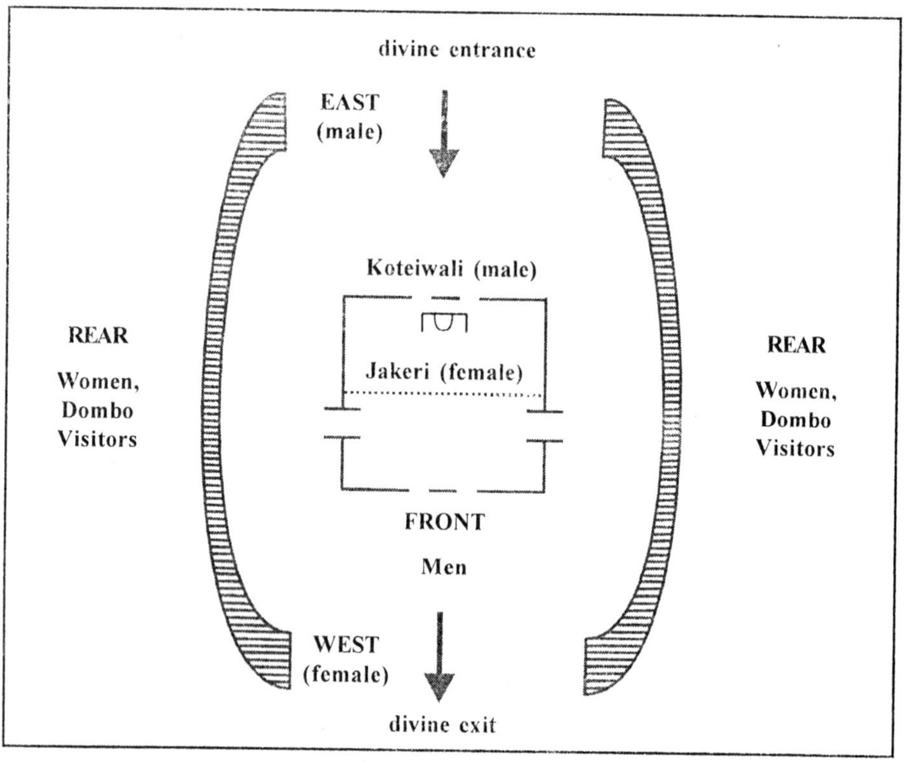

dormitories[10], which, like the houses of the Dombo, lie behind the two rows of houses. These are the places where the girls meet with young men coming from other villages. A girls' dormitory is referred to as *daaska hada* or "hut of the young girls" as it consists of one room only, except perhaps in those places where the female youth of a village stay with a widow or have taken over a deserted house. Some dormitories have cooking places used at the time of marriages and village festivals when the young girls prepare food for their visitors. During the day, the dormitory remains mostly empty, except when the girls have to husk rice or millet. For this work, most of these huts have one or two holes (*heni*) in the ground, into which the girls rhythmically pound (*uhpoli*) the wooden pestle to mash the grains. Only in the evening do activities in the dormitory increase when the girls meet to comb their hair, put on body decorations, and talk about the events of the day.

The dormitory system organises sexual relations between male and female youth from different villages and clans. Upon reaching maturity, a girl will join her female friends and share a dormitory or the house of a lone widow. Boys, on the other hand, have to leave their own village and search for girls of a clan distinct from their own. They leave their village in the evening, spend the night in the dormitory where they talk, sing, and perhaps have sex with their hosts, and return early next morning before sunrise.

In summary, while married men are permanent to the village, unmarried boys are expected to leave the village every night. On the other hand, while married women are strangers to the village when taking up virilocal residence after the wedding, unmarried girls receive their lovers in their native place. However, these meetings of the young people take place in a marginal place lying between the proper village and the forest. They occur at night and without the knowledge of the parents, who, however, tolerate them as long as the rules of clan exogamy are observed. In relation to the village as a "house" occupied by the village family (*kutumb*) consisting of the "mother" (*jakeri*), the "father" (*koteiwali*) and the "children" (male Dongria), the meeting places and huts of the young are clearly located in a liminal space which marks the border to the outside world, *i.e.*, the forest and other villages. It is also the space where Dombo setup their houses. Like the young people, the Dombo as traders link the "kin community" with the outside world, *i.e.* with the market towns in the valleys.

Conclusion

This paper addresses two issues discussed in previous literature on the Indian village: firstly, the question of how territory, descent and residence are related to one another in the social organisation of the Dongria Kond, and secondly, the question of how the village layout and the social practices of the inhabitants reflect a village's dependency on outside forces and agents.

With reference to the first question, I come to the conclusion that the territorial principle has two dimensions. I speak of "transcendental villages" in which territory is intimately linked to descent and the worship of the Earth goddess and defines a unit that exists relatively independently from concrete individuals. These units are not timeless, but are at least not as short-lived as the "empirical villages" where it is not territory, descent and the Earth goddess which define membership, but common residence and joint action.

While territory is an attribute of clans (*kuda*), residence does not define the membership of an individual in the exogamous *kuda* category. However, residence can be a factor in changing one's affiliation to a particular descent group (*punja*) but only to another descent group of one's own clan category (*kuda*). One may, therefore, state that in the system of opposed clans, territory-cum-descent always overrides residence, while within the clan, residence may override affiliations created by descent. This is best understood within the context of marriage rules. Rules of exogamy apply to the clan category (*kuda*), while rules prohibiting the repetition of marriage are observed by local lines (*punja* or *ijo*). The first rule tolerates no exception, as clan incest is considered to be the gravest mistake a person can commit and is punished by expulsion from the community. Repetition of marriage with certain local lines is not met with the same sanctions and does occur from time to time, but it can be hidden by claiming an affiliation with another local line or by contesting the descent relations between local lines.

With reference to the second question, I come to the conclusion that even though Dongria Kond villages may exhibit a certain autarky in terms of political decisions and subsistence, they are clearly conceived of as elements in a complex exchange network which involves spiritual beings and humans in the contexts of rituals, marriages and trade. The village as a whole is structured like a "house", with the parents—Earth goddess and her husband—residing in the centre, and the Dongria, their "children", inhabiting the two rows of houses. The village as a "house" is connected to the "outside world", *i.e.* spiritual beings, unmarried boys and other communities by various rituals, the dormitory system and the Dombo. The east-west axis marks the dependency of the "house" on spiritual forces which are controlled by rituals. The opposition between the centre and the rear of the "house", on the other hand, is linked to the dormitory system and the trading activities of the Dombo.

NOTES

1. I am grateful to Kate Sullivan for the language correction. I also thank Diane Mines and Stuart Blackburn for comments on earlier drafts of the paper.
2. Recently, Vandana Madan (2002), for example, edited a reader including a number of important writings on the Indian village.
3. Bailey does, however, recognise the importance of villages when he writes about the "Kond clan-territory and its *constituent* villages". (Bailey, 1961: 12, my emphasis)
4. In Middle Indian tribal societies these exchanges are to my knowledge not interpreted in the context of complex indigenous conceptions of "substance-codes" as has been reported for other regions of India. The act of exchange itself is constituent of the social order and the most important aspect of substances are not their "biomoral codes" but the fact that they can be given away or distributed in contexts that define and create social relations. Peter Berger convincingly illustrates this point on the basis of his ethnographic data collected among the Gadaba of Koraput District Orissa (Berger, 2007).
5. The situation is different among the Dongria Kond, who spread their marriage relations over the whole area they occupy and intermarry with a large number of different villages. For details *see* Hardenberg forthcoming.
6. Now-a-days, Dongria villages are freely accessible. Only at the time of the buffalo sacrifice will the whole village be fenced and the entrances be guarded by the villagers.
7. For example, while a shaman (*beju/bejuni*) will normally face east when performing a ritual in a village built according to the "ideal model", he or she will face towards the south in a village aligned on the south-north axis.
8. Dongria jokingly call the Dombo *dhumba*, the Oriya word for dead people.
9. It is tempting to interpret the stone arrangement of the earth goddess itself as a kind of hearth consisting of conical stones to hold the pot and a slab with a grinding stone to prepare the food. However, I have no indications that Dongria themselves conceive of the stones in this way.
10. For an overview on youth dormitories in the whole of India *see* Fürer-Haimendorf 1950. For detailed descriptions *see* Sarat Chandra Roy (1915) for the Oraon, Charles McDougal (1963) for the Juang, Verrier Elwin for the Muria (1991 [1947]), and Bondo (1950) as well as Simeran Gell (1992) for the Muria Gond.

REFERENCES

Bailey, F.G. 1957. *Caste and the Economic Frontier: A Village in Highland Orissa.* Manchester: Manchester University Press.

_____. 1960. *Tribe, Caste and Nation: A Study in Political Activity and Political Change in Highland Orissa.* Manchester: Manchester University Press.

_____. 1961. " 'Tribe' and 'Caste' in India," *Contributions to Indian Sociology*, V: 7-19.

_____. 1994. *The Witch Hunt; or, The Triumph of Morality*. Ithaca/London: Cornell.

Berger, P. 2002. "The Gadaba and the 'Non-ST' Desia of Koraput," (pp. 57-90) in G. Pfeffer & D.K. Behera (ed.), *Contemporary Society: Tribal Studies* (Vol.5). New Delhi: Concept Publishing Company.

_____. 2007. *Füttern, Speisen und Verschlingen. Ritual und Gesellschaft im Hochland von Orissa/Indien.* Berlin, LIT Verlag.

_____. 1997. *Human Sacrifice and Religious Change: The Kondhs.* (Tribal Studies of India Series T 180) New Delhi: Inter-India Publications.

Boal, B.M. 1999. *Man, the Gods and the Search for Cosmic Wellbeing.* Bhubaneswar: NISWAAS.

Campbell, J. 1864. *A Personal Narrative of Thirteen Years Service amongst the Wild tribes of Khondistan for the Suppression of Human Sacrifice.* London: Hurst and Blackett Publishers.

Cohn, B.S. 1959. "Law and Change (Some Notes on) North India," *Economic Development and Cultural Change*, 8: 79-93.

Daniel, E.V. 1984. *Fluid Signs: Being a Person the Tamil Way*. Berkeley: University of California Press.

Dube, S.C. 1955. *Indian Village*. London: Routledge and Kegan Paul.

Dumont, L. & D. Pocock. 1957a. "For a Sociology of India" *Contributions to Indian Sociology* 1: 7-22.

_____. 1957b. "Village Studies," *Contributions to Indian Sociology* 1: 23-41.

Dumont, Louis 1983. *Affinity as a Value. Marriage Alliance in South India, with Comparative Essays on Australia.* Chicago and London: The University of Chicago Press.

_____. 1998 [1966]. *Homo Hierarchicus. The Caste System and its Implications.* Complete Revised English Edition. Delhi: Oxford University Press.

Elwin, V. 1991 [1947]. *The Muria and their Ghotul.* Bombay: Oxford University Press.

_____. 1950. *The Bondo Highlanders.* London: Oxford University Press.

Frazer, J.G. 1968 [1890]. *Der Goldene Zweig: Eine Studie über Magie und Religion.* Köln/Berlin: Kiepenheuer & Witsch.

Fürer-Haimendorf, Chr. von 1950. "Youth-Dormitories and Community Houses in India," *Anthropos*, 45: 119-144.

Fuller, C.F. 1989. "Misconceiving the Grain Heap: A Critique of the Concept of the Indian Jajmani System" (pp. 33-63) in J. Parry & M. Bloch (eds.), *Money and the Morality of Exchange.* Cambridge: Cambridge University Press.

Gell, S.M.S. 1992. *The Ghotul in Muria Society.* Chur: Harwood Academic Publishers.

Hardenberg, R. 2005. *Children of the Earth Goddess: Society, Marriage, and Sacrifice in the Highlands of Orissa (India)*. Unpubl. Habilitation. Submitted to the Westphaliant Wilhelms University, Münster.

Inden, R. 1990. *Imagining India*. Oxford: Basil Blackwell.

Israel, M. 1979. *A Grammar of the Kuvi Language*. Trivandrum: Dravidian Linguistics Association.

Jena et. al. (Jena, M. K., P. Pathi, J. Dash, K. Patnaik and K. Seeland) 2002. *Forest Tribes of Orissa. Lifestyle and Social Conditions of Selected Orissan Tribes. Vol. 1 The Dongaria Kondh* (Man and Forest Series 2). New Delhi: D.K. Printworld.

Kanungo, A.K. 2004. Problems in Educating Tribal Children: The Dongria Kondh Experience. www.anthroglobe.ca/docs/Dongria.pdf (20.10.2004)

Karve, I. 1994 [1953]. "The Kinship Map of India," (pp. 50-73) in P. Uberoi (ed.), *Family, Kinship and Marriage in India*. Delhi: Oxford University Press.

Lewis, O. 1958. *Village Life in North India*. Urbana: University of Illinois Press.

Madan, V. (ed.) 2002. *The Village in India*. Delhi: Oxford University Press.

Marriott, McKim & R. Inden 1977. "Towards an Ethnosociology of South Asian Caste Systems," (pp. 227-38) in K. David (ed.), *The New Wind. Changing Identities in South Asia*. Chicago: Chicago University Press.

MacPherson, S.C. 1863 [1842]. *Lieut. Macpherson's Report Upon the Khonds of the Districts of Ganjam and Cuttack*. Madras: Graves, Cookson & Co.

_____. 1852. "An Account of the Religion of the Khonds in Orissa," *Journal of the Royal Asiatic Society of Great Britain and Ireland*, 13: 216-74.

_____. 1865. *Memorials of Service in India: from the Correspondence of the late Major Samuel Charteris Macpherson, C.B., Political Agent at Gwalior During the Mutiny. Formerly Employed in the Suppression of Human Sacrifice in Orissa, edited by his brother*. London: John Murray.

Mathur, K.S. 1959. "Village Studies in India," *Man in India*, 39 (1): 44-52.

Mayer, A.C. 1958. "The Dominant Caste in a Region of Central India," *Southwestern Journal of Anthropology*, 11: 407-27.

McDougal, C.W. 1963. *The Social Structure of the Hill Juang*. Ph.D. thesis. The University of New Mexico.

McLennan, J.F. 1970 [1865]. *Primitive Marriage. An Inquiry into the Origin of the Form of Capture in Marriage Ceremonies*. Chicago & London: Cambridge University Press. (reprint)

Moore, M.A. 1988. "Symbol and Meaning in Nayar Marriage Ritual," *American Ethnologist*, 15 (2): 254-73.

_____. 1990. "The Kerala House as a Hindu Cosmos," (pp. 169-202) in McKim Marriott (ed.), *India through Hindu Categories*, New Delhi: Sage Publications.

Nayak, P.K. 1989. *Blood, Women and Territory. An Analysis of Clan Feuds of the Dongria Kondhs*. Delhi: Reliance Publishing House.

Niggemeyer, H. 1964. *Kuttia Kond. Dschungel-Bauern in Orissa*. Frankfurt am Main: Klaus Renner Verlag.

Padel, F. 1995. *The Sacrifice of a Human Being. British Rule and the Konds of Orissa*. Delhi: Oxford University Press.

Pfeffer, G. 1997. "The Scheduled Tribes of Middle India as a Unit: Problems of Internal and External Comparison," (pp. 3-27) in G. Pfeffer and D.K. Behera (eds.), *Contemporary Society: Tribal Studies. Vol. 1: Structure and Process*. New Delhi: Concept Publishers.

____. 2000. "Tribal Ideas," *Journal of Social Sciences (Special Volume: Asian World Views: Context and Structure, ed. by R. Hardenberg)*, 4 (4): 331-46.

Randeria, S. 1992. *The Politics of Representation and Exchange amcng Untouchable Castes in Western India (Gujarat)*. Berlin: Unpubl. Ph.D. Thesis. Freie Universität, Berlin.

Roy, S.C. 1915. *The Oraons of Chota Nagpur. Their History, Economic Life, and Social Organization*. Ranchi: Man in India Office.

Sax, W.S. 1991. *Mountain Goddess. Gender and Politics in a Himalayan Pilgrimage*. New York: Oxford University Press.

Srinivas, M.N. (ed.). 1955. *India's Villages*. London: Asia Publ. House.

Vatuk, S. 1975. Gift and Affines in North India. *Contributions to Indian Sociology*, 9 (2): 155-96.

EIGHT

THE "LOST" SOUTH AFRICAN TRIBE: Rebirth of the Koranna in the Free State

PIET ERASMUS

Introduction

There is uncertainty surrounding the origins in place and time, as well as the migration (reasons for this and routes that were taken) of the Khoekhoen (*see* Boonzaier, Malherbe, Berens & Smith, 1996: 4-27; Buys, 1989: 6-18; Engelbrecht, 1936: ix-xii; Elphick, 1973: 2-84; Malherbe, 1984: 1-48; and Penn, 1995: 2-45). For various reasons different tribes/clans were formed with the passing of time; one of which were the Koranna[1] (Gorachouqua). As with the Khoekhoen, the origins of the Koranna are also uncertain (*see* Buys, 1989: 6-27; Engelbrecht, 1936: 1-79; and Maingard, 1932b: 108-111), making it impossible for the outsider to come to any solid deductions on the matter.

In comparing the Koranna with other Khoekhoen groups (Boonzaier *et al.*, 1996; Carstens, 1966 & 1985; and Schapera, 1965), one starts to doubt whether a unique Koranna culture, as postulated by Engelbrecht (1936: 83-194) and Schoeman (1985: 25-26), ever existed. Tobias (1955: 263), however, refers to what he terms a "racial basis of the modern Korana". An own Koranna dialect (Ora/Goragowap), distinct from other Khoekhoen dialects such as Xirigowap/Gri (Griqua) and Khoekhoegoawab (Nama), is said to have existed (Engelbrecht, 1936: 197-231; Maingard, 1932b; Trail, sa: 23; and Strauss, 1979: ii). It is alleged, however, that Ora disappeared over time[2].

Various (sub)groups with their own identities are found amongst the Koranna. According to Tobias (1955: 263), there were already 17 different sub-groups in existence by approximately 1850. Buys (1989: 33) and Engelbrecht (1936: 55) refer to the following groups of the Koranna, during the period 1820-30, as the most important of these: Cloetses, Linkse, Regshande, Katse, Springbokke, Skerpioene, Pampiere, Karosdraers, Afrikander, Towenaars, Slaparms, Bitterboschse, Taaiboschse. etc.

By 1932, Maingard (1932a: 103) maintains that none of the Koranna or any of the above mentioned subgroups were in existence. A range of factors contributed to what Marks (1972: 77) has called "the ultimate disappearance of the Khoi-San as an ethnic entity". In all probability, colonialisation is the greatest reason for the disintegration and "disappearance" of the Koranna. Initial Dutch occupation of the Cape (1652) drove the Koranna from their original place of habitation to the North, thus rendering them the first "frontier" community in South Africa. When the British extended the Northern most colonial boundary from the Buffels to the Orange Rivers (1847), the Koranna were once again placed under the colonial yoke. As nomadic cattle herders and hunters, the Koranna were no longer able to practice their traditional mode of existence, and two destructive wars (1868-69 and 1878-79) with the colonial authorities left the Koranna beside the Orange River without a leader. Under the false pretence that the colonial spokesmen wanted to enter into peace negotiations, the Koranna leadership agreed to a meeting. Virtually all of the Koranna were captured by the colonial authorities and were banned to Robben Island.

Marks (1972: 77) States that another reason for Koranna extinction was their tendency towards acculturation. She claims that the Koranna "literally acculturated themselves out of existence", ascribing this to the fact that the social organisation of the Koranna had not formed a close and integrated unit. The publications of Legassick (1970), Lye (1970), and Lye and Murray (1980) make noteworthy references to the mutual interactions between the Koranna, the Griqua, the Tswana, the Sotho and whites in the Transgariep[3]. These were mostly interactions of trade, war or intermarriage. As a matter of fact, intermingling with other groups seems to have been such a common occurrence, that Beach (1937), as quoted by Buys (1989: 55), states it impossible "to find a pure representation" of the Koranna. Schapera (1965: 47) and Kies (1972: 34-36) are of the same opinion.

Schoeman (2002: 100) illustrates the role that missionaries and westernisation have played in the destruction of the Koranna's tribal cohesion and identity. He refers to the incomprehension, impatience, disapproval and flagrant antagonism of the missionaries towards the Koranna (1985: 77), as well as the way in which their haughtiness, insensitivity and intolerance detracted from their good intentions (1985: 88). The discovery of diamonds (1869-71) was an important catalyst in the process of westernisation. Apart from the labour that the Koranna supplied in the diamond diggings (Buys, 1989: 101-102; and Van der Merwe, 1984: 57), they themselves came to a quick realisation of the economical value of diamonds and involved themselves in the diamond trade. According to Shillington (1985: 35-44), the Koranna, Griqua and Tlhaping found the largest share of diamonds next to the Orange River in the early years. The Koranna of Jan Bloem played an important part in the diggings at Gong Gong next to the Vaal River.

In spite of the general view that the Koranna had become extinct, two factions identifying themselves as the Taaibosch Koranna made appointments with the researcher on the same day (without being aware that the other group had done the same). They both requested for research to be conducted on the history and genealogy of the Taaibosch family of the Free State.

According to Marks (1972: 55) and Strauss (1979: v), the history of the Koranna people has mostly been written by whites. On this subject, Strauss (1979: v) feels that "their ethnocentric and 'anti-Hottentot' bias is evident. They looked upon the Koranna as an uncivilized, morally degenerated and lazy people with an innate desire to steal cattle". Coertze (1983:111) endorses this view, while contributions by authors such as Buys (1889: 65), Coertze and Coertze (1996: 157), Kies (1972: 32), Marais (1968: 94) and Pretorius (1963: 36) confirm the negative characterisation of the Koranna.

Given the negative historical characterisation of the Koranna, a decision was made, on accepting the request of the Taaibosch Koranna, to adopt an inclusive approach to the study in question. An agreement was made with the involved persons that they would share partnership in the research and writing process, and would accept mutual responsibility for the final product. The structure and objectives of the research report were negotiated and a decision was made to focus the research on the involvement of the Koranna in the early history of the Free State, as well as recent developments, identity issues and the genealogy of the Koranna. The researcher has undertaken to remain unbiased, and to avoid verifying or falsifying individual suppositions or conflicting interpretations and deductions. It was anyway not possible to verify the "truth" in all cases.

Involvement in Events in the Orange Free State

During the 16th to 17th centuries the Koranna were established in a region more or less west of the present-day Stellenbosch (Marks, 1972: 64-65 and

Schapera, 1965: 47). Kora (Gora/Chora) was the chief (Khoeseb) of the Koranna at the time of Jan van Riebeeck (1652). He was succeeded by his son Eikomo, who, together with his followers, left the Cape area for good between approximately 1661-86 (Maingard, 1932a: 108-112). Their route from out of the Cape extended in a northerly direction and out of Namaqualand. They had reached the southern banks of the Orange River by approximately 1750 (Kies, 1972: 31). They moved along the Orange River in an easterly direction until they reached Prieska, where the Taaibosch and Links families (these were two half brothers) established themselves. Under Klaas Lukas, the Kats Koranna were diverted to the regions of Upington and Keimoes (Marais, 1968: 92-93; Engelbrecht, 1936: 31; and Lye, 1970: 113).

The Koranna were at the forefront of the northerly migration, with white "trekboere" and "Basters" following at a later stage. The resources that were available came under pressure, resulting in clashes and conflict. The Koranna were systematically forced to move yet further North and East. In the Taungs region (between the Vaal and the Harts Rivers), the Koranna made contact with the Tlhaping (a Tswana group). The two groups intermarried freely and extended trade relations were established (Lye & Murray, 1980: 41-42). When the Rolong (another Tswana group) created conflict by invading the Thlaping region under the command of Tau, the Koranna hastened to the side of the Tlhaping, driving out the Rolong (Lye, 1970: 114, 141). At the end of the 18th century conflicting trade interests destroyed the peaceful relations between the Tlhaping and the Koranna. The Koranna drove the Tlhaping (settled in Nokaneng at the time) out to Kuruman (Lye & Murray, 1980: 42). Between 1813 and 1820 the Koranna relocated to the Mamusa region (Schweizer Reinecke) (Maingard, 1932a: 121). It was here that the Links and Taaibosch families went their separate ways. The pious (Backhouse 1844:393) leader of the Taaibosch family, Hanto Taaibosch, moved to the Platberg, South of Ladybrand (Dreyer, 2001: 92) via Boshof[4] during 1833. From here he moved to Umpukani[5], between Clocolan and Marquard in the following year (1834) (Engelbrecht, 1936: 35; Kriel, 1982: 27; and Buys (1989: 17). Hanto was killed by a lion in 1839 (Backhouse, 1844: 393 and Buys, 1989: 51) and the son who was to be his successor was a minor at the time, and was being schooled at Farmerfield, Albany. As a result of this, Gert Taaibosch, Hanto's brother, assumed chieftainship of the Taaibosch family (Germond, 1967: 165), later became a well-known figure in the Transgariep and much of this contribution is focused on Gert and his descendants[6].

Maingard (1932a: 120) describes the Taaibosch family as the 'largest and most important' of the various Koranna families and they are thus known as the Kei (Big) Koranna[7], or the "Bolanders"[8]. Jan Taaibosch (I) was the ancestor of the Taaibosch family and the oldest son of Kora and his first wife (Ktanghy) (*see* genealogical chart I). He had four sons, namely Jan Taaibosch (II) (also known as Hanto or Jan Kaptein), Gert Taaibosch, Johannes and Jacob. It was during their stay at Prieska that Jan Taaibosch (I) was murdered by the San (Maingard, 1932a: 120) and succeeded by his son Hanto.

According to Kriel (1982: 27) and Lye and Murray (1980: 48), the Koranna in the Thaba 'Nchu and Thaba Bosiu regions had launched a number of marauding-expeditions against Moshweshwe and his followers by 1836. This obligated Moshweshwe to react violently against the marauders, driving them out into different regions. The Koranna fled, attacking the Tlokwa of Sekonyela in the process. According to what has been reported, Sekonyela was very impressed with the military capabilities of the Koranna (they possessed horses and rifles), and immediately saw the possibility of using their skills to outdo Moshweshwe. As a result of this, Sekonyela invited the Koranna to teach his people to horseride and shoot; an invitation gladly accepted by them. Quarrels broke out between Sekonyela and the Koranna, who relocated to the Korannaberg (at Excelsior and Marquard, Schoeman 1985:53) in the meantime. The Koranna succeeded in driving Sekonyela across the Caledon River and virtually all of his cattle were carried off. A year later there was another clash between the two groups and the Koranna drove Sekonyela deep into the Maluti mountains, once again stealing his cattle from him.

According to the treaty signed between Sir George Napier and Moshweshwe on 13 December 1843, the region between the Caledon and the Orange Rivers was to reside under the authority of Moshweshwe. According to Barnard (1965: 369), Moshweshwe was greatly advantaged by this treaty. However, Gert Taaibosch and the Griqua chief, Pieter Davids, laid claim to areas in the same region[9], and the treaty could not be implemented (Germond, 1967: 167-170; and Kriel, 1982: 29). With the Maitland treaty three years later (1846), Gert Taaibosch's land claims were officially acknowledged (Buys, 1989: 64). In all likelihood, a variety of reasons contributed towards this. According to Germond (1967: 187-192) and Buys (1989: 83), there was the good mutual understanding between Gert Taaibosch and Major Warden. In fact, Gert Taaibosch assisted Warden against Moshweshwe, the BaTaung of Moletsane, and the Koranna chief Gert Links during the Battle of "Viervoet" (30 June 1851). Gert Taaibosch also had

TAAIBOSCH GENEALOGY (I)[20]

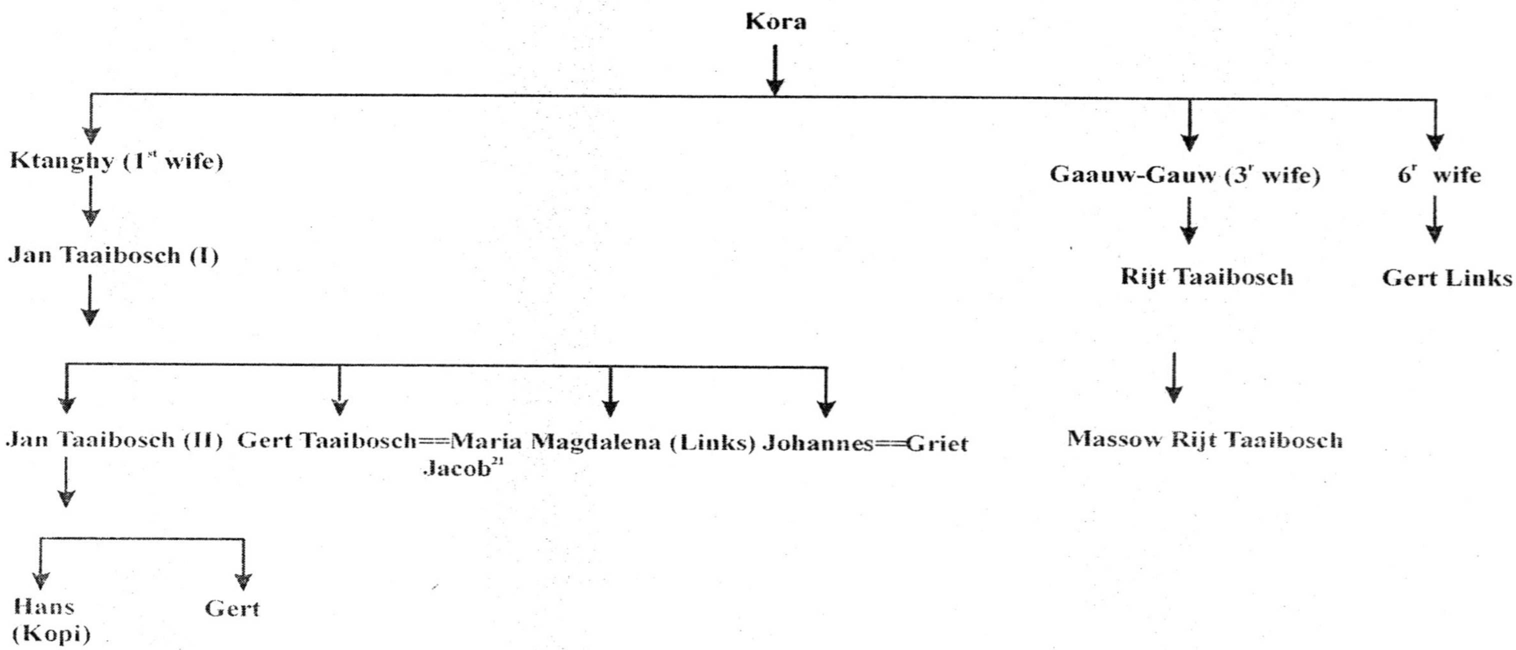

[20] Apart from the details provided by informants, Moncoe (1934) was an additional source of information.
[21] His descendants reside in the vicinity of Barkley West.

good relations with the white farmers. He assisted the "voortrekker" leaders Potgieter and Maritz against the Ndebele of Mzilikazi during December 1838 (Rasmussen, 1975: 277), and never attacked any whites on their farms (Buys, 1989: 64)[10].

According to Barnard (1965: 414), Gert Taaibosch and Sekonyela were reconciled during May 1849, and Taaibosch became actively involved in the struggle between Moshweshwe and Sekonyela[11]. Gert Taaibosch and Sekonyela launched various attacks on Moshweshwe and Moletsane (Kriel, 1982: 32). Moletsane, who was also an ally and friend of Gert Links, had some of Gert's cattle in his possession and these were unknowingly plundered by Gert Taaibosch (Engelbrecht, 1936: 37). The Links group took their revenge by raiding the cattle of Gert Taaibosch.

After the attack on the Basotho living near to the Phuthiatsana River during July 1849, Warden intervened and tried to bring about a peaceful agreement. A meeting was arranged in Bloemfontein for 27 August 1849. The most prominent roleplayers, namely Moshweshwe, Sekonyela and Gert Taaibosch did not turn up for the meeting (Attree, 1949: 230), and Sekonyela and Taaibosch launched an attack on the Basotho on the same day. On 1 September 1850, Warden received permission to take military action against Sekonyela so as to put an end to his ongoing attacks on the Basotho and the BaTaung. However, Gert Taaibosch and chief Moroka of Thaba 'Nchu mediated discussions between Warden and Sekonyela. Sekonyela voiced his remorse over the attacks and agreed to pay a fine of 300 cattle. Sekonyela and Taaibosch, who in the meantime came to learn that Warden was planning military action against Moletsane, also offered to assist Warden; an offer gladly accepted by the latter (Barnard, 1965: 425).

After the battle of Berea (20 December 1852), Gert Taaibosch and Sekonyela attacked the BaTaung of Tulu (in the Winburg region) and the Kgolokwe under Wetsi in the Harrysmith region (Kriel, 1982: 34). Moshweshwe saw this as an opportunity to unite the conflicting chiefs of the Orange River Sovereignty under his authority, and decided to take action against them. In the ensuing struggle during November 1853, Gert Taaibosch was killed at Dawidsberg[12] (Germond, 1967: 217–221 and Buys, 1989: 82). He was succeeded by his son Jacob Taaibosch, who moved nearer to Thaba 'Nchu (Buys, 1989: 100).

The Republic of the Orange Free State was established in 1854, at the time of the Bloemfontein convention. The second article of the Bloemfontein convention determined the government's internal policy with respect to the regulation of the relations between the various population groups. One of the matters that the Volksraad took responsibility for, was the discontinuation, as they saw it, of the migration of indigenous population groups. By means of this the freedom of movement necessary for the indigenous Khoi-San to practice their economies of existence was finally destroyed, causing the issue of land ownership to grow in importance. In a time when their downfall was inevitable, the Koranna no longer had a place in the rapidly changing landscape of the Transgariep.

Further information on the history of the Taaibosch family could not be found in documents. Interviews with informants also did not provide much information, and thus it seems that for a period of more than a 100 years there is virtually no information on these people.

Recent Developments: Leadership and Identity

The identity of the Khoi-San was undervalued during the apartheid regime, thus furthering the disintegration of the Koranna. According to the Population Registration Act (No. 30 of 1950), all people not typified as whites or blacks, were classified as "coloureds". The term "coloured" was an umbrella concept for the "rabble" of society—those who did not belong anywhere else. As the number of population groups grew, sub-groups such as the Cape Coloureds, Malays, Griqua, the Chinese, and the Indians were later identified. No mention, however, is made of the Koranna; a clear indication that their existence remained unacknowledged by the apartheid Government.

Khoi-San identity was contaminated. Informants tell of the ways in which they were forced—politically, socially and economically—to renounce their descent. For instance, the Department of Coloured Education prohibited the use of Khoi-San languages by the children on the school grounds (a practice of the early mission schools), and the Khoi-San descent and culture were ridiculed (the "Jolly Hotnot" image of comical rowdiness). In many cases parents felt ashamed to speak their mother-tongue in front of their children for fear of being thought "backward".

The present Government grants constitutional accommodation and recognition to traditional communities and their leadership, including the Khoi-San (*see* Traditional Leadership and Governance Framework Amendment Act, 2003 [No. 41 of 2003]). Together with the Government's land reform policy (*i.e.* to return land to the individuals/communities who lost it through racially discriminatory practices), these developments have been a powerful stimulus in the revival of traditional Khoi-San leadership and identity. National and regional organisations geared towards gaining political recognition and linguistic or cultural revival have come into being all over the country. This is also true for the Koranna, who were thought to be extinct.

During 1998-99, Jaftha Davids, a self-confessed successful building-contractor at the time, developed an awareness of the Koranna case and joined the Free State Koranna Community Committee (FSKCC), led by Mr. Raymond Beddy[13]. Although they convened on a regular basis, Davids felt that nothing constructive came out of these meetings. Together with a colleague, Willem de Wee, Davids started to register Koranna people as members, although this was not met by a great deal of enthusiasm by members of management. In fact, a committee member felt it necessary to warn Davids that he was being overly hasty in promoting awareness of the Khoi-San identity, in that it would take the Government a long time to address the issue.

According to Davids, the leaders of various Khoi-San groups in the Free State did not see eye to eye. The poor understanding between Mr. Johannes Kraalshcek of the Free State Griqua Council[14] and Beddy of the FSKCC disadvantaged the unity of the Khoi-San. Davids sought greater clarity on the aforementioned differences and approached Mr. Johannes Kraalshoek to speak about the matter. Kraalshoek stated his side of the matter and Davids undertook to apply himself to achieving greater unity amongst the Khoi-San. He was supported in this by Mr. Hansie Johannes Mathews and Mr. Willem de Wee. Apparently though, their intentions were not supported by the FSKCC.

During 2001, Johannes Kraalshoek's son, Mr. Leonard Kraalshoek, delivered a message from Prof. Jattie Bredenkamp (University of the Western Cape) to Davids, Mathews and Wee. Bredenkamp asked whether the recipients of the message wouldn't be interested in representing the Free State Koranna at a Khoi-San conference in Oudtshoorn. Davids was under the impression that Bredenkamp had already contacted Beddy in connection with the conference, but that Beddy was unwilling to co-operate, thus necessitating the invitation extended to Davids himself. Davids informed Mr. Job Buffel about Bredenkamp's request, asking him to contact Beddy. Davids delivered Bredenkamp's message to Beddy, who made it clear that he wanted nothing to do with the conference[15]. Davids reacted to this by saying that he would obey Bredenkamp's request on behalf of the Koranna people and their future.

Together with delegates from the Free State Griqua Council, Davids, Mathews and de Wee attended the conference in Oudtshoorn from 29 March to 1 April 2001. The National Khoi-San Consultative Conference of South Africa (NKOC) was established during the conference[16]. After the conference

Davids asked Bredenkamp for advice and was told to establish a council that would dedicate itself to raising awareness of Koranna identity. Bredenkamp even went so far as to suggest that the council be called the "Vrystaat Koranna Kultuur en Erfenis Raad" (Free State Koranna Culture and Heritage Council).

Back in Bloemfontein, Davids, Mathews and de Wee got to work, and family members recognised Jaftha Taaibos-Davids[17] as chief (Khoeseb) of the Koranna in the Free State on the basis of his supposed genealogical seniority. This position was recognised by the chairman of the Khoi-San Council (Khoeseb Joseph Little) and the Koranna House, North Cape (Khoeseb Josiah Katz) on 29 October 2001. Subsequently, 46 family members gave their written support of this move on 17 December 2001.

Taaibos-Davids bases his claim to leadership on matrilineal descent. He is the eighth child of Marie (Toebaai) and Jacob Davids (*see* genealogical chart IV) and has the support of his older, living brother and two sisters. Marie, in turn, was the oldest child of Isaac and Ellen Taaibosch. Taaibos-Davids makes use of a reference from Engelbrecht's publication (1936: 191-192) to justify his allegation that Marie is Isaac Taaibosch's rightful heir. The relevant reference reads: "Male children had preference over female in the sense that if the family consisted of several daughters and but one son the latter, even if he was the youngest child, would still succeed his father as head and also be his chief heir". Taaibos-Davids argues that there was not only one, but two sons in the case of his mother, and thus Marie is the rightful heir.

Taaibos-Davids registered the Free State Koranna Culture & Heritage Council Trust (IT 803/02) on 14 May 2002. According to this the Free State Koranna Culture and Heritage Council (FSKCHC) has the highest authority, and provision is made for a Traditional Council. On request, the FSKCHC attended the meetings of the National House of Traditional Leaders, taking part in discussions on the accommodation of traditional leaders. As a result of these discussions, consultations with communities in the Free State were initiated, and the FSKCHC decided to found the Taaibos-Davids Koranna House (TDKH). On 2 August 2003, the TDKH was established in Bloemfontein with the acceptance of a constitution. The TDKH's constitution makes provision for an elected council (Council of the Elderly) with an executive committee existing of a chairman (R. Dodds), Vice-chairman (T. Peterson), secretary (D. Davids), treasurer (vacant), and two additional members (A Sandt and Johanna Taaibosch). Furthermore, there is a "Women's Association", "Youth League", and a "Language and Cultural Association".

Taaibos-Davids and the elected council members also paid visits to Government offices and institutions such as the National Museum. Cultural events were undertaken in cooperation with the Heidedal Police Station, and community institutions such as Dr. Blok Secondary School and Credence Primary School were addressed on the issue of Koranna identity.

Taaibos-Davids called the Taaibosch family members together to ask them to work together in promoting the interests, culture and identity of the Koranna. However, his leadership was not undisputed and led to much discord and disunity. There were members of the Taaibosch family[18], and especially Mr. C.H. Taaibosch (Chris), Taaibos-David's nephew and Mr. Johannes Taaibosch's son, who voiced their disagreement with Taaibos-David's leadership. In this case it is argued that genealogical succession traditionally takes place from the father to the oldest son, and therefore it should be calculated on this basis for the Free State's Taaibosch family. According to this, as Johannes is Isaac's oldest son, Johannes is the rightful heir. In turn, Chris is Johannes's oldest son and thus is to be his successor (*see* genealogical chart IV).

A number of attempts were made to resolve the ongoing family disputes. For instance, Taaibos-Davids arranged a meeting at the home of Chris which, amongst other things, dealt with the leadership issue. A second meeting was arranged but Chris did not attend. At a later occasion Chris and Taaibos-Davids had a chance meeting at the home of Mr. Raymond Loff, where Chris requested a family meeting in order to hold further discussions on the leadership issue. Taaibos-Davids agreed to this request and a meeting was arranged for 6 December 2001. The meeting took place at the home of Veronica Taaibosch in Rykmanshoogte, Heidedal. However, Chris, his brother and his father did not attend the meeting and the gathering proceeded without them. Taaibos-Davids informed those present about the leadership issue and the family members present at the meeting expressed their full support of Taaibos-Davids. During this meeting, 15 January 2002 was decided upon as the date for the following meeting. On this date, family members from Heidedal and from the surrounding squatter camps gathered together, while members of the Griqua Council were present as mediators. It is alleged that a class distinction caused the meeting to be disrupted. Family members from Heidedal (with a higher socio-economic status) did not want to allow the family from the squatter camps, and who were in favour of the leadership of Taaibos-Davids, to declare their support of him. The attendees did not reach consensus and the meeting ended on an unsavoury note.

Shortly after the above mentioned meeting, Taaibos-Davids received a letter from Chris requesting a meeting between himself, Taaibos-Davids, David Davids, Leon Taaibosch, Johannes Taaibosch with two members of the FSKCHC (Mr. Julien Jackson and inspector Francis of the Heidedal Police Station). The latter were intended to be neutral mediators. The meeting took place at the Heidedal Police Station, was recorded, and dealt with ways in which the distastefulness surrounding the leadership issue could be resolved.

At a later meeting (21 October 2003), at the home of Chris, Taaibos-Davids suggested that Chris, Pat Buffel and Leon Taaibosch were to be offered positions on the Council of the Elderly or the Executive Committee. However, Chris turned down the offer, stating that although Taaibos-Davids had made much progress with the Koranna case, he preferred to establish his own case. Lydia Harris chaired the meeting.

Research Findings

It is, firstly, evident from the research that the section Taaibos-Davids quotes from Engelbrecht (1936: 191-192) to confirm his leadership claim deals with the inheritance of property and the estate of a deceased, and not with the succession of chieftainship. Regarding the succession of chieftainship, Schapera (1965: 328) declares that it was never transferred to a daughter, while Engelbrecht (1936: 90) states that in case a chief passes away without a son, the chieftainship is carried over to his brother and the brother's sons. This information was presented to the relevant parties and Taaibos-Davids admitted to being misguided, thus abandoning the claim he had wrongly based on Engelbrecht.

Secondly, according to the genealogical data compiled in consultation with the two relevant parties (*see* genealogical chart II), not one of Gert Taaibosch's sons remained in the Free State, and thus he could not be succeeded. The leadership was thus transferred to the lineage of Gert's younger brother, Johannes (married to Griet). Following on Thomas and Hans, Isaac (married to Ellen) was the third oldest son of Johannes (married to Marie). It was pointed out to the relevant family members that it is not possible for Isaac's son Johannes (married to Martha) to be the successor, as alleged by Chris. In the first instance, descent is to take place from the home of Thomas, and then from that of Hans. Chris responded by saying that the houses of Thomas and Hans produced no living descendants. This information was presented to Taaibos-Davids, who denied it strongly. He arranged a meeting with Thomas's descendants (*see* genealogy chart III) on 1 April 2004 and provided them with an exposition of the descendancy

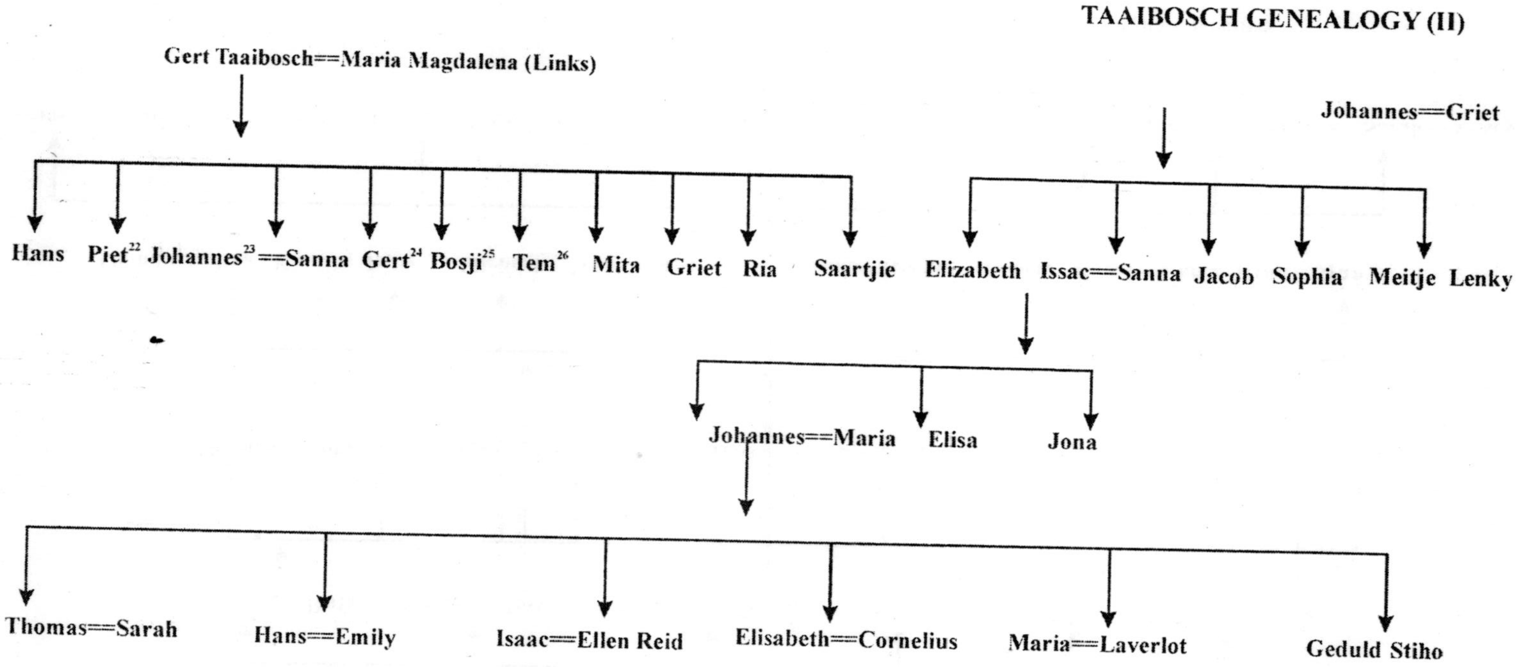

[22] He was so 'pale' that he became white.
[23] He succeeded his father but relocated, together with his family, to the vicinity of Worcester.
[24] He spread out to Namibia.
[25] He moved to Springbok.
[26] He established himself somewhere in Namaqualand.

TAAIBOSCH GENEALOGY (III)

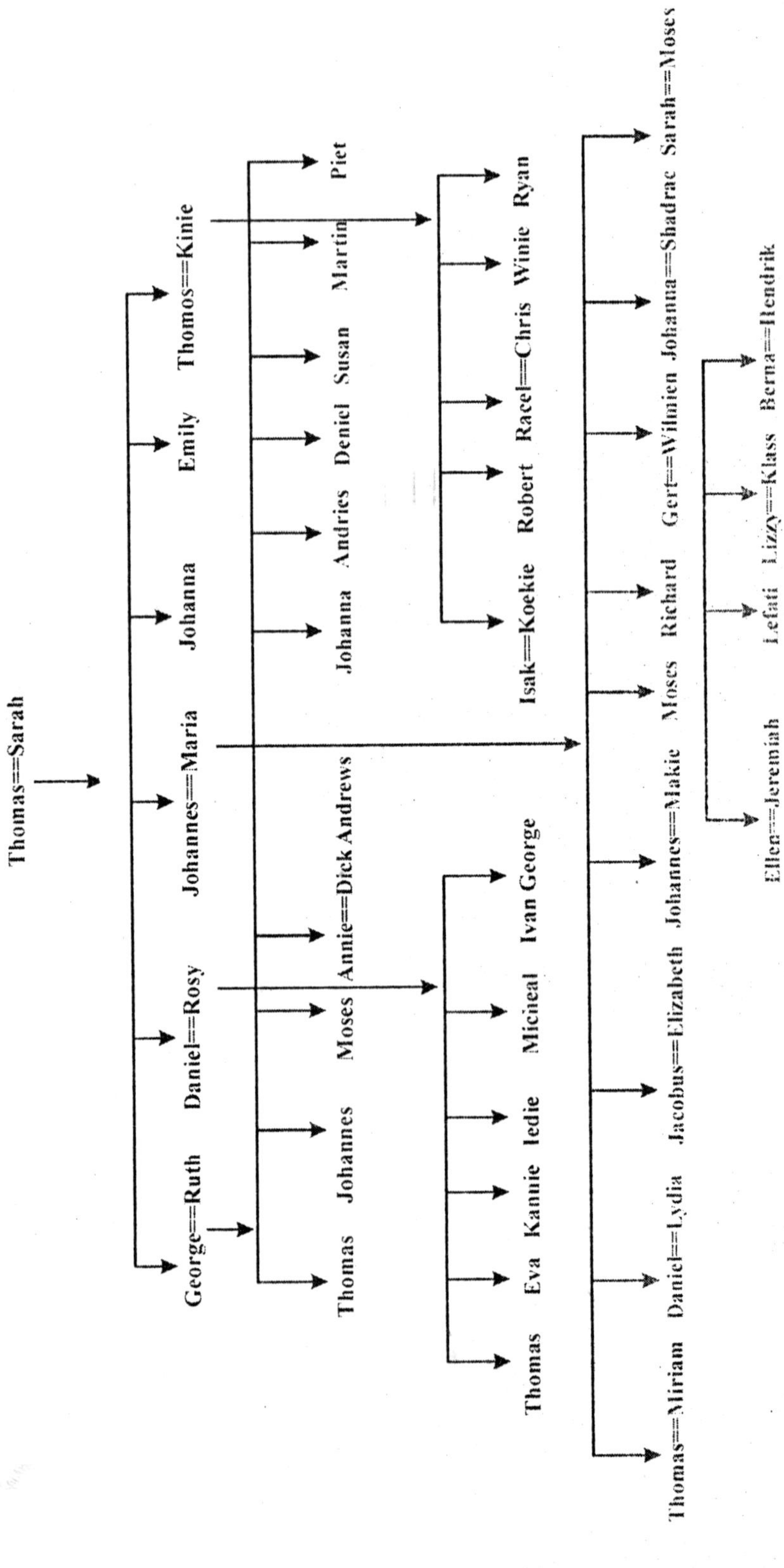

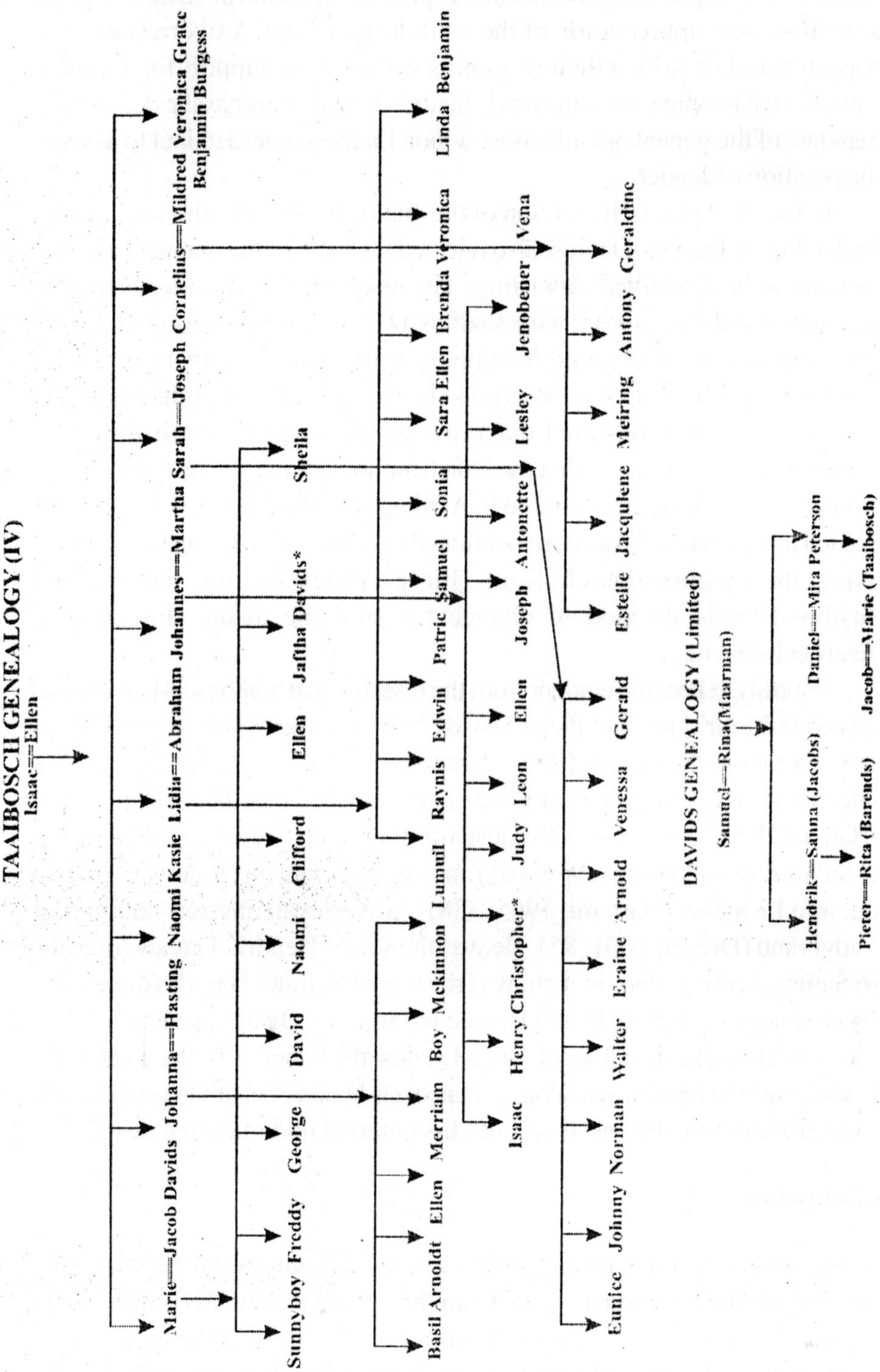
TAAIBOSCH GENEALOGY (IV)
Isaac==Ellen
Marie==Jacob Davids
Johanna==Hasting
Naomi Kasie
Lidia==Abraham
Johannes==Martha
Sarah==Joseph
Cornelius==Mildred
Veronica Grace
Benjamin Burgess
Sunnyboy
Freddy
George
David
Naomi
Clifford
Ellen
Jaftha Davids*
Sheila
Basil Arnoldt
Ellen
Merriam
Boy
Mckinnon
Lumuil
Raynis
Edwin
Patric
Samuel
Sonia
Sara Ellen
Brenda
Veronica
Linda
Benjamin
Isaac
Henry
Christopher*
Judy
Leon
Ellen
Joseph
Antonette
Lesley
Jenobener
Vena
Eunice
Johnny
Norman
Walter
Eraine
Arnold
Venessa
Gerald
Estelle
Jacqulene
Meiring
Antony
Geraldine
DAVIDS GENEALOGY (Limited)
Samuel==Rina(Maarman)
Hendrik==Sanna (Jacobs)
Daniel==Mita Peterson
Pieter==Rita (Barends)
Jacob==Marie (Taaibosch)

situation. Those present at the meeting expressed their faith in Taaibos-Davids as well as their appreciation of the work he had done. A sworn statement was prepared, in which their origins as well as their support for Taaibos-Davids's leadership was confirmed. Taaibos-Davids thus has the democratic mandate of the genealogically most senior Taaibosch descendant to assume the position of leader.

In the third place, the section of the Taaibosch family who rejected the leadership of Taaibos-Davids, also rejected his view of the manner in which they are to be described in writing. The researcher took a closer look at this matter and discussed it with Taaibos-Davids. He was informed that no substantial proof was found in support of his insistence that the typical Afrikaans spelling of "Taaibos" must be recognised. All of the historical sources that were consulted make use of the original Dutch form, *i.e.* "Taaibosch". It is unlikely that the Dutch authorities in the Cape at that time would have written the surname in Afrikaans as the language had not yet existed at the time. For the aforementioned reasons it was decided to continue using the original Dutch form (for purposes of this report), and Taaibos-Davids decided to change his surname again, this time to Taaibosch-Davids.

Fourthly, it became evident from the research that Taaibosch-Davids was related to the Griqua Chief Pieter Davids[19] on his father's side. Pieter Davids was married to the Griqua Chief, Barend Barendse's daughter (her name is uncertain and could be Rita or Elsie), and they lived together at Danielskuil (Barnard, 1965: 338). After Barendse was murdered, Pieter Davids assumed chieftainship (Germond, 1967: 165) and, together with his followers, moved out into Lishuane (Barnard, 1965: 338)—a Wesleyan mission station near Ladybrand (Dreyer, 2001: 85). He was the son of Hendrik Davids (married to Sanna Jacobs), who, in turn, was the son of Samuel Davids (married to Rina Maarman). Samuel Davids's second son was Daniël Davids (married to Mita Peterson), the father of Jacob Davids, the father of Jaftha Taaibosch-Davids (*see* the Davids genealogy). Taaibosch-Davids's claim to genealogical seniority can thus be based on both his paternal and maternal descent.

Discussion

In this contribution the focus has firstly been on the history of the Taaibosch Koranna in the Free State. Apart from the negative characterisation of the Koranna, the scarcity of information is worth noting and causes one to question whether the Taaibosch Koranna were sufficiently important to justify the accurate keeping of records. Not surprisingly then, references which indicate that the "disappearance" of the Koranna is a cultural, ethnic and linguistic loss to South Africa cannot be found. Figuratively speaking, not a tear has been shed for the loss of the Koranna.

Secondly, this contribution has dealt with the revival of Koranna identity and leadership. Although various authors (Bekker, 1993: 24-28; De Beer, 1998: 38; Kriel, 1998: 23; and Slabbert, 1999: 61-62) have alleged that the post-apartheid disposition is generally disinclined towards the identity issue, the current Government's constitutional accommodation and recognition of traditional communities and leadership, as well as the land reform policy have stimulated the revival of Koranna identity and leadership. Apart from the aforementioned (national) factors leading up to the revival of Koranna identity, authors such as Kuper (1994: 537) and Darnell (1994: 7) hold that the contemporary international climate is favourable for the recognition and debate of indigenous linguistic, cultural and identity rights.

Thirdly, a closer look has been taken at the role of specific individuals. Accusations of own gain, enrichment and power hungriness have passed between the opposing factions. Whatever the reasons for the involvement of certain individuals in the case of the Koranna, their involvement has been instrumental to the revival of Koranna identity. Regarding the value of the individual in the construction of cultural patterns, groups and identities, it is important to note the following: Although social pressure can be overwhelming, it is the voluntary relationships which determine the singularity of the person, his/her relationships with others, and with groups. When the initial pattern of relationships between individuals changes for some or the other reason, the individual's connectedness with a specific group is bound to change. The individual finds himself situated in a bringing along, as well as a marginal position with respect to the group. As a result of this, group membership and the extent to which the individual conforms to group culture is adaptable (*see* Banton, 1994: 2; Bekker, 1993: 12-13; and Segar, 1989: 97). Authors such as Bates and Rassam (1983: 85-88) and Sharp (1988: 80) have reported that ethnic identity is in a constant state of flux due to the fact that individuals fulfil complementary roles determined largely extent by the essence of that which the group does for survival. Seen in this light, the definition of ethnic boundaries varies according to the context, and individuals make conscious or subconscious choices between alternative sources of identity in order to manipulate social and economical situations.

The individual is confronted with innumerable situations where a decision has to be made on whether he/she identifies with a certain group or not.

Logically speaking it is the individual who conceptualises the meaning that is attached to the notion of "identity". Regardless of the implications of the individual's decision (choosing to accept or reject groups; preparedness for active or passive participation in symbolic systems, etc.), authors such as Bates and Rassam (1983: 85-88), Bekker (1993: 12) and Martin (1995: 14) feel that identification is a personal affair representing the result of an exercised choice. Furthermore, multiple identities exist not only because the individual may alter his identification during the course of his life, but because he is able to relate different identities and reconcile contradictions between identities.

In keeping with the above, ethnic groups and boundaries are similarly not permanent fixtures. In this regard, authors such as Barth (1969), Bates and Rassam (1983: 85-88), Banton (1994: 2), Martin (1995: 5), Peoples and Bailey (2000: 307-309), Sharp (1988:80) and Weber (quoted in Segar, 1989: 97) focus our attention on the fact that the origin, creation, maintenance and disbanding of ethnic groups is similar to the origin, creation, maintenance and disbanding of any other type of group, and thus may be explained in the same terms. Thus, the Koranna have "disappeared"(disbanded) because the connectedness of individuals has weakened. Stated differently, the Koranna are experiencing a revival because individuals are prepared to make the effort to promote their case.

In revival scenarios, and this is the fourth point of this discussion, Martin (1995: 5) states that different identity narratives are generated and offered to the individual exercising his/her choice. Certain values are proclaimed within these narratives, and attempts are made to convince the individual to identify with these values. In this regard, undisputed truths, promises, feelings, emotions, fears and anxieties are combined. The research requested by the various Taaibosch factions may be seen as an attempt to create an identity narrative; 'something' which may be upheld as proof of the 'truth', or as a justification of the allegations, but which may also provide the basis for identifying with the case of the Free State Koranna.

NOTES

1. The Koranna peoples' spelling of their name is used in this contribution, *i.e.* 'Koranna' as opposed to the more generally used form 'Korana'.
2. According to Trail (sa: 25), Ben Kraalshoek was one of South Africa's last! Orą speakers. In an interview with Mr. H.C. Taaibosch (19 February 2004), he has claimed that there are still a number of people living in Heidedal

(Bloemfontein) and Boshof who speak the language fluently. Mrs. Susan van Wyk from Heidedal confirmed this allegation in an interview (1 July 2004), stating that she still speaks the language.

3. Areas of the central interior occupied by the Koranna included: the southern area of the North Cape from Augrabies in the West to the Caledon River in the Free State; the South-easterly areas of the Free State excluding Griekwastad and Douglas, as well as next to the Vaal and Harts Rivers (in the vicinity of Taungs), the Modder and Riet Rivers, and North of the Kuruman River.
4. Frans Taaibosch and a few of his family members remained here.
5. This mission station was established for Hanto and his descendants by Thomas Jenkins during 1833. According to Dreyer (2001: 96), missionaries made attempts to relocate the Koranna from Umpukani to Merumetsu (between Marquard and Winburg) during 1836 and 1837. Both of the aforementioned mission stations were attacked by Moletsane during 1850, after which the stations were abandoned.
6. A section of the Taaibosch family who became well-known in the former Transvaal were the followers of Massow Rijt Taaibosch. He was Kora's grandson from the house of his third wife (Gaauw-Gauw). Together with approximately 300 of his followers (according to Backhouse, 1844: 461 many of his followers abandoned him when he was converted), Massow Rijt Taaibosch lived at Patuni/Nukuni, Northwest of Kuruman during 1839. From here he moved to Zendelingsfontein between Klerksdorp and Wolmaransstad, where he remained until approximately 1850 (Engelbrecht, 1936: 35-39). He lost his ground after a land dispute with the Republic of the Transvaal in 1873 (*see* Buys, 1989:102 and Shillington, 1985:129-130, 133-135). He was succeeded by his son David Massow, who died during the battle of Mamusa (Schweizer Reinecke) in 1885.
7. According to Buys (1989: 23), the Koranna referred to the main group as the 'Bigt' Koranna, and to those that later broke away from them as the 'Small' Koranna.
8. This term is used to refer to those who first reached the Orange River, while the "Ondervelders" were those who arrived later (Lye, 1970: 113 and Lye and Murray 1980: 40).
9. At that time Gert Taaibosch was living at Nieuweland (Engelbrecht, 1936: 37; Maingard, 1932a: 127; and Buys, 1989: 101). This was the name of the region surrounding the Wesleyan mission station Platberg, South of Ladybrand (Schoeman 1985: 53).
10. Skeelkobus (Skeelkoos or Kousop Kousopson) and a number of his followers attacked farms in the Boshof district, murdered whites, and plundered property in 1858. White researchers generally view this type of behaviour as that which may typically be expected of the Koranna (*see* Van Aswegen 1977: 67-77; Malan, 1929: 372-385; and Van Heerden, 1908: 15-44 for details). Conflicting land claims and confusing land transactions were the main contributing factors to this unrest.
11. According to Attree (1949: 41), Gert Taaibosch was deeply offended by Moshweshwe's invasion of his territory by 1847, and by the number of cattle

posts he had established there. In all likelihood, the aforementioned chain of events influenced Gert Taaibosch's decision to join forces with Sekonyela.

12. Dawidsberg (also known as Yoaloboholo) was the home of Sekonyela's mother, Mantatise. It is situated at Marabeng, Sekonyela's hill fortress near Ficksburg (Dreyer, 2001: 89).
13. According to Beddy (interview held on 16 July 2004), the Koranna Royal Family (descendants of the Regshande family) have held annual meetings on 16 December) at the home of Mr. Esegiël Meyer (1599 Dilape Street, Batho) since the Koranna afsetting from Bethany during 1925 (Van der Merwe, 1984: 58). At these meetings, the members of the Koranna Royal Family sang the Koranna hymn (Sorop se !!am Broekoe ye wakoe ye wakoe ye !!am Broekoe ye) in Ora, discussed family matters, and informed the children about Koranna traditions and practices. The FSKCC's constitution was approved by representatives of the Koranna Royal Family on 22 January 2000.
14. The Kraalshoek family are originally of Koranna descent. According to Engelbrecht (1936: 49, 55), they joined the Koranna people living with Piet Witvoet and Goliath Yzerbek in the region of Brandewynsfontein beside the Riet River (later known as Bethany, 20 km. North of present-day Edenburg in the southern Free State). According to Schoeman (2002: 276), however, the Kraalshoek family broke away from the Koranna at Bethany, and Adam Kok granted a farm to Jan Kraalshoek as lawful property in 1833 (Schoeman states that the farm's name is unknown but according to Kraalshoek informants it may have been called "Bloubank"). This agreement was renewed on 13 September 1842 (Schoeman, 2002:166). According to Johannes Kraalshoek (interview held on 27 November 2003), the Kraalshoek family have—since the family broke away from the Koranna at Bethany and the agreement with Kok—identified themselves more strongly with the Griqua tribe than with that of the Koranna, thus regarding themselves to be Griqua. He stresses, however, that this does not mean that the Koranna origin, history or identity is to go unrecognised (Erasmus, 2004: 9-10).
15. This matter was discussed with Beddy on 16 July 2004. According to him, he was involved with the initial arrangements for the Oudtshoorn conference, and the misunderstanding revolved largely around the administering of funds to the Free State delegation. It was felt that the manner in which the matter was dealt with, their independence, and the struggle against apartheid had been misjudged.
16. The NKOC strives to represent the South African Khoi-San both nationally and internationally. Furthermore, it aims to promote and co-ordinate their culture, heritage and economic empowerment.
17. At this stage, Davids decided to change his surname to Taaibos-Davids, and applied for a new identity document. He was convinced that the family surname was to be written as 'Taaibos' and not 'Taaibosch', basing this view on the fact that his mother's (Mary Magdalena) surname is indicated as Taaibos (not Taaibosch) on her birth certificate and identity document (Identity No. 1409280060015).
18. Interviews held with Ms. Lydia Buffel and Veronica Taaibosch, as well as Messrs. Johannes Taaibosch and Chris Taaibosch (27 February 2004).

19. According to Barnard (1965: 338), Campbell has wrongly typified Barend Barendse and Pieter Davids as Griqua. In fact they are of Koranna descent.
20. Apart from the details provided by informants, Mancoe (1934) was an additional source of information.
21. His descendants reside in the vicinity of Barkley West.
22. He was so 'pale' that he became white.
23. He succeeded his father but relocated, together with his family, to the vicinity of Worcester.
24. He spread out to Namibia.
25. He moved to Springbok.
26. He established himself somewhere in Namaqualand.

REFERENCES

Attree E.M. 1949. "The Closer Union Movements between the Orange Free State, South African Republic and Cape Colony (1838-1863)," *Archives Year Book for South African History*, 12 (2). Pretoria: Government Printer.

Backhouse J. 1844. *A Narrative of a Visit to the Mauritius and South Africa.* London: Hamilton, Adams and Co.

Barnard B.J. 1965. "n Lewensbeskrywing van majoor Henry Douglas Warden," *Argiefjaarboek vir Suid-Afrikaanse gekiedenis*, 11 (1). Pretoria: Staatsdrukker.

Banton M. 1994. "Modelling Ethnic and National Relations," *Ethnic and Racial Studies*, 17 (1): 1-19.

Bates D. & A. Rassam 1983. *Peoples and Cultures of the Middle East.* Englewood Cliffs: Prentice-Hall.

Barth F. 1969. *Ethnic Groups and Boundaries: The Social Organization of Cultural Difference.* London: Allen & Unwin.

Bekker S. 1993. *Ethnicity in Focus. The South African Case.* Pietermaritzburg: Indicator.

Boonzaier E., C. Malherbe, P. Berens & A. Smith 1996. *The Cape Herders. A History of the Khoikhoi of Southern Africa.* Cape Town: David: Philip.

Buys J.J. 1989. *Die oorsprong en migrasiebewegings van die Koranna en hul rol in die Transgariep tot 1870.* Ongepubliseerde MA-verhandeling. Bloemfontein: Universiteit van die Vrystaat.

Carstens W.P. 1966. *The Social Structure of a Cape Coloured Reserve.* Cape Town: Oxford University Press.

_____. 1985. *The Social Organisation of the Nama and Other Essays by Winifred Hoernlé.* Eeufeesbundel. Johannesburg: Witwatersrand University Press.

Coertze P.J. 1983. *Die Afrikanervolk en die Kleurlinge.* Pretoria: HAUM.

Coertze P.J. & R.D. Coertze. 1996. *Verklarende vakwoordeboek vir Antropologie en Argeologie.* Pretoria: Coertze & Coertze.

Darnell R. 1994. "Comments on Wolf, E.R. 1994. Perilous Ideas, Race, Culture, People," *Current Anthropology*, 35 (1): 7-8.

De Beer F.C. 1998. "Ethnicity in Nation-states with Reference to South Africa," *Suid-Afrikaanse Tydskrif vir Etnologie,* 21 (1): 32-40.

Dreyer J. 2001. "Thomas Arbousset and Francois Daumas in the Free State: Tracing the Exploratory Tour of 1836," *South African Humanities*, 13: 61-96.

Elphick R.N. 1973. *The Cape Khoi and the First Phase of South African Race Relations.* Michigan: Ann Arbor.

Engelbrecht J.A. 1936. *The Koranna. An Account of their Customs and their History with Texts.* Cape Town: Maskew Miller.

Erasmus P.A. 2004. *Die geskiedenis van die Kraalshoek-familie van Bethanie in die Vrystaat.* Bloemfontein: Kraalshoek-familie.

Germond R.C. 1967. *Chronicles of Basutoland.* Morija: Morija Sesoto Book Depot.

Kies C.W. 1972. Die Kleurlinge van Noord-Kaapland, Noord van die Oranjerivier. D.Phil.-proefskrif. Pretoria: Universiteit van Pretoria.

Kriel J.D. 1982. "Die lotgevalle van die Batlokwa ba okotleng vanaf die aanvang van die Difaqane tot 1853," *Suid-Afrikaanse Tydskrif vir Etnologie*, 5 (2): 21-36.

Kriel M. 1998. "Taal en identiteit, en die alternatiewe Afrikaanse musiekbeweging," *Suid-Afrikaanse Tydskrif vir Taalkunde*, 16 (1): 16-26.

Kuper A. 1994. "Culture, Identity and the Project of a Cosmopolitan Anthropology," *Man, The Journal of the Royal Anthropological Institute*, 29 (3): 537-554.

Legassick M.C. 1970. The Griqua, the Sotho-Tswana, and the Missionaries, 1780-1840: The Politics of a Fronteer Zone. Ph.D. Dissertation. Los Angeles: University of California.

Lye W.F. 1970. The Sotho Wars in the Interior of South Africa, 1822-1837. Ph.D. Dissertation. Los Angeles: University of California.

Lye W.F. & C. Murray 1980. *Transformations on the Highveld: The Tswana and the Southern Sotho.* Cape Town: David Philip.

Maingard L.F. 1932(a). "Studies in Koranna History, Customs and Language," *Bantu Studies*, 6 (2): 103-162.

____. 1932(b). "Koranna Names of Animals and Plants," *Bantu Studies*, 6 (4): 309-322.

Malan J.H. 1929. *Die opkoms van 'n republiek: of die geskiedenis van die Oranje-Vrystaat tot die jaar 1863.* Bloemfontein: Nasionale pers.

Malherbe C. 1984. *Men of Men.* Pietermaritzburg: Shuter & Shooter.

Mancoe J. 1934. *The Bloemfontein Bantu and Coloured People's Directory.* Bloemfontein: AC White P & P Printers.

Marais J.S. 1968. *The Cape Coloured people 1652-1937.* Johannesburg: Witwatersrand University Press.

Marks S. 1972. "Khoisan Resistance to the Dutch in the Seventeeth and Eighteen Centuries," *Journal of African History*, 13 (1): 55-80.

Martin D.-C. 1995. "The Choices of Identity," *Social Identities*, 1 (1): 5-20.

Penn N.G. 1995. The Northern Cape Frontier Zone, 1700-c.1815. Unpublished Ph.D. Dissertation. Cape Town: University of Cape Town.

Peoples J. & G. Bailey 2000. *Humanity. An Introduction to Cultural Anthropology.* New York: West Publishing Company.

Pretorius RdeV. 1963. *Die geskiedenis van die "Vrystaatse" Griekwa 1825-1862.* Ongepubliseerde MA-verhandeling. Bloemfontein: Universiteit van die Vrystaat.

Rasmussen R.K. 1975. Ndebele Wars and Migration, c. 1821-1839. Ph.D. Dissertation. Los Angeles: University of California.

Schapera I. 1965. *The Khoisan Peoples of South Africa.* London: Routledge & Kegan Paul.

Schoeman K. 1985. *Die huis van die armes: die Berlynse Sendinggenootskap in die O.V.S., 1834-1869: 'n bloemlesing/geredigeer en vertaal deur Karel Schoeman.* Kaapstad: Human & Rousseau.

____. 2002. *The Griqua Captaincy of Philippolis, 1826-1861.* Pretoria: Protea Book House.

Segar J. 1989. *Fruits of Apartheid. Experiencing "Independence" in a Transkeian Village.* Bellville: Anthropos Publishers.

Sharp J. 1988. "Ethnic Group and Nation: The Apartheid Vision in South Africa," (pp.79–99) *In* E. Boonzaier, and J. Sharp (eds.), *South African Keywords. The Uses and Abuses of Political Concepts.* Cape Town: David Philip.

Shillington K. 1985. *The Colonization of the Southern Tswana 1870-1900.* Pretoria: Sigma Press.

Slabbert F. Van Zyl. 1999. *Afrikaner Afrikaan—Anekdotes en Analise.* Kaapstad: Tafelberg.

Strauss T. 1979. *War along the Orange. The Koranna and the Northern Border Wars of 1868-9 and 1878-9.* Cape Town: Centre for African Studies.

Tobias P.V. 1955. "Taaibosch Korannas of Ottosdal," *South African Journal of Science*, 51 (9): 263-269.

Trail A. sa. *South African Khoisan Languages*. Johannesburg: University of the Witwatersrand.

Van Aswegen H.J. 1971. "Verhouding tussen blank en nie-blank in die Oranje-Vrystaat, 1854—1902," *Argiefjaarboek vir Suid-Afrikaanse gekiedenis*, 34 (1). Pretoria: Staatsdrukker.

Van der Merwe W. 1984. "Bethanie in die Oranje-Vrystaat – 'n terugblik na 150 jaar," *Lantern*, Julie: 50-58.

Van Heerden P.S. 1908. *Herinneringen uit den tijd der Vrijstaatsche Voortrekkers.* Stellenbosch: Pro Ecclesia Drukkerij.

SECTION IV

DESCENT PATTERNS: MIDDLE AND NORTH EAST INDIA

NINE

THE SEGMENTARY LINEAGE SYSTEM AMONG THE SAORAS OF ANDHRA PRADESH

M. SURYANARAYAN

Introduction

The Saoras, classified among the so-called PTG within the *Scheduled Tribes* of Andhra Pradesh, are mainly distributed in the Srikakulum and Vijayanagaram Districts. They are also widely found in the neighbouring State of Orissa. The Saoras speak their own language belonging to the Mundari language family. Their descent organization is patrilineal. Unlike many of the Mundari speaking tribes, Saoras do not possess clans, but their social structure is characterized by segmented lineages (*kulam marangi units*).

Fieldwork among the Saoras was conducted in different periods of time, *i.e.* intensive fieldwork between 1965-1967 followed by short field trips in the years of 1976-1991 and in 2001. In all more than fifteen months were spent in the Saora villages where I also developed a working knowledge of the Saora language. The major scope of the study is to highlight the segmented lineage systemamong the Saoras with the following specific objectives:

(i) Present a brief profile about the Saoras,
(ii) Describe the endogamous and exogamous divisions among the Saoras with a special emphasis on the lineage system, and
(iii) Highlight the role of segmented lineages in the organization of various rituals and socio-economic life in context of the kinship interaction.

The Saoras

Saoras are one of the ancient tribes of India. Various earlier scholars who have worked on the Saoras like Ramamurthy 1931, Sithapathi 1938—1943, Elwin 1955 have stated that they are Pre-Aryan and Pre-Dravidian. Ramamurthy has studied the language of the Saoras and published a *Manual for Saora Language* in 1931. His son G.V. Sithapathi has made an ethnographic study of the Saoras and published the same in a series of articles in the *Journal of the Andhra Historical Society.* Elwin (1955) has made an elaborate study of the religious life of the Saoras. Except Ramamurthy others did not mention the existence of the lineages among the Saoras. Ramamurthy, in the context of the ancestor worship, referred to the *kulam maranji* unit equating it with that of lineage.

Saora economy is characterized by shifting cultivation. The people also practice terracing, dry and wetland cultivation. Food gathering and hunting are important subsidiary occupations. Agricultural services in Saora villages are seen operating at different levels and accordingly we find obligatory services between members of the same lineage, reciprocal services between the co-villagers as well as paid services. Obligatory services are predominantly confined to the lineage unit, expressing the underlying principle of assistance. The rendering of assistance works mainly on the basis of kin obligations. These mutual services help in strengthening the solidarity among the kinsmen and suggest the mutual benefit in corporate living. As the kin relationship becomes distant, the obligation for services decreases.

Social control in Saora villages is mainly maintained through an organized political system. Each village is characterized by the existence of status-oriented groups like the *gamong*, the *buya* and the *parja*. The *gamong* is the chief as well as the civil head of a village, the *buya* the religious leader and the *parja* are the common people of the village.

Saoras are generally monogamous but polygamous marriages are not uncommon. The various types of marriages found are: marriage through negotiations, marriage through elopement, marriage by capture, marriage by service and marriage by intrusion of the bride. According to the Saora conception, every normal individual in a society is expected to marry to gratify sexual inclinations and to have children for perpetuating the *kulum marangi* unit. In all marriage forms, especially in the marriage by negotiations, the *kulum marangi* unit plays the central role. Every member of the *kulum marangi* is expected to contribute some amount to the bride as a presentation when she leaves her natal house for her husband's place.

Marriage payments are invariably made in all regular cases. The word marriage payment is used to convey the transfer of goods to the bride's parents made by the bridegroom's side. This is called *voli labu*. Only such a payment makes the marriage legal and valid. In case a woman elopes with another person or a widow remarries, the *kulum marangi* of the former husband demands a marriage compensation which is called *danda*. Though the presentation of *voli labu* is accepted by the parents and the brothers of the bride, they should not take it and utilize payment for themselves. With this amount they are supposed to purchase an animal and liquor and give a feast to all of their members of the *kulum marangi*. The same is the case with regard to the *danda*. The celebration of the feast with this amount may be considered as an expression of the unity of the *kulum marangi* whose members actively participate in such a marriage and also in the collection of the *voli labu* or *danda*. Gluckman (1950) mentions that marriage payments bind the reproductive capacity to the perpetuation of the agnatic lineage and this is exactly the case among the Saoras.

An individual's basic needs are primarily met with at the level of the family only. The Saora family is corporate in its character. Further, through the dyadic relationships of the constituent members of a family, such corporate character is preserved. Every member of the family has certain privileges and duties over other members. Through exercising these privileges and duties, the family functions properly and thus achieves its integration into the society. A Saora child passes through different stages of life which are of ceremonial importance. People take great care in bringing up their children as they consider them to be the perpetuators of the *kulum marangi* unit. The Saora family is characterized by patrilineal descent, patrilocal residence, and patripotestal authority. The senior most male controls all the activities in the Saora society. These conditions are also clearly reflected in their kinship terminology. The kinship behaviour and jural authority have a profound impact on the kinship terminology of Saoras as is the case in some of the other Mundari speaking tribes and accordingly we find an overruling of the generation principle and terminological equation of the following sets of the relatives:

koein: younger brother's wife = daughter-in-law; *reyamyen*: younger sister's husband = son-in-law

The reasons for equating the two categories of relatives in terms of reference, or the resulting in the overruling of the generation principle from the point of view of the Saoras may be:

(i) Saora society is based on patriarchal authority and accordingly the jural authority is vested in the hands of the senior most male members. As long as one's father is alive in an extended family, he will be the controlling authority and also taking up the responsibilities of looking after the son and daughters. After his death, the jural authority and responsibility rests on the senior most brother in looking after his younger siblings. Even after the split of the extended family the same jural authority and responsibility continues to exist. Just because the roles of a father and a senior brother are one and the same and with the associated behavioural pattern the terms *koein* and *reyamyen* might have been applied to relatives belonging to two different generations.

(ii) In association with more responsibilities, the eldest male sibling is given a greater share (primogeniture) at the time of division of property.

(iii) The emphasis on the jural authority of a senior male is also quiet understandable from the lineage organization wherein we find an emphasis on seniority.

(iv) In view of the same responsibilities of a father or a senior brother, perhaps we do not find the practice of a person marrying his deceased younger brother's wife.

The lineage system of the Saoras is seen as the structural basis of the ritual organization and jural authority, while the domestic organization is found to be the basis of the organized person-to-person relationships to meet the needs of the individuals. Their kinship system as a whole reflects jural authority emanating from the lineage system and the kin obligations originating from the family. The articulation of their religious institution with their kinship system can be seen in the importance they attach to the worship of ancestral spirits. Such worship among the Saoras is always to be organized by the senior members of the lineage. Saoras have an elaborate pantheon of Gods and Goddesses. Ancestor worship is more predominant and widely practiced. The *buya* officiates all the rituals relating to the village, and *kudammar* (male)/*Kudam boi* (female) officiates the rituals relating to the lifecycle of an individual.

Endogamous and Exogamous Groups: Saora Sub-divisions

Saoras are endogamous and I have not come across any violation of this rule. As many as 23 endogamous groups were reported among them. The following is the list of the various sub-divisions among the Saoras as mentioned by the earlier scholars (Sitapati, 1938-43; Elwin, 1955):

Arsi Saora	Jara Saora	Luang (Luara) Saora	Tekkali Saora
Based Saora	Jati Saora	Male Saora	Tudum Saora
Bhimma Saora	Jurai Saora	Mara Saora	
Bobbili Saora	Kampu (Kapu) Saora	Moni Saora	
Dondiya Saora	Kimsed (Kindal) Saora	Muli Saora	
Gontora Saora	Kumbi Saora	Sarda Saora	
Jadu Saora	Lambo Lanja Saora	Sudda Saora	

The interesting feature we find is the principle on which the various sub-divisions among the Saoras are formed. For a few sub-divisions there is no information in the existing literature as to how these names have been formed, but for others the name itself indicates how the sub-division is derived. A few are formed on the principle of the main occupation such as: Kindal Saora (Basketry); Kumbi Saora (Pottery); Arsi Saora (Weaving); Luara Saora (Blacksmithy); Gantora Saora (Metal Workers).

A few sub-divisions of the Saoras are formed on the basis of the territory they inhabit: Bobbili Saora; Tekkali Saora, Based Saora (Saoras inhabiting coastal areas). A few others are formed on different other principles: Lambo Lanja (Toka) Saora who wear a loin cloth which hangs behind like a tail; Jati Saora Saoras of par excellence, Sudda Saora, Bhimma Saora and Kampu (Kapu) Saora are names referring to the more Hinduized groups.

An overall distinction is generally made among the Saoras as:

(a) The Saoras of the hills (who are popularly called as Pauri Saoras) as against, and
(b) The Saoras of the plains.

The former categories are studied in the present context. The various sub-divisions are not strictly endogamous. From their genealogies it is found that the Saoras are not strict about bringing spouses from the other sub-divisions. We also find a sort of social mobility among the Saoras as many of the hill Saoras are calling themselves as Kapu Saoras in the course of the present study, *i.e.* claiming a higher status among the different sub-divisions. Hence, for an investigator, it will be a rather painstaking job to identify exactly to which sub-division they belong. Elwin (1955) also says that the distinctions between the sub-divisions are vague.

Status Groups and Martial Relations

One important feature about the institution of marriage among Saoras was that certain persons with status in the society should select their spouses from similar status groups. For example, a *gamong* or a *buya* were expected to marry the daughter of another *gamong* or *buya* respectively of another village but within the same sub-division. But a *gamong* or *buya* could also marry the daughter of a *buya* or *parja.* On the other hand, a *parja* would not be allowed to marry the daughter of a *gamong* or a *buya*. This corresponds to the hypergamous marriages of caste Hindus. However, this rule is not being strictly adhered to at present.

Exogamous Units

Unlike many other Mundari speaking tribes, unilineal descent groups like clans and septs are absent among Saoras. The *kulam marangi* unit, *i.e.* the lineage is the principal exogamous unit controlling marriage. It is the pivot of the social organization of the Saoras. Besides being primarily an exogamous unit, it is also a corporate unit. Saoras refer their lineage members as *kulam marangi.* There is no term to refer to a Saora lineage as such. The *kulam marangi* represent the group of lineal descendants. There is male emphasis in the designation of the term. *Kulam* literally means lineal descent and *marangi* refers to a group of male members. It is because women members go out of the lineage after marriage due to lineage exogamy and thus leaving only male members to become active participants in lineage activities, although it actually consists of all the agnatic descendants, both male and female.

It seems, that the earlier scholars have overlooked the existence of the lineage among the Saoras. Ramamurthy (1931), however, mentioned the word *kulam marangi*, but did not talk about its composition and function; perhaps he was primarily concerned with the analysis of the Saora language. It did not catch the attention of either Sitapati (1938-43) who was more interested in giving an ethnographic account of the Saoras nor of Elwin (1955) who completely overlooked Saora social structure and its relation to religion.

It is in fact in the religious life of the Saoras, one finds the existence of the Saora lineages.

In Saora society lineage is primarily defined by the canon of agnatic descent. All the *kulam marangi* can trace their genealogical relationship from one another. Though all the agnatic descendants both male and female of the founder ancestor belong to the lineage group, in actual conduct of lineage affairs, the male members have the dominant role and the *de facto* corporate unit is the group of the male members. This can clearly be noticed in the word associated with the members of the lineage group—*kulam marangi*.

A Saora lineage is not only an agnatic genealogical unit; it is also an *ipso facto* ritual unit. The importance of the lineage is emphasized through the ancestral worship, which is made effective by the elaborate death rites. The *kulam marangi* have to erect menhirs in honour of the dead ancestors at one place in accordance with the age, to be followed by buffalo sacrifices. In various other rituals, associated with life crises and harvest festivals, the lineage is a major source for integration. In marriage by negotiation *kulam marangi* have a role to play at different phases of marriage, and in other forms also their participation is necessary. In the economic and political spheres the *kulam marangi* have a respectable role to play.

The basic identification of an individual in the absence of clans is with the lineage. Though there is no specific name for a lineage group the members are called as *kulam marangi* and the non-*kulam marangi* relatives are referred to as *somandi mar* (male) and *somandi boi* (female) respectively. This distinction helps to some extent in identifying the different lineages and also helps in knowing whom one can marry. With whom one can marry are referred to as *somandi mar* and *somandi boi.* The organization of the lineage is not only confined to intra-village level but also to the inter-village level especially when a lineage is dispersed in different villages. In short, lineage is the 'pivot' in many affairs of the Saora social structure. In the absence of clans, lineage shoulders many of their responsibilities.

The simple family forms the basic unit for the lineage which is expanded through various segments over a few generations and includes the agnates within the village as well as those from outside. The dispersion of the lineage members to different villages leads to its inter-village organization. The various members of the lineage often meet together in times of crisis situations. The solidarity of the lineage group is unique. Thus the genealogical kinship ties of the *kulam marangi* of different villages through a common ancestor unite them for sharing of sorrows and pleasures equally.

Saora lineages seem to be originally localized. This can be seen by the interpretations given by the earlier ethnographers about the village exogamy. Sitapati (1938-43) reported the practice of village exogamy among Saoras. Writing about the village and exogamy he states that 'there is no trace of totem or sept or barga or any other group of exogamous nature except the village. The general rule relating to exogamy is, therefore, with reference to the village community. Elwin (1955) writes that "neither the village nor the quarter is an exogamous unit. There is no territorial exogamy among the Saoras. There may once have been". Fawcett, writing in 1888, says a Saora may marry a woman of his own village or of any other village. Razeq (1966) also did not observe village exogamy among Saoras. Out of 439 marital unions recorded in the present study 205 (46.69 per cent) marriages have taken place within the village. This shows that the village is not an exogamous unit. Probably Sitapati might have wrongly interpreted the practice of village exogamy. It can be presumed from his writings and also from the continued habit of the agnatic kin living in a single village or in near by hamlets, this might have made him to mention the practice of village exogamy.

Sitapati (1938-43) at a later stage writes that "the man and woman of the same village should not inter-marry because according to the conception of the Saoras they stand in the relation of brother and sister. In every village the tradition goes to say that this rule was strictly observed in the past...". But I have noted several instances where this rule is violated. A young man of Bontelda said he had married a girl of the same village and explained that he had been permitted to do so because, the girl's parents came from another village and settled there in recent times, within the memory of the elders of the villages. But in reality the Saoras have been observing lineage exogamy only. From the above observations of Sitapati, we can conclude that Saora villages in course of time became multi-lineage settlements, thus facilitating marriage within the settlement and outside the lineage.

This fact can further be substantiated by the practice that lineage members from one village go to that village from where they have migrated to participate in *guar* ceremony, which is performed in honour of the dead. All such lineages that go out of a village for such participations may be considered as immigrant lineages.

In some areas due to the influence of Dravidian language speaking tribes and castes, *i.e.* the Jatapus as well as various Telugu castes, the Saoras began to name their lineages especially on the pattern of the Jatapus. Though by tradition Saoras have no name for lineage or to designate a lineage group, the Saoras of the Bhadragiri area under study have adopted the clan names of the neighbouring tribe Jatapu to identify their lineage groups. Some of the Jatapu clan names found among Saoras are: Nimmala, Toika, Biddiki, Pattika, Kadraka, Mandangi, Mootaka, Yapparaka and Arakollu which are characterized by exogamy. Stray instances of marrying within the named lineage groups are recorded which may be because the adoption has not yet been fully integrated with exogamy. In Malluguda Toika Lakkai eloped with Toika Sukki of Jammu. The villagers say that the two did not belong to the same designation "Tokia". The argument was strengthened, because people in these two Saora villages adopted the same clan name—tokia (of the Jatapu caste) independently. But in Seethampeta and Mandasa areas, no such change has taken place in the Saora *kulam marangi* unit. Since the units there do not bear any names in these areas, a person is referred just as Saora Lakki, Saora Addai and the like.

Fission of Lineages

When a lineage is established first at a new place by the dispersion of a group of agnatic kin of one village in search of livelihood, they assume rights over all the areas suitable for cultivation under the guidance of the senior member of the group that come over to the place to settle. The later immigrants will have rights over the areas left by the original settlers. Thus a lineage among Saoras becomes corporate as in course of time, the rights over the land are passed on to descendants of the original settlers. Only after two or three generations they sever their links with the core and establish their new lineage which is marked with the independent erection of menhirs at their new place.

Identification of Lineage

In Saora villages the different lineages present can be identified by enquiring where each lineage erects its menhirs. It is customary among Saora lineages to erect their menhirs separately. Those who migrated to a new place invariably come to the place where they traditionally erect menhirs. Whenever *guar* is performed for the erection of menhirs to the dead, all the *kulam marangi* are informed well in advance to make necessary arrangements for participating in the *guar* ceremony. In the course of time as and when the members of a lineage migrate to another village and when the members of a lineage grow sufficiently, they start erecting menhirs in their own village with a ritual sanctification and a severing of the ties with their parental lineage, thus resulting the fission of a lineage.

Segmented Lineage System

The Saora lineage is poly-segmentary and is divisible into three segments, *i.e.* maximal lineage, major segment and minimal lineage. The maximal lineage generally covers five to six generations depth and stands at a higher level. Within the maximal lineage there are two segments—major segment and minimal lineage. The domestic group forms the basis for the lineage organization and it has generally two to three generations' depth and it can be identified as minimal lineage. More than one such minimal lineage constitutes the major segment, which stands in an intermediary position between minimal lineage and maximal lineage. More than one major segment constitutes the maximal lineage. The segmentation of lineages can clearly be conceived in various situations and mainly in ritual interactions. The lineage and its segments are always seen functioning as a combination of segments but not as mere collections of individuals linked through common descent. The distinction discussed above are not made by the Saoras but can be perceived in their various socio-religious interactions.

The minimal lineages are seen in operation in various contexts in routine life and rituals performed at domestic group level. A minimal lineage is basically a food producing and consumption unit among Saoras. The major segment comes into action in certain contexts of economic life where co-operation is required among the members of the unit. Certain categories of rituals, which do not require the presence of all the *kulam marangi*, also operate at a higher level than the minimal lineage, *i.e.* the major segment. In the majority of the cases the minimal lineages and major segments function within the boundary of a village. In actual life, the different agnates belonging to the major segment live in the same village. A major segment is mainly a cooperative unit. The maximal lineage may be associated exclusively to a village or as in a number of instances may spread over to nearby villages. The *kulam marangi* of the maximal lineage are united through various socio-religious activities which cover the whole lineage. Most important of the activities being, the rites associated with the ancestors, and life cycle ceremonies.

The various deities and ancestors always keep in touch the Saoras through the *shaman* or in dreams and express their feelings and desires and control the activities of the living. The Saoras believe that the dead are to be properly attended to and accordingly various ceremonies are to be performed in order to satisfy the dead, lest they may turn into hungry ghosts or malevolent spirits wandering in the mundane world in search of food and causing harm first to the immediate kin and later to the entire *kulam marangi*.

The Saoras strongly believe that the living depend upon the ancestral spirits. They consider that these spirits are powerful and are capable of doing good as well as harm in accordance with the treatment given to them. They also guide the agricultural operations of the descendants; bestow their blessings and sanctify the seeds they broadcast. Thus the Saora religious structure and the social structure are intimately related. It is very important to note that in the religious sphere Saoras have a good number of practitioners and specialists who play a vital role in the religious organization of the society.

Turner (1967), while reviewing Saora religious data writes, "it is primarily in ritual that discrepancies between structural principles are overlaid or feigned not to exist. One way in which the Saora do this is by ritualizing each crucial principle in isolation from others. Thus we find period rituals each of which celebrates the importance of a different principle of grouping. These rituals are performed at different periods in the annual cycle. Each of them asserts the par amounting of a particular principle of grouping in connection with a specific set of activities and motivations".

The various ceremonies pertaining to the life cycle and a few others are mostly based on the segmented kinship groupings starting from that of minimal lineage level passing through major segment level and ending at maximal lineage level. The principle of grouping that is in operation varies from ritual to ritual depending on the nature of the ritual. The interactions of the people at various levels bring them closer and bind them together at the times of distress as well at the time of pleasure, thereby helping for the integration of these people at various levels (*see* Table 9.1 and Table 9.2).

The rituals that operate at the minimal lineage level are confined to the domestic family level participation, whereas the rituals that operate at the major segment involve the agnatic kinsmen living in a village. A maximal lineage comes into operation mainly in the context of an entire lineage involving the interaction of agnatic kinsmen living in different villages. The whole village acts as an integrative unit mainly at the time of celebrating the harvest festivals because it is relevant for everybody. There, the *buya*, generally presides over the religious rites and festivals. Turner (1967) rightly interpreted in this connection: "In harvest festivals, presided over by the *buya* priests, the principle of unity of the village is stressed over and above its internal divisions. The emphasis here is one of the maintenance of the social order, not as in curative ritual, on its re-establishment after breaches have occurred". In the absence of any ritual embracing the whole sub-division of this tribe—or the whole tribe itself—the village plays a major role in the maintenance of social order; correspondingly we do not find any over all

Table 9.1: Rituals at Different Levels of Lineage

Name of the Ceremony/Festival	*Type of Religious ceremony*	*Level of participation of the **kulam marangi***	
Kanniboipur (Ceremony for a healthy child)	Lifecycle	Minimal	Lineage
Aje ban (a purification ceremony after delivery)	,,	,,	,,
Asandae boung/abbungyo pur/kannipur (a ceremony to take the child outside the house)	,,	,,	,,
Akottalayan (ceremony to protect a child against malevolent diety-*Akottasum*)	,,	,,	,,
Kaduenyopur (Ceremony to protect the child from epilepsy)	,,	,,	,,
Agottal kadaenyo pur (Ceremony to protect the child from fever)	,,	,,	,,
Adolging pur (Ceremony to protect the child from fever)	,,	,,	,,
Asiyaranyo pur (Ceremony to protect the child from cough)	,,	,,	,,
Ajerejanyodan pur (Ceremony to recover from ill-health)	,,	,,	,,
Aduboi pur (Ceremony to recover from ill-health)	,,	,,	,,
Lijap (Ceremony connected with the dead)	,,	,,	,,
Kittung pur (Ceremony for children to prevent infantile mortality)	,,	,,	,,
Moyun pur (Ceremony to make the delivery easy)	,,	,,	,,

Contd...

Name of the Ceremony/Festival	*Type of Religious ceremony*	*Level of participation of the* ***kulam marangi***	
Lolopur (Ceremony performed before hoeing the barun)	Economic*	Minimal	Lineage
Udanadur (Ceremony for the first use of mangoes in the season)	"	"	"
Buroinadur (Ceremony for the first use of a variety of millet in the season)	"	"	"
Varadapasam (Rain producing ceremony)	"	"	"
Gamtada (Rain producing ceremony)	"	"	"
Abbanadur (Ceremony for the first use of mahwa flowers in the season)	"	"	
Tankunadur (Ceremony for the first use of mango seeds in the season)	"	"	
Usanadur (Ceremony for the first use of pot herbs in the season)	"	"	"
Kondemnadur (Ceremony for the first use of a variety of paddy-kondem in the season)	"	"	"
Kuroinadur (Ceremony for the first use of a variety of millet in the season)	"	"	"
Kamburnadur (Ceremony for the first use of a variety of millet in the season)	"	"	"
Gelwal (Ceremony before weeding in the season)	"	"	"
Rogonadur (Ceremony for the first use of a variety of pulse in the season)	"	"	"

Contd...

Name of the Ceremony/Festival	*Type of Religious ceremony*	*Level of participation of the **kulam marangi***	
Kurtari tung pur/ sandinyopur/Ajolaemae (Ceremony to save mother in difficult delivery)	Life-cycle	Major	segment
Kum kum bob pur (Tonsure Ceremony)	"	"	"
Solapur (Ceremony to sanctify weapons and agricultural implements)	Economic		
Jammolpur (Seed sanctification ceremony)	"	"	"
Puberty ceremony	Life-cycle	Maximal	Lineage
Marriage (*sirrung*) ceremony	"	"	"
Kuddipuram (Name giving ceremony)	Life-cycle	Maximal	Lineage
Jamnae juran (Purification ceremony after death)	"	"	"
Limma (Ceremony connected with the dead)	"	"	"
Sikunda (Ceremony connected with the dead)	"	"	"
Guar (Ceremony connected with the dead and for erection of menhirs)	"	"	"
Karja (Ceremony connected with the dead)	"	"	"

*Most of the ceremonies and festivals mentioned under 'economic' are also performed at the village level where *buya* officiate.

Table 9.2: Religious Practitioners and Specialists, their Duties in Relation to Different Levels of the Lineage

Sl. No.	*Type of Religious Practitioners and Specialists*	*Important Duties*	*Level of Participation*
1.	*Buya*	Religious head of a village, major role in marriage ceremonies and harvest festivals	Inter-lineage
2.	*Kudammar/ Kudamboi*	Diviner, decease detector, medicine man and attending routine rituals	—
(A)	*Raudakumbmaran/ Raudakumboi*	Qualified to perform great rituals like, Jammolpur. Never assists in funeral	Minimal Lineage and Major segment
(B)	*Guarkummaran/ Guarkumboi*	Mainly confined to funeral rites —guar, karja etc.	Maximal-lineage
(C)	*Tonaimar/ Tonaiboi*	To perform Tonaipur (Sorcerey rites)	Inter-lineage
(D)	*Regamaran/Ragaboi*	Medicine man	" "
(E)	*Idaimaran / Idaiboi*	To attend funerary rites like Lijap, cannot sacrifice a buffalo and routine domestic rituals	Minimal lineage
3.	*Siggamaran*	Cremation of corpse and performing other duties at the funeral	Minimal lineage
4.	*Ittalmaran*	To draw ikons	Inter-lineage
5.	*Desari*	Person who prescribes auspicious days	" "

*Details do not correspond to Elwin (1955) due to regional variation.

political authority based at the above levels. With this background, let me discuss the interaction of kinsmen at the time of death and ancestor worship, which plays an important role in Saora life.

Death and Ancestor Worship

Death results in the loss of a living member to the *kulam marangi* unit. The dead has to be properly admitted into the ancestral world by observing various rites and he or she has to be worshipped from time to time. Hence death ceremonies are observed very strictly and are performed elaborately among Saoras. Death is informed to all the *kulam marangi* of the other villages by a messenger. After all the *kulam marangi* gather, the corpse is given turmeric water bath. At the time of death water is poured into the mouth to open the doors and allow the souls to leave the body. The whole body is coated with oil and turmeric. Around the corpse grains are poured in a row and these grains are to be cooked by the *siggamaran* on the third day after the ashes are collected from the cremated place. The *siggamaran* carries fire. Grains are to be thrown behind the corpse throughout while carrying it to the cremation ground. The *siggamaran* sets fire to the corpse.

In many places, *gamong*, *buya* and *parja* each have their separate cremation ground. If a woman dies, she will be taken back to her parents' village and is cremated there. In case the village is at a long distance she can be cremated at her husband's village and the ashes and bones will be taken to her parent's village to perform further rites. At the time of cremation all the *kulam marangi* go to the cremation ground. After the corpse is completely burnt, the *kudammar* invokes all gods and ancestors and asks the cause for the death of the person. A fowl and liquor are offered to the deity or spirit who caused the death and he appeals the deity to be pleased with it and not to do further harm to anybody. Food is prepared by mixing *limma* (neem) leaves and after eating and drinking there; they return to their villages.

The purification ceremony falls on the seventh or twelfth day, which is called *jamanae puran.* All the *kulam marangi* contribute rice and money to this rite and cook in a new pot and a small portion of the cooked food will be taken to the cremation ground. A fowl is sacrificed there. A small portion of the food, brought by each male *kulammar*, will be placed there with the expression: "Here we have given you food and a fowl. So please don't do any harm to us". All of them take a bath and cook food and eat together. Then they return to the village after drinking liquor.

Limma is a rite celebrated generally on the third day, when the burial of ashes and bones will be done. As food on this day is to be cooked with *limma* leaves, the ceremony is called as *limma.* All *kulam marangi* in particular attend this. A miniature hut is constructed there in the cremation ground to make the soul rest protected. After this is done a fowl is sacrificed to the dead and food is cooked with *limma* leaves. Eating and drinking follows. The *sikunda* ceremony supercedes *limma* at irregular times and makes the *guar* and *karja* ceremonies to be postponed.

If a number of persons die in a *kulam marangi* unit this rite—*sikunda*—is celebrated collectively at a particular house. One day before the *kudammar*, followed by instrumental music, gather all souls of the dead in a pot by visiting the houses where death has taken place. A long thread and a ladder are placed over the pestle in the house and it touches the roof above and the thread is placed in the pot. They believe the soul enters the pot through the ladder. All the *kulam marangi* attend with rice and money for performing the rite. *Kudammar* invokes all the dead persons and ancestors to offer a buffalo to them. A small religious rite is also performed at the cremation ground where a buffalo is sacrificed.

The next elaborate and most expensive rite is *guar* where honorific sacrifices of buffaloes are made. The *guar* ceremony is more significant and prominent of all rites for the dead. *Guar* ritually means the erection of stones (*gu* = to plant, *ar* = a contraction of *arangen* = a stone). *Guar* is performed after a good harvest year. The souls of all the dead in the *kulam marangi* unit after the last *guar* ceremony are to be admitted to the underworld ceremonially with the performance of a *guar, i.e.* the *guar* is performed to enable the souls to rest permanently in an ancestral abode. It is generally believed that the soul will be hungry till *guar* is performed.

Each *kulam marangi* unit has its own group of menhirs just as each has its own cremation ground. They are generally outside the village under any tree. If more lineages erect menhirs under the same tree they, however, erect them distinctly. The height of the menhirs to be erected is not specified. It is a common practice to erect big stones for the elders and smaller ones to their juniors in honour of them.

As mentioned earlier, all the *kulam marangi* have to erect menhirs only at one place. The day of celebrating the *guar* is informed to all the *kulam marangi* well in advance. The seniors of the *kulam marangi* organize the proceedings. All the lineage members have to contribute for conducting the *guar*. After ceremonially invoking the dead, liquor is offered to the dead and at least one buffalo will be sacrificed in honour of each dead. Then they erect stones.

If there is a death(s) in his sister's house, it is obligatory on the part of a man to bring a buffalo, a goat, or a fowl and sacrifice it before his sister's house at the time of conducting a *guar* ceremony for the dead to express his solidarity. The dead man's friends *gadi mar* may also bring an animal each for sacrifice to boost up their friendship.

After the ceremonial erection of the menhirs, the *kulam marangi*, the participating affinal kin and guests have a feast and consume much liquor. The rest of the time is spent in dancing. Another common ceremony to be performed to the dead is *karja*. Generally to avoid expenses at a many places this is mixed along with *guar* and celebrated at a time. During this rite also slaughtering of buffaloes is a common feature.

Lijap is the last ceremony which is generally performed after the harvest to persuade the ancestors to give good crops in future. It is not a common rite for all the *kulam marangi* and is performed by individual families. The soul of a dead person is believed to cause harm until they perform all the above mentioned ceremonies.

As stated earlier, it is interesting to observe that among Saoras that the part played by the minimal lineage is great during the ceremonies concerned with the early stage of a person's life. As an individual grows, his interaction with wider kin unit of the *kulam marangi* is taken note of by the Saora society and accordingly we observe the participation of the wider kin unit in the later and final stages (*i.e.* in marriage and death) of the life of a person.

Conclusion

Elwin (1955) writes, "the most remarkable thing about the organization of the Saora society is its lack of organization". But in the present study, we find at the domestic level, the person-to-person relationships are being organized and maintained through dyadic relationships. The corporateness of the lineage is strengthened through the organized participation of the *kulam marangi* in various socio-economic and religious activities. As discussed earlier in this study, we find at the village level inter-lineage activities. With the clear-cut organization at all these levels and the organized functioning of the descent groups, it is difficult to agree with Elwin's statement about the organized life among the Saoras.

There are religious specialists to perform various religious practices in the Saora society. The occupational specialization of the various Saora religious specialists is as follows:

But for the *buya, siggamaran, ittalmaran* and *desari* for all other male religious specialists, there are female counterparts who either assist the male religious specialist or perform duties independently when required. A *guarkum boi* should not marry and should lead a life of celibacy.

REFERENCES

Sitapati, G.V. 1938-43. "Saoras and their Country," *Journal of the Andhra Historical Research Society.*

Elwin, V. 1955. *The Religion of an Indian Tribe.* London: Oxford University Press.

Ramamurthy, G.V. 1931. *A Manual for Saora Language*. Madras: Government of Madras,

Turner, V. W. 1967. "Aspects of Saora Ritual and Shamanism: An Approach to the Data of Ritual," In A.L. Epstein (ed.), *The Craft of Social Anthropology,* London: Tavistock

Razaeq, Khaja A. 1965. "Aspects of Saora Culture," *TheBulletin of the Anthropological Survey of India, Calcutta.*

Suryanarayana, M. 1977. Marriage, Family and Kinship of the Saoras of Andhra Pradesh, Unpublished Ph.D. thesis, Andhra University, Waltair.

Fawcett, F. 1888. "On the Saoras: An Aboriginal Hill People of the Eastern Ghats of the Madras Presidency," *Journal of the Anthropological Society,* Bombay.

Gluckman, M. 1950. "Marriage Payments and Social Structure among the Lozi and Zulu," In J. Goody (ed.), *Kinship.* Baltimore: Penguin.

TEN

THE NAGA SEGMENTARY SOCIAL SYSTEM

N.K. DAS

The main objective of this paper is to portray the structural foundation of a Naga tribe specifically as "a pyramid of social groups" ("a segmentary system"), which operates as a decentralized political system under its headmen/ Big Men. The paper intends to elucidate the jural and political manifestation of social structure by examining the principle of descent in the wider context of Naga kinship. In doing so it critically explores the jural functions of kinship in regulating rights and duties, and further examines the function of non-kinship institutions in decision-making and the multiple roles of headmen who emerge as key figures in establishing jural order in this acephalous society. The paper also discusses the devious non-kinship measures often employed by certain rich men/Big Men to boost political power in wider kinship sphere.

I

The data used in this paper were collected during 1980s from Viswema and adjoining villages, located in the Kohima district of Nagaland. The first visit to the village of Viswema was made in 1977 for two months. Prolonged fieldwork was conducted subsequently during 1988-89 in the same and adjoining villages. More than nine months' fieldwork was thus conducted during three visits amongst the Zounuo-Keyhonuo. The author spoke with the respondents in Nagamese, the local *lingua franca* understood by the majority of the Zounuo-Keyhonuo, even though a local elderly person was regularly employed to assist in interpretation and explanation of minute details of customary laws, kinship behaviour and practices. A short re-visit was made in 1990 to these villages to ascertain the nature of culture change. The data collected have been used in several publications, including a monograph *Kinship Politics and Law in Naga Society*, published by the Anthropological Survey of India in 1993. The 1990 visit had helped to update existing material and to gain fresh insights. An attempt is made here to reinterpret the data collected during these several visits to Nagaland.

II

What social anthropologists call structural analysis began with the study of lineage systems in societies where descent is the most important principle of grouping in political matters as well as the source of individual rights and liabilities. This type of analysis distinguishes the lineage structure from that of kinship. It was necessary to achieve such a level of abstraction to make the distinction between the domains of politics and kinship. The major advance in kinship theory since the Radcliffe-Brown era has been this analytical separation of the political and the domestic domain. The publication of *African Political Systems* (Fortes & Evans-Pritchard, 1940) and of the *Dynamics of Clanship among the Tallensi* (Fortes, 1945) for the first time established the political perspective in relation to social structure (Das, 1993: 6-7). Meyer Fortes, a noted Africanist, particularly regards the politico-jural aspect as complementary to familial aspect of kinship relations (Fortes, 1969: 73). Since some anthropologists have argued that corporate descent groups are only found in Africa, Jean La Fontaine however rejects the view that the descent model is non-applicable beyond Africa. She suggests that such vision will only destroy much of the unity of kinship theory (Hershman, 1981: 234 and Das, 1993: 145-46). The concept of "jural" employed in this paper is in line with the authoritative analysis of law in tribal society advanced by Hoebel (1954), Gluckman (1955) and Fortes (1969). The notion of politics implied here is that of "relations between or within large groups" (Fortes and Evans Pritchard, 1940: 5-7). Descent, for Fortes is fundamentally a jural concept and forms the connecting link between the external, that is political and legal aspect of unilineal descent groups, and the domestic aspect (1953; 1970: 84). The Marxist anthropologist Godelier (1973) moreover argued that kinship was not merely jural and or ideological in nature, but also formed an integral part of the relations of production.

III

Anthropologists use the category of tribe with two meanings: as a type of society and as a stage in social evolution (Godelier, 1974: 198-222). The latter was dropped till Sahlins (1969) and other neo-evolutionists re-defined tribe with same dual meaning (Das, 1993: 16) despite distrust, such as that by M. Fried, nurtured periodically about the utility of concept of tribe. For Service (1962) a tribe is defined evolutionarily and distinguished from a band or a mere association of nuclear families. By comparison, a tribe combines a much larger number of kinship segments, tied more firmly together than any band. According to Sahlins, the social organization of various levels is reflected in various gods or spirits who function at one or the other of these levels. At one evolutionary end of this decentralized social setup are the segmentary tribes proper, at the other are chiefdoms. The sociological categories of big man and chieftain are both seen among tribes (Sahlins, 1968: 21-25). Many economic types may also be found as the varied ecological adaptations of different kinds of tribes.

In India the category of tribe has not been developed as a conceptual category. The matter becomes puzzling when Indian scholars claim that a tribe is a tribe, because it is included in the administrative list of *Scheduled Tribes*. By contrast, my intention has been to portray the tribal social formation in the Naga Hills analytically in terms of a pyramidal genealogical superstructure. In doing so I will examine the segmentary system of interlocking descent groups which are of varying depth and spans and which ultimately shape the decentralized political system of the Zounuo-Keyhonuo people.

IV

The Nagas, scattered in Nagaland and adjacent parts of Manipur, Assam and Arunachal Pradesh and Myanmar, do not form one homogeneous tribe but rather a constellation of numerous tribes. Each Naga Tribe is in possession of its distinct territory in these states, where it enjoys all traditional rights over land, forest and water resources both at a collective level and in a private capacity. The fact remains that the tribes of no other state enjoy special protective measures and privileges to such an extent. At the same time the so-called *Inner Line Regulation*, operationalized since colonial days, till today continues to prohibit unauthorized entry of non-Nagas into Naga area.

The Nagas regard themselves as 'independent' and autochthonous people historically and ethnically. On the eve of Indian independence the Nagas had generally protested against their inclusion into the Indian Union and later they launched one of the most effective movements led by their English educated middle class leaders who had voiced apprehension on various forums. This construction of Naga ethnicity and the anxiety for its preservation continues to form the essence of the current appeal of Naga leaders negotiating with the Government of India.

All Nagas share a common core of cultural traditions and material traits, but unique customs, laws, dialects and other social institutions differentiate them from one another. Seventeen tribes in Nagaland and seven tribes in Manipur are notified as Naga *Scheduled Tribes*, but such ethnic categorization, a legacy of colonial constructions, does not match with the peoples' own ethno-cultural classification. The deconstruction of colonial categories and the recognition of ethnic self-perceptions of the Naga Tribes is the foremost prerequisite to gain a better insight of Naga history and culture. The popular labels such as Ao, Angami and Sema are names arbitrarily given by outsiders to various sections of Naga people. Even though the J.H. Hutton accepted the Tengima Nagas to be the true Angamis, he included as many as six tribes (Tengima, Chakroma, Chakrima, Dzono-kehono, Memi and Kezami) within the category Angami (Hutton, 1921, 1969). The Dzono-kehono now identify themselves as the Zounuo-Keyhonuo who form the subject of the present article. Remarkably these six tribes never formed an interactive network and, what is more, any one of these would interact more frequently with other tribes rather than those mentioned among the so-called Angami constellation. The possession of distinct hill ranges on part of these six tribes had furthermore generated the sharp differences of cultural usages and dialects. The people who identify themselves as "Zounuo-Keyhonuo" in all circumstances are usually called "Southern Angamis" in administrative parlance though the Zounuo-Keyhonuo resent this latter designation.

The Zounuo-Keyhonuo Naga territory forms an irregular plateau with elevated ridges and peaks in the Kohima district of Nagaland. The adjoining Japfu peak touches almost 3,050 M. The hill-streams are many hence it is possible for the tribe to pursue wet terrace cultivation along with shifting cultivation. Distributed in ten principal and several offshoot villages, these people are not only conscious of their tribal boundary, they conceive their tribe as a giant patri-clan descended from Zounuo and Keyhonuo, their twin apical ancestors. The Zounuo-Keyhonuo villages are located near the Japfu mountain hence these people call themselves also as Japfu Phiki. Their legend has it that Zounuo and his brother Keyhonuo had lived in Tengife and their sons Kigwe and Viswe had established the two most prominent villages of Kigwema and Viswema respectively. Here we shall deal with one of these villages, Viswema.

The ecological setting of the Zounuo-Keyhonuo country provides the foundation of their economic life. Villages located in the summits of hills are systematically drained and manured. Hence the succession of fine terraces of paddy where fields have been maintained for centuries by traditional skills and by, with the help of headmen, employing customary laws of kinship properly. The wet rice is planted first in a specially prepared seedbed where it is allowed to grow till the seedlings have reached the height of several inches. Early in the rainy season the seedlings are transplanted from these seedbeds to regular fields. The most laborious task now is to regulate the flow of water and to keep the dikes in repair. All the rivulets and the streams are well taped and led through long channels to flood the terraces. Though there is an adequate supply of land there are nevertheless disputes over claims and counter claims on land and water-channels. In those forest areas where the terrain is not suitable for the construction of terraces shifting cultivation is done by the villagers.

A village may be defined as a cluster of independent clans. It is through the clan organization that the village itself emerges as a structural unit. There are a large number of settlements today but all people recognize the ten original Zounuo-Keyhonuo villages. Viswema, the studied village, is the oldest village having been established by one of the ancestors of tribe.

V

Unlike villages in peninsular India, a Naga village is not a cohesive interacting entity. A Naga village may be defined as a cluster of independent clans anchored to their bounded and permanent territories, which date back for many generations. In the pre-colonial period the clan was a politically more significant unit. It was united for war and self-protection against any common enemy. Indeed, large and independent clans had acted as independent war-groups. The independent status of the clan within a village was not only acknowledged by its occupation of distinct forest and arable field areas, water resources, fishing areas, *dzulye* (water-channels) and the clan gate, but also in the ultimate jural and ritual unity of the clan and the capacity of its headmen to establish peace between hostile parties. Thus *clan endogamy* was the rule in the pre-colonial period of the Naga Hills mainly owing to the prevalence of inter-clan inter-village animosity, head-hunting and local warfare. In the post-colonial era however, *tribal endogamy* has become the rule, at least in theory if not in practice (Das, 1984, 1993: 62). The social groups of village such as *thevo-tepa*, *thenu*, *sarra* and *putsanu* are portrayed here as representing the level of moiety, clan, lineage and sub-lineage respectively. Portraying the localized *sarra*, the exogamous group, as lineage is based on the requirement of the structural analysis of the Naga data, the fuller outcome of which has been reported elsewhere (Das, 1985, 1989, 1993).

VI

Kinship has a wide range of application in the Zounuo-Keyhonuo Naga Society. A clear-cut segmentary principle is operative and relations between interlocking descent groups are envisaged in terms of a pyramidal genealogical superstructure. Descent emerges not only as a basic principle of social grouping, but also as source of individual and collective rights and liabilities. Based on the principle of descent there exists a definite continuity in the structural progression of jural relations from the domestic domain to the domains of lineage and clan. Lineages and clans are anchored to their fixed territories and thus the segmentary structure of social groups implies a segmentary structure of social space. Both the descent principle and the territorial principle contribute to the determination of the politico-jural field. Indeed in the absence of any political or governmental institution, the diffused political functions are observable in the interplay of the clan-lineage-sub-lineage structures, territorial structures and age-sets. In fact, in the absence of a distinct political authority, the lineage elders/headmen emerge as key figures in maintaining social control and jural order.

VII

In Viswema a clan varies from one group to another in terms of population size and territorial span. It maintains an integrated balance amongst component lineages. Both clan and lineage are constituted by the same patrilateral principle and their structural linkages are observable in the village genealogy. There are four clans in Viswema named Zherima, Rochuma, Kirhazuma and Pavoma, which are neatly distributed in distinct territories on the village landscape. The term *thenu* is used to denote both the social and territorial unit of the clan, hence we shall use the term *thenu*-district to describe the latter. In Viswema the Pavoma *thenu* is smallest in territorial span and population size (70 houses with 420 individuals) while the other three *thenu*-districts are comparatively large (Kirhazuma *thenu* with 154 houses and 986 individuals, Zherima *thenu* with 166 houses and 1128 individuals, and Rochuma *thenu* with 159 houses and 1119 individuals).

In the wider genealogical chart we discover that each segment is divisible into several segments which are themselves perceived and actually generated only through genealogically traceable segmentary processes until we come to the lowest level of kilokhro (family). Thus the Rochuma *thenu* of Viswema has nine *sarra* segments named as pusatso, rhutso, ichotso, theyonu, kuhotso, sothunu, kinnu, neikhatso and krahonu. Likewise, the Zherima *thenu*, as revealed in the Tribal Genealogical Chart, also consists of nine lineage groups and the Kirhazuma and Pavoma *thenu* consist of twelve and eight lineage segments respectively.

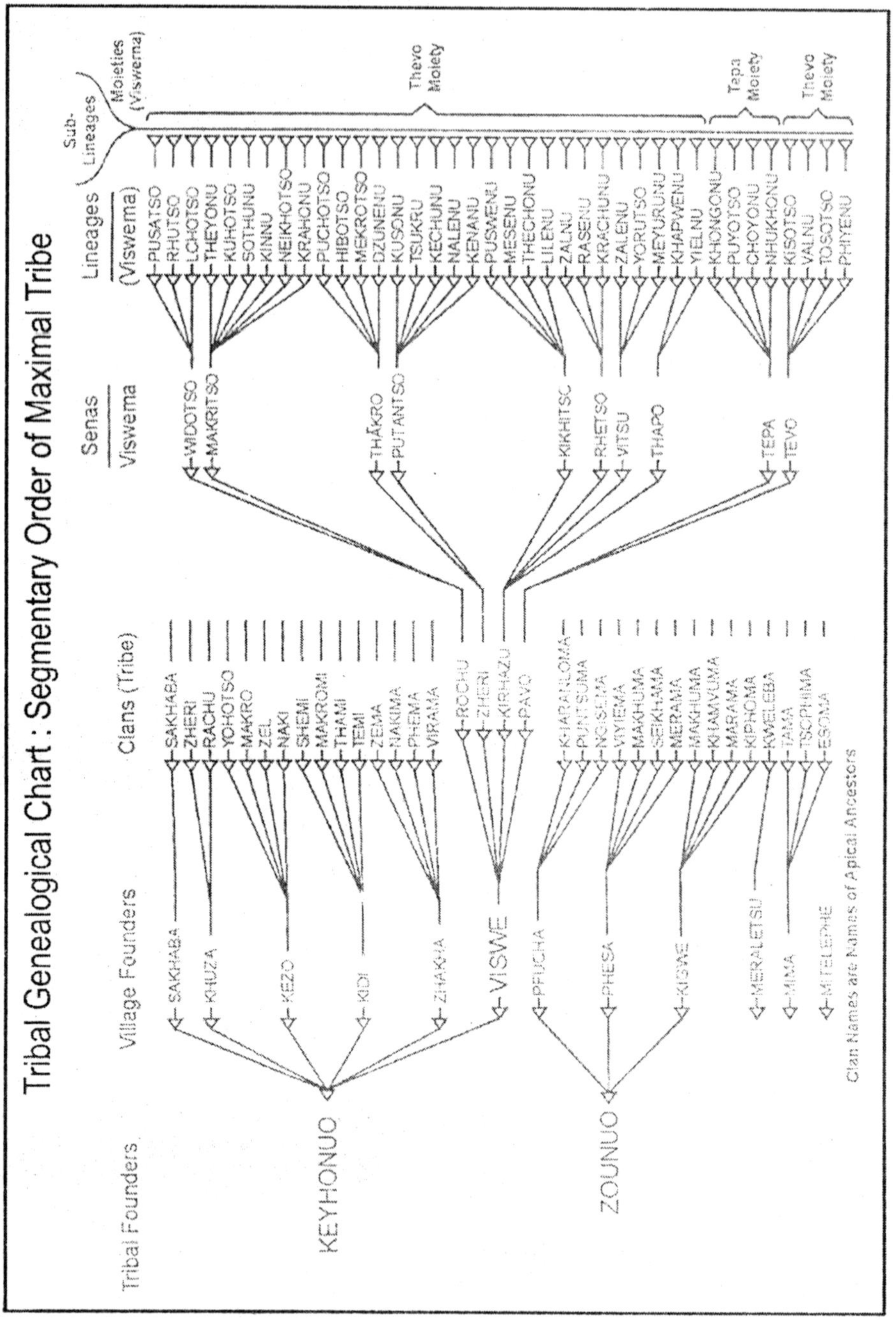

All the lineage or *sarra* units are named groups and in each *thenu* it is possible to trace genealogical links between the founders of different *sarra* groups and the founder of the clan. Within the *thenu* a strong feeling of solidarity binds all individuals because within the clan district all the important politico-jural and ritual interests and purposes are served. A clan acquires the jural cohesion on account of the balancing mechanisms derived through the social-territorial segmentary system, its 'ritual' unity and the age-set system.

A structural unit called as *khonsa-seba* or *sena* exists between the clan and the lineage. It is a multi-lineage segment with very limited forms of group action. The *sena* group solidarity is visible during the mourning period. At the event of the death of a *sena* member the whole *sena* group expresses its solidarity by observing *kenu* (taboo to work in the field or to visit the house of a non-*sena* person). The recognition of *sena* categories in village genealogy helps to trace the direction of actual segmentation leading to the constitution of several component lineages within the *thenu*. At the level of *thenu* we can thus observe that the internal constitution is neatly tied to a segmentary model both in terms of 'the nesting attribute of segmentary series' (Barnes. 1954: 49), and the characteristic of being in a state of continual segmentation internally. Segmentation as a process, however, affects only the inner constitution of the *sarra* since through segmentation a *sarra* merely divides in certain contexts and retains its collective identity in others.

The segmentary processes operating at *sarra* and *putsa-lokro* levels are important in the historical evolution and formation of *thenu* groups. The increase in population size of a cluster of localized sub-lineages, such as putsanu and lokro, over a longer period leads to the formation of a new lineage, but such a localized lineage is only distinguished from another by maintaining its place within its localized clan structure. Lineage segments thus exist only in terms of the *thenu* system.

VIII

The local group of *sarra*, the lineage, is the most extensive group of people belonging to either sex all of whom are related to one another by common patrilineal descent traced from a known founding ancestor through known agnatic antecedents. The exact agnatic relationship between all the members of a *sarra* can be ascertained by genealogical reckoning. A *sarra* is divided into a number of segments, which are more or less of the same structural form as the whole *sarra*. Each segment is identified by reference to its founding ancestor who marks the point on the genealogical tree of the whole lineage at which that segments' line of descent gets connected with the other lines of descent sprung from the founding ancestor of the lineage.

Thus, every lineage is divisible, in the first instance, into two or more *putsanu* segments. Each *putsanu* embraces all the agnatic descendants of one of the sons of the founder of the *sarra*. At the next level each *putsanu* is itself divisible into segments known as *lokro*. Each *lokro* embraces the agnatic descendants of one son of the founding ancestor of the *putsanu*. In some *sarra* there are segments which embrace descendants of one of the supposed sons (not real descendents) of a *sarra*. Such segments are potential parts of a *sarra*. The lowest order of segmentation, at the other end of the lineage scale to that represented by the *sarra*, is that of the *punumi*. This is the narrowest agnatic group to which a person can belong.

It is clear from the above description that every person belongs to a hierarchy of segments ranging from the minimal one to the maximal limits of her or his *sarra*. Different orders of segmentation become relevant for his conduct in different degrees and in accordance with variations in the social situation. As a farmer, for instance, his productive activities are mainly determined by his membership of his maximal lineage (*sarra*) which is also one of the factors limiting his choice of a bride; but the completion of the jural formalities is governed by his membership of the much wider segment of *thenu*.

At the same time a very important aspect of the lineage system is the fact that even when only a segment of a lineage emerges in any corporate activity the total politico-jural field of which it is part and which includes, at the maximal limit, the field of clanship, influences its status and functions.

A lineage segment emerges in action indeed only as a relatively autonomous unit, but it always functions as a combination of segments, not as a collection of individuals sharing common descent. Every lineage in fact represents a dynamic equilibrium of mutually balancing segments. The ultimate pattern that emerges is that the segments of a lineage trace their descent from the sons of their common founding ancestor. In consequence, after induction of several generations, co-ordinate segments of a lineage are referred to as 'brother-lineages', and their reciprocal rights and obligations as well as the conventional patterns of sentiments holding between them, are regulated and shaped in terms of the mutual relations of brothers. The *sarra* indeed do not have a stereotyped structure and growth. Thus, the Pusa lineage of Rochuma clan consists of only one putsanu, Hocho-putsanu, two lokro groups—Kamu lokro and Vabio lokro—and several sub-lineages. On the other hand the Kikhitso lineage of Kirhazuma clan consists of as many as five pustanu segments, twelve lokro segments and over thirty punumi groups (Das, 1993: 110).

The rhetso lineage of the Kirhazuma clan presents a somewhat unique structural pattern. It consists of two distinct social groups, A or Yedu as well as Zhokhri lokro and B or Krachunuo lokro. The exact genealogical relationship between A and B is not traceable but they form one sarra and marriage alliance between these two segments is prohibited. The heavy number of deaths among male members in every generation had resulted in an unusually small number of sub-lineage segments both in the A and in the B group. It is further observed that these two groups of A and B are aware of having their separate kayie estates. Theoretically then we could speak of these two groups as almost autonomous corporate groups who are soon to become two different lineages.

The Kschuno *sarra* of the Zherina clan shows yet another pattern of lineage formation. It has three putsanu segments, seven lokro segments and as many as ten punumi segments. While the three pustanu segments (Heviru, Lopongol and Hoswen), six lokro segments and eight punumi segments form the major section of the lineage, there is one additional segment of Tamo-lokro formed by the cognates, who have now been completely absorbed in the Kechunuo lineage. Another significant aspect of Kechuno lineage is that along with Tsukru lineage of the same clan it forms "a single exogamous group". No marriage union between members of these two lineages could take place.

In most cases it is found that no single lineage consists in its genealogical chart for more than seven or eight generations. Beyond seven generations we find that the former lineage has segmented into two distinct ones who have then become separate exogamous groupings allowing intermarriage between them. An old Viswema villager thus rightly stated that "we marry in our own sarra". The different patterns that emerge in the formation of lineage segments have structural links with the processes of segmentation and unification. Thus all the lineages do not tend to have a stereotyped structure and development. There are considerable variations in the growth and constitution of different lineages. While at one level there exists a hiatus in reckoning the exact genealogical connections between different segments of some lineages, in some other cases, two separate lineages form a single exogamous unit as discussed above.

In fact, we witness three distinct types of lineages in terms of their internal constitution, development and the exogamic rule. The first is that lineage in which its genealogically traceable sub-lineages are the basis of its existence.

This is the commonest type. The second is the lineage of which distinct segments are no longer able to trace their connecting relationships back "to the founder and the third is the exogamous unit" of two closely associated lineages who have made it a point not to inter-marry as a strict rule.

In the past a certain geographical mobility of a descent unit, though extremely limited, also took place to solve the problem of unusual growth of kinsmen in one locality. Thus a few kinsmen of Zherima *thenu* in the past settled in a new territory which later came to be known as Khuzama village, the literal meaning of *khuzama* being "those pushed away". The role of exogamy remains in force among close agnates of these two villages who still trace their common genealogical relationships. The solidarity between *Viswema* and *Khuzama* villagers is also expressed through the common observance of birth and death taboos which are applicable to agnates through *seba* relationship, as described earlier. But in practice the *Viswema* and *Khuzama* villagers do not have any corporate and effective relations since they are territorially dispersed.

The Zounuo-Keyhonuo *see* religious observances as the supreme safeguard for the basic needs of their existence, such as land, cattle, rain and health. Though all lineages are equal to each other in the village a certain ritual hierarchy is maintained. Thus, the lineages of Zaphu, Kiso, and Phiye (all belong to Tepa moiety) of the Pavoma clan are regarded as the most significant lineages of the village. They regard themselves as "brother-lineages" and hence no marital alliance can be established between their members (Das, 1993: 149). Kemovo from Zaphu lineage and Kiso-pithimi are regarded as chief religious specialists.

Within each clan-district, every segment of component lineages is anchored to a local sub-division of the clan-settlement. Each lineage thus has its members living in one particular locality, called as *sarra-zhu* and none of its members is dispersed to other localities. Again, within a specified territory of a lineage different sub-lineage segments have their distinct residential areas, a series of *compounds*, which given the present growth rate of population, are slowly loosing their distinct territorial identities. The smallest of such compounds within a lineage is that occupied by a single punumi segment. It is referred to as *punumi-zhu*, (the local term *zhu* means a settlement of kinsfolk). Several *punumi-zhus* are component territorial segments of a lineage territory. Since the Viswema people have adopted many non-kinsmen as their sons, it is customary on part of the former to help such 'outsiders' by giving arable land as well as residential areas in their respective *punumi-zhu*. The dwelling area of any person is thus known to any other person from any distant group. This is mainly possible on account of the neat segmentation of social groups and their localities which are simultaneously perceived in terms of genealogical linkages and socio-territorial segments.

In Zounuo-Keyhonuo society each individual's social status is determined and influenced by the facts of birth, adoption and marriage and jural claims of such an individual is linked with intra-family reciprocal jural obligations and laws of property and the rules incorporating inheritance and succession. Though there are sufficient plots of land and enough sources of water to irrigate terrace fields in Viswema, a number of disputes nevertheless keep arising on account of the claims and counter-claims of land as well as water channels in Viswema (Das, 1993: 82-83).

This village is self-sufficient economically as people get adequate produce by depending on both *pani-kheti* (wet terrace rice cultivation) and *jhum-kheti* (shifting cultivation). The terrain of the hills does not offer enough scope for a large scale conversion to terrace fields hence the Viswema villagers eke out their food supply by growing potatoes in *jhum* or shifting fields. Great efforts are required to develop and maintain terraces. They either have some natural source of water supply (*i.e.* streams) or man-made irrigational water channels—*dzuye*. The water flows down from the upper terrace to the one below and a complicated system of water rights governs its distribution. The fields close to the water sources and at the upper part of hills are always sought after and sold at high prices. Water is thus a valuable property. Channels used to draw water and streams become the subjects of all sorts of rights, of purchase and inheritance. Indeed water in Viswema is a cause of many disputes. In questions involving water, water channels, streams and claims over *kayie*, the agnates, siblings and neighbours often tend to be rivals.

The lineage estate of *kayie* is established through shares received from childless male agnates on their death. The *kayie* estate derives its jural individuality through its vital link with a descent group and not through links between individuals. The distribution of *kayie* land for use (generally among poor families) is done by lineage elders. Even married female agnates and their children (cognates) under certain conditions enjoy the right to use such *kayie* property (Das, 1993). An adopted son, as long as he lives in the compound of his adopter, also has such a right.

IX

The lineages provide the conceptual framework of the political system within which they also function as its organizing principle in relation to the wider tribal structure. The identification of *sarra* segments in the political context is brought about by the acknowledgement that the lineages emerge as corporate groups. In defending their social and economic interests they behave and act as one jural personality, one body. The term corporate has been restricted to be used for those kin groups within which property, in the shape of either land or wealth, is transmitted (Goody, 1990: 70). As a member of a *sarra* group indeed one's claim is not limited only to land that one's father had actually cultivated but also to that part of the land or the forest that belongs to the lineage. Depending on the individual need, each *sarra* member enjoys the right to make direct use of such common *kayie* property.

In Zounuo-Keyhonuo society clearcut economic rights and jural liabilities exist in unison with descent principles and kinship rules, but different interests of members of separate segments often lead to conflicting individual claims based on certain customary allegiances though they are ultimately restrained through other allegiances enjoined on them by custom.

It is observed that at the level of lineage the management of the corporate *kayie* estate and particularly the allocations of *kayie* arable land and forest areas are not always made according to jural rules and the genuine needs of agnatic members. Prominent headmen and rich individuals always articulate their demands and priorities by influencing some obliging kinsfolk. Some actors even redefine the lineage pedigree and capitalize on the support base gained through allies (obliging kinsfolk) *vis-à-vis* rivals (or other agnates) and thereby make strategic choices with support of their allies. As yet another example of such decisions we may cite here the strategic initiatives made by wealthy individuals in adopting poor kinsfolk or even non-Zounuo-Keyhonuo young men. Such newly introduced members are for all practical purposes considered as the children of the man who patronizes them. They are encouraged to develop arable lands and increase other economic resources in order to maximize the profits of the patron. These actions also help to increase the base of the *khrohi* (labour pool) formed at the sub-lineage and lineage levels during collective endeavours. The *khrohis* are often employed by manipulating the situations to serve the economic interests of the rich. The *punumi-zhu* of Vinol was one such segment which had several adopted children and hence a strong base of the *khrohi* which also included friends.

The incorporation of outsiders as children of smaller descent groups and family units is ultimately directed towards maximization of the pre-existing economic base. The incorporated outsiders indeed protect and expand the private estate and other sources of income of their patrons. The latter use part of such profits indeed for giving feasts to the villagers in order to expand the prestige base even further by acquiring the rank of Zhodimi. Attempts made by actors to vie for giving feasts in order to achieve the status of Zhodimi may be seen as the struggle for political power. Barth has described the phenomenon of such individual efforts as adaptive strategy. He tried to understand the Pathan social structure through the concept of strategic choices as expressed by the Pathans through the idiom of descent (1959a, 1959b, 1966). We therefore witness that the individual actor, through his strategic choices and manipulations of pre-existing descent links, emerges as an equally great factor in the Zounuo-Keyhonuo social system by establishing positions of leadership. This example is identical with what Barth called "political prestations of submission" from followers (Barth, 1966).

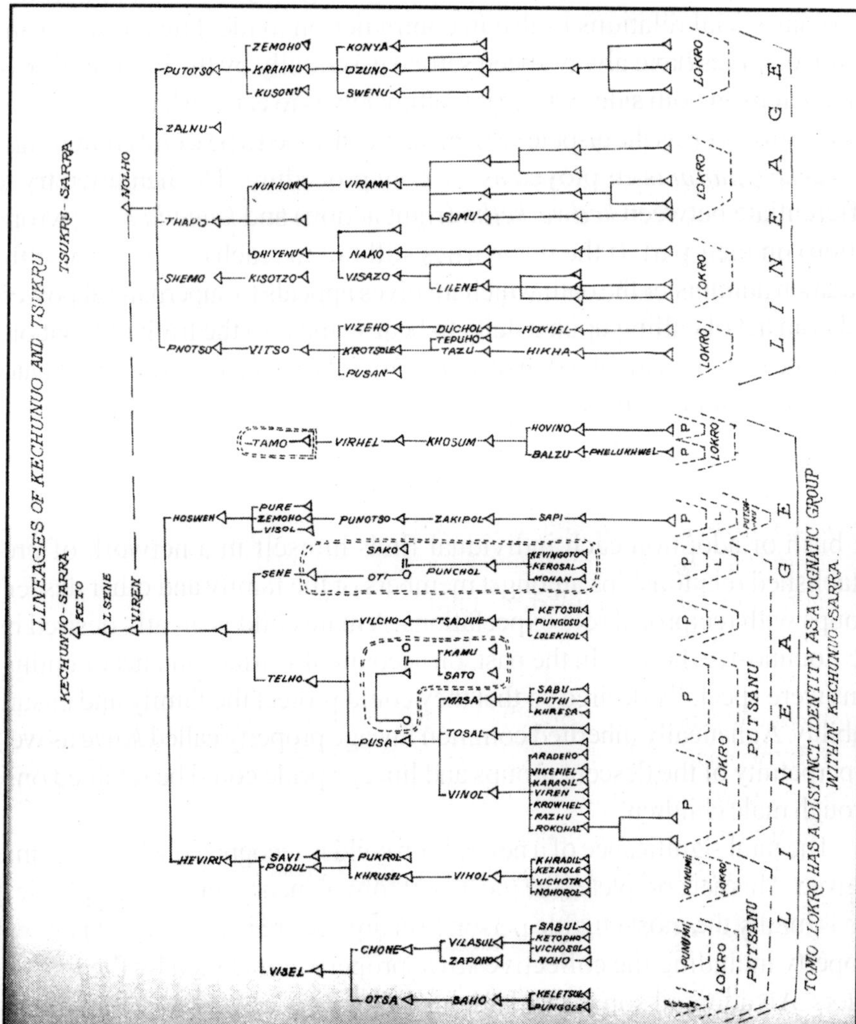

X

Every person in Zounuo-Keyhonuo society belongs to a hierarchy of descent groups lying between the limits of punumi and putsanu in his lineage and such varied orders of segmentation become relevant for his conduct in different degrees. A lineage which functions as a combination of segments, represents a dynamic equilibrium of mutually balancing segments. There are instances however when such sub-lineage segments, in the non-ritual sphere, assert their independent economic statuses and hostilities between them lead to open conflict. Elsewhere this author has elucidated actual cases of such hostilities and disputes (Das, 1985; 1993: 108-109).

Since a prolonged and widespread fighting may lead to disruption of everyday social relations is also in contradiction to ideal ties of *sarra* and *thenu*, disputes have always been settled essentially by the intervention of headmen from both sides whose job ultimately is to establish peace through discussion. As far as the dispute settlement is concerned a peaceful compromise or *kezekevizhonu* is employed as the core procedure. The headmen try to differentiate between *kedwe-ketho* (right action) and *kemeda dwe* (wrong action) on their part. If the two parties still fail to reach a compromise the headmen administer the oath which involves appeals to supernatural powers and is an act of calling upon a deity to bear witness to the truth of what one says. The headman involved in dispute settlement is an informal adjudicator who acts as a go-between.

XI

At birth or adoption each individual finds himself in a network of pre-established relationships amongst members of the family and other descent groups with reciprocal role expectations. A male child is greatly desired by the Zounuo-Keyhonuo. In the past, on account of warfare and headhunting, sons were specially desired so that they could protect the family and ensure stability. Agnatically inherited common lineage property called *kayie* as well as perpetuity of the descent groups and lineage pride could be retained only through male children.

The jural significance of a newly born child is recognized when the name is given. This act completes the process of formal incorporation. The physical son is jurally the most eligible person to claim a share in all kinds of paternal property including the collective *kayie* property controlled by the lineage elders. An adopted son is easily deprived of his jural claims to adopter's property as soon as he leaves the compound of his adoptive parents. The mere idea of the extinction of the lineage is utterly abhorrent to the Zounuo-Keyhonuo mind.

It is by the act of marriage, on the other hand, that the other set of rules come into force whereby women are transferred and recruited into new households. Of course tribal endogamy has become a strong preference nowadays among Naga Tribes. Village endogamy was always the rule and a dominant norm particularly in pre-British era mainly owing to the strong antagonism between villages. Thus, a Naga village remained largely a closed group often even further divided within itself due to inter-clan rivalry.

The bridewealth amongst the Zounuo-Keyhonuo of Viswema normally consists of one or two pigs, some fowls, a few hoes and a spear. It is a prerogative and a privilege of a clan or *thenu* member to receive the spear. The fact remains that the spread of Christianity and formal education among these people has not altered these traditions. Bridewealth indeed has only a symbolic value particularly as the married daughter's jural right to inherit shares of immovable property of the both parents, exclusively, including terrace fields and highly valued water channels called dzulye provides an unique dimension to the Naga social organization. One of the important obligations of the married woman is to participate in the village festivals of Sekrinyi and Terhunyi representing her agnatic core as member of father's patrilineage (Das, 1993: 64-67).

Events like divorce and death of a father often prompt his children to take up residence in mother's agnatic compound where they, by the time become adults, become absorbed as resident-cognates. Such cognates also acquire full jural status in their adopted matri-lineage (Das, 1993: 70). A woman, therefore, in order to sustain herself and her children, exploits the landed property of pozuopu and tepumi kitsa received through marriage. This observation is to stress the importance of matri-filiation as an alternative framework as recruitment of cognates to the agnatic core of their mother though it is not to construe that a widow has no right of residence in her diseased husband's house.

Despite the jural recognition of matri-filiation in the Zounuo-Keyhonuo society, patrifiliation is accorded the highest value. It is because the patrilineal descent is the vehicle of the continuity and stability of social organization. It is the men who hold the reigns of authority and control the informal legal-political institutions.

XII

If one critically considers the Zounuo-Keyhonuo political system in all its manifestations two important features emerge. On the one hand independent lineages maintain their 'corporate' identities, as discussed. On the other hand, informal politico-jural authorities, such as the razu-pithi (village-headman), pithimi (headman of lineage), sechomi (arbitrator, peace maker) Zhodimi (big man) and Kemovo who are recognized as custodians of customary laws and rituals. These two features of the polity, based on kinship and non-kinship principles respectively, are not contradictory but complementary. The mechanisms of social control, the rules of conduct and the customary laws are all concerned with the maintenance of the jural order. The notions of "jural" and "politico-jural" exercised in this paper are used mainly to emphasize what is described as the "jural institutions of stateless societies" (Fortes and Evans-Pritchard, 1940: 14-15; Fortes, 1945, 1969; Tait, 1961). In Zounuo-Keyhonuo customary law is not upheld by legal institutions (formal judicial methods and courts) but through informal headmanship and other legal institutions and procedures that embody the jural consensus of society such as the age-set system.

In Viswema all persons of same sex and of about the same age are formally grouped into distinctive age sets. Each age-set or *thechu*, is a named group of age fellows such as nhachu-chu, khrisa-chu, khrisa-mehu-chu, mehu-chu and pithi-ketsami. The salient features of these age-sets may be described in brief here.

1. *Pithi-ketsami*: Included under this age-set are the senior most elders, who generally occupy either religious or the secular positions of headmen, *gaon-bura*. The senior most village-headman (Razuo-pithi) is also chosen from this set. In general, the people above the age of 70 are included in this age-set.
2. *Mehu-chu*: Included under this set are people between the age range of 50 to 70. The elders belonging to this age-set are mostly responsible for carrying out the jural duties as pithimi (headman) and sechomi (tribal adjudicator).
3. *Khrisha-mehu-chu*: The people in this age-set are mainly responsible for all manual work associated with village festivals. Adult members of this age-set (between 30–50 years of age) are responsible for singing and dancing during important events.

4. *Khrisha-chu*: Included in this age-set are adults of 15 to 30 years of age. The duties performed by the members of *khrisha-mehu-chu* are also performed by people of this age-set.
5. *Nhachu-chu*: Young boys and girls below the age of 15 are included in this age-set . These boys and girls have no specific job to perform.

Except the age-set of Nhachu-chu the women do not form core groups in any age-set.

In a society in which kinship provides formal framework of social as well as economic relations certain organizational aspects of social relationships are bound to be complex and jurally significant. Each individual's jural status is determined and influenced by the facts of birth adoption and marriage .The issue of jural authority is directly connected with the individual ties, intra-family jural obligations and laws of property, which incorporate the rules of inheritance and succession. Effective enforcement of these rules is imperative for the maintenance of jural order. At a wider societal level the subordination and super-ordination based on the fact of birth are also reinforced through the recognition of *thechu* or age-sets.

Today the formal constitution of an age-set in the village does not involve any military purpose or any collective ceremonial initiation. In the past, when head-hunting was common and wars were frequently fought between the Naga villages, the age set system served the purpose of recruiting young men for military education. The bonds of age fellowship however continue to unite the sets of men of a wide area and which cut across those of lineage boundaries.

The whole population of Viswema has always been organized predominantly on the basis of age-sets. Age was always a factor in determining the rank and in conferring rights and privileges. The age in the life of Viswema villagers even today confers authority in matters of customary law and jural duties and the headmen belonging to *mehu-chu* age-set have the decisive voice in all matters that concern the regulation of public life.

In this acephalous society there are no holders of political office apart from those who hold primarily domestic authority such as the pithimi. Within this authority is embedded some form of politico-jural leadership which is reflected mainly in the context of dispute settlement and peaceful compromise. The pithimi of different descent groups are informal leaders who assemble from time to time to resolve disputes arising between the *sarra* members or between sub-lineages and also to supervise ritual activities. The *sarra* pithimis also bear jural authority over the kayie estate. Thus the senior elders-belonging to the top age-sets of *mehu-chu* and *pithi-ketsami*-being the headmen are not only responsible for ordering jural relations within and between the lineages, but they also supervise and arrange the rituals.

XIII

During their lifetime the Zounuo-Keyhonuo organize several expensive feasts in order to achieve the rank of Zohdimi—the pre-eminent man, big man. One has to organize at least four feasts for the villagers to attain the status of Zohdimi, though there are altogether twelve feasts in the whole series of feasts, each ensuring a step upon the ladder of social status and prestige. The salient features of these feasts—divided into five categories—may be described in brief.

The feast of tem-za is the beginning of the series. It is the first feast which can be given by any newly married couple. Some three or four pigs are killed and their meat along with rice-beer is distributed among the own clan members. Close friends who render services are also given meat. At the second stage of the feast of *zhotho-keda* three oxen are killed (one provided by the feast giver's father; one by his wife's father and one is by the giver himself and his wife). In this feast also one's own clan members and friends receive the meat along with rice-beer. After this feast the prestige symbol of special post, called as *ye-kenava*, is put on the house gate of feast giver. After the death of such a feast giver a special basket called as *likhunu* will be hung on his grave.

The next feast of zhotho-kehi is considered to be very significant since some ten to fifteen oxen are killed and the whole village is invited. Every villager gets a share of flesh and rice-beer. It is in Zhotho-kehi feast that the 'Zhodimi' or the prominent men who have already given several feasts and who are classified into 'seven grades' are specially honoured. Each type of joint is given to a Zhodimi of a particular class. After giving the next feast of tsusu one can place kika (a big wooden-house-horn) over the house roof. From the fourth to the tenth feast the same term zhotho-tsusu is used. Most of the Zhodimi attain their big man status generally by organizing a zhotho susu feast in their life time. The eleventh and twelfth kind of feast are called ezade. It is very difficult to find people who have given ezade feasts. One who does so is regarded as very fortunate and entitled to erect a monolith, "zhotho-tsusu", in the outskirts of the village in the name of himself and his wife. Such a stone remains a "memorial" for many generations to come.

Since the values of prestige, privilege and to some extent power are measured by such old standards in Zounuo-Keyhonuo Society, new couples vie with each other in producing more and more paddy from scarce resources in order ultimately to attain the status of Zohdimi through these graded feats. For the distribution of food through such feasts, a surplus is needed which requires several years of hard work by men and women associated with a bit of good fortune. Women in Naga Societies normally carry out major portions of agricultural work. In the past these feasts served various political purposes being the ladder to attain successive stages of pre-eminence and positions of prestige. The rank of Zohdimi in the remote past could be acquired by one who organized at least ten successively large feasts in five different stages, such as tem-za, zhotho-keda, zhotlho-kehi, zhotho-tsusu, and ezade, but now a person even having organized a lesser number of feasts could attain the status of Zohdimi. Thus, Tsupa of Zerima clan obtained the rank of Zhodimi by arranging the following feasts: First Temza (by offering rice, rice beer and meat) for all members of his own Zerima clan, then keda by inviting all members of his own and wife's clan to cross the stage of keda, then Zhotho-kehi by inviting all the four clans of Viswema. In this feast about ten cows and pigs were killed and divided in a series of recognized joints, each of which was handed over to former Zhodimi.

The status of Zhodimi in the past was achieved by one who gave all the twelve feasts inviting at different stages one's own lineage members, clan members, own and wife's clan members, all the clans of the whole village, neighbouring friendly villages, and ultimately the whole tribal population. On account of inter-village animosity inviting people from outside one's village was practically impossible, hence only ten feasts were regarded as enough.

The most important feature of these feasts is the method of killing the animal and the division of the meat. The flesh of the animal is not cut at random, but is divided into a series of recognized joints, each of which has its own name. Moreover, each type of joint must be handed-over to a particular class of headmen.

In this complicated scheme of distribution we see that three main sets of people receive meat. One set includes the kinsfolk of the feast giver, another friends and people who have performed rituals and provided religious services such as Kemovo, the former givers of feasts. The people belonging to last set are regarded as true Zohdimi and they are specially honoured. The ceremony exhibits how a free use of perishable goods in the society becomes an enduring fact. The category of flesh called thulikra is given to the lowest zhodimi, who has given only one feast at his clan level. The Puobo portion is regarded as most important. Those Zhodimi who have given all the graded feasts to villagers are given the flesh of puobo. In fact Tsupa organized the kehi feast in such large scale that the title of Zhodimi was

Distribution of Flesh Among the Headmen

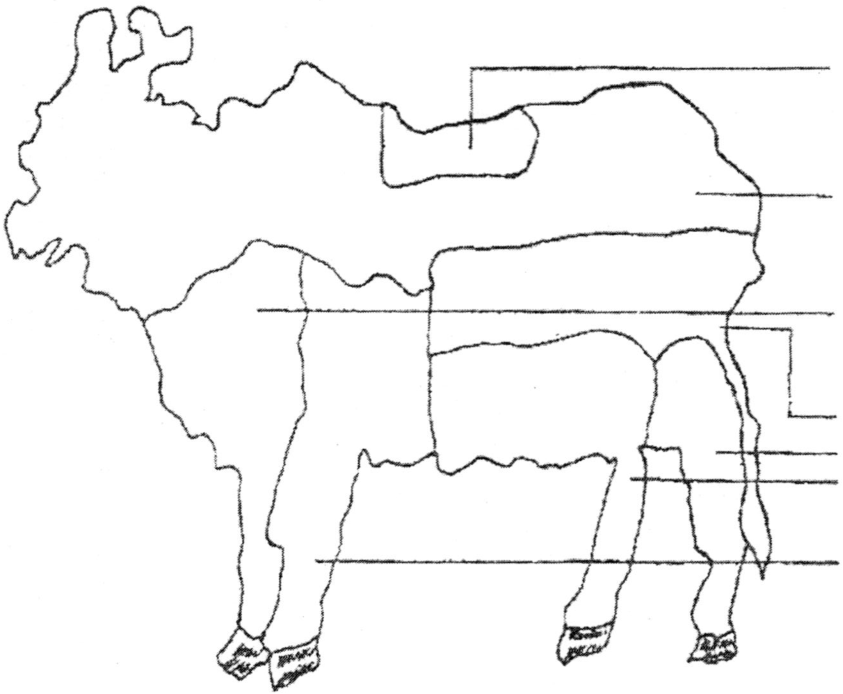

Portion of Pocu is given to one who has given maximum of two feasts.

Thulikra is the part of flesh which is not distributed widely. A small portion of this flesh is given to a Zhodimi (bigman) of a lower rankie. A Zhodimi who has given only one or two feasts.

This portion is called as *Pangu-Data*. This portion is given to a bigman who has given the feasts for three times. Paws are retained by the owner.

Puomei and Bokhi

Puophi

Puophi-Bokhi

This portion is called as *Puobo*. Those elders who have already given four or more than four numbers of prestige-gaining feasts are given flesh of *Puobo*. Even paws are to be given away.

conferred on him with all privileges. Thus, Tsupa became entitled to display a Kirhuva post on his house roof. At the same time he became entitled to install otsusu—the large memorial stone in the ontskirt of the village and also to fix a kika-(house-horn) in his house. Only a Zhodimi is customarily entitled to wear shawls with special designs and to possess specially crafted mugs for drinking rice-beer. Tsupa could enjoy even these privileges. Thus we see that the big-men—Zhodimi essentially owe their status to their material economic success and their generosity. The Zounuo-Keyhonuo believe that it is more blessed to give than to receive.

The feasts and connected rituals are the traditional means of elevating the status of an individual and position of a household in the local hierarchical scale, outside the realm of kinship. Closely associated with the status of Zohdimi are certain otherwise enjoyed only by the reputed headmen-pithimi-sechomi. Those who perform the eleborate feast-rituals are honoured throughout their lives and even after death within and outside their village areas.

The Zounuo-Keyhonuo use the term Pithimi alternatively while referring to an elder punumi-headman, lineage-headman (*sarra-pithi*), or the tribal arbitrator (*sechomi*). A single individual may hold these offices, but the nature and extent of authority of such an individual and his powers of representation may vary widely according to the situation. The pithimi who emerge as peacemakers may be called expert headmen. They are differentiated from religious functionaries who are also lineage-based pithimi (headmen).

XIV

In order to maximize the pre-existing economic base prominent headmen and rich individuals often foist their gain by making strategic choices with the support of their allies. Adopted children help to manipulate pre-existing descent links and also develop arable lands thereby expanding the private estate of their patrons. The patron uses part of such profits indeed for giving feasts to the villagers in order to further expand his prestige base by acquiring the rank of Zhodimi. Actors vie for giving feasts in order to boost political power. Barth studied Pathan social structure through the concept of strategy and strategic choices expressed by the Pathans through the idiom of descent. The Zounuo-Keyhonuo example is identical with what Barth called "political prestations of submission" from followers (Barth, 1966).

In this uncentralized Naga Society, however, the entire gamut of the political field cannot be defined only in terms of the system of descent, because strategic choices made by individuals, often deviating from jural rules, generally assume political significance. One such choice is noticeable in attempts made by actors to maximize their economic resources by forming labour pools, and thereby to indulge in the competition to host graded feasts to acquire the high rank of Zohdimi, a position in the local hierarchy of informal leadership. Such leaders indeed owe their status to their material success and generosity.

Each individual's jural and economic status could only be perceived in terms of kinship status hence all adopted children are clearly declared to be the so. With marriage each individual male receives his share of land and other facilities. However, one is free to make use of his physical capabilities in order to cut jungle areas and develop the own terrace fields to maximize yields. Ideally the institution of khrohi (labour pool of patrilineage) is to help during house construction and even building new terrace fields. But with a greater number of male members one has the capacity to increase economic gains. Thus men like Vinol often go on adopting male members into their families. They all work in the large estate of the patron.

Matri-filiation provides an alternative framework for the recruitment of cognates with full economic rights and jural status. The cognates enjoy rights by virtue of residual claim which married woman possesses on her patrilineage property.

In the case of this Naga Tribe it is observed that politico-jural relations between local groups are controlled as much by the holders of statuses in the age-set system as by elders emerging as big-men through the institutionalized prestige-gaining give-away ceremonies. Despite the adoption of Christianity these basic cultural traits and their traditions continue to unite the Naga people.

XV

The diffused political system of the Zounuo-Keyhonuo people, as discussed, is based upon a segmentary system of interlocking descent groups. Lineage segments are of varying depth and span and non-kinship institutions—the age-sets and the assembly of headmen. In this paper analytic relationships between territory and descent ideology, corporateness and genealogy and headmanship and jural norms are elucidated in order to determine the processes of social control and jural order in this Naga Society. Descent ideologies, descent dogmas and more particularly the descent relationships indicate and involve politico-jural aspects of rights and duties transmitted lineally by virtue of descent—succession, inheritance and group membership. Descent, as argued by Fortes, is fundamentally a jural concept and the total social system is primarily a politico-jural entity, in which the corporate descent groups constitute both the moral and legal elements (Fortes, 1953; Dumont, 1971: 76; Barnard and Good, 1984: 74).

Not much attention is paid to the descent theory in anthropological studies of South Asian Tribal Societies. Refuting Goody's argument that fully corporate descent groups are only found in Africa, LaFontaine has observed that rejection of the descent model as non-applicable to societies outside Africa would destroy much of the unity of the present theory of kinship (1973, also see Hershman, 1981: 234; Das, 1993: 15). Indeed, as discussed, the Zounuo-Keyhonuo Naga do provide an example of a society which has a system of unilineal descent and, to be more specific, comprising a segmentary lineage system alongside patri-virilocal residence, where the general devolution of productive and immovable property is agnatic. In fact, as we observed *kayie* estate derives its jural individuality through its vital links with a particular descent group and not through links with the individuals.

The lineage system among the Zounuo-Keyhonuo Naga is built up largely on the recognition of the agnatic line of descent and it provides the framework of corporate groupings upon which political notions and jural institutions are founded. The *sarra*—lineage is divided into a number of segments, which are more or less of the same structural form as the whole lineage. Every lineage or lineage segment, in fact, represents a dynamic equilibrium of mutually balancing segments.

The descent groups, territorial divisions and age-sets provide the main fields of political relations in Zounuo-Keyhonuo Society. Identities, positions and interests of social and territorial groups could not be tormented or weakened by colonization or modern transformations. This may be partly because Naga areas are characterized by a low population density and surplus land. Indeed the connection between kinship and rights over land is fundamental in this segmentary society where the genealogies are the foundation both of claims to land and descent status. In fact, special constitutional safeguards provided to Naga Tribes in respect of their customary laws, rights over land/forest areas and religious beliefs have re-enforced the jural norms of kinship and clanship.

In Zounuo-Keyhonuo Society the age-sets establish not only the efficacy of the adult males; but by the order of seniority inherent in the system an organism of ranking and an obligation of leadership in politico-jural and ritual domains. Thus the village headmen as described are entangled in the web of kinship links and yet have statuses of a dissimilar kind, either as Pithimi-headmen or as the Zohdimi-privileged big-men in relation to the same set of people. Clear distinctions are witnessed between headmen in terms of their statuses, roles and authorities. Thus, while the lineage "Pithimi" and "Sechomi" owe their status and authority to their "descent position" and "knowledge of customs" respectively, "Kemovo" and "Zohdimi" owe their statuses, roles and authorities to their hereditary religious position and material prosperity and generosity, as discussed. Ritual specialization does not confer unequal rights but certain privileges and prestige (*Genna bura-Kemovo*, rain-maker) during and after their lifetime. The grave of a Kemovo, regarded as very sacred for example cannot be damaged or shifted to a new site.

XVI

In fact the diffused political life of the Zounuo-Keyhonuo people is revealed through interplay and interposition of such ritual specialization, virtuosity of sechomi and statuses emanating from age-sets as also through various dynamisms of competition—rivalries for prestige and influence—resulting in inequalities—big-men *vis-a-vis* common-men.

In Zounuo-Keyhonuo Society the clans and lineages are not ranked in any hierarchical order. These localized descent groups are structurally-functionally equivalent and politically equal. The headmen—pithimi, sechomi, zohdimi, kemovo—repressenting these descent groups in various capacities belong to the chapi (assembly of headmen) but they all lack formal authority. They cannot enforce rigid compliance of their decisions. Though one pithimi among the elders is nominated as sechomi—the adjudicator—on account of his being a skilful orator and for his impartial convictions he is not a very influential man personally. As a matter of fact, in the gathering of headmen-*chapi*—no single headman—not even sechomi—is ever declared as the formal chief. The politico-jural authority thus ultimately rests with the entire group of headmen, *i.e.* their capacity to dominate public opinion. One of their tasks is to give expression to the public opinion reflecting both moral and politico-jural values. The principal roles of the headmen ultimately are to limit the disorder by preventing the extension of the quarrel and to establish the jural order.

XVII

Conclusion

In India the category of tribe has not been developed as a conceptual category. The present intention has been to portray the social formation of a Naga Tribe analytically in terms of a pyramidal genealogical superstructure. The people who identify themselves as Zounuo-Keyhonuo in *all* circumstances are actually called as Southern Angamis in administrative parlance. The Zounuo-Keyhonuo resent this latter designation. This example has helped us to re-establish the analytical utility of the concept of tribe using some of the basic theoretical leads provided by concerned anthropologists. In this society the segmentary principle is operative and relations between interlocking descent groups are envisaged in terms of a pyramidal genealogical superstructure. Descent emerges not only as a basic principle of social grouping, but also as source of individual and collective rights and liabilities. Based on the principle of descent there exists a definite continuity in structural progression of jural relations, from domestic domain to that of lineage and clan.

In this society the descent principle and the territorial principle both contribute to the determination of the politico-jural field. Indeed in the absence of any political or governmental institution, the diffused political functions are observable in the interplay of clan-lineage-sub-lineage structures, territorial structures and age-sets. In fact, in the absence of a distinct political authority, the lineage elders/headmen emerge as key figures in maintaining social control and jural order. Each individual's jural status is determined and influenced by the facts of birth adoption and marriage. The issue of jural authority is directly connected with the individual ties, intra-family jural obligations and laws of property which incorporate the rules of inheritance and succession. Effective enforcement of these rules is imperative for the maintenance of jural order. In the case of this Naga Tribe it is observed that politico-jural relations between local groups are controlled as much by the holders of statuses in age-set system as by elders emerging as big-men through the institutionalized prestige-gaining grand give-away ceremonies. The entire gamut of the political field can not be defined only in terms of the system of descent, particularly because strategic choices made by individuals, often deviating jural rules, generally assume political significance. One such choice is noticeable in attempts made by actors to maximize their economic resources by forming labour pools, and thereby to indulge in the competition to host graded feasts to acquire the high rank of Zohdimi, a position in the local hierarchy of informal leadership. Such leaders indeed owe their status to their material success and generosity. The paper also discussed the devious non-kinship measures employed by certain rich men /big men to boost political power in wider kinship sphere. Author employed the theory of structural analysis to study of lineage system of Naga Tribe where descent is the most important principle of grouping in political matters as well as the source of individual rights and liabilities.

The headmen—pithimi, sechomi, zohdimi, kemovo—representing these descent groups in various capacities belong to the chapi (assembly of headmen) but they all lack formal authority. They cannot enforce rigid compliance of their decisions. Though one pithimi among the elders is nominated as sechomi—the adjudicator—on account of his being a skilful orator and for his impartial convictions but he is not a very influential man personally. As a matter of fact in the gathering of headmen-*chapi* no single headman, not even sechomi is ever declared as the formal chief. The politico-jural authority thus ultimately rests with the entire group of headmen. The mainspring of the power of the headmen rests on their capacity to dominate public opinion. One of their tasks is to give expression to the public opinion reflecting both moral and politico-jural values. The principal roles of the headmen ultimately are indeed to limit the disorder by preventing the extension of the quarrel and to establish the jural order. In fact the diffused political life of the Zounuo-Keyhonuo people is revealed through interplay and interposition of such ritual specialization, virtuosity of sechomi and statuses emanating from age-sets as also through various dynamisms of competition—rivalries for prestige and influence—resulting in inequalities—big-men *vis-a-vis* common-men.

REFERENCES

Balandier, G. 1970. *Political Anthropology*. Harmondsworth: Penguin Books Ltd.

Barnard, Alan and Good Anthony. 1984. *Research Practices in the Study of Kinship*. London: Academic Press.

Barnes, J.A. 1954. "Class and Committee in a Norwegian Island Parish," *Human Relations*, 7.

Barth, F. 1959a. *Political Leadership among Swat Pathans*. London: Athlone.

____. 1959b. "Segmentary Opposition and the Theory of Games: A Study of Pathan Organization," *Journal Royal Anthropological Institute*, 89 (1): 5-21.

____. 1966. *Models of Social Organization*. Royal Anthropological Institute Occasional Paper 23.

Das, N.K. 1984. "Agnatic Descent, Matrifiliation and Endogamy: Implications of Descent Group in-marriage among the Naga," in B.B. Goswamy, D. Danda and J.K. Sarkar (eds.), *Marriage in India*. Calcutta: Anthropological Survey of India.

____. 1985. The Politico-jural Aspects of the Zounuo-Keyhonuo Social System, Ph.D. Thesis, Gauhati University.

____. 1989. *Ethnic Identity, Ethnicity and Social Stratification in North East India*. New Delhi: Inter-India Publication.

____. 1993. *Kinship, Politics and Law in Naga Society*. Calcutta: Anthropological Survey of India.

Dumont, L. 1971. *Introduction 'a deux theories d' anthropologie socialae.* Paris: The Hague: Mouton (quoted in Barnard and Good 1984).

Elwin, V. 1969. *The Nagas in the Nineteenth Century.* Bombay: Oxford University Press.

Fortes, Meyer. 1945. *The Dynamics of Clanship among the Tallensi.* London: Oxford University Press.

____. 1953. "The Structure of Unilineal Descent Groups," *American Anthropologist*, 55: 17-41.

____. 1969. *Kinship and Social Order: The Legacy of Lewis Henry Morgan.* London: Routledge and Kegan Paul.

Fortes, M. and E.E. Evans-Pritchard (eds.). 1940. *African Political Systems.* London: Oxford University Press.

Goody, J.R. 1990. *The Oriental, the Ancient and the Primitive.* Cambridge: Cambridge University Press.

Hershman, P. 1981. *Punjabi Kinship and Marriage.* Delhi: Hindustan Publishing Corporation.

Hutton, J. H [1921]. 1969. *The Angami Nagas.* Bombay: Oxford University Press.

La-Fontaine, J. 1973. "Descent in New Guinea : An Africanist View," (pp. 35-51) in Goody, J (ed.), *The Character of Kinship.* Cambridge: Cambridge University Press.

Lehman, F.K. 1963. *The Structure of Chin Society.* Urbana: University of Illinois University Press.

Middleton, John. 1970. "The Political System of the Lugbara of the Nile-Congo Divide," in J. Middleton and D. Tait (eds.), *Tribes Without Rulers: Studies in African Segmentary Systems.* London: Routledge and Kegan Paul.

Tait, David. 1961. *The Konkomba of Northern Ghana.* (ed. by J. Goody). London: Oxford University Press.

Winter, Edward. 1970. "The Aboriginal Political Structure of Bwamba," In J. Middleton and D. Tait (eds.), *op.cit.*

Vivelo, F. Robert. 1978. *Cultural Anthropology Handbook.* New York: McGraw-Hill Book Company.

ELEVEN

ORISSAN TRIBAL SOCIETIES: Commonalities and Variations

GEORG PFEFFER

Before Culturalism

At the end of the last century, the *Annual Review of Anthropology* asked Marshall Sahlins for the general outlook of the discipline which he had, during the past five decades, influenced rather decisively. The author of *Culture in Practice* (2000) responded with characteristic scepticism:

> "contrary to notions of progressive development the surviving victims of imperial capitalism have neither become all alike nor just like us". Moreover, "(r)eports of the death of indigenous cultures have been exaggerated" (Sahlins, 1999: i).

His essay opposed a somewhat antique notion of progress as well as a rather trendy "sentimental pessimism" (*ibid.* vi). In fact, Sahlins was happy to note the widespread habit of "cultural usurpation" (*ibid.* ix), *i.e.* the indigenous use of foreign wealth for the local conception of human existence:

> "Unified by the expansion of Western capitalism over recent centuries, the world is also being re-diversified by indigenous adaptations to the global juggernaut.... Thus one complement of the new global ecumene is the so-called culturalism of very recent decades: the self-consciousness of their 'culture', as a value to be lived and defended, that has broken out all around the Third and Forth Worlds. Ojibway,

Haiwaiians, Inuit, Tibetans, Amazonian peoples, Australian Aborigines…: Everyone now speaks of their culture…." (*ibid.* x)

While I will make no attempt to conceal my lasting sympathy with this view of increasing, if innovative, cultural diversity, my paper will offer certain qualifications by exempting those who, as yet, have *not* been reached by Western capitalism, being encysted within a particular kind of state that is still largely influenced by Hindu values. The numerous tribal peoples of the South Asian subcontinent have simply been ignored by Western anthropology. Sahlins' "culturalism" may be widespread elsewhere but has so far *not* reached tribal middle India[1], even though a particular blend of Hindu-*cum*-Western impact may have influenced some, creating specific reactions which may, in their own specific way, be also part of a cultural "re-diversification" of the subcontinent.

Conspicuous and concerted public references to the own culture, emphasizing the own cultural distinctions, is a very obvious aspect of South Asian *castes*, as exemplified by the proponents of Jat values[2], Yadav resistance[3], or Maratha heroism[4]. In fact this self-conscious propagation of particular caste achievements is very much the subject of contemporary Indian politics[5], but it is *not* found in tribal middle India, if we leave aside a very limited number of Santal and Munda urban intellectuals.

Not surprisingly, this lack of conspicuous claims to cultural distinction goes together with a general deficit in public relations. Indian tribal society is practically unknown in Western anthropology, leave alone news media, one reason for this being the fact that tribal women and men do *not* make a fuss about their status, another being the disposition of their fellow citizens to ignore the tribes and play down the fact of their existence. Such policy is shared by the country's Westernized citizens, by conservative caste Hindus, or Muslim, Sikh and Christian ideologues. All unite in their tendency to devalue and marginalize tribal society. Frequently this is done in the form of apologies indicating a general embarrassment over the lack of "development" among those "backward" sections of the population. The people I will, following the rules of Indian English, call "tribals" in this paper, are discreetly added to the category "downtrodden"[6] and "exploited" by public sympathizers, just as they are "primitive" or "uneducated" for the less compassionate observers. Both clichés hardly hide a general lack of interest in the indigenous cultures of the forest, or of those regions that used to forested a century ago.

But then 84 million people are officially counted as members of *Scheduled Tribes (ST)* in 2001 (*The Hindu,* 07/11/2004), *i.e.* many more than the inhabitants of Germany. Anyone living in the tribal areas can furthermore witness the "tribal" character of numerous groups, *e.g.* weavers, listed as *Scheduled Castes (SC)* or *Other Backward Classes (OBC), i.e.* listed in *other* administrative brackets to reduce the official number of the tribal population. Tribals have never opposed such camouflaging operations, just as they have failed to find any sort of common political platform. In fact, they have little access to the multiplicators of publicity. Wherever vociferous claims[7] to official tribal status have been forwarded, spurious motives are immediately suspected, since any *ST* registration implies certain governmental benefits of the financial type such as job and scholarship reservations, or the official protection of tribal land against any non-tribal efforts of appropriation.

Why has the self-conscious claim of cultural achievements not been heard in tribal India? How can we explain tribal modesty in contrast to all that noise made by natives of New Guinea or Hawaii, Canada or Australia? Any answer will, of course, be speculative, but a reference to the state in Indian history may be helpful, *i.e.* the kind of civilization that has been known on the sub-continent over the last five thousand years. We do know, for example, through the testimony of Asoka's rock inscriptions of the third century B.C. that the tribes of middle India challenged and disturbed the borders of historical empires, just as imperial expansions must have contacted the tribal society. However, armies crossing the forests *en route* to other states lacked the impetus, characteristic of European colonizers, to convert and transform the tribal people into co-religionists, peasants of the plough, or obedient tax payers. There being no Hindu dogma, leave alone a dogma of conversion, tribal religion was left untouched just as tribesmen appear as proud, if uncivilized, bowmen in the Hindu epics.[8]

India was an *under*-populated land for most of history, so the vast forests in the hilly middle of the subcontinent could remain the grand asylum of the untamed and the untaxed. If, once in a while, an adventurer was able to control a piece of jungle by his trained troops, he might have imported Brahmins and accountants to inaugurate temples that were financed by the revenues forced out of the neighbourhood's cultivators. However, these patches of land, hardly surpassing the walls of the mud forts, remained isolated in the forests, even though the inhabitants of the hills might have come down once in a year for the royal ritual and offered token gifts of recognition in order (*see* Otten's contribution in this volume) to depart immediately after the show. State expansionism, mostly unrecorded, was of a very limited kind and confined to the plains or, at the most, to the plateaus and not the steep sides of the hilly areas. Accordingly, very little is heard of tribal resistance.

The late Morton Fried's theory of the tribe as a "secondary socio-political phenomenon" (1975: 114) simply looks out of place in this setting, just as the more recent Friedian researches by Ferguson and Whitehead (1992) suffer from their ethnocentric concentration on European imperial expansion. Rome, Spain, Britain, France, and Russia were not the only imperialist powers in the world. Perhaps the tribes of India have been ignored by Western anthropology, because they were mostly out of reach for European armies and European epidemics. The tribal way of life did *not* usually cause the concern of the traditional Hindu state, so the tribes had less reason to fear its atrocities and less motives to assert their respective culture by more expressive acts of publicity.

If India, during the last century, has turned into an *over*-populated country, the Hindu manner to keep the uncivilized at a distance—rather than to expand and exterminate in European style—has not changed in a similarly significant manner. In fact, the famous "culture lag" is at work. Though quite a number of plains' people have recently migrated into the malaria infested hills to grab tribal land and sell the junk of the developed lowlands to those locals they could convert to a moderate kind of consumerism, the influx might have been far greater. It might have been a flood. Immigrant traders and administrators have also, with unnoticeable exceptions, made it a point *not* to fraternize with the tribals, and *not* integrate them or be integrated, since any such intimacies run against the fundamental values of Hindu purity and status.

Tribal not Caste Society

As long as Indian history is recorded, the king has been known to regulate the estates of his realm. Mohenjodaro in the third millennium B.C. or Pataliputra two thousand years later were governmental centres that classified the status of their subjects. Contrary to notions of "postcolonial" ethnohistorians[9], caste was not invented by the British. It was the organizing principle of the pre-modern state. Hereditary duties of philosophers and accountants, soldiers and merchants, artisans, peasants and multiple service categories were assigned and enforced by the sovereign at the centre. The *Lord of the World* in the coastal town of Puri, *i.e.* Jagannath (who, by Marx and others, was adopted as *juggernaut* into the English language), stands to this day in the sanctum of the royal temple to classify and insure status variations of the many temple services, ranging from the purest type of Brahmins to untouchables. Though today the republic has taken over his empire, the King of Puri continues to act as the "moving Vishnu", or as Jagannath's representative, to implement the proper world order (*see* Hardenberg, 1999, 2000), and the leaders of the republic, along with millions of pilgrims, make it a point to worship him in public during the major annual festivals. The Hindu state was structured and inspired with meaning by caste ideology whereas the tribal constitutions in middle India were of the "kinship" kind, or not very different from other "kinship constitutions" in Asia and the rest of the world.

Traditionally, Hindu states of the plains and those which, at times, existed on the plateaus implied fuzzy borders towards the stateless tribes of the hills, until British empire builders, starting in the eighteenth century, introduced a certain administrative rigor. Expanding their Bengal Presidency, the troops of the East India Company conquered the narrow strip of Orissa's coastal plains by 1803, but in the Western Hills they were able to install "indirect rule" effectively only since the middle of the 19th century. In practice such imperial policy raised former non-descript adventurers claiming royal heritage to the status of micro-kings of jungle kingdoms, as long as these "recent royals" ensured their loyalty to the European power. As the immediate consequence of Christian interference, Hindu traditionalism broke out in the forests. Booming construction activity led to palaces and temples, unknown in pre-European days. Whereas, in pre-British days, the Gajapati rulers of the land disallowed any other temple of Lord Jagannath besides the huge centre of pilgrimage in Puri, this symbol of royalty spread like measles throughout the little jungle kingdoms once Queen-Empress Victoria and the so-called "evangelicals" of Westminster ruled over India. For the new courts and temples, Vedic Brahmin masterminds could be lured away from Puri and into the wilderness by offers of rent-free land and prestigious positions of the royal priesthood (Pfeffer, 1976).

Until the formal removal of princes from power in 1949, Hindu titles and traditions flourished in the midst of the jungle, or rather in those tiny patches cleared for the micro-courts. However, national independence did away with the dozen, or so, royals of western Orissa. Over night everyone was said to be free and equal, even those millions of unimpressed slash-and-burn cultivators surrounding the royal theatres. The tribals were then exposed to development. In the following overview I hope to show that they have neither all become alike, nor like the dominant Hindus of the coastal plains. Sahlins' proposition is elaborated with reference to the specific Indian case. However, 'culturalism' has yet to break out, because in India, tribal society on the periphery of the administrated territories has always been a self-understood, if inconspicuous, part of the Hindu way to conceive territory—like numerous other domains—as a matter of hierarchical gradation.

Contemporary tribal Orissa, unchallenged by any major effects of modernity, is still in the "pre-culturalism" stage. Nobody doubts that the Kond,

Sora or Gadaba as tribes are culturally different from non-tribal inhabitants of the province and represent, each in their own particular way, a *specific* social structure fused with a matching worldview and economy, rather than one of many castes within an overall hierarchy, or individual citizenship of a universalist political and philosophical persuasion. There being no dispute over particular tribal identities, any self-conscious defence or expressive claim to a cultural uniqueness can be dispensed with. At the same time anthropologists are sure to note certain "family resemblances" between the many different tribal cultures, or commonalities indicating a marked contrast to the values of caste society. Shared basic value-ideas become obvious within an otherwise wide variety of tribal cultural features.

Commonalities of Tribal Cultures

Tribal Constitutions

Many more than the officially registered 62 *Scheduled Tribes* of Orissa live in anarchic communities of a "generalised" structure, as is characteristic of tribal society (Sahlins, 1968: 15). Policemen and foresters may intervene, election agents and social workers may campaign, or school teachers may, as they like to do, convey the joys of vegetarianism: all score results of very a limited success. Badly enough, factories of the most polluting industries have—perhaps due to the lack of local resistance—been planted by the state (in the socialist phase) and by private enterprise (in the phase de-regulation) in some tribal areas, just as tribal cultivators have learned to take an occasional time-out for the sake of wage-labour in cities and plantations of modern India. However, the specific tribal constitutions and tribal community life have mostly remained in tact. As in other parts of the globe, these constitutions classify and evaluate the universe of communal roles in the guise of seemingly natural and thus undisputed "kinship" relations.

Very obviously, the tribal "kinship" vocabulary differs from the patterns found among the castes of either north or south India. I will not go into the subtleties of this specific middle Indian deep structure, shared by *all Scheduled Tribes* and non-scheduled tribal neighbours between Ganges and Godavari, but it should be clear that such an order is at the same time complex and holistic, refined as well as closed in the sense that it includes all those marked by clear juxtapositions rather than the fuzzy external boundaries of Hindi, Oriya, or modern European terminologies. Categories[10] of middle Indian 'kinship' invariably divide a tribal universe into several types of agnates and affines of the three central genealogical levels while simplifying, and sometimes fusing, the levels of grandparents and grandchildren. Tribal terminologies are *systems*, not just vocabularies like those of north India, but they are systems of a highly differentiated kind, when compared to the simplicity of the so-called Dravidian system in south India. It should also be clear that such a "deep structure". of the terminology[11] is invariantly the same, whether the language spoken is of the Indo-Aryan, the Dravidian, or the Munda family. Other *overt* features of the numerous tribal "kinship" constitutions indicate common trends within the local variations to be described below.

Age and Seniority

Tribal concepts of age and authority are diametrically opposed to those of caste society. In the last century, the major ethnographers of tribal communities, *i.e.* Sarat Chandra Roy (*e.g.* 1915 for the Oraon) and Verrier Elwin (*e.g.* 1947 for the Muria Gond) described so-called youth dormitories in most of their many monographs, but today, under external influence, the institution seems to disappear gradually. The traces though are still very obvious: in 1980 I lived for months with Kuttia Kond boys in their *kure*, now abandoned, and in 1987 the Gadaba gave me the hut of their village girls since the latter agreed to shift to a widow's home. The *majang* of the Juang males is still the biggest and most decorative building of any Juang settlement, just as the Hill Bhuiya construct the largest house of the village for their boys and men. In the last decade I have also seen such dormitories for male Jhoria and Elwin (1950) describes those for female Bondo, but by far the most elaborate and pertinent descriptive analysis of a youth dormitory—in this case for females—has been supplied by Roland Hardenberg (2005, 2006) in his recent work on the Dongria Kond, based on 14 months of fieldwork in 2002/3.

These fierce people of the mountain slopes have been able to remain aloof of most outsiders and, having once accepted the ethnographer and his wife, did not bother to conceal the communicative aspects of the girls' huts that are positioned behind the binary rows of adults' homes. Hardenberg found that tribal feuds and politics ran along the complex lines of affinal relations—including elaborate marriage negotiations, bridewealth excesses, abductions, elopements, and huge compensation payments—which were dominated by male householders. However, a parallel system linked the youth dormitories of mutually affinal villages, and in this context, male visitors had to—and did—submit to female decision making. Not surprisingly, the family prospects, as negotiated by the married Dongria for their children and infants, frequently contradicted those developed by independent efforts of the younger generation. When facing the other village or descent group in conflict parents and children would stand together, but within the family a youth had the tendency to play her or his own game during the nocturnal excursions of young males into dormitories governed by young females. The resulting complexities and contradictions formed much of the content of local conflicts and conciliations.

Hardenberg's observations confirm the general point I wish to stress: young, unmarried tribals always operate very much as a part of the village community, but once they are about ten years old, they do not necessarily follow the inclinations and strategies of their parents. At the same time young people are close to their grandparents, practicing *Joking Relations* with some of them and even, in the context of classificatory kinship, marrying a "grand-parent" who are said to be of the same age-set, as Skoda describes in this volume. For the youngsters, the peers are more important. Many ethnographers report a special closeness of alternating, rather than adjoining, generations. Similarly, the Berlin research group has, during the last decade, noticed several cases of parricide and not infrequent physical violence against aged men as were carried out by their adult married sons in several tribal societies. Parents were, at times, also kicked out of their homes, abused and intimidated.

All of this diametrically contradicts the value-ideas of *caste* society demanding strict obedience of children, unquestioned authority of parents, and special care and respect for the aged irrespective of their children's age. The famous "Hindu Joint Family" experiences a sense of crisis, whenever married sons or grandsons vaguely indicate intentions to set house on their own, while it is self-understood for tribal India that any couple gets a separate hut after marriage and that unmarried children, once old enough to do so, move out of their parents' way. Spending the nights on the verandas of friends or on elevated platforms in the fields to guard the harvest against bears and elephants, or seeking the company of age-mates in own or other dormitories is their proper nocturnal activity. The forest is a source of food and firewood, not—as in common Hindu understanding—a source of fear. Teenagers conceive no problems when sleeping in tree-huts or hiking across mountain ranges in the short hours of the night. Filial independence is the tribal value, filial submission that of caste. Whereas neither the parents nor anyone else can be said to exercise authority in tribal Orissa, paternal authority is the first and foremost of several highly authoritarian levels in caste society, the latter being a rather pure version of an authoritarian model.

Food, Drink, Dress, and Dance

India's culinary code has always been one of the most exciting public issues.

In 1857, the "First War of National Independence"[12] broke out over questions of diet[13] and recently, to offer just one of many examples, the Hindu nationalist movement offered "political asylum" to all European cows threatened by slaughter during the "mad cow disease" of the nineteen-nineties. Apart from such well-known efforts of cow protection, vast sections of the Indian society, whether Westernized or conservative, explicitly favour a total ban on any form of animal sacrifice. In this context, the low castes want to rise by adopting vegetarianism and the lowest castes have mostly abandoned the consumption of beef for the same reason. Milk, butter or other products of the cow are the religiously recommended food.

Tribal markers offer an inversion of this value: milk and milk products are generally avoided, whereas most tribals make no bones about their beef consumption. True, the inversion is once again turned around by the *junior* or Dudh Kharia who, guided by their specific myths and in contrast to their *senior* agnates, the Dhelki Kharia, drink milk and avoid beef, just as, for similar mythological reasons, Rona, Bhumia and Boro Porja of the Koraput District shun the flesh of the cow. Basically, however, it is clear that all over India "animals are good to think and to prohibit" (Tambiah, 1969) and that tribal culinary classification diametrically opposes that of caste. At a number of grand feasts, for example, I have met Rona eating buffalo meat while proudly proclaiming that they would have nothing of the beef stew which their Gadaba friends, sitting a few yards away, were consuming so joyfully. Such a scene would be quite unthinkable in a caste context.

Alcoholic beverages are a more complicated issue of discussion. In coastal Orissa I could easily find close by liquor vendors and liquor dens whenever I looked for them, not to speak of the regular customers. However, drinking alcohol is an extremely polluting exercise and accordingly, all aspects of it are camouflaged as best as is possible. Addicts make it a point to hide whenever they go for intoxication and otherwise hide the fact that they are addicts. The situation is the very opposite in a tribal village where liquor is required in everyone of the innumerable rituals and not just male inhabitants openly compete to get drunk and proudly demand drinks in public. People try, whenever they can, to distil their own liquor within the village for all to see, since alcoholism is in no way polluting, but rather an accepted way of life. Sobriety, on the other hand, is far from being a public virtue.

Tribal people, as such, and as the members of a particular tribe, used to be recognized by their dress. Tribal women would cover their hips only and British Census ethnographers were fond of relating how officers forced the Juang to abandon their leaf dress for textiles provided by the champions of progress. Today, the inner-Indian development agencies are eager, in this respect more than in others, to supply cheap mill made textiles to the tribal women of whom some, like the Kuttia Kond, have cut the cloth in their own particular fashion, *i.e.* as aprons with a miniskirt for the unmarried and simply skirts for housewives, while all are still recognized as tribal, having considerably shortened the length. The Bondo women, however, stick to their—mythologically prescribed—miniskirt as the sole garment while female Dongria Kond of the high mountains cover their entire body, but do so in their own conservative style which is quite different from the fashions of the caste women in the plains.

Finally, the concept of dancing is relevant. Classical Odissi dance is one of the palace entertainments in India. Outstanding individual artists are trained from early childhood onwards to perform in temples and during festivals on tours and for the television. Hereditary professional musicians accompany them during a performance. By contrast, tribal music and dance have a "participatory value". Throughout winter, the young engage themselves as dancers on a good number of festive occasions, and normally their elders remind and encourage them to practice on the threshing floor. No status bars disqualify any human male or female desiring to join or leave the dancing chain without interrupting the fun. Hundreds of step varieties are usually experienced in a circle, with each dancer tying her or his arms behind the adjoining back to the alternating person in the row. The girls engage in singing while the boys take shifts in drumming. Only the oboe-like *moira*, the leading melody maker, is restricted to a player of the weaver category, *i.e.* the landless artisans that are found in all tribal villages. In fact the man is called "*the moira*", being responsible for the music of all life cycle ceremonies in a village.

Whenever a male outsider, coming from caste society, watches such dancing, his standard comment would condemn tribal "immorality" and the "sensual" inclinations. In fact the many joyful occasions of tribal festivals are the source of basic cultural misunderstandings on behalf of caste Hindu observers who like to imagine unrestricted tribal sexuality. Such fantasies not infrequently lead to violent crimes against tribal women.

Reincarnation

Tribal culinary, dress and dance codes express social values which are far removed from "inner-worldly asceticism". Providence is not an issue. In fact, tribal India does not conceive cumulative social achievements. People live in "cold" societies of which the "internal environment borders on the zero of historical temperature" (Lévi-Strauss, 1973: 29). As a shortcut to a long chain of evidence, we may examine tribal concepts of reincarnation (for details *see* Pfeffer, 2001). After death and various forms of intervals, a person is finally reborn within the same status and village community to re-open an existence in the immanent world, before once again passing into the world beyond and then continuing in the cycle. The crucial difference in caste society is the *post mortem* evaluation of the life performance which is likely to lead to individual promotion or relegation of status. The Hindu *karma* concept offers transcendental sanctions and re-enforcements for the individual actor, whereas *no* such evaluation and *no* such individual mobility—ranging from the status of bacteria to that of Vedic Brahmins—has been known in Indian tribal societies.

Variations

Given the obvious "family resemblances" between all middle Indian tribal cultures, the point is that they refer to the "deep structure", to existential ideas, and to the spirit of the community—the basic values—rather than to the overt institutions. The latter tend to vary from tribe to tribe, just as they have been exposed to a variety of historical circumstances. I shall sketch some of them all the same, because these cultures "have not become all alike". For simplicity sake, I will try to demonstrate these variations *only* in the south of the river Mahanadi which is bifurcating the hilly regions and their inhabitants. A similar exercise could easily be conducted in the northern tribal areas.

The Sora Complex

A good number of different tribes (*e.g.* Lanjia Sora, Arsi Sora and others, *see* Suryanarayan in this volume) are included within about half a million people called Sora by the Census[14] who, speaking a Munda language, live in the south-eastern hills of the province—and in the mountains of neighbouring Andhra Pradesh—side-by-side in the villages with their Pano weavers. As is generally the case in tribal India, none of these Sora units ever appears as a tribe in any sort of joint social action or obligation, be they physical or symbolic. The village is the unit to reckon with, or, on the highest behavioural level, the assemblage of agnatic and affinal villages. Within each settlement, shallow local descent groups[15] (or LDGs) of the commoners (*Porja*) and those of elevated status, either sacred (*Buyya*) or secular (*Gomango*), who operate as ritual units (Elwin, 1955: 128), the members being allowed to marry into either one of these *kinds* as long as village exogamy is observed. Each of these local descent groups also conducts the grand secondary funeral (*guar*) with the erection of megaliths for sacrificial buffaloes, as related by

Suryanarayana in this volume. However, as Suryanarayana further explains, unnamed smaller patrilineal units organise marriages, and for those I met in the mountainous Mahendragiri region the rule allowed a repetition of intermarriage between such units only after an interval of three generations. In other words, the smaller local descent group is referred to unit by the marriage rules whereas clans are conspicuous by their absence. To my knowledge, only the Maler of the Daman-i-Koh mountains in the Santhal Parganas District of Jharkhand manage, like the Sora, without clans, all other tribal communities base their social structure on such large patrilineal descent categories.

Perhaps because of this exceptional social order, *i.e.* the obvious lack of larger institutions and the territorial identities that frequently go along with such a tribal system, the gradual breakdown of the old socio-religious order has been registered among the Sora during the last three decades. This process was accelerated under the influence of Tibetan refugees who were settled by the Union Government in Sora country since 1960 and were also quick to gain the economic upper hand. Similarly, I have noticed the successes of Hindu Vaishnavi sects coming from the lowlands to build temples and propagate vegetarianism as well as the *bhakti* version of the cult, *i.e.* ecstatic dances by males only following the rhythms of brass instruments of percussion. Moreover, conversions to Christianity have also taken place under the influence of "evangelical" missionaries from North America who have radically outlawed former instruments of worship, whereas the Vaishnavi intruders banned all leather items.

These interferences have, of course, caused a major break with the past. In one of the very few impressive monographs on Orissan tribes, based on fieldwork in the nineteen-seventies, Vitebsky (1993) had been able to introduce us to the highly sophisticated spiritual world and the rather introverted cults. Apparently, much of this inner world has now gone under missionary influence, while the Sora outer world has in no way been improved, or become the source of "culturalism". Whereas Shamans, as related by Vitebsky, used to draw events of their cosmological journeys on the clay walls, to be washed away when phases of possession had past, these fabulous drawings, now decorations of match boxes and t-shirts, are being sold by clever merchants on the coast in tourist centres. The Sora do *not* advertise such pieces of their cultural heritage. To my knowledge, they do *not* react at all. Perhaps their spiritual sophistication had led them to a certain disregard or neglect of dangers in the immanent world, but we will never know for sure.

The Kond Complex

Orissa's central mountains are almost entirely inhabited by more than a million people speaking the Dravidian dialects of the language applied by numerous Kond tribes who, along with their Pano weavers, form a new "local society" of every 30 to 40 kilometres, or the walking distance of a day. Territorial clans order the landscape and even the higher territorial level of *muta*, that includes a number of such clans, is still known and discussed. In British days the *patro*, the tax farmer of the micro-king, used to operate on this level, sometimes aided by a staff of non-Kond tribesmen. Judging from the name, a fixed number of clans made up a *muta,* or a "local society", since each appellation mentioned the number of constituent clans, *e.g.* "eight *muta*" or "twelve *muta*". In the Phiringia area of the northwest of Kond country, two fraternal clans, one senior and one junior, would always control a single patch of clan land implying territorial exogamy, but if one of these clans was represented in several pairs of this kind, each of the two could, away from home territory, contract marriages with the other, as long as the two clans involved did not *both* represent either senior or junior status. Today these rules are discussed but no longer strictly observed. The same holds true for the explicit commandment prohibiting the repetition of intermarriage between two household within an interval of seven generations. Presently, a clan-pair is still dominating a limited territory, but the rules of exogamy have been reduced to clan level. Similarly, the grand sacrifice of buffaloes (formerly humans) devoted to the Earth Goddess, *i.e.* a fertility festival connecting mutually agnatic and affinal clans within a *muta* year after year (*see* Hardenberg in this volume), has been discontinued since the nineteen-seventies[16].

Every Kond villager carries a title indicating sacred or secular leadership. Further south, among the shifting cultivators known as Kuttia Kond, two such titles (*jani* and *majhi*) demarcate the local descent groups as the ritual units of a village. They are without affinal reference, as long as village exogamy is observed. While the co-resident Pano weavers practice cross-cousin marriage, the Kuttia households must not repeat intermarriage as long as memory lasts. To this day they have retained their grand buffalo sacrifices carried out in harmony between agnates and affines. In memory of the human *meriah*, each village has also kept for worship the metal chains and tools for torture (*maladipa*) as my friend Albert Götzelmann found out during repeated stays in the 1980s. His hosts, very casual and friendly men, were kind enough to show them to me. Similarly, Niggemeyer (1964) related two decades earlier how, in their prayers, the Kuttia Kond would apologize to the Goddess for the modern substandard victims, blaming by name each of the two 19th century Scottish officers who had put an end to human sacrifice.

Higher up on the mountain slopes and further to south, similar clans, local descent groups and marriage rules have been recorded for the Dongria Kond by Hardenberg (2006). They go together with frequent violence and feuding, particularly in connection with the regular and omnipresent buffalo sacrifice, as a mark of contrast to the other Kond. Along with the Bondo of Koraput these shifting cultivators are the least influenced by caste people, but on the plateau, *i.e.* much below their peaks of the Niamgiri Mountains, local societies named Desia or Porja Kond are fully pacified and adjusted to state administrators, even if they regularly conduct the grand buffalo sacrifice and retain their systems of gift exchange plus an occasional intermarriage with their more aggressive cousins of the high mountains. Only these plateau Kond practice cross-cousin marriage, not the Dongria, even though such immediate repetition of intermarriage is *not* allowed among the caste Hindus of Orissa.

The Koraput Complex

Many Kond also inhabit the southern (old) Koraput District, the "tail" of Orissa, as well as the adjoining areas in Andhra Pradesh. Along with them, some 20 other tribes live in the south, speaking tongues of all the three major Indian language families. All—except the Bondo who disallow it—are practicing bilateral cross-cousin marriage in south Indian style, though all relationship terminologies, by comparison, represent much more sophisticated patterns of symmetry. All of these tribes are unknown or only superficially known to anthropology, if we leave aside two recent monographs[17] and Elwin's older Bondo book of 1950.

Apart from the weavers, omnipresent in all tribal areas of the province, almost all[18] tribals of Koraput cultivate their own fields with ploughs and bullocks after the British colonial Government deforested the huge area in the nineteen-thirties to provide sleepers for the major railway lines in the coastal lowlands (Mohanty, 1997: 4-5). Now the landscape is treeless and exposed, not dissimilar to the surface of the moon, though one can find occasionally interspersed agaves, eucalyptus and cashew nut patches, the witnesses of widely propagated development policies in the 1950s. The tribal memory still recalls the good old days of vast forests and shifting cultivation, but people had to adapt to the recent blessings of civilization. As one result of this state organized deforestation, corpses must now be burned with cashew nut wood. When, in the two to three months of winter, temperatures approach freezing point, only straw fires can provide warmth, but the relatively "advanced" technique of ploughing has mostly substituted hoe cultivation in the rain-fed fields. At the same time the absence of mud roads between the villages has, to this day, prevented the introduction of bullock carts. Heavy goods are being carried on the backs of the animals, as they always have been. On the two or three thinly metalled roads, built in the 1940s when some huge hydro-electric power plants were developed in the region, occasional trucks used to ply, as well as the two Government busses of the day, until, in the 1990s, the privatisation policy lured up from the plains numerous busses that destroyed what was left of the roads and numerous petty entrepreneurs who have made some villagers grow chillies and other cash crops. So far, all of this has had limited effect upon the social life or the value-ideas in common to some 20 indigenous (*desya*) tribes.

The features of this social structure can only be sketched here: No clear-cut territorial boundaries separate the major tribes and yet geographical centres of gravity are easily discernible for each one of them. Social hierarchy is another omnipresent value. When, half a century ago, Dumont (1957) started his arduous—and probably unsuccessful—efforts to convince anthropology of a difference between hierarchy and power, he could hardly have imagined that Indian tribal societies would provide the best examples for his point. All indigenous people of Koraput can be said to be equally poor and without political influence. At the same time all are aware of—and constantly confronted with—unequivocal status differences that are self-understood. In the rather large area of the old Koraput District toured by me[19] some tribes (Rona, Boro Porja, Bhumia, Boro Mali) are known to be the seniors of the indigenous *ryot* (cultivator) category, namely the Gadaba, Sano (Jhoria) Porja, Matia and Sano Mali. Didaye and Bondo, each counting only about eight thousand members and inhabiting the forested hills on the fringes of the high plateau, are again the seniors of their neighbouring Gadaba, but they have never had, like the Rona, a link to the "jungle king" in Jeypur town on the lower plateau. Following the standard line of "hierarchical segmentation", the Gadaba, one of the largest tribes of the region, are again sub-divided into a senior and a junior branch, each with geographical centres of gravity but without clear territorial boundaries. All Gadaba are also the seniors of the Parenga, just as this principle, unilaterally demanding formal respect but not tribute from the juniors, is subsequently extended within all units.

The many different indigenous tribes, including the weavers, *i.e.* the omnipresent landless clients, all share the same eight clans, *i.e.* major totemic patrilineal descent categories, though some have only four or two of them. If an occasional love marriage will make a woman marry a man of a different tribe, this will be tolerated, but I have never heard of marriages within the same clan. The issue may become thorny. More than a hundred thousand members of Bhumia tribe, for example, only belong to either the *tiger* or the *cobra* category so that, in the usual demographic dilemma of moiety societies, one of the two (in this case the *cobra* half) by far outnumbers the other. The Bhumia solution is not surprising, since they bifurcate senior and junior *cobras* and formally, allow intermarriage between them.

In a major ethnographic breakthrough, Peter Berger has, among the Gadaba, recently discovered discreet village units or spatial clan concepts below this totemic level, the so-called "village-clan" (*see* Berger in this volume) which the people themselves call *the twelve brothers, thirteen seats*. This unit is of tremendous ritual relevance and is activated in assemblies when normative crises interfere with the "anarchical regulations" of the tribe. Perhaps such a technically inconspicuous, though sociologically central, patterning of the landscape is a regular feature of all tribes, as future research may show. For the time being, we are only aware of the inclusive endogamous and exogamous social categories, as elaborated by Berger in this volume, with local descent groups segmenting the village community and, for example, performing the specific obligations during the Gadaba grand give-away festivals of fertility and secondary funerals called *gotr* (Pfeffer, 2001).

Some authors have applied the term "lineage" to these intra-village units, but I hesitate to do so, since such phrasing would imply similarities with the constitutions of the well-known African or Middle Eastern tribal societies that—at least according to the classical Africanist literature—depend upon focal ancestors, extended pedigrees, and regular forms of segmentation according to the genealogical lines which also determine the set "complimentary oppositions". All of this is absent in Koraput and middle India in general. The territorial dimension is relevant to the extent that tribes as well as totemic clans have territorial and local centres of gravity which, in the case of clans, may be institutionalised by ritual markers, just as the village as such (or the "village-clan") is bound to a timeless deity, represented by an unshaped stone. Gadaba intra-village local descent groups each refer to a different platform where—in exchange for a buffalo—agnates of another village have, as reciprocally obliged "brothers", planted a megalith in memory of a deceased member. These platforms attain ritual relevance only during the secondary funerals (*gotr*). Such memorials are lacking in other tribes but all of the latter have similar local descent groups that, except for those of the weavers, are associated with honorific titles. In fact, some individuals also bear such leadership appellations, though all of these elders must display modesty in public and be inconspicuous in dress and behaviour. Only then villagers might, or might not, listen to them.

On the Koraput plateau I have found the most expressionistic and vigorous tribal cultures of India. Quite a few individuals, perhaps two or three per cent of the population, have adopted an ascetic religious movement of the plains called *Mahima Dharma*, even though, as Lidia Guzy (2003) has shown, they have remained members of the regular communal life and inspired the adopted creeds with their own characteristic ecstasy so that these creeds bear little resemblance with the nominally—the same convictions of the caste people in the lowlands who had sent their missionaries. In fact, tribals have not 'usurped' the *Alekh* movement but transformed it into an indigenous cult in spite of the roots in the plains. Rather than, in the style of "culturalism", pronouncing their own identity to the rest of the world, they add a local imprint to the imported creed without much ado. All people of the plateau, being separated from the plains of caste India by steep passes through barren hills, have little to fear and less cause for a defensive stance. Deforestation may have accelerated the inner communication and strength of the indigenous people, *i.e.* facilitated the exchanges between the many different tribes in contrast to the—otherwise similar—obvious parochialism in the forest villages within the Kond and Sora complexes.

The Gond Complex

In the southwest of Koraput (now Malkangiri District) and at the very "tail-end" of the province and beyond in Andhra Pradesh, *i.e.* in the steppe and the forested area of the adjoining Bastar District, lies Gond country. It used to be almost exclusively inhabited by a number of different Gond tribes such as Dorla, Dhurwa and Koya. During the last decades, however, major irrigation projects for the benefit of newly settled refugees from Bangladesh have been developed to the disadvantage of the locals who used to, and sometimes still do, shift their villages after the soil is worn out. All Gond peoples structure their local societies by four or five totemic and exogamous phratries which again are said to be subdivided into numerous totemic clans[20], as elaborated by Demmer in this volume. However, each one of the phratries is usually represented on the village level so that *intra*-village marriage, being quite impossible in the previous three tribal complexes, is common and usually of the cross-cousin type. In fact, the relation between phratry and clan is far from clear in the ethnographic accounts and my own repeated visits of the villages have not brought any further light. All written reports mention a multitude of clans, but anyone visiting a Koya a village today would be impressed by the huge menhirs or wooden poles, bearing witness of the grand secondary funerals and representing the dead according to the particular phratry rather than distinguishing clans. My impression is that the phratries, all represented in a village, have taken over the ritual functions of the local descent groups as described above among the Sora, Kond and Koraput tribes. As to the clans, the literature mentions them and my informants have named them, but I have simply failed to see them operate on the local level. As a general conclusion, it may be obvious that future research must raise all of the Radcliffe-Brownian questions, *e.g.* those on the close ritual and sometimes jocular link, in life and death, between maternal uncle and sister's son, since Elwin and others offer many anecdotal observations in this direction which are lacking a structural perspective. But then current anthropology is not really interested in the question of an ordered anarchy that is publically executed by millions of tribal people in southern Orissa and the adjoining regions.

The New Peasant Complex

Further North, after a small strip of Chhattisgarh province, the plains on Orissa's western borderland, surrounded by the Gandhamardhan Hills, are the home of a large society which I associate with the peasantry of the world (*see* Wolf, 1966) rather than the tribal order. My description will be confined to a few externally observable issues. The tax-paying cultivators are small landowners belonging mostly to several different *Scheduled Tribes* (*ST*) and a minority of *general* castes (including the weavers of fine cotton cloth). Their subordinate *Scheduled Caste* (*SC*) weavers work as plough servants and as manufacturers of coarse cotton blankets and loin cloths. All speak only Oriya and Hindi, the Indo-Aryan languages, and the owner-cultivators, irrespective of administrative status, respect one another as equally energetic and successful peasants.

Of the *Scheduled Tribes*, the Binjhal (or "sweatless") and the Gond used to have "kings" in their rows who, during colonial days, collected taxes from the cultivators on behalf of the British sponsored jungle-kings, in return for a tax-free estate. In fact, the then tribal leaders occupied an administrate level below the theatre monarchs of the jungle, but such positions indicate that these two *ST* were always, as they are today, of a slightly higher status than the Kulta peasants said to be a *general* caste these days and the other two local *ST* known as[21] Kond and Sora but without any known historical or cultural resemblance with the above mentioned tribes of the Kond and Sora complex. The status difference between the higher ranking Binjhal and Gond and the lower ranking Kulta, and Weavers, Kond and Sora may be minimal and may have absolutely no practical implications, but it is publically alluded to. Like the subordinate weavers, all of these ethnic units are subdivided into numerous exogamic clans *within and between* the large multi-ethnic villages with preferential cross-cousin marriage[22] being the only regular affinal feature.

However, the Gond are an exception, though they too manifest numerous clan categories in every village. When I asked their elders for the totemic phratries (of the "Gond complex"), they failed to understand me. Remembering then how von Fürer-Haimendorf (1956: 500) had discovered a numerical, rather than a totemic order of phratries in Adilabad, I touched these numbers, and they indeed referred to five phratries in numerical order (3, 4, 5, 6, and 7[23]) with the additional nos. 1 and 2 being reserved for the Gond priests. Without any clear territorial order, these phratries included the multitude of clans. Given these conditions, my impression is that the situation of "the Gond complex" with a single tribe and different phratries practicing ordered intermarriage *within* the village could have been transformed by two externally induced factors:

1. The population of any village has grown to the tenfold size, without any of the—otherwise usual—classification differentiating communal units into "jungle-clearers" and "latecomers". As a consequence numerous ethnic groups of about the same social status inhabit a single village without clear and significant communal entities such as local descent groups.
2. The order of the pre-modern state with hereditary taxation and tax-farmers is self-understood but absent elsewhere.

All of these peasants, irrespective of their *Scheduled Tribe* status of the contemporary administration, bear little resemblance to the anthropological category of tribal society. At the same time, several reasons also speak *against* their status as caste people. The ideology of caste that envisages far-reaching concepts of purity and pollution and intricate status differences is absent. As far as social groups are concerned, Brahmins and Brahmanical classification are nowhere in sight. All of the locals, including the *general* caste of Kulta, employ the services of non-Brahmin priests who are, like everybody else, small landholder-cultivators as well as ritual specialists within each of the ethnic units. In fact, the Kulta history may not have been different from that of the Binjhal, Gond, Kond and Sora of the region save some accident that had excluded them from the governmental *Schedules* during the constitutional reforms of 1935. In short, neither the tribal relational patterns and rituals, found in the other four zones, can be detected in this region, nor the caste system and Hindu temples and festivals. A regional peasantry based on large families and local cults has developed.

Furthermore, all of the local endogamous units mentioned pay bridewealth in tribal style rather than following the rules of *kanyadhan* to offer a 'free gift' of a virgin and a dowry to the bridegroom, as is the all-India norm of Brahmanical Hinduism. All eat pork but not beef in a kind of culinary compromise code, and all lack the—typically tribal—economic self-sufficiency of the village. One could add, as a "survival" of the tribal stage, the elaborate displays of music and dances, linked to the local deities. This form of entertainment has, due to the general geographic mobility, become popular all over the province now that the modern audio-visual media have adopted, and perhaps tamed, the fascinating melodies. In fact, Orissan radio and television, not the people themselves, make a big issue out of this "tribal" music.

As a kind of a minor culturalism, some Gond leaders are members of an *All-India Gond Association* with the practical consequence of networking and politicking within the context of *ST* political representations in elected assemblies. In contrast to the people of the other zones, all of these peasants are literate and well aware of markets and prices, political parties and educational institutions as well as technical innovations. At the same time, I was quite unable to notice ritual barriers between the different units in the same very obvious manner that is found in coastal caste Orissa. My observations leave the impression of a people *neither* associated with the values of tribal society, *nor* with those of caste. The lack of Brahmins, temples, and Brahmanical rituals just as the indifference regarding commensality rules and other ritual discriminations, important in both tribal and caste contexts, implies the existence of several very similar endogamous groups who, united by the common interests as small landowners, supervise agricultural workers of lesser means and status while religion and the ritual concepts of all units are developed and upheld by internal specialists in a non-spectacular manner, *e.g.* without the grand megalithic secondary burials of the Gond complex.

Overview

Certain institutions of the *Scheduled Tribes* in the southern part of Orissa have been described above to indicate variation and different developments, as can be demonstrated on the table below:

ETHNIC COMPLEX.	*Sora/Southeast Orissa*	*Kond/Central Orissa*	*Koraput/South Orissan Tribes*	*Gond/South-west Orissa*	*Peasants/ West Orissa*
Language Family	Munda	Dravidian	all three	Dravidian	Indo-Aryan
Phratries in Village	no	no	no	yes	Yes + no
Territorial Clans	no	yes	yes + no	no	no
Totemic Clans	no	yes	yes	yes	yes
Local Descent Groups	yes	yes	yes	no	no
Village Exogamy	yes	yes	yes	no	no
Cross-Cousin Marriage	no	yes + no	yes + no	yes	yes
Fertility Rituals	yes	yes	yes	yes	no
Clan Megaliths or Poles	yes	yes	yes	yes	no
Shifting Cultivation	yes + no	yes + no	yes + no	yes + no	no
Missionaries	yes	no	no	no	no
Refugee Settlers	yes	no	no	yes	no

The examples of certain external institutions in western Orissa south of the Mahanadi seem to indicate that the tribal character of a community is very closely linked to the concept of territorial clans and ritual unity, as symbolized by grand give-away ceremonies such as the Sora Guar, the Kond buffalo sacrifice or the Gadaba Gotr. The village community is manifesting such symbols of such ritual unity in the form of megaliths and/or wooden poles representing the clan affiliation. Local descent groups, or local representations of phratries in case of the Gond complex, physically manage the ritual interaction of the tribal village. These markers of identity is underlined by the territorial clans of the Kond and Gadaba (in Koraput) or by marriage rules that are non-pragmatic in the sense of perpetuating diachronic affinity either by immediate repetition of intermarriage or—like those of the Sora, the Bondo and the high mountain Kond—by demanding a long interval before the repetition of intermarriage is allowed, with the result of systematically dispersed affinal links and ritual bonds.

The end of slash-and-burn cultivation as a result of the Koraput deforestation did *not* lead to the collapse of the rather homogenous society of many different tribes in the region, whereas missionaries and settlers appear to have accelerated the deterioration of Sora culture, just as the Bangladeshi influx did not improve conditions for the Koya in the Gond complex of the extreme south. The people of the western plains, many being *Scheduled Tribes* for the Government, lack the communal intensity and discretion of tribal society, being open to the socio-political influence of the market and the state. Having become peasants with tax obligations and governmental benefits, they do not seem to have adopted the Brahmanical caste system which can be observed in full force in the coastal plains of Orissa. The new peasants have retained old rules of ethnic endogamy and quasi-tribal priests of each unit, but these "family matters" are a separate domain and seem to have little to do with the public institutions of "kinship", *i.e.* the ritual, affinal, and descent rules that regulate tribal society. The peasant public sector is provided by the state in the form of administrative and educational or political institutions, not that of tribal rituals and or Hindu temples. Though manifestations of "culturalism" are not in sight, the cultural differentiation of the province is obvious and obviously not endangered by either the forces of Westernization or by those of caste.

NOTES

1. The situation in Nagaland and other states of Northeastern India is quite different and, at least partially, more "culturalistic".

2. These have, for example, been praised during huge public rallies of this cultivator caste dominating much of Northwest India.
3. *Yadav* is the modern honorific name employed by the cow herder caste of the Gangetic valley that dominates the politics of the vast provinces Bihar and Uttar Pradesh.
4. *Maratha* is the most populous cultivator caste (or collection of castes) in the Western state of Maharashtra.
5. In Orissa, the castes of landholders and scribes (Khandait and Karana) conspicuously oppose the highest Brahmins. The former seem to have the upper hand in politics, the latter in the administrative services.
6. This word is usually added when the former "untouchables" and present *Scheduled Castes* are being mentioned.
7. For examples, the Badaga peasants of the Nilgiris have articulated such claims (F. Heidemann, personal communication).
8. Usually the composition of these epics is dated at the beginning of the Christian era.
9. The best known is Dirks (2001).
10. For the experts, I offer the following characteristic equations: WPa=HPa; FZ=MBW^1 SpM; MB=FZH^1 SpF; FeB=MeZH; MeZ=FeBW; PassSbCh=Sb; SpssSb^1 PaosSbCh; SWPa=DHPa; PaosSbCh^1 ChSpPa; SposSb^1 ChSpPa; BCh(ms)=ZCh(ws); BCh(ws)=ZCh(ms); osSbCh^1 ChSp; DH=SWB; SW=DHZ. Other features, such as intra-level age differentiation (in the central generations) and equations in alternating genealogical levels are frequent but not regular. North of the river Mahanadi PaosSbCh=Sb is frequent, while to the south it is PaosSbCh^1 Sb.
11. For details *see* Pfeffer (2004).
12. British Historians used to call it the "Sepoy Mutiny".
13. Indian soldiers of the British East India Company were made to bite cartridges that had been greased with a mixture of cow and pig fat.
14. The name is related to the Sanskrit Sabara meaning "savage". In their own Munda language, the Sora call themselves 'humans' as usual.
15. I have, of course, adopted the terminology of Leach (1961: 56) in his "basic assumptions...".
16. Similar information is given by Bailey (1960: 48/49) for the Kond living about 100 km. further east.
17. Otten (2006) on the Rona and Berger (2007) on the Gadaba.
18. As exceptions, Bondo and Didaye of the high hills practise shifting cultivation in the mountains having only a few fields for ploughing.
19. In the Western region of the vast old Koraput District (*i.e.* the new Nowrangpur District), the Batra people (administratively and *Other Backward Class*) seem to hold the highest status of the many indigenous tribal categories, but I have not spent much time in that area.
20. See Grigson (1938: 306/7); Buradkar (1940: 272); Elwin (1947: 61); Dasgupta and Sarkar (2003: 46).
21. Neither Kond nor Sora are indigenous appellations. Tribal people everywhere refer to themselves simply as "humans".

22. For the specialists it may be of interest that such marriages go together with a terminology that equates cross-cousins with siblings. Thus the difference between the terminological and the normative systems is obvious.
23. The Adilabad Gond did not have a phratry numbered "3".

REFERENCES

Bailey, F. G. 1960. *Tribe Caste, and Nation. A Study of Political Activity and Political Change in Highland Orissa.* Manchester: Manchester University Press.

Berger, Peter. 2007. *Füttern, Speisen and Verschlingen. Ritual and Gesellschaft im Hochland von Orissa, Indien.* Münster: LIT.

Buradkar M. P. 1940. "Totemism Among the Gond," *Man in India*, XX (4): 268-289.

Dasgupta, Samira and Amitabha Sarkar. 2003. "New Dimension on Social Organization of Abujh Maria of Tribal Bastar: Communion between Celestial and Terrestial Life," *Journal of the Indian Anthropological Society*, 38: 41-54.

Dirks, Nicholas B. 2001. *Castes of Mind. Colonialism and the Making of Modern India.* Princeton: Princeton University Press.

Dumont, Louis. 1957. "For a Sociology of India," *Contributions to Indian Sociology*, 1 (1): 7-22.

Elwin, Verrier. 1947. *The Muria and their Ghotul*. Bombay: Oxford University Press.

____. 1950. *Bondo Highlander*. Bombay: Oxford University Press.

____. 1955. *The Religion of an Indian Tribe*. Bombay: Oxford University Press.

Ferguson, R. Brian and Neil L. Whitehead. (eds.). 1992. *War in the Tribal Zone*. Santa Fe, New Mexico: School of American Research Press.

Fried, Morton H. 1975. *The Notion of Tribe*. Menlo Park: Cummings Publishing Company.

Fürer-Haimendorf, Christoph von. 1956. "The Descent-Group System of the Raj Gonds," *Bulletin of the School of Oriental Studies*, 18 (3): 499-451.

Grigson, W. V. 1938. *The Maria Gonds of Bastar*. London: Oxford University Press.

Guzy, Lidia Juliana. 2002. *Baba-s and Alekh-s – Askese and Ekstase einer Religion im Werden. Vergleichende Untersuchung der asketischen Tradition Mahima Dharma in zwei Distrikten Orissas (Dhenkanal and Koraput)/östliches Indien.* Berlin: Weissensee Verlag.

Hardenberg, Roland 1999. *Die Wiedergeburt der Götter. Ritual and Gesellschaft in Orissa.* Hamburg: Verlag Dr. Kovac.

____. 2000. *Ideologie eines Hindu-Königtums. Struktur and Bedeutung der Rituale des, Königs von Puri' (Orissa/Indien).* Berlin. Das Arabische Buch.

____. 2005. "Mädchenhäuser, Schöpfung und Empfängnis: Kulturelle Konstruktion der Geschlechter bei den Dongria Kond (Indien/Orissa)," *Zeitschrift für Ethnologie*, 130 (1): 69-98

____. 2006. *Children of the Earth Goddess: Society, Marriage, and Sacrifice in the Highlands of Orissa (India).* Unpublished Post-doctoral Thesis of the Wilhelm's-University Münster, Germany.

Leach, E.R. 1961. *Rethinking Anthropology*. London: Athlone.

Lévi-Strauss, Claude. 1973. *Structural Anthropology 2*. Harmondsworth: Penguin.

Mohanty, Bibhuti Bhusan. 1997. "State and Tribal Relationship in Orissa," *Indian Anthropologists*, 27 (1): 1-17.

Niggemeyer, Hermann. 1964. *Kuttia Kond. Dschungel-Bauern in Orissa.* Munich: Renner.

Otten, Tina. 2006. *Heilung durch Rituale. Vom Umgang mit Krankheit bei den Rona in Hochland Orissas, Indien.* Münster: LIT.

Pfeffer, Georg. 1976. *Puris Sasana Dörfer; Basis einer regionalen Elite.* Unpublished Post-doctoral Thesis. Ruprecht Karl University of Heidelberg.

____. 2001. "A Ritual of Revival among the Gadaba of Koraput," (pp. 123-148) In Hermann Kulke and Schnepel Burkhard (eds.), *Jagannath Revisited. Studying Society, Religion and the State in Orissa.* Delhi: Manohar.

____. 2004. "Order in Tribal Middle Indian 'Kinship'," *Anthropos*, 99: 381-409.

Roy, Sarat Chandra. 1915. *The Oraons*. Ranchi: Man in India Press.

Sahlins, Marshall D. 1968. *Tribesmen*. Englewood Cliffs: Prentice Hall.

____. 1999. "What is Anthropological Enlightenment? Some Lessons of the Twentieth Century," *Annual Review of Anthropology*, 28: i-xxiii.

____. 2000. *Culture in Practice. Selected Essays*. New York: Zone Books.

Tambiah, Stanley J. 1969. "Animals are Good to Think and to Prohibit," *Ethnology*, 8 (4): 424-59

Whitehead, Neil L. and R. Brian Ferguson (eds.). 1992. *War in the Tribal Zone*. Santa Fe, New Mexico: School of American Research Press.

Wolf, Eric. 1966. *Peasants*. Englewood Cliffs: Prentice Hall.

SECTION V

ADMINISTRATIVE "TRIBES" OR ANTHROPOLOGICAL TYPES

TWELVE

SOCIAL EVOLUTION: History or Ideal Types?

GEORG PFEFFER

One of the timeless, though controversial, textbooks of socio-cultural anthropology was published in 1960 by Sahlins and Service, the students of Leslie A. White at the University of Michigan. Against the dominant school of the day, the Boasian "historical particularism" and other proponents of cultural relativity, the brilliant young minds opted for a return to evolutionism, a school that had been ousted under the impact of Franz Boas and his many students, *i.e.* the representatives of an anthropological discipline understood as being one of the humanities in the sense of *Geisteswissenschaften* of Boas' German mother-tongue. The Michigan evolutionists who, to this day, are mistakenly called neo-evolutionists wanted scientific clarity and scientific standards. Holding out against the tide, several universities of the United States, Europe, or India continue until the present to teach socio-cultural anthropology as a science which, in fact, under-scores their materialist approach of what the Germans would call *Naturwissenschaften*.

Their basic formula had been proposed by Tylor (1871) and was, as such, only reintroduced 90 years later. On the one hand the "adaptive specialization"—or history—of a particular population was said to advance its "specific" evolution in the phylogenetic perspective. Its societal structure would be diversified and its members put into a position to utilize functional improvements. On the other hand, societies and their cultures were supposed to be taken *out of* their respective histories and grouped into several timeless types which represent successive levels of all-round progress, or "general" evolution (Sahlins and Service, 1960: 14-16). The authors make it very clear that here the term "progress" is understood in a purely functional and not in any moral sense. The ability of a state to destroy the whole world through atomic or hydrogen bombs, for example, rather than "only" 20 crore people, as in the last world war, is seen as "progress" in this evolutionary context.

The isolated "general" types of evolutionary levels had been named "savagery", "barbarism" and "civilization" by Messrs. Morgan, Tylor, Lubbock and the likes, and as such adopted by Messrs. Marx and Engels, all of the 19th century. The latter two, in an indirect manner, had popularized the concepts in the late "socialist block" as well the socialist minds of India and many other countries. However, because of the nasty pejorative aspect of such an arrogant Victorian terminology, the labels had to be changed and refined by the "progressive" authors appealing to readers of liberal societies in the subsequent century.

The "general" or non-historical types are now known as those of "gatherer-hunters", "tribal peoples" and "peasants" in a very broad sense. Sahlins and Service, following White, had forwarded these comparative levels at a time when Marxism was on the rise in Western and Indian academic circles. They were also able to move beyond the schematic handling of such an arid typology under the direct influence of Karl Polanyi[1] (1968). Perhaps due to these circumstances, the professional public neither tarred nor feathered them in those days, but times may have changed by now.

The dominant trends of current anthropology advocate moral and historical arguments at a global level and subjective or situational ethnographies of the local scene. Levels in-between used to be relevant in the past and were debated as "culture" or "social structure". However, these intermediary concepts, between the global and the local, have been facing a rapid decline ever since the interventions of politicians like Margaret Thatcher who, as a newspaper reported, had "never seen a society—only real people" and who consequently sought either to change or to abolish the social sciences. Irrespective of these trends of the discipline, *en vogue* since the late 1980s, the above named levels or societal types continue to be—deliberately or not—used by some anthropologists, in India more than elsewhere because of the—terminological—proximity between the administrative label of *Scheduled Tribes (ST)* and the evolutionary level of tribal society. Accordingly, a short reminder of the latter's anthropological meaning may not be out of place in the context of this volume. The question will be whether these evolutionary labels are to be misunderstood in the "specific" sense, *i.e.* as historical concepts, or correctly applied in the "general" sense, *i.e.* as Weberian "ideal types".

My experience of several large anthropological conferences in metropolitan India and a simple look at the national weeklies and dailies would lead to phrases like "backward" and "forward", just as the original idea of the Constitution in 1950 was to remove the "backwardness" of the *ST* within a decade by means of "protective discrimination" and then remove the latter. As a result, the established "reservations" have to be renewed by Parliament every decade. In yet another effort, Government has declared certain *ST* communities of India as *Primitive Tribal Groups* (*PTG*) in the 1970s and earmarked additional funds[2] for their "uplift", compared to the "non-primitives". In other words, most anthropologists of the Indian governmental institutions and universities do understand the term "tribe" in the historical sense of people being "backward" and—if one follows their public appeals—in need to be advanced to a "forward" position, whatever that means. Such historical reasoning, *i.e.* the idea that "tribes" are people who must be "developed", is considered to be a condescending and wrong generalization of specific situations and as such reproachable in most "Western" anthropological publications, even though the policies of the "Western" governments make it a point to pass on "development aid" to others in order to—if one follows the public appeals—advance the lot of the citizens of these countries. Mainly because of the above mentioned reproaches, the term "tribe" as such has been discarded by much of "Western" anthropology.

The ideal types have no moral or political connotations but rather refer to certain criteria of the economy, morphology and ideology among the concerned people.

1. Economically the domestication of plants and animals is at issue. Those who avoid cultivating the earth or raising of animals are gatherer-hunters, while the members of a tribal society do live on such pursuits as independent owners, just as peasants plough the land and/or milk the animals but have to part with some of the returns as dues for encompassing institutions such as those of landlords, temples or tax collectors, all exercising their superior demands under the protection of the state. There is no economic inequality among gatherer-hunters and sharing between equals is self-understood, while tribal people organize reciprocity in many rituals of gift exchange, the most prominent being the grand give-away ceremonies. Such reciprocal gift exchange is less spectacular among the peasants. Being a *partial* society, they face the dilemma that any of their investments also allows their superiors to benefit from it, or those who cream off the peasants' surplus product (Wolf, 1966).

2. Morphologically gatherer-hunters operate in loosely organized egalitarian migrant bands of a rather limited size and conceive, at the most, associations of bands that co-operate only very occasionally (Barnard, 1992). Most members of such a band are related to some others through kinship in some way or the other, but the principle of "flux" (Pedersen and Waehle, 1986: 75-90) prevents any rigorous ascription. When dissent arises or harmony declines, bands split or individuals part with the rest, just as individualism rules in all other spheres. At the same time, gatherer-hunters of Africa and India are never alone in some territory. Their social organization "is best understood as a product of encapsulation" (Woodburn, 1986: 31-64). A tribe, on the other hand, is usually much more populous than an ethnic unit of gatherer-hunters, just as a tribe may very well have its own territory or share it with several others living interspersed. These large tribal units may be organized on a territorial basis and/or on the basis of descent. Their ritual and affinal exchanges, not a "law enforcing agency", articulate and carry out rules and thus structure the societal whole which is characterized by numerous inequalities of status—but not of power and property. In the sense of Lévi-Strauss (1973: 28-29), tribes are "cold" societies who, by their institutional setup, are trying to ignore the effects of history. Peasants, on the other hand, experience the very explicit effects of conquest and subjugation or historical change. Like tribes, they may be—or may partially be—organized and regulated through ties of ritual, kinship and affinity, and yet regular interventions "from above" continue to interfere with their relative autonomy. Without such external demands, tribal society is characterized by being "at once structurally decentralized and functionally generalized" (Sahlins, 1968: viii). Kinship institutions are *multivalent*, *i.e.* equally relevant for production, politics and ritual.
3. As far as religion is concerned, gatherer-hunters are said to experience "the giving environment" (Bird-David, 1990) as a quasi-parental or unilateral source of unlimited provisions. Supportive ancestors are bound to return from the underworld which, in many ways, resembles conditions of the living (Demmer, 2001). Beyond such limited sanctions and interferences by transcendental forces, the tribal religion reveals highly influential local and territorial deities, those of environmental interventions and those of social dangers, those of cultivation and those of the chase. All over middle India, the maternal earth goddess

> exercises more power than any other deity, whereas the supreme male god of heaven (or the sun) reigns in a style that is withdrawn from mundane obligations and powers. The aniconical deities are contracted or bound by ritual sacrifices and gifts underscoring their reciprocal exchange relations with humans. Peasants, on the other hand, provide the tribute for many smaller and bigger, at times even huge, palatial buildings of the revered deities or saints holding court in temples and shrines. These sacred palaces, and the multiple services they offer for their divine masters, are highlighted as the models for the less influential secular power-holders who are "the first servants" of gods or saints utilizing for themselves analogical services by the subjects. Peasants have supralocal institutional and hereditary as well as trained priests being part of a hierarchy of clergymen. Tribal people choose specialists on the village level to facilitate transcendental communication, while both peasants and tribals utilize the aid by possessed individuals. Such spirit media are the only communicators with the world beyond in gatherer-hunter societies.

Given this typology—to be applied with the usual reserve regarding "ideal types"—Indian anthropology must choose between the home-grown administrative label and logic on the one hand and the general typology on the other, if at all the term is to be applied. The issue may be rather relevant since no other country of the world is the home of more gatherer-hunter communities and more tribal people than India and nowhere in the world, such large gatherer-hunter communities and such large tribal communities, *e.g.* five million Santhal, are to be found, even though our ethnographic knowledge is, as yet, highly limited. In case the migrant communities continue to be treated as "tribes", international exchanges with the specialists of such researches are unlikely to be productive.

The fact that gatherer-hunters live and work interspersed with numerous other people of castes and tribes had been the source of a most pronounced critique of gatherer-hunters theory (Fox, 1969) and yet, as Gangadhar's work on the Chenchus in this volume illustrates, such an "encapsulation" is a defining criteria for such migrant communities. India has many of them, as are known from the work of Sudhakar Rao (1991) or that of Gardner (*e.g.* 1982; 1991) and Morris (*e.g.* 1981), but more intensive work could be done to counterweigh the sad story of the Andaman Islanders under Indian administration (Venkateswar, 2005).

Similarly, S. Narahari's contribution on the migrant Yerukala in this section refers to one of the few studies on Weberian *guest tribes* or a category that is represented in all Indian provinces but hardly noticed by anthropology. These migrant specialist, minutely differentiated rather than "loosely structured" in gatherer-hunter style, occupy certain niches of the complex caste society, preferably those in urban centres, but until today they are the most obvious "*out*-castes" and as such on the margins of all types of societies found on the subcontinent. In fact, the government of the state is quite unable, and perhaps unwilling, to reach these migrant people even by measures intended for their own "development". This section of our book thus reintroduces some marginal cases as well as Demmer's morphological comparison of a tribal society and one of gatherer-hunters in the anthropological sense, even though both are know as *Scheduled Tribes* in administrative terminology.

NOTES

1. Of Polanyi's many publications, I only refer to the extract of Fried's reader (1968) in the hope that it is accessible and read in Indian departments.
2. Some observers note that if—in the first decade—these funds had been given to the concerned individual members of the *PTG* in cash, such an act would have made the receivers quite prosperous and independent of any further aid. However, the past three and a half decades have not witnessed an increased prosperity among them.

REFERENCES

Barnard, Alan. 1992. *Hunters and Herders of Southern Africa. A Comparative Ethnography of the Khoisan Peoples*. Cambridge: Cambridge University Press.

Bird-David, Nurit. 1990. "The Giving Environment: Another Perspective of the Economic System of Hunter-gatherers," *Current Anthropology*, 31: 183-96.

Demmer, Ulrich. 2001. "Always an Argument: Persuasive Tools in Jenu Kurumba Death Rituals," *Anthropos*, 96 (2): 474-90.

Fox, Richard. 1969. " 'Professional Primitives': Hunters and Gatherers of Nuclear South Asia," *Man in India*, 49: 139-60.

Gardner, Peter. 1982. "Ascribed Austerity: A Tribal Path to Purity," *Man*, 17: 462-69.

_____. 1991. "Pragmatic Meanings of Possession in Paliyan Shamanism," *Anthropos*, 86: 367-84.

Lévi-Strauss, Claude. 1973. "The Scope of Anthropology," In Claude Lévi-Strauss (ed.), *Structural Anthropology 2.* Harmondsworth: Penguin.

Morris, Brian. 1981. "Hill Gods and Ecstatic Cults: Notes on the Religion of a Hunting and Gathering People," *Man in India*, 61: 203-36.

Pedersen, Jon and Espen Waehle. 1986. "The Complexities of Residential Organization among the Efe (Mbuti) and the Bangobi (Baka): A Critical View of the Notion of Flux in Hunterer-gatherers Societies," (pp. 75-90) In Tim Ingold, David Riches and James Woodburn (eds.), *Hunters and Gatherers. Vol. I History, Evolution and Social Change*. Oxford: Berg.

Polanyi, Karl. 1968. "Anthropology and Economic Theory," (pp. 215-38) In Morton Fried (ed.), *Readings in Anthropology* Vol. II. New York: Thomas Y. Crowell Co.

Rao, Sudhakar Nemalladinne. 1991. *Marriage Alliance, Family and Kinship in an Island Community: A Case of Yanadi of Sriharikota Island.* Unpublished Ph.D. Thesis, Deptt. of Anthropology, University of Hyderabad.

Sahlins, Marshall D. 1968. *Tribesmen*. Englewood Cliffs: Prentice Hall.

Sahlins, Marshall D. and Elman R. Service. 1960. *Evolution and Culture*. Ann Arbor: The University of Michigan Press.

Tylor, Edward B. 1871. *Primitive Culture*. 2 Vols. London: Murray.

Venkateswar, Sita. 2005. "An Ethnographic Overview of Policies of 'Planned Change'." *In* Deepak Kumar Behera and Georg Pfeffer (eds.): *Contemporary Society: Tribal Studies Vol. 6 Tribal Situation in India*. New Delhi: Concept.

Wolf, Eric R. 1966. *Peasants*. Englewood Cliffs: Prentice Hall.

Woodburn, James. 1986. "African Hunter-gatherer Social Organization: Is Best Understood as a Product of Encapsulation?" (pp. 31-64) In Tim Ingold, David Riches and James Woodburn (eds.), *Hunters and Gatherers. Vol. I History, Evolution and Social Change*. Oxford: Berg.

THIRTEEN

COMMUNITY-SOCIETY: Models of Social Life in Tribal India

ULRICH DEMMER

Introduction

This chapter is concerned with Adivasi people in India perceiving and conceptualising the social world they live in. In particular I want to ask how tribal communities imagine and construct their social fabric. Empirically the chapter focuses on the Koya of Southern Orissa and, on the other hand, the Jenu Kurumba, a gatherer-hunter and forest trader community of south India. These cultures will be compared with respect to the quest of how they model society and social relationships.

How people represent and conceptualise their social relations is one of the central issues of social anthropology at large (cf. Kuper, 1992) and of South Asian anthropology as well (cf. Dirks, 2001). With respect to South Asia two scientific models dominate the discussion: One is, of course, the one articulated most prominently by Louis Dumont (1970). As is well known he views Indian society as being organized in terms of a homogenous total system, with a consistent single pattern and a prime value. Moreover, social relations are patterned by a clear-cut structure of oppositional ideas like purity/impurity, hierarchy/equality and others. The other prominent model is associated with praxis and discourse oriented approaches and, as represented by anthropologists like Gloria Raheja (1994), points out the openness, the flexibility, the negotiated and contested character of relationships and values in contrast to the terms of structure or system as forwarded by Dumont.

Yet, unless these models are tested against indigenous conceptions of social life both are in danger of essentializing anthropological ideas. While we can all agree, in other words, on the most general thesis that models (scientific and indigenous ones) are constructed, empirically we surely need to show on empirical grounds the terms in which, for example, Adivasi people, do in fact conceptualise their social world. This chapter, therefore, explores Adivasi conceptions of social life and seeks to analyse on empirical grounds whether indigenous models see social relations as being negotiated, flexible and contested or as systematic, fixed and rule-guided. Drawing on fieldwork among two Indian Adivasi cultures it investigates what kind of models these people conceptualise.

A Plurality of Views

It is in particular the late R. Burghart (1978, 1983) and G. Pfeffer (1997) who seriously began to take up those questions. Burghart (1983) explicitly argued for a hermeneutic and what he called an "intra-cultural" approach. He forwarded the fact that social relationships are not only the object of scientists but of the people 'on the ground', so to say, as well. Notwithstanding the fact that empirical models will always be subject to a retranslation into the language of scientific discourse, from this point of view, rather than starting from a uniform and total concept of society we expect a plurality of social representations "on the ground".

His analysis of eighteenth century documentary sources from the kingdom of Nepal modifies Dumont's model and shows the extent to which local and regional perspectives vary and even may compete with one another. Seen from this angle it becomes clear "that Dumont's theory, for example, only pertains partially to Hindu Society as it actually existed in its recent but pre-modern past. The evidence from royal, ascetic, *and* brahmanical sources indicates", so Burghart, "that the value of purity, far from being a sole fundamental value, both relativised and was relativised by other values". In other words "the brahman, ascetic, and king each presented a hierarchical model of Hindu Society and that each person claimed the supreme rank according to his own hierarchical model of social relations" (1978: 519).

Based on extensive field research among Adivasi societies in Orissa Pfeffer (1997) too argues for a comparative perspective that takes the diversity *and* unity of ideas and social practices as an object of study and not as a "theoretical given". Because Dumont's single system approach, expressed as it were in terms of the *varna* system tends "to remove tribal categories from the agenda" (*ibid.*: 5) he empirically explored tribal ideas that follow a "different rationale when compared to the Hindu or 'Western' order, and pleaded that we concern ourselves with the tribal idea of life" (*ibid.*: 25-26).

Both approaches, then, mark a shift from a single systemic perspective to local perceptions and interpretations. They thus encourage the empirical study of the plurality and variety of models and social representations "on the ground". This does not preclude, of course, that Dumont's or Rajcha's models do match the facts—it only demands that we account for them in each specific case before we begin comparison on a higher cross-cultural level. As Vincentnathan's (1993) study shows, for example, the social concepts of higher castes do closely correspond indeed to the ideas of Dumont.

This is also confirmed by Hardenberg's (1999) research on the Orissan *nabakalebara* ritual where actors in the course of performance obviously represent central ideas of the social order quite in Dumontian and classical Hindu terms. This holds true in particular for the contrasts between "people out of the world" and "people in the world," between ascetic and householder, between individual and society, between egalitarian relations and hierarchy and also for the opposition of purity and impurity (1999: 417).

When we turn to the Adivasi regions, however, we often find quite different models of the social order and its values. Thus Vincentnathan (*ibid.*) also shows that ideas of low caste Dalit or Harijan groups do not seem to follow the hierarchical and binary logic that is taken by many to be inherent in the Hindu System. This seems to be the case for many tribal societies as well where we encounter rather specific conceptions of society. As Pfeffer (1997) reveals "a vast array of tribal and so called scheduled caste people do not necessarily follow the *varna* model of social relationships". The difference between coastal and tribal Orissa with respect to the level of ideas is in fact evident: "The *varna* model is the frame of reference for all castes of the coastal area, but it cannot be discovered in the tribal hills at all. No estate of intellectual ritualists is opposed to the holders of secular power or segregated from the general peasant community" (*ibid.*: 11). If we only concentrate on inter- and intra-tribal relations it is the ideas of seniority and affinity resp. reciprocity that govern tribal conceptions. Thus seniority is seen to order relations "between sub-tribes and between clans and even at the village level members of a single clan subdivide into closely interrelated ritual groups of different standing....status categories and groups are seen interrelated, mutually dependent seniors and juniors...." (*ibid.*: 25). And with respect to affinity, reciprocity and symmetric exchange we can see that "the relationship between intermarrying lineages or between the living and the recently deceased is that of an overall symmetry. Temporarily the "wife-givers" will have a status advantage that will be levelled [however] because of the rule of [...] reciprocity." (*ibid.*). In the following sections of this chapter I will explore two further views about how contemporary Adivasi people conceptualise society and social life, namely the Jēnu Kurumba and the Koya.

The Koya

Linguistically the Koya belong to the Dravidian family of languages that includes in Orissa tribal cultures like the Khond or Oraon and the many sections of the Gond (cf. Tyler, 1969, 1965). The Koya communicate easily, however, also in other local languages, in particular in Telugu. In fact the Koya language itself is, as Tyler (1969) shows, though without doubt a distinct language of its own linguistically closer to Telugu than to any other idiom in the region.

Also known in the ethnographic literature under the name Bison Horn Maria (cf. Grigson, 1938), the Koya settle in the southernmost part of Orissa in what is today the Malkangiri District. Large sections of this tribe also live in the eastern parts of the neighbouring state Bastar. The Koya I'm referring to in the present chapter live in the southernmost part of Malkangiri district, in settlements close to Mottu village.[1] As traditional slash and burn cultivators they are farmers who practice cultivation (*e.g.* rice and millet), but they also herd cattle and buffalo or work in the fields of neighbouring farmers.

The Koya organize their social order in terms of a "group model" of society and represent their social organization as a clear cut network of kinship based groups. According to that model, their social organization consists of five exogamous phratries, namely *kōvsi*, *mādi*, *sōdi, markami* and *podiāmi*.[2] Each phratry in turn is constituted by a number of patrilineal clans (*katta*) with each phratry and clan having its own totem. Both units, that is phratries and clans, are exogamous units to the effect, that all of the phratries intermarry while marriage within the clan or the phratry is prohibited. While actual kinship on the personal level surely is the dominant factor in the structuration of domestic and local units, locality is no longer thoroughly structured by clan affiliation. Even in the times of the early ethnographer Grigson (1938) this was no longer the case (1938).

Fig. 13.1: The Koya Group Model of Society

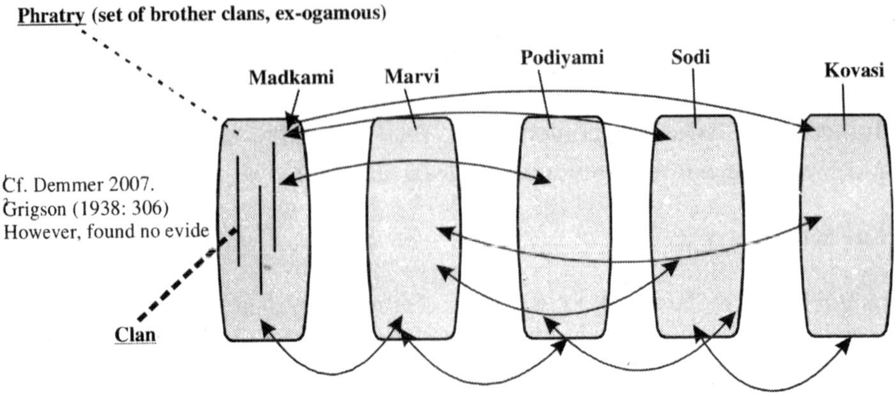

The linkages between the segments are determined by the kinship system, which is of the Dravidian type, differentiating all kin people in two categories, namely those with whom one can have marriage ties and those with whom one cannot. The former category, what we call the affinal relatives, is termed *akomāma*. The latter category, those with whom marriage is forbidden, are the *dadabhai* (cf. also Grigson, 1938: 244-45).

Table 13.1: Koya System of Kinship Classification

Parallel Relatives	*Cross Relatives (Affines)*
dādā (FF), emma (FM)	Tātā (MF), kāko (MM)
tappe (F, FB), evva (FBW, M, MZ)	māmā (MB, FZH, WF, HF), pōye (FZ, MBW, WM, HM)
enna (eB, FBeS), ekka (eZ, FBeD) tammundu (yB, FByS), e:la:di (yZ, FByD)	bātā (FZeS, MBeS, eZH), enge (FzeD, MBeD, eBW) erundu (FZyS, MByS, yZH), ēnda (MByD, FZyD, yBW)
marri (S, BS), maya:di (D, BD)	āne (ZS, DH), kodiya (ZD, SW)

This classificatory system is employed on the clan level as well, so that an ego has a number of *dadabhai*—clans, with whom he/she cannot intermarry and a number of *akomāma*—clans with whom marriage is conducted. This confirms to an overall Middle Indian pattern where, as Pfeffer (1982) has pointed out, affinity is a key social principle organizing the society as a whole.

This is the case among the Koya too where the category of *akomāma* plays a central affinal role. Moreover, not only are the phratries seen as affinal categories because you can talk, *e.g.* of *akomāma* clans but, as the analysis in the present article shows, actual kinship relations and social as well as ritual life are also based on "affinity as a key value". However, those kinship based social structures are not fixed *per se* but have to renewed and maintained. It is in rituals like the death ritual where the meaning and significance of that principal value is reinforced and kept alive.

The same holds true for the relationships between humans beings, the departed and the deities, all of which are seen as members of the society. The later has, in fact, an extended character. As among many other cultures in the world so in this culture too the society is not confined to human beings but includes the dead and deities as well. Among the latter it is in particular the clan deities (*pen*) and the Earth, worshipped as the village mother in every settlement. All of these deities, *i.e.* the clan deities as well as the village mother, influence the well being of the community and are worshipped in the course of the many rituals (*padum*) associated with the fertility of the soil, prosperity and agriculture. Moreover, people also communicate and talk with them in times of difficulties. This 'divine discourse' is only practiced in the séances where Koya shamans embody the deities and act as their medium.

As the deities so the dead too are regarded as important and active members of the society. In fact, they are really a part of everyday life. In every hut of the Koya a part of the storage room (*wijalon*) is kept apart where the "pot of the departed" (*hanal kunda*) as well as the "hearth of the departed" is setup. Usually the dead are thought to live in the underworld, but in times of ceremonies and rituals they are regarded to reside in the pot, in front of which they are offered food, drink and the smell of incense sticks. Moreover, in most of the *padum* associated with the prosperity of the land the Koya also seek to maintain good relationships with the dead in order to secure fertility and well being. The burning down of bushes on the land can also be done only with the help of the dead, because it is a burning log from their hearth that must be used to kindle the bush fire. But even in everyday life the dead are recognized as active beings with whom good relationships must be secured.

In sum the Koya have a rather clear cut idea of what their society looks like. According to the image represented in the death rituals, it is seen as a system of exchange and of marriage relations between groups, namely the phratries and clans. Society, then, is seen here in terms of a group model of social order that consists of five phratries, all of which are connected through exchange and marriage relations. Those relationships include also the other than human-beings and, build on the kinship system and its normative implications, are seen to constitute the basis for the exchange of services and gifts. Society is therefore conceptualized as a rule-guided system of exchange relations with relatively clear outlined structures. Imagined as a network of exchange and alliance among rather clear- cut social categories, it is conceived to rest primarily on values like seniority, exchange and affinity. The findings correspond clearly with a whole spectrum of other tribal societies in Middle India where affinity and exchange relations are the central parameters of the society (cf. Pfeffer, 1982). In some cases, however, the idea of a group model of society is less pronounced and eventually shifts towards a notion of moral community that is primarily based on interpersonal kinship relations rather then on groups and exchange.

The Orissan sections of the gatherer-hunting Birhor, for example, seem to articulate such a social concept. According to the study of Adhikary (1984), the Birhor draw a sharp contrast between their own internal relations and the broader Indian Society. The former are conceptualized not in terms of a segmented society but in terms of personal relations in a moral community.

> "They divide their universe on the earth into *disum* and *muluk*. By *disum* they mean the region of hills and forests, their own territory, and by *muluk*, the peasant villages and the markets, the territory of 'other people'. The Birhor have developed adaptive strategies of participation and social interaction in these two sets of environment: A morally ordered gemeinschaft in *disum* and a rationalist-utilitarian gesellschaft orientation in *muluk*" (1984: 22).

Taking Adhikary's view into account it seems clear that the Birhor have worked out two quite distinct models of social life. One—*muluk*—is related to the world of society and, though one needs not to agree with him that this is a rationalist-utilitarian model is conceptualized as a segmented model of group relations, making frequent reference to terms like groups and what we call hierarchy, status, system and the like. The *muluk* seems indeed to refer to what we have called a group model of society. The other concept—*disum*—serves to imagine the internal personal relations and is based on moral values of a community. Unfortunately we don't have more details about the Birhor conception of community and we must look at the utmost periphery beyond Orissa to get a fuller idea of how a moral community is conceptualized in contrast to "society". The Jēnu Kuṟumba in Southern India, for example, present those ideas very explicitly.

The Jēnu Kuṟumba

The Jēnu Kuṟumba are the numerically largest gatherer/hunter people (around 15,000 to 20,000 people) in South India. Their home range stretches along the western side of the ghat forests, forming today a part of Kerala, Tamil Nadu and Karnataka. These forests constitute the traditional foraging areas of the Jēnu Kuṟumba but since the establishment of reserve—and forest areas and the wildlife sanctuaries of Mudumalai and Bandipur (in the middle of this century), the Jēnu Kuṟumba have been deprived of their rights to forage in these forest regions. Today they are forced to live in settlements (comprising from one to twenty-five conjugal families each) at the periphery of the sanctuaries and reserve forest areas. In the latter they are, however, entitled to gather minor forest products (honey, tamarind, tree-moos, soap nuts et al.). Moving through the reserve forest areas in small, flexible camps, the Jēnu Kuṟumba gather these products throughout the year and they usually sell them to non-tribal (private or public) agents. In addition they are employed as wage labourers in tea or coffee plantations, on farms or in wildlife sanctuaries.

As is typical for many gatherer-hunter cultures, they have no political or juridical institutions like a chief, a tribal council, a village assembly, court, nor do they have any corporate and stable groups like clans, moieties or the like. Social life is thus not based on a group model of society but unfolds exclusively on the level of the community and interpersonal relations. The Jēnu Kuṟumba live in communities of approximately 300 to 400 people, scattered over a wide area. Sociality within the community is predominantly based on kinship relations but in contrast to the micro-castes, the networks of the Jēnu Kuṟumba are neither denoted by names nor situated in a hierarchical organization—therefore, they do not exist as indigenous categories of the social order.[3] This, in turn, is related to the fact that an explicit representation of their society as a totality (be it as a verbalized model or in mythology) does not exist. Likewise the Jēnu Kuṟumba do not conceptualize a clan or moiety system for the network or for the *jāti* as a whole.

Since there are no lineages, unilinear or agnatic descent groups, that act or define themselves as corporate units, the social order is not framed in a group model of society but rather in terms of interpersonal sociality. People in the network are situated in a chain of mutual obligations, in a moral order of kinship that stresses filiative and affinal bonds. Affines, *bā-mayika*, *i.e.* all those who are bound through repeated marriage (genealogical and terminological cross-cousins: ZH-WB, MB-ZS, FZ-BD, WF-DH, HM-SW) should share among themselves, the Jēnu Kuṟumba say. They should support each other if one of them runs into difficulties (having no cloths, no money, no cigarettes, no food provisions, etc.).

As it is typical for many gatherer-hunters the Jēnu Kur̲umba have no headmen, no tribal council or any other institution of political authority. Though all these features clearly differentiate them from the Koya, what they share with the latter is that concepts of social life and community are constructed most explicitly in death rituals. In fact, their death rituals[4] are organized around three "key metaphors" which articulate a performed allegory of a moral community. In a first metaphor, the performance depicts social order in terms of a moral community and a cooperative household. A second image presents it as an encompassing community that not only consists of the living but also of the ancestor-deities and the deceased as well. Finally, the third metaphor represents this encompassing community as a "tradition of argumentation" where people are continuously required to engage in verbal debates on the values of community and on the quality of actual social relations.

The first image—community as a household—is enacted in a series of ritual acts, since a death ritual proceeds in a succeeding number of symbolic sequences or scenes. In the first sequence, called the "*cutting and bringing of leaves*," all male participants walk in a kind of procession to a nearby river or a waterhole. Guided by musicians who play a special tune of music they are going to get branches with green leaves that are needed later on to build a small hut with. Into this hut the ancestor and the spirit of the dead person will be made to sit, entertained with music, dance and food and thus, be made happy.

After reaching the river, the ritual priest (*yajman*) selects a special tree (*onge-mara*) with green leaves and performs a *puja* at the root of this tree. A bit later one of the younger participants climbs the tree up and cuts down enough green branches to build a small hut with. Thereafter all other participants carry these branches ceremoniously back to the ritual place. Holding the branches above their heads and accompanied by music they walk in a line and shout joyfully. Once they have reached the ritual place they circumambulate (anti-clockwise) a prepared wooden frame three times and put the leafy branches on that frame or simply down onto a heap. Then the musicians stop to play and the first sequence ends.

After some time of rest the second scene, called the *bringing of water*, is performed. In this sequence all people present walk back to the river and again they walk in a kind of procession led by the music. The women carry water vessels, while the ritual priest brings two small clay pots. After reaching the river bank, the *yajman* performs a *puja* [as before an offering of bananas, coconut, incense, and parched rice] in front of the water vessels and the small clay pots.

Then one of the small clay pots is ceremoniously filled with water and from now on the ancestor is said to reside in it. Later on the whole group ceremoniously returns to the ritual place. Two children carrying the small clay pots walk in front, in front of them walk the musicians and three to four women follow carrying big water pots on their head that were filled with water from the river before. When they approach the ritual place other male participants join them with foodstuff (bags of rice, oil, vegetables, etc.) and firewood. Finally, the group circumambulates the wooden frame and the heap of green branches three times, screaming loud and joyful in a rhythmic voice.

Immediately after the circumambulation, the small clay pots, the foodstuff and the big water pots are put down and a fire is made with the burning firewood. Then the ritual priest builds a small hut (*udi-mane)* with the green branches and the two small clay pots are put in its centre. If green branches are left, they are used to build a bigger leaf-hut side to side with the small one. In that bigger hut the cooking, undertaken by some of the male participants, takes place. Finally, the *yajman* erects a wooden pole (*ranga kamba*) in the vicinity of the *udi-mane,* adorns it with small green branches and performs a *puja* in front of it. Then, gradually, the musicians start to play and the people start to dance in circles around the *ranga kamba*. This dancing lasts the whole night, and the dancers will only make a break when the food is ready. First, the ancestor as well as the spirit of the dead will get an offering of cooked food and incense. Thereafter, the living too will be served by the people who cooked it. As every other action in ritual context this communal eating is ceremoniously performed and the people are sitting and eating in a quadrangular.

The following day the unification of the dead and the deity is ceremoniously enacted. The spirit and the deity, both still in their clay pots, are now brought in a procession, again led by music, to a tree in the forest. At the bottom of the tree, the ritual priest erects a small stone (approx. 7 inches in height) performs a *puja* (as usual with incense, bananas, coconut and parched rice) and then pours the water of both pots down on the stone. This is interpreted by the participants as their ultimate contribution to, as they say, "making the spirit to sit in the company of the deity".

As these performances make clear the ritual articulates a key metaphor of that culture namely the community as a co-operative household. In the ritual process people actively construct an image of the community as a space of actually lived solidarity and co-operation. This concept is further developed in the wake of the discourses and dialogues within the performance. Thus, a good social life is imagined verbally as the "pleasant and protected camp," as the "cool spot," the "shady place in the forest" or it is likened to the "calm and peaceful camp under trees that offer shade". Other verbal images depict it as a nest wherein humans are supportive to one another "like eggs in a nest that mutually support one another and prevent that one tips over" and so forth...

The second main image—the encompassing community—is also performed in the death ritual. This metaphor depicts the community as an encompassing social fabric including not only the living but also the ancestors and the dead. According to the Jēnu Kuṟumba worldview the ancestors and the dead live in the underworld. Nevertheless the latter can interact and verbally communicate with the living. This, however, happens only in ritual contexts. In ritual performances the ancestors as well as the souls of the deceased can embody themselves in the shamans of the tribe and thus embodied they are able to interact and to talk with their living relatives.

In the death ritual this is performed in several scenes. In the first sequence it is the ancestors who distribute the green branches to the living. In fact, they need the ancestor's co-operation to perform the first scene and bring the branches to the ritual place. The same holds true for the second phase. When the living have performed the *puja* at the river bank they invite the spirit of the dead person to join the ritual. Moreover, when they come and embody themselves in the shaman, they also fetch the water from the river and distribute it to the women. Without the support of the dead the living cannot enact this second scene and are unable to bring the water to the ritual place. Thus, the ancestors and the dead demonstrate their solidarity with the living and their belonging to the moral community.

However, their relationship with the living is no one-way-street. The ancestors and the dead not only help and support the living but they also demand solidarity and assistance for their part. Thus, as the performance proceeds the ancestors may indicate with gestures that they want to drink a cup of water or the dead may demand to smoke a *bidi*, *i.e.* a kind of local cigarillo. Usually the living provide both to them. Apart from those "worldly" desires the supernaturals, and in particular the dead, show to have also very human feelings. Thus they point out their suffering and their need for help, they bent down and hold their paining side, they are given a stick to walk because they indicate their weakness and they complain, cry or even embrace their close relatives. At other times, however, they also show their happiness and start to dance in a circle with their living relatives.

The most important act of solidarity, however, is the achievement of the death ritual itself. According to Jēnu Kuṟumba believe, a person continues to live after its death. Yet the spirit of the dead needs to reach the underworld where the ancestors and the other dead are already "at home". Otherwise the deceased will henceforth exist as angry and lonely spirits roaming around in the forests of the upper world. It is therefore the ultimate aim of the death ritual to help the dead to reach the underworld and its inhabitants. From this it follows that the dead need the help and solidarity of their living relatives. This image is celebrated most elaborately in the final scene of the ritual.

After the nightly performance of good and happy relatedness between the living, the ancestors and the dead, the living help the dead to move down into the underworld and to join the ancestors. To achieve that the people bring both of the small water-filled jags, in which the ancestor and the dead still reside, to a tree in the forest. Once the procession reaches the tree, a small stone is decorated and a *puja* is performed. Finally, the *yajman* pours the water of both jags on that stone and with this act, the Jēnu Kuṟumba say, the ancestor and the dead go down together into the underworld.

Another mode of visualizing the significance of the ancestors and the dead for the community is to underline and dramatize their presence. The act of embodiment itself is already a dramatic performance. When the shamans are getting possessed they tremble violently, tumble, throw their arms up or fall to the ground. This, however, is always prevented by some of the relatives who stand close by and quickly catch them. Once the shamans embody the supernatural beings their peculiar style of moving serves to focus attention on them. At those times the ritual place becomes a kind of arena in the centre of which the shamans pace back and forth. Sometimes they stop walking but even then they appear restless, their speech is chopped off and breathless. Many of the living, in contrast, are accorded the role of spectators keenly observing the shaman in the centre. Others, however, are picked out by the shaman. They are brought forward to stand in a row and face the shaman in order to talk with the ancestors and the dead.

These performed images make clear that the moral community not only rests on co-operation and solidarity but that it is basically an encompassing unit unable to exist without the support and moral guidance of supernatural beings. The 'good community' is only realized as an encompassing order which includes the ancestors and the dead as active negotiating members of the social fabric.

This idea also emerges in verbal dialogues. People describe themselves as "the children of the deities" or they address the shamans as the "favourite children" of the deities "sitting in their lap and being taken care of nicely". In turn the deities are imagined as parents who hold the human beings "like children by their hand" who keep the living "like infants in their lap", "weigh them into sleep like children" and so forth.

A third image being performed in the ritual depicts the community as a negotiated community, a social fabric that is based on the discursive engagement of persons in dialogue. This is made visible in the very performance of the dialogues which are not only public but also highlighted, dramatized and in fact "staged" as an arena of debate. But this idea, what one might call "dialogic sociality", is a crucial topic in verbal discourse as well. In fact, the reason why moral sociality must be dialogic in character, is explained in discourse itself. First, speakers frequently express that they are in need of moral knowledge and orientation. Only if they are able to speak with the non-human beings about "what is good and bad" can they walk on the "right and good footpath", as they say. Without it, they lament, there is no justice, no allocation of responsibility, one can't see the correct way of living with other people, etc.

One of the crucial features of social life that these dialogues point out, then, is that communal life is inherently dilemmatic and uncertain. Its outcome and overall development is always open and at stake. The consequence is that, in order to live in a good (!) way or, as the Jēnu Kuṟumba say, in a "shady and protective camp" people are required to *morally* attend to one another. Moreover, to live such a moral life in a good way, people must respond to one another and constantly negotiate and justify relations and behaviour. What emerges in the death ritual is a concept, according to which moral sociality is kept alive only through continuous engagement in public debate. What the Jēnu Kuṟumba discourse tells us, then, is that without debate there can be no foundation (*nele*) for the moral community. The latter can thus be seen as a "tradition of argumentation" where people continually argue with each other over who or what they are.[5]

Conclusion

This chapter investigated empirically local conceptions of social order and society among two Adivasi cultures in contemporary India and it explored how they are represented in the course of ritual performance. As it turns out, the Koya perform an image of society that corresponds in some aspects to the Dumontian theory. Like other Orissan tribal people they conceptualize their social fabric in terms of a kinship based model and as a system of exchange. In the course of the death ritual they represented it in terms of a relatively clear structure of interrelated segments and thus articulate the social order as being organized in terms of a group model of society.

The Jēnu Kuṟumba of South India, in contrast, and probably the Birhor of Orissa as well, imagine their social world as a moral and discourse-based community and foreground the active dialogic construction of relationships on the interpersonal level. Coming close to Raheja's conceptualization of social life as an ongoing process of negotiation and contestation they imagine their social order in terms of a moral community that needs to be reworked again and again through debate and argumentation.

NOTES

1. Cf. Demmer, 2007.
2. Grigson (1938: 306) mentions the *kuhrami* (or *kadiari*) phratry instead of *podiyami*. My own inquiries, however, found no evidence of the former.
3. For those aspects and the general ethnography, cf. Demmer 2001b.
4. Cf. Demmer, 2001 for a detailed description and analysis of the performance.
5. I have explicated this concept in more detail in Demmer 2006.

REFERENCES

Adhikary, A.K. 1984, *Society and Worldview of the Birhor: A Nomadic Hunting and Gathering Community of Orissa.* Calcutta: Anthropological Survey of India, Government of India.

Burghart, R. 1978. "Hierarchical Models of the Hindu Social System," *Man* (N. S.), 13: 519-36.

____. 1983. "For A Sociology of Indias. An Intracultural Approach to the Study of Hindu Society," *Contributions to Indian Sociology* (n.s.), 17 (2): 275-299.

Demmer, U. 2001. "Always an Argument: Persuasive Tools in Jēnu Kuṟumba Death Rituals," *Anthropos*, 96: 475-90.

____. 2001b. "The Social Structure of the Jēnu Kuṟumba". In G. Pfeffer and D.K. Behera (eds.), *Contemporary Society, Tribal Studies Vol.* 4. New Delhi: Concept Publishing Company.

____. 2006. "The Rhetoric and Poetics of Ritual Performance: The Jēnu Kuṟumba. A interactive Multimedia CD-Rom," In Ulrich Demmer (ed.), *Rhetorik, Poetik, Performanz. Das Ritual und Seine Dynamik bei den Jēnu Kuṟumba (Südindien).* Berlin, Muenster: LIT.

____. 2007. "Memory, Performance and the Regeneration of Society among the Koya (Middle-India)," In A. Malinar, (ed.), *Time in India. Concepts and Practices.* Delhi: Manohar.

Dirks, N. 2001. *Castes of Mind: Colonialism and the Making of Modern India.* Princeton: Princeton University Press.

Dumont, L. 1970. *Homo Hierarchicus: An Essay on the Caste System.* Chicago: Chicago University Press.

Grigson, W. V. 1938. *The Maria Gonds of Bastar*. London: Oxford University Press.

Hardenberg, R. 1999. *Die Wiedergeburt der Götter*. Berlin: Verlag Dr. Kovac.

Kuper, A. 1992. "Introduction," In A. Kuper (ed.), *Conceptualizing Society*. London, New York: Routledge.

Pfeffer, G. 1982. *Status and Affinity in Middle India*. Wiesbaden: Steiner.

____. 1997. "The Scheduled Tribes of Middle India as a Unit: Problems of Internal and External Comparison." In D. K. Behera and G. Pfeffer (eds.), *Contemporary Society: Tribal Studies*, Vol. 1. New Delhi: Concept Publishing Company.

Raheja, G. G. and A. G. Gold. 1994. *Listen to the Heron's Words. Re-imagining Gender and Kinship in North India*. Berkely, London: University of California Press.

Tyler, S. A. 1965. "Koya Language Morphology and Patterns of Kinship Behaviour," *American Anthropologist*, 67: 1428-1440.

____. 1969. *Koya: An Outline Grammar*. Berkeley, Los Angeles: University of California Press.

Vincentnathan, L. 1993. "Untouchable Concepts of Person and Society," *Contributions to Indian Sociology*, 27 (1): 25-53.

FOURTEEN

GATHERER-HUNTER CHENCHU OF NALLAMALAI FORESTS, ANDHRA PRADESH

V. GANGADHARAM

Introduction

Social life and the mechanisms including the structures facilitating social relations in the Hunter Gatherer (H-G) communities have been quite challenging as well as intriguing. These communities are leading a life with a simple technology. Their social organization is very simple eluding the attempts to grasp some of the fundamental features and principles in substantive terms. Though the contemporary H-G communities are not identical with those of their ancestors, studying them from different dimensions and perspectives is expected to yield some useful insights for the theorizing of society and social life as such. H-G studies in India are very meagre, in spite of the existence of excellent fieldwork opportunities. Apart from the recent contributions (Demmer, 1993; Bird-David, 1992; Morris, 1982; Adhikari, 1984), much more may be explored from these societies. This article deals with the Chenchus of Andhra Pradesh. The major issues dealt with are:

1. Salient features of the social structure of the Chenchu as reflected in various kin, social and territorial groups;
2. The nature of Chenchu social relations as existing within and between these groups;
3. The distinction of their social formation; and
4. Their evaluation compared to the H-G band.

The state of Andhra Pradesh is the traditional homeland of thirty-three *Scheduled Tribes*. Most of them inhabit the mountainous areas along the

Eastern Ghats starting from Kadapa district to those of Visakhapatnam and Srikakulam. A spectrum of occupations is seen in the tribal economy. While plough agriculture is the most predominant occupation for many of these groups, occupations like shifting cultivation, animal husbandry, horticulture, fishing and food gathering are also reported (Rao, 1993). The Chenchu is the only *Scheduled Tribe* in Andhra Pradesh that traditionally led a life of gatherer-hunters.

The Chenchu

There are several ethnographic and analytical studies concerned with the Chenchu (Newbold, 1846; Thurston, 1909; von Fürer-Haimendorf, 1943; Census of India, 1961; Bhowmick, 1989; Sastry, 1993; Gangadharam, 1999; Turin 1999). In spite of these studies, these people seem to have eluded the gatherer-hunters scholarship in anthropology. The above studies are very rarely quoted in the H-G literature.

The Chenchu do not conceive themselves as a recently formed unit, but rather as a traditional community living on food gathering and hunting. Von Fürer-Haimendorf (1943) singles them out as the most simple tribe, *i.e.* devoid of an elaborate or complex socio-political and ritual organisation. Food-gathering and hunting suffuse the people's lifestyle, in spite of professing several new occupations. A substantial number of Chenchu are anchored to the woods cherishing a life in its most simplest form.

History

Very little is known about the history of the Chenchus. The Hindu epic *Manusmriti revealed* that they are the first dwellers of the Andhra region, having settled here much earlier than the people known as the Dravidians. Various explanations are in vogue regarding the meaning and origin of the name Chenchu (Census, 1961). These interpretations are shown on Table 14.1:

Table 14.1: Explanation of the Meaning and Origin of the Name Chenchu

Sl.No.	*Dimension/ Interpretation*	*Explanatory Meaning*
1.	Ecological	Habit of living under a *chettu* (tree).
2.	Economic	Habit of *chanch* (wandering-seasonal migration) for the collection of food resources.
3.	Racial	Chenchu hair was like *chendu* (ball).
4.	Cultural	Habit of eating *chunchu elaka* (a kind of rat).

The Chenchus were in relative isolation until about the middle of the nineteenth century, the British encroached the Nallamalai and the Chenchus, for the first time, faced a power prohibiting their age-old calling of foraging. Consequently the Chenchus turned restive and resorted to plundering grains from the neighbouring agricultural communities. In order to contain this law and order problem the British, after the futile attempts of punitive actions, launched programmes of income generation for the Chenchus, such as wage labour in the plantations, crop-watching in the peasants' fields, collecting taxes (*metta mirasi*) from pilgrims in return for accompanying them through the forest during their visits to the Sri Sailam Temple and the like. The most significant aspect is that, in spite of these efforts, the Chenchus did not totally detach themselves from the forest. They continued to depend upon its product variety for different purposes, including medicine, food and household equipment. At the same time, the Chenchus treated the forest without change, *i.e.* as a place for recreation, sexual gratification and an abode of ancestral spirits and deities. Moreover, they derived the meaning of social life from the forest that supported communal activities and discouraged an individualistic life with selfish motivations. Thus the Chenchus, to this day, continued to retain their connection with the forest.

The Nallamalai: Ecological Context

The middle section of the eastern Ghats, falling almost in the middle line of south Andhra Pradesh, is formed by highlands known as the Nallamalai. These constitute the most impressive chain of rolling hills laid in north to south and south-west direction in tune with the western coastal belt of the Bay of Bengal. Geographically these hill ranges are located roughly between 15° 10′ and 16° 30′ northern latitude and 78° 30′ and 80° 10′ eastern longitude. The northern most boundary of the Nallamalai lies in the Palnadu basin of the Guntur District and the southern boundary lies in the Tirupati hills.

The total length of the Nallamalai from the northern edge to the south is 430 km. The average width from east to west is 30 km. The elevation of the Nallamalai ranges between 275 metres to 915 metres with an average of 750 metres. The altitude thus varies considerably within the Nallamalai. The total area of the forest is 5161 sq. km. with 39 per cent of the forest seen on flat and rolling hills and 61 per cent on hill ranges (Parthasarathy, 1978: 91).

The Nallamalai hosts a deciduous type of forest. The altitude, terrain, soil quality and rainfall determine the quality and type of vegetation. The topography of the Nallamalai is characterized by a variety of features ranging from small mounds to big hills, flat plain grounds to plateaux, narrow steep valleys to broad basins, gentle tapering hill slopes to steep gorges and ravines, rocky terrain to fertile black soil grounds and high to low altitude zones. The forest types vary from a bushy inferior type to patches of evergreen forests and several large stretches of grass lands interspersed by inferior tree coverage. This topographical variation imposes certain contrasting conditions within the Nallamalai:

1. A relatively wide variety of floral resources of a deciduous nature occur. Most of these floral resources are evenly distributed throughout the Nallamalai so the Chenchus of different places are acquainted to them more or less evenly notwithstanding the geographical distances between settlements. However, a few resources are endemic and their availability is confined to specific zones;
2. Depending upon the topographical, altitudinal and soil conditions, superior and inferior vegetation occurs; in terms of quantity and quality, the vegetation also differs between different zones;
3. The floral resources are usually dispersed, *i.e.* in any given area the number of members per species may be less than the number of species. However a few species tend to grow in high density (*e.g.* tamarind, gum tree, bamboo);
4. Some plants occur in abundance in some areas whereas the same plants are found to be scarce in some other localities (*e.g. Chenchu gadda*, honey, gum trees, tamarind); and
5. Moreover, most of the floral species are season-specific.

In some specific ways, the above ecological features entail certain constraints and risks. The constraints are mostly in the nature of depletion or non-availability of resources. In response, the Chenchu community has adopted two basic strategies, namely flux and sociability. These are reflected in the social organization.

Social Organization

Social relations among the Chenchus are organized through various corporate groups. It has been suggested that some H-G are not organized in terms of a group model of society that stresses institutions, corporate groups etc. (*see* Demmer, 1993). However, among the Chenchus certain groups are clearly recognized. Each of them is featured in specific ways. The following Table 14.2 shows the names of groups and their distinct features.

Table 14.2: Type and Organizing Principle of Groups among the Chenchus

S. No.	*Name of the Group*	*Type*	*Organizing Principle*
1.	*Gudem*	Territorial, Bilateral	Birth, Migration
2.	*Mirasidar*	Quasi-proprietary	First settlers
3.	*Punnapollu*	New entrants	Visiting relatives:Temporary residence; post-marital residence
4.	*Tega*	Chenchus as a whole	Language, cultural practices and more or less similar life-styles and territory.
5.	*Ilaka*	Kin segment (families inhabiting in separate groups either within a *gudem* or in the neighbouring *gudems*)	Consanguinity and affinity
6.	*Kulam*	Patrilineal kin group	Exogamy
7.	*Annadamula varsa kulalu*	Patrilineal kin group	Real and putatively reckoned through filiation
8.	*Bammardula varsa kulalu*	Affinal kin group	Marriage (real and putative)
9.	*Gumpu*	Kindred and action group, agnatically inclined	Food sharing and provisioning; sociality; mutual security and obligation in work; non-kinship parameters like age, skill, status, leadership (All supported by the moral order)
10.	*Kutumbam (family)*	Familial kin group (couple and their unmarried children)	Marriage and procreation; mutual provisioning of food
11.	*Gudese (hut) and illu (Household)*	Familial kin group including one/two other relatives	Filiation, affinity supported by the moral order; temporary occupation.

Tega (Community)

The Chenchus are well known for their skills at honey collection from rocky cliffs and gorges. Another significant feature of their image is their extreme sense of reserve. Adults are said to be usually seen together as couples, wherever they go or whatever they do. They maintain a geographical identity of living in the forest area, though contact with and mobility into the neighbouring farming/rural and urban centres have been increasing at different intensities.

The Chenchus inhabiting the Nallamalai fall into a culturally and linguistically identifiable endogamous social group since they exclusively speak an indigenous form of a Telugu dialect. They call themselves by the name Chenchollu. Their term *tega*, in popular parlance, is roughly equivalent to community or "tribe" (as understood in the Indian context), *vis-à-vis* caste, though there may be other meanings associated with it. One such meaning is a division, or a distinct and unique group, largely marrying within it and exhibiting a sense of sociality.

The neighbouring peasant communities as well as some settlers (*i.e.* outsiders living among the Chenchu) attribute some distinct features or stereotypes to the Chenchus:

- The latter are supposed to be highly unstable and unpredictable in respect of their whereabouts and residence;
- Women and men, it is reported, tend to have multiple single-pair marriages, not caring much for their children;
- Paternity is not said to be strictly valued;
- A reputation of being lazy and incapable of working for long hours (unlike agricultural labourers) is attached to them;
- Mate selection is conducted on a personal and independent basis, *i.e.* a highly disreputable behaviour according to caste Hindu standards;
- Subsistence is said to be maintained on a day-to-day basis;
- Work is supposed to be discontinued until the food reserves in the hut are exhausted;
- They are said to be capable of living in isolated place all alone or with wife and children; and
- Lack of trust between the siblings is also narrated, *i.e.* the fear that one's spouse may elope with the other siblings along with other tales of disrepute.

These external observations are neither corroborated nor denied nor recognized as significant or dominant features by the Chenchus themselves.

On occasions when Chenchus spoke to me about these issues, they discussed such attitudes without any derogatory connotation. However, their self-image offers certain other features which they claim to possess, *i.e.* that they:

- Are proud to be forest-dwellers gaining a subsistence on account of the benevolence of Mother Earth and *Devara*, a blanket term for the forest deity;
- A people who never deny food to those lacking it;
- A people who never dominate or override children, not only those of one's own but children in general;
- A people who consume food to quench their hunger;
- A people who hate or disapprove the destruction of the forest;
- A people who cherish personal values of freedom and liberty in matters related to mate selection and conjugal life;
- A people who believe in the complementary role performance as well as role swapping by largely suppressing gender discrimination; and
- A people who desist personal aggrandizement and cherish polycentric leadership roles.

Thus these special features of their self-image and their discrimination by others single them out as a distinct cultural group. The people maintain their identity by means of endogamy and by leading certain specific life-style as listed above.

Kinship

Central to Chenchu kinship is affinal alliance and *kulam* exogamy. *Kulam* is an organ that promotes exogamy and regulates alliances to the extent that relationships—agnatic, uterine, cognate—are defined and established between individuals. But the *kulam per se* do not prescribe mates in a positive manner, but operate through proscriptions. In fact, the individuals themselves articulate marriage preferences.

The kinship system can be labelled as bilateral rather than strictly unilineal, though there is a perceptible but moderate emphasis on agnates in the group membership. However, the kinship terminology is based on a shallow reckoning wherein ancestors dead for some time are ignored. In fact the ideas of ancestors are rather amorphous in the sense of a blanket term including many ancestors of both the paternal and the maternal side. On the other hand living relatives are given due importance. They are informed about social events such as life cycle ceremonies and personal adversities or an experience of prosperity.

Particularly maternal relationships are always kept active. Following Murdock (1949) the social organization of the Chenchu can be said to resemble that of a Bi-Dakota type. The salient features of Chenchu kinship are given below.

1.	**Descent**	:	Ideally patrilineal but bilateral reckoning is also found.
2.	**Cousin terms**	:	Iroquious (parallel *vs.* cross-cousins).
3.	**Residence**	:	Bilocal/optional.
4.	**Clans**	:	*Kulam*—Patrilineal clans, exogamy.
5.	**Other kin groups**	:	*Gumpu*—agnatic; *gudem*—bilateral.
6.	**Exogamy and incest**	:	Bilateral extension of incest taboo.
7.	**Marriage**	:	Monogamy; serial.
8.	**Family**	:	Nuclear (virilocal or uxorilocal).
9.	**Aunt terms**	:	Bifurcate merging.
10.	**Niece terms**	:	Bifurcate merging.

A classificatory kin terminology is applied to relations on the father's and the mother's side by distinguishing parallel cousins and cross-cousins. An important feature in Chenchu kinship is its orientation towards alliance and not descent. This is due to the practice of single pair marriage and serial monogamy wherein a woman can be a mother to children of two or more persons serially, *i.e.* one after the other, from different *kulam*. Women are not tied down to the *kulam* into which is married first. In the event of divorce or death, the woman has the freedom to choose a partner in a secondary marriage from any other eligible *kulam*. In this respect women are not transferred from one lineage or clan to another. There are several lines of descent which form the basis for brotherly related *kulams* (actually individuals). Naturally the bondage between such individuals is not very strong. Alliance relations, on the other hand, are more specific and hence strengthen the bond between individuals.

Territorial Groups

The H-G literature suggests that communities coming close to "pure H-G" had occupied definite territories or definite places in which they either foraged or at which they assembled seasonally. It is necessary to take a closer look at "being migrant" and "being territorial", *i.e.* confined to a territory and also to a site, and also to clarify who occupied individual tracts and how the territory is maintained. The earliest reports (Newbold, 1846; von Fürer-Haimendorf, 1943) observed that the Chenchus lived in settlements comprising very few low-lying conical huts erected in cleared spots amidst the jungle. In Scott's Ferista, the Chenchu are said to have lived in caves or under the shade of trees. Von Fürer-Haimendorf (*ibid.*) recorded the peoples' memory of the days during which their ancestors roamed through the jungle living under trees or rock shelters without any hut. But it is not clearly known whether such movements were residential flux or a lack of any physical settlement. Today the Chenchus live in "permanent" settlements and have sufficiently and solidly built huts. These are small in size, locally known as *gudem* or *penta.* It was mentioned in the *Census of India* (1961) that the emergence of permanent habitations which were fixed at one place and bearing a proper name must have been a later development. Customarily each Chenchu *gudem* possessed a territory known as *polam* (a common collecting or foraging ground). These territories, though loosely defined, are marked by boundaries. The following account gives some details regarding spatial and social groups.

Gudem

The terms *gudem, polam* and *kandava* throw some light onto the manner the society as such and the communities in particular are organized among the Chenchu. Firstly, the term *gudem* means a lodge derived from the root word *goodu.* More precisely the term conveys a meaning of coalescence, because it is the place to which any inhabitant has to return, being identified with it. This term has to be understood in relation to *polam* and *kandava. Polam,* among several other meanings, is a site or region where resources can be procured, particularly food. This is a beat where the Chenchus roam as foragers. *Kandava* should also be translated as a place or region, just as *polam,* but it signifies two additional or annexed meanings. Firstly, it refers to an isolated place or a place known by certain land marks and secondly, it connotes a *tega* or a *sangamu* which has to be understood, in this context, as a place where other individuals belonging to the Chenchu *tega* (or community) also meet. Then *kandava* specifies that an individual has been away from his or her *gudem* for some time, usually for days, staying in the forest alone or having temporarily putup with the relatives.

Gudem and *polam*—are the two fundamental organizing units among the Chenchus for procuring two important or basic necessities—*koodu* (food) and *goodu* (shelter). These two are procured through social arrangements. Social life is also facilitated by these arrangements. While both the terms refer to a territory, they also signify a livelihood characterized by social action of food gathering, sharing and mobility. At the most elementary level, the *gudem* and *polam* are the basic arrangements adapted to the foraging life style of the Chenchus. The *polam* is gleaned for food and the site of sex and entertainment.

Gudem is understood to be the retreat from *polam* for resting and meeting others who habitually assemble at that place for social life. *Gudem* also facilitates contacts in the form of occasional visits and other social obligation, being the stage for public life and the site for multiple occasions of contact between individuals and families.

The *gudem*, which might be translated as the camp of the band, consists of several clusters of huts, each one is loosely known as *gumpu*. Moreover, a *gudem* comprises of several *kulam* or patrilineally defined groups. Each *gumpu* may in fact be organized agnatically by an affiliation to a single *kulam*. Even then some affinal relatives are also likely to reside in the *gumpu*. And some *gumpu* may—within the camp—stand in an affinal relationship with other *gumpu*. Together *gumpu* and *kulam* are the relevant sub-units of the *gudem* community.

Territoriality is a matter of community interest. At any point of time there are a certain number of core members (*mirasidars*) who have been established since long within the *gudem*. The notion of community and its allegiance to its territory is upheld by these members. The newcomers (*punnapollu*), however, are in no way disadvantaged. Territorial ownership is always a matter related to the community at large and to the people of the *gudem* irrespective of temporary or permanent residence. In principle, any member of the *gudem* is free to forage and collect any resource with the few exceptions of tamarind, soap-nut, and honey which are under the control of the *mirasidars* whose tacit permission is required for the collection of these resources. The strong norm of sharing food, pooling resources and redistributing them reflect the feeling of oneness in the spirit of a communally owned resource base.

The territory is sub-divided into smaller named zones recognized mostly on the basis of geographical location, topography and the nature of the available resources. Another important feature of the territory is the existence of buffer zones which are exploited along with neighbouring *gudem*. Most of the summer camp sites can be categorized as buffer zones. In other words, the territory comprises broadly two divisions—one which is exploited exclusively by the *gudem* community and another comprising multiple sites which are simultaneously exploited by neighbouring *gudem* communities. Thus exclusive territorial rights of the *gudem* community are relevant only to the former division. Among the Chenchus, the social aggregate (*gudem, gumpu*) is characterized by a territorial range with exclusion rights rather than permanent membership as stipulated by Steward (1969: 187).

Though the community of the *gudem* exhibits relative permanence, members may not for ever remain within the same *gudem* or camp. A part of the total adult life span of almost every individual is spent in other territories. Entering into these becomes a necessity due to:

(a) Strife misunderstanding in one's own community,
(b) The scarcity conditions in one's own territory,
(c) The absence of any relatives in one's own territory,
(d) Pull factors like employment opportunities,
(e) Kinship obligations, and
(f) Marital dissolution and the concomitant dispersal.

However the *gudem* or camp is not necessarily pitched permanently to a site. It may be shifted within its range or its *polam*. Whenever, the Chenchus feel inconvenient due to a suspicion that evil spirits may be wandering close by or due to the occurrence of frequent deaths, they shift residences to a new place. Even within the *gudem* individuals shift their huts from one place to another or transfer it to other *gudem* due to clashes with neighbours, the death of a family member and frequent illness of close relatives, or for the sake of convenience in day-to-day dealings.

Mobility

Though the Chenchus are hunter-gatherer they are no longer a migrant community at present. When von Fürer-Haimendorf (1943) worked among them, seasonal migration was in vogue. He felt that the Chenchus were influenced by migratory leanings. Contemporary Chenchus, however, exhibit varying types of special mobility, mainly operating from the *gudem* or *penta*. The most predominant mode of movement is:

(1) Daily trips to the forest, followed by,
(2) Temporary camps in summer and during special seasons of wage labour, and
(3) *Kandava* or *nidra polam*, a stay in the forest the duration of which may vary between one night and two to three months.

The Chenchus usually stay back in the *gudem* during the rainy season while mobility is high during summer. As pointed out earlier, the range is sub-divided into named zones, between which the *gudem* community disperses. The group of a camp is characterized by relatives who are primarily a mix of agnates and affines, but the group's kin composition is far from being rigid.

The camp members need have been original members of the *gudem* or *gumpu* community.

Blood-relatives are preferred associates but real brothers and to a certain extent classificatory brothers are unlikely to settle at a single camp. However, this is not a rule and there are instances where real brothers do stay in a single camp. Thus composition of the *gudem* is flexible. Seasonal migration usually begins by mid January. Camps are raised in the jungle to last for three to four months. However, towards the end of March or early April, when the *mahuwa* (*Bassia latifolia*) flowers start blossoming, the Chenchus may choose to return to the *gudem* or shift to the place where the *mahuwa* trees are in plenty. Groups of the *gudem* usually split into smaller ones tending to establish separate camps which will be joined by some relatives for a brief time or stay until summer camping comes to an end.

Social Groups

Kulam

The Chenchu tribe comprises several exogamous patrilineal groups known as *kulam* or *inteperu*, *i.e.* surname. The members of one's own *kulam* are called *kulapollu* by the member. Customarily, the Chenchu fix the *kulam* name before their respective personal names and a woman, after marriage, acquires her husband's *kulam* name. Though the *kulam* can be considered as a clan, no other distinguishing feature except for the rule of exogamy is noticeable. No ancestors, unknown or putative, are traced by the *kulapollu*. The distribution of *kulam* within the *gudem* is characterized by:

(1) Numerical preponderance of one or two, sometimes even three, *kulam,* and
(2) Several *kulams* represented by very few households.

However, by no means the numerically preponderant *kulam* is supposed to exercise some power or superiority with regard to the others. While some of the *kulam* members could be the first settlers, the newcomers from different other *kulams* might in due course of time outnumber them. Von Fürer-Haimendorf (1943) says that *kulam* are simultaneously regional units (p.89), and local units (p.96), though according to Newbold's account, appearing about 100 years earlier, a *gudem* may contain several *kulam*. This means that, even as early as mid 18th century, the *gudem* contained multiple *kulam* in the current manner as observed by me. The relevance of the *kulam* category seems to be with regard to alliances, *i.e.* marriage regulations, and the expansion of kin relations rather than the operation of a corporate unilineal descent group. Reckoning filiation is usually bilateral and any form of unilineal reckoning is highly limited.

There are very few occasions when the solidarity between *kulam* members becomes the point. The mutual loyalty and co-operation existing between the members of one *kulam* are in no way qualitatively different from those between the members of the entire *gudem* community. In fact, as it will be shown later, the most intensive social relations occur among the members of the *gumpu*. Those of the *kulam* exhibit tend to disperse rather than concentrate spatially. There is no clan council or leadership role nor any other institution regulating and controlling the behaviour of the *kulam* or clan members. von Fürer-Haimendorf adds: "nor are there ceremonial occasions, aimed at strengthening clan-solidarity....Visiting other villages, a man is not offered more hospitality by the people of his own clan than by other friends, nor do clans-people, unless actual blood relations, grant each other rights of free chase and collection on their land" (1943: 95).

Marriage between *kulapollu* is forbidden. Moreover, this prohibition is extended to a few other *kulams* who are considered to be fraternally related. Accordingly, a few *kulam* are grouped as *annadammulla varas kulalu* or agnates in a general manner. In the scheme of marriage alliances, an individual classifies some kinsmen of some *kulam* as a group of common connubium known as *bammardul varsa kulalu* or affines in general terms. However, this classification is neither dichotomous nor uniform throughout the Nallamalai. Neither a single *kulam*, as an unit, nor the larger group of exogamous *kulam* enter into an empirical alliance. In fact, it is the segment, at least a family, of a single *kulam* that is responsible for marriage. Each one maintains its own pathways of arranging alliances with other *kulam*. In fact the fundamental rule in arranging marriages is the custom for a man to take a wife from his mother's kin and *gudem*. These segments of operational units have no particular names. The individuals and families belonging to the *kulam* segment may reside in a single *gudem* or be distributed in neighbouring *gudem*. Within the *gudem*, the households of the *kulam* segment may or may not live in a cluster of huts. Depending upon their numerical strength they are seen distributed across different clusters of huts. The composition of one such cluster is not based on *kulam* membership, but rather on known genealogical relations.

If the Chenchu *kulam* were local groups, the patrilocal rule would also have been in operation. However, in all fairness, also vouched by von Fürer-Haimendorf, the rule is mostly optional. In absolute figures, virilocal residence

(56%) is more preponderant than uxorilocal. However, the occurrence of the latter type, amounting to about 33 per cent is far from insignificant. On the other hand, a change of residence is also very common, atleast during the young age of individuals. If these *kulam* were local, *i.e.* at that patrilocal units, and also patrilineal, a system of *kulam* corporatedeness and ownership rights would have emerged. In fact, some resources are actually "owned", but not in terms of the kind of "property" when an individual A owns a resource *against* an individual B. In fact, the individual, on behalf of the community, is only to guard the resource from theft or other forms of illegal appropriation. The sharing of honey in fact transcends the *kulam* that is supposed to be the owner (*mirasidar*) of the honey combs.

In effect, a *kulam* among the Chenchu does not have any function in ritual, economic, or political contexts. It only regulates the marital connection between individuals. *Kulam* may be composite and flexible local groups (as a *gudem* community) observing local exogamy. Hence they are not like the clans or surnames found among the caste communities of Andhra Pradesh.

Gumpu

If the *kulam* is not a corporate unit, which unit, among the Chenchu, is the one to operate functionality? *Kulam* is not a residential kin unit though a few families belonging to *kulam* reside in *gudem* along with other families belonging to few other *kulam.* These families are not separated on the basis of *kulam,* nor are all the families of all *kulam* freely mixed in the site of the *gudem* or camp. To be sure each family of each *kulam* has a separate hut. However, the huts are not randomly dispersed. One of the most striking features of the Chenchu *gudem* is the existence of clusters of huts—each cluster being separated distinctly from the other. These sub-camps are called *gumpu* and each of them may contain 5 to 10 households mostly comprising genealogical relatives alongwith a few others relatives who have sometimes come as guests. Each *gudem* may contain several *Gumpu* which would usually be formed around a person, though, the links may not always begin and end with an individual. The membership in the *gumpu* is not permanent and rigid. Though blood relationship seems to be the criteria for recruitment, alliance is also a determining factor. Frequent interactions take place among the members of each *gumpu* concerning day-to-day activities. The membership is sustained by a spirit of mutuality, co-operation and common interests in work participation. Though kinship is important, other criteria such as age, skill, leadership qualities, knowledge on technology, the forest, faunal behaviour, medicine and the like are important considerations for the formation of a *gumpu.* However, membership is voluntary though kinship may facilitate and attract persons into the *gumpu.* Sometimes, individuals are even invited by their respective kin.

The members of the *gumpu* are quite familiar with each other, though many of them might have not have grown up together in the same *gudem*, though they might have earlier been in contact with each other owing to visits to each other's *gudem* and alliances or other social events including disputes and sharing episodes. The kin composition in the *gumpu* gives an indication that it is a group consisting mostly of blood relatives most of them being agnates. However close and distant affines are also seen, though less compared to genealogical relatives. The *gumpu* composition is given for a few *gumpu* in different *gudems* below.

Kin Composition of Selected Gumpu (terms as referred to by Ego; only household heads)

1. *G-1 of Peddamanthana*
   Third S; FeB; FeBSS; MZS; MZDS
2. *G-8 of Guttalachenu*
   ZS; WB; WZ; FBDH; DHB; BS; BD(divorced); FZHZH; FaHM; ZHB; WB;
3. *G-3 of Palutla*
   M; B; Z; Z; Z; FBS; FZH
4. *G-2 of Pechhruvu*
   FZHM; half B; FBDH; MZS; MZD; MZDS; FZH
5. *G-1 of Nekkanti*
   Z (Widow); Z (widow); ZS; WB; B; DH; WD (of 1st marriage)
6. *G-3 of Bairulutigudem*
   S; M; B; FFBeSW; WZ; DH; BSS; ZH

It can be seen from the above composition, that *gumpu* is constituted of blood relatives such as real agnates and classificatory agnates. Wife's brother, wife's sister; wife's father, daughter's husbands, called "immediate affines" by Dumont (1983), are rarely seen residing in the *gumpu.* Furthermore, MB, MBS as separate heads of family are also conspicuously absent. Wife's brother is considered to be a significant person to a Chenchu. The former is assigned a very important role in honey collection from *serri* (cliff and ravines). This shows that the Chenchu *gumpu* are patrilaterally organized. However, too much emphasis should not be given to this point, because son-in-laws are also seen residing in the *gumpu* in significant number. This relative is mostly the frequent co-resident along with another frequently occurring one, namely ego's sons. This indicates that post-marital residence may be both virilocal and uxorilocal. Another important feature is the fact that, though patrilaterality is seen in the kin composition, ego's *kulam* is not dominant, because there a substantial number of children of ego's sisters is present. In other words, the organizing principle behind the formation of the *gumpu* is not a kin unit like a clan or a lineage, but follows a variety of individual genealogical relationships.

Another important feature of the *gumpu* are its spatial and temporal linkages with the affinal relatives. Intensive social contacts between agnates and affines occur during special occasions or *times*, *e.g.* honey collection from a *serri* or collection of *mahuwa* flowers for liquor brewing, tamarind, gum, platter leaves etc., contract labour in the forest etc. Also during the summer camps or *locations* when the *gumpu* members may meet their affines or split up with some of their affines. And as such summer camps and honey collection expeditions are organized by *gumpu* which are predominantly structured according to affinal relations. Sometimes this restructuring does not occur and each may maintain operate on its own, but the spoils are shared. As these camps are in a state of flux, they offer a complex pattern that is difficult to fit into any rigid model. Honey collection is one excellent example.

The collection of honey from the cliffs and gorges or ravines yields great quantities. These sites are named, imbued with folklore, and histories of homicides as well as startling episodes of collection. They are also owned by some individuals, *kulam* and the communities who are spread across *gudems*. Usually real brothers tend to disperse to different sites, or concentrate on separate locales. The preparation involves some seventeen tasks such as a ritual, a sacrifice, cooking, rope and ladder making, rolling in smoke bundles, the processing of honey and the guarding of the rope by the brother-in-law of the chief honey collector who would descend into the valley from the hill top to reach the comb.

These activities not just require practice, knowledge and skill but also honesty and a moral qualification. Hence the group is carefully chosen to be combining kinship, friendship, skill and a feeling of integrity. Any number of people may flock together at the site, being are disallowed to draw near to the actual spot of the honey collecting activity. The moral order seems to be important among the constituent members of the task group particularly when it comes to the distribution of honey and the safe-guarding of the honey collector's life.

The kin composition of the *gumpu* indicates that the constituent families are closely linked with each other through sharing and co-operation. The division between relatives is not marked by a close or a distant relationship. MZDS is equated with FBSS and one's own sons and they are not only referred to by the same kin term but also treated equally without any discrimination. The *gumpu* can be seen as one single large household the members of which have collective access and equal rights in the exploitation of resources. But it is not a single unit of housekeeping because the membership is so flexible. While a genealogical relationship appear to be the chief organizing mechanism, it is one that exists between individuals and not between families causing fission and fusion. For instance, widows return to their natal *gudem* to join their brothers. Sometimes this also happens in the event of temporary absence of their spouse. If the family were the integrating unit, the sisters should have stayed with the families of the respective husbands, as is the case in regular caste communities. Among the Chenchus, sisters and daughters occupy prime positions in the relationship network. Brothers and sons have mostly passive roles in the sense that they tend to adjust their residence according to the sisters and daughters of their own *gudem* and those of the *gudem* of their prospective brides. This practice is different from the one Levi-Strauss (1949) expounded when discussing his "generalized exchange". Chenchu women are indeed exchanged. But such transfers are not in themselves initiating or terminating actions. It is not that women are simply given away in marriage as reciprocations of earlier transactions. When it is necessary, women stay back in the native place and their husbands join them. Quite often sister's children settle in their mother's native place to which their mother (the sister) also returns in the event of her husband's death. Common practice among the Chenchu is also the rearing of orphan children by their MZ or FZ even though a FB may still be alive, an unthinkable responsibility in the Hindu caste context. This structural arrangement seems to be emanating from the important female role of gathering food which is regarded to be much more significant than men's hunting.

Service (1962: 33-5) held that agnatic relations in the H-G band are male centred. He said that male agnates come together because having grown up together, trust and familiarity is presupposed. Among the Chenchu, however, male agnates tend to fall apart and to suspect each other of eloping with their respective wives. Furthermore, the *gumpu* kin composition reveals that out of 23 types of agnatic relationships, 13 has a female as the base whereas only ten had a male. It appears that women are equally or even more important in the formation and maintenance of the *gumpu.*

The Chenchu case also differs from Steward's patrilineal band (1955: 122-50) which is said to comprise male agnates with their wives. The Chenchu *gumpu,* as mentioned earlier, has a firm female base. Furthermore, the constituent families of the *gudem* also include individuals who are not agnates. In other words some *gumpu* are not agnatically related to one another. This arrangement existed even when von Fürer-Haimendorf studied the Chenchus in 1940. Such an arrangement continues to exist until today because the *gudem* contain multiple *kulam* and each *gumpu* represents one *kulam.* Thus at the level of *gudem,* several patrilaterally organized *gumpu* are each related to the other mostly in terms of fraternal *kulams* and sometimes as affinally related *kulam.* Such an arrangement at the level of *gudem* resembles that of a composite band. The *gudem* also satisfies two fundamental features of the composite band since:

1. The *gumpu* are affiliated bilaterally with each other; and
2. Membership within and between *gumpu* is not permanent but fluctuates as individuals make fresh choices in response to the ecological rhythm or to conflict management and group adjustment owing to death, disease or other personal inconveniences.

The *gudem* as a whole is a comparatively large aggregate though *not* exactly in terms of Steward's criteria namely "many unrelated nuclear or biological families" and "constant association and co-operation rather than actual or alleged kinship" (1955: 143).

Family

The Chenchu family is their smallest social unit consisting husband wife and unmarried children. A few polygynous families and nuclear families with additional relatives as well as single individual households are also encountered. Married children usually establish independent families, mostly at the initiative of the elders themselves. A family does not exist as a unit detached from others by selfish interests and it is not wholly organized by the division of labour between its members. In fact, the Chenchu family is not entirely equipped to cope-up with production and distribution and is not exclusively controlling the produce because productive resources are not owned by the household. At first it might appear that the Chenchu family is quite an independent unit of production and consumption. However, it is not the sole owner of the resources, as the following examples may illustrate:

1. Game after being killed is not immediately claimed by its hunter. Any person nearby may volunteer to butcher it and, as many others may

more join, the hunter may be pushed to the back stage. In the course of the restless activities which include butchering as well as separating the shares and offerings to the forest deity before the final distribution, it is not so important to assign the different tasks to specific individuals but rather what is or what ought to be done. As soon as the meat has been distributed, the site vacated since everybody will return to the respective *gudem* including the hunter with an extra share.

2. Another interesting case happened in Appapur *gudem*. The *paddamanishi*, *i.e.* the elder of the *gudem*, had sown horse gram and at the time of the abundant harvest, the *gudem* members came to reap the crop each taking home what could be collected. This went on for three days. Thereafter, what was left to the *peddamanishi* could be kept in a single bag.

These two examples may explain how resources are communally owned and a household has no autonomy or sole claim over the goods for consumption even if produced by nobody else. Households are "independent" not because they are self-sufficient but because no estates or manorial rights are vested in any individual. The resources are common property resources (CPR) and *not* open access resources. The chief characteristics of CPR are the right of exclusion and assurance. The territorial resources are in spirit meant for the *gudem* people and the latter are assure each other that they will avoid any excess collection so that no individual share is subtracted. Even if the collection is meagre, it is to be shared with any individual member lacking food.

Each household depends upon others for various services which include among others, baby-sitting, caring for the disabled and the diseased and the like. For the same reason a family need not be permanently anchored to one place. Seasonality invariably forces such a unit to be mobile. Family members are located in the web of social relations having multiple strands extending across the *gumpu*, *gudem* and neighbouring localities.

Summary and Conclusions

The Chenchu are gatherers and hunters of the Nallamalai forest of the Eastern Ghats in Andhra Pradesh. Their society is organized in certain groups which may be broadly categorized under territorial and social considerations. These groups, like segments, are spatially segregated and socially divided. If we examine them within the temporal dimension, these segments appear to be in a constant flux. The spatial group—*gudem* or camp—seems to contain the band and to be broad based in the sense it bilateral kin groups. Agnatic and affinal groups do not live in separate quarters but geographically contiguous, they may be said to form a geographical connubium.

The social groups—*kulam* and *gumpu* are agnatically defined. *Kulam* is a shallow descent group defined by exogamy rather than corporateness. In the band-segment or *gumpu*, membership is far from rigidly assigned which means that a temporary recruitment is possible and any new member can choose to become a permanent resident. Such persons may also be affines, or uterine relatives. Such an affiliation to the band segment *gumpu* is effected through the co-option by at least one relative being an established member of the group. Thus a group as camp or band (*gudem*) and camp or band segment (*gumpu*), can be conceptualised to be an association of individuals with their families related to each other agnatically, cognatically or affinally and occupying a particular territory. At the same time such a group membership is characterized by a high mobility rate resulting in perennial fission and fusion. This kind of a band organization of the Chenchus indicates a rather simple social order while, at the same time, the Chenchus cannot altogether escape the pressures of the general Indian caste society, a highly complex social order. Thus, on the continuum ranging between band simplicity and nation state complexity, the Chenchus are bound to experience both contexts of social order.

REFERENCES

Adhikari, A.K. 1984. "Hunters and Gatherers in India: A Preliminary Appraisal of their Structure and Transformation," *Journal of the Indian Anthropological Society,* 19(1): 8-47.

Bhowmick, P.K. 1989. *The Chenchus of the Forests and Plateau: A Hunting-Gathering Tribe in Transition.* Calcutta: Institute of Social Research and Applied Anthropology.

Bird-David, N. 1992. "Beyond 'The Hunting and Gathering Mode of Subsistence': Observations on the Nayaka and other Modern Hunter-Gatherers," *Man*, 27 (1): 19-44.

Census of India. 1961. *The Chenchus: A Scheduled Tribe of Andhra Pradesh.* Census of India. Vol. I, Monograph Series, Part V-8 (VI).

Demmer, U. 1993. "The Structure and Structuration of Gathering Camps among the Jenu Kurumba Gatherer-Hunters of South India," *Journal of the Anthropological Society,* 28: 249-259.

Dumont, L. 1983. *Affinity as a Value. Marriage Alliance in South India with Comparative Essays on Australia.* Chicago and London: The University of Chicago Press.

Fürer-Haimendorf, C. von. 1943. *The Chenchu: Jungle folk of the Deccan* (The Aboriginal Tribes of Hyderabad. I). London: Macmillan.

Gangadharam, V. 1999. *Fertility Behaviour in Tribal World: Anthropological Perspective.* New Delhi: Reliance Publishing House.

Levi-Strauss, C. 1969. *The Elementary Structures of Kinship.* Translated James Harle Bell and John Richard von Sturmer and ed. by Rodney Needham. Boston, Beacon Press.

Morris, B. 1982. *Forest Traders: A Socio-economic Study of the Hill Pandaram.* London School of Economics: Monographs on Social Anthropology. New Jersey: The Athlone Press.

Newbold, C. 1846. "The Chenchwars: A Wild Tribe Inhabiting the Forests of the Eastern Ghats," *Journal of Royal Asiatic Society of Great Britain and Ireland,* 8.

Parthasarthy, V. 1978. *Andhra Pradesh Forest Souvenir.* Forest Department, Government of Andhra Pradesh.

Rao, M. 1993. *Socio-cultural profile of Tribes of Andhra Pradesh.* TCRTI: Tribal Welfare Department. Government of Andhra Pradesh.

Sastry, V.N.V.K. 1993. "Chenchu Food Gatherers and Hunters of Nallamalai Forests: Problems of Transition," *Man and Life,* 19 (1-2).

Service, E.R. 1962. *Primitive Social Organization: An Evolutionary Perspective.* New York: Random House.

Steward, J.H. 1955. *Theory of Culture Change: The Methodology of Multilinear Evolution.* Urbana: University of Illinois Press.

____. 1969. "Observation on Bands," In D. Dams (ed.), *Contributions to Anthropology: Band Societies.* National Museums of Canada Bulletin, 228. OhaWa: Queen's Printer.

Thurston, E. 1909. *Castes and Tribes of Southern India.* Vol. II. Madras: Madras Government Press.

Turin, M. 1999. "Chenchu," In. R. Lee and R. Daly (eds.), *The Cambridge Encyclopaedia of Hunters and Gatherers.* UK: Cambridge University Press.

APPENDICES

Appendix I: Kin Composition in the Camp

1. **Ego**
2. **ZH/WB** (Affinal)
3. **Z (widowed)** (Agnatic)
4. **B-in-law (H of Ego's Z)** (Affinal)
5. **BS** (Agnatic)
6. **FBS (whose wife is in other gudem)** (Agnatic)
7. **BW (widowed) & her D** (Affinal)
8. **ZDD (Affinal)**
9. **eZS** (Affinal)
10. **FBS** (Agnatic)
11. **ZD & ZDH** (Affinal)

Appendix II: Kin Composition of Gumpu

MATERNAL AND PATERNAL KIN:

F eBS
F yBs
FBSS
Half B
FFB eSW
B
Z
STEP S

M
MZS
MZD
MZDS

AFFINAL RELATIVES

DH
WB
ZHB(dead)WH
FZH
ZS
ZH
FZHM
FZHZH
Half BWM

FIFTEEN

SOCIAL STRUCTURE OF THE YERUKALA: A Migrant Tribe of Andhra Pradesh

S. NARAHARI

Introduction

The social structures of Dravidian speaking South Indian tribes, particularly those of Andhra Pradesh, reveal a similarity although these tribes differ from one another with regard to their ecological niche, way of life, ethnic background and numerical strength. The evidence presents a four phratry system in each with an additional ramification of clans.

There are 33 *Scheduled Tribes* in Andhra Pradesh forming 6.31 per cent of the state population in an area of 11,595 sq. miles that includes a forest belt, hilly slopes and plain lands. Ethnically, most of the tribes belong to the Proto-Austrialoid category and they speak diverse dialects of their own. Occupationally, they can be categorized into food gatherers, pastoralists and cultivators. The present paper reports social structure and mating patterns among the Yerukalas of Andhra Pradesh. Specific schedules, designed for this purpose, have been employed. Relevant data were collected on a total of 474 Yerukala unions from 72 villages of Guntur, Nellore and Anantapur districts of Andhra Pradesh. Extensive interviews were also held with elderly Yerukalas (60 years and above) to substantiate the information wherever necessary.

The Yerukala are known as a migrant tribe of Andhra Pradesh distributed in the coastal and Rayalaseema Districts and numbering 162,560 persons according to the Census of India in 1971. They are known by different names such as "*Korcha*" or "*Koracha*" in Tamil Nadu, "*Korava*" in Karnataka and "*Kaikadi*" in Maharashtra. The people trace their origin from Mahabharata and believe '*Ekalavya*' to be their ancestor. Their dialect is "*Oodra*" or

"*Yerukala Bhasha*" or "*Kulatha*" or "*Kurratha*" which is a conglomeration of Tamil, Telugu and Canarese and akin to a typical Dravidian language in its "agglutinative" structure. The traditional occupation of the Yerukalas is basket-making and pig rearing. Their womenfolk are experts in sooth saying. As many as 15 divisions exhibit some of the characteristics of sub-tribes whose names are derived from the particular occupation they follow as a means of livelihood for over generations, as listed on Table 15.1.

Table 15.1: Yerukala Sub-tribes

Serial No.	*Name of the Division*	*Occupation*
1	SUVVI (or) Yeethapulla Yerukala	Wild-date Basket-makers
2	BADDA (or) Dabba Yerukala	Bamboo Basket-makers
3	Uppu Yerukala	Traders in salt
4	Kunchapuri Yerukala	Makers of Weavers' Brushes (Kunchelu)
5	Yaddu Yerukala	Carriers of merchandise on Bullocks
6	Karivepaku Yerukala	Sellers of curry leaves
7	Kavali Yerukala	Watchmen
8	Voora Yerukala	Pig Rearers and Agricultural Labourers
9	Parika Muggula Yerukala	Story tellers
10	Nara Yerukala	Rope makers
11	Kothula Yerukala	Monkey-men and Beggars
12	Koot Yerukala	Tattooers
13	Bhajantri Yerukala	Musicians
14	Pedditi Gollalu	Snake Charmers
15	Setrament Yerukala	Petty Criminals

The first four of these units are numerically dominant while the others show scanty distribution with small numbers in Andhra Pradesh.

Social Structure

As stated above, the entire Yerukala people is divided into as many as 15 endogamous divisions named after their traditional occupations of which the first four are numerically dominant in the State of Andhra Pradesh, *viz.*, Suvvi Yerukala, Badda Yerukala, Uppu Yerukala and Kunchapuri or Kunchi Yerukala. The first two divisions are found in good numbers in Guntur and Anantapur districts and practise a semi-migrant way of life. The Uppu Yerukalas are highly concentrated in Nellore while the migrant Kunchapuri Yerukalas are found in small numbers but distributed in almost all the districts.

The Phratries

Each division again is split up into four common exogamous Phratries (Figure 15.1) which appears to be a typical Dravidian tribal social structure as observed by earlier anthropologists working with some of the tribes of Andhra Pradesh. These phratries are *Kavadi*, *Sathpadi*, *Manapadi* and *Mendragutti* or *Kothadi* or *Thukothadi*. It is said that these terms are corrupted Tamil words and the meaning of them is obscurely connected with the various services performed to the God, Lord Venkataramana Swami. For example:

> *Kavadi*, is meaning a pole carried on the shoulders with two baskets, pended from its ends, in which are contained offerings for a deity or temple.
> *Sathpadi*, is a corrupt form of Sathepati, meaning adorning a Hindu deity with flowers, jewels and vestments.
> *Manapadi*, is another corrupt form of the word Manapati, meaning singing in praise of God.
> *Mendragutti*, is a corrupt form of Menrikutti, meaning stitching a pair of shoes and presenting them to the temple, a custom still prevalent at Tirupati and other temple shrines.

There is a small but famous epithet on the strength, nature and status of the phratries as informed by an eldest Yerukala to the author during the field work, as follows:

Manam Gatta Manapadi
Sagam Gatta Sathpadi
Nitya Kavadi

This means that Kavadi is the most powerful and dominant group as far as numerical strength is concerned, followed by Sathpadi. The other two phratries—Manapadi and Mendragutti are relatively smaller and resulted intermarriage of the former groups with non-Yerukalas. The mythological assumption, popularly believed by the Yerukalas but without recorded evidence, reveal that a Kavadi boy fell in love with a girl of another caste and, marrying her, he was not socially accepted by Yerukala "*Kulapanchayat*". Therefore, Yerukalas separated their children and considered them as Thukothodi (split phratry group) or Kothadi or Mendragutti. Similarly, a Sathpadi girl, one a fine morning ran away with an outcaste boy and begot children. Since she had lost her chastity, the children were considered to be Manapadi or Manampoyindani pillalu. Apart from these stories, the difference from the nature of religious services to God is to be noticed. Moreover, neither are any numerals associated with these phratries nor any symbols in the form of animals or plants to convey a totemic distinction. Therefore, the status inequality and non-totemic nature of four phratries is the characteristic feature of Yerukala society.

The exogamous phratry among the Yerukalas is an agnatic descent group with a maximal span and its members conceive their unity also sharing a few economic and emotional interests during their daily lives as known from the Gond society. However, it is unclear whether the phratry is a ritual unit or not. Two constituent principles are always given:

(a) Descent, vertical axis following the division into four phratries originally from the services performing to the God Lord Venkataramana, and
(b) Fraternal solidarity, a horizontal dimensional aspect of relationship between contemporary members of the agnatic group and their wives.

The Clans

Each phratry in each division consists of a number of clans (Fig. 15.1) locally known as intiperlu (surname). Like other Dravidian languages one can find these clans in Yerukala usage, preceding the personal names and determining the social relationship of two men and the kinship terms by which they should address and refer to each other. Earlier clans are said to have been restricted to a particular area and group but now-a-days they are seen to be spread into different regions. The Yerukalas treat the members of a clan as a fraternal group. Accordingly, we find the usage of kinship terminology in par with the Dravidian kinship systems (Dumont, 1957). The clans are non-totemic viable patrilineal groups although some of the clans may be named after birds or grass varieties or a God.

A man's clan membership is immutable and persists from birth to death while a woman attains the status of her husband's clan after her marriage. The prevalence of "*Katta*" and "*Garika*" clans in Kavadi and Sathpadi phratries respectively and their unions appear to be numerically dominant. During the survey the belief was revealed that *Katta* (bank or "gattu") is a basis for originating *Garika* (a grass species) while another version indicates that the presence of *Garika* on *Katta* not only provides natural beauty but also strengthens the latter and hence the claim of a different status arises. Whatever the case may be, some interdependence appears to exist between these two clans. Except for them no other clan's people within any phratry claim a higher rank or status compared to others.

It is interesting to note that the number of individuals in a particular clan varies according to the particular Yerukala social division, habitat and degree of migration. Thus, a clan may be considered as a territorial unit regulating marriage alliances. Marriage within a clan is practically unheard off. Similarly, absolutely no evidence suggests the clan to be a ritual unit.

Mating Pattern

The clan system of Yerukala society is a complex governing the patterns of mating among them. The Yerukalas, irrespective of division, are said to be divided into two broad mating groups—"*Pothu*" and "*Penti*," literally meaning male and female respectively. All the families or clans included in the *Kavadi* phratry are *Pothu* and those being in *Sathpadi* are *Penti*. The *Pothu* section is said to have arisen from men going in search of brides for themselves and *Penti's* men going in search of husbands for their daughters. Moreover, the 'alliance' is seen taking place more frequently between these two phratries and similarly particular clans are giving and receiving daughters in a specified way. Relatively, the role of other two phratries, *Manapadi* and *Kothadi* or *Mendragutti* in marriage alliance is nominal, due to their supposedly degraded origin, intermixture, as has been noticed from a sample of 474 unions. Such sort of mating system of organized type recalls the process of 'Homogenization' (Karve, 1961, 1965; Burkhart, 1978) among the Yerukala phratries.

The graphic representation of the marriage network among the four endogamous divisions of Yerukalas reveals that about 50 per cent of the marriages are concerned with daughter-exchange between particular clans of the Kavadi and Sathpadi phratries like Katta and Garika in Suvvi Yerukala (*Figure 15.1*), Gujjala and Saka in Badda Yerukala (*Figure 15.2*), Avula and Kandrakunta in Uppu Yerukala and Jagannatham and Dasari in Kunchapuri Yerukala. This preference may be compared to marriages of other clans of the same phratries, and may be due to the localization of certain clans in the respective divisions. The next order of preferred alliance is between the phratries of Kavadi and Manapadi, Sathpadi and Mendragutti. Moreover, the incidence

Fig. 15.1: Representation of Marriage Network among Endogamous Divisions of Yerukalas

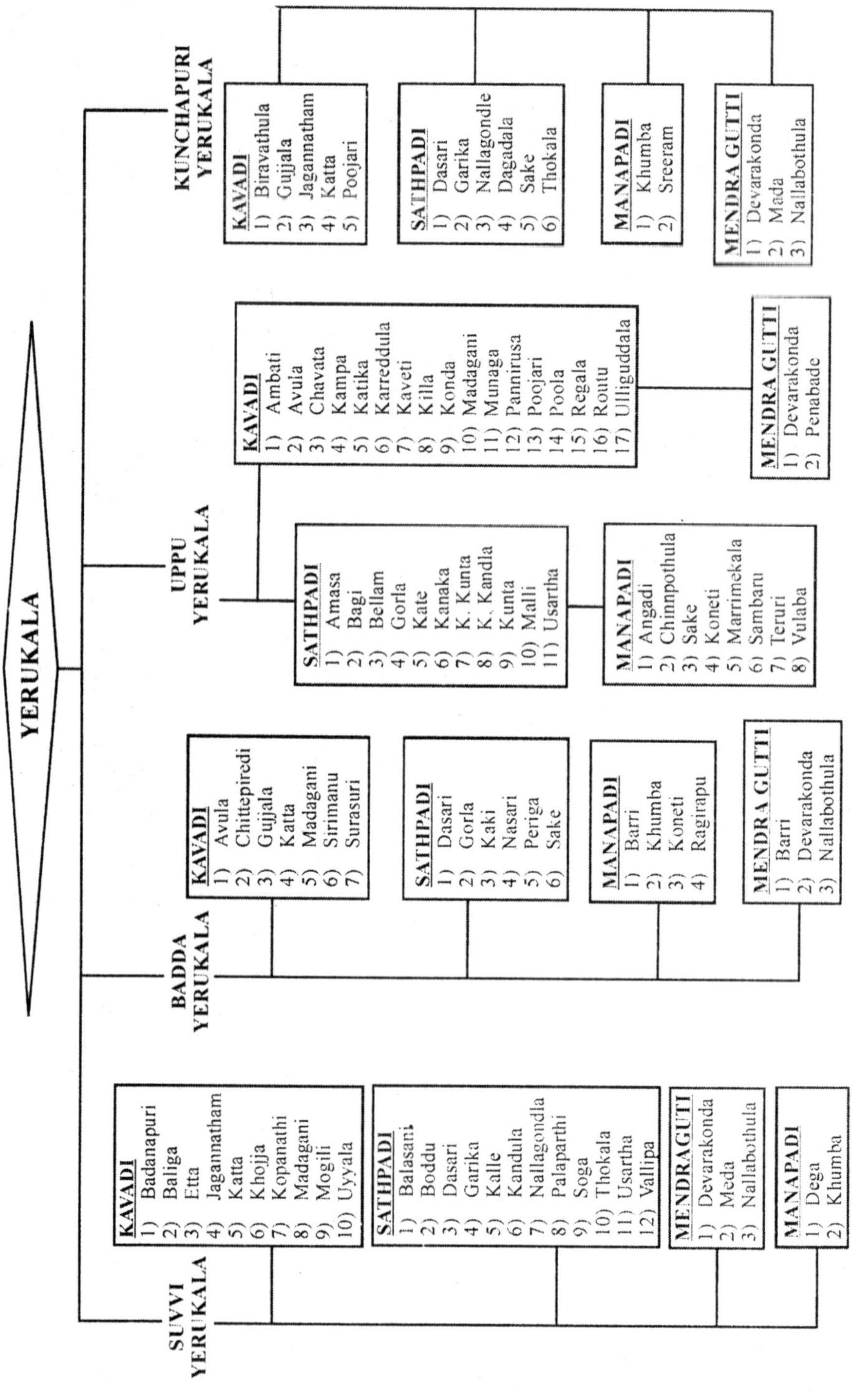

Fig: 15.2: All Marriage Ties among the Badda Yerukalas (N=61)

		KAVADI														MANAPADI				MENDRAGUTTI		
		1	2	3	4	5	6	7	8	1	2	3	4	5	6	1	2	3	4	1	2	3
KAVADI	1												1						2			
	2																					
	3													1	10						1	
	4																					
	5																					
	6																					
	7																					
	8																					
SATHPADI	1																					
	2																					
	3				1																	
	4			1			1															
	5																					
	6			20	1				1												5	3
MNP	1																					
	2		1																			
	3																					
	4	1																				
MDG	1							1														
	2		1												5'							
	3														4							

LEGEND

I. KAVADI

1. Avula
2. Badanapuri
3. Baliga
4. Etta
5. Gurunatham
6. Jagannatham
7. Katta
8. Khojja
9. Kopanathi
10. Madagani
11. Mogili
12. Uyyala

II. SATHPADI

1. Balasani
2. Boddu
3. Dasari
4. Garika
5. Kalle
6. Kandula
7. Nagaleru
8. Nallagondla
9. Palaparthi
10. Sake
11. Soga
12. Thokala
13. Usartha
14. Vallipa

III. MANAPADI

1. Dega
2. Khumbha
3. Sajja

IV. MENDRAGUTTI OR KOTHADI

1. Devarakonda
2. Meda
3. Nallabothula

of consanguinity recorded among these four Yerukala divisions indicates that, depending upon the system of preferential marriage, there is a structural basis for alliance formation and maintenance.

Primary Marriage Preferences

Among the Yerukalas, the most preferred marriage is that of a person with the MBCh or FZCh, *i.e.* the closest cross-cousin or an affine's child with due weight given considerations of consanguinity and descent. Uncle-niece (MyB=eZD) marriages (6–12%) are not uncommon either and therefore, we find a certain variation in kinship terminology.

The persistence of various types of consanguinity among the Yerukalas could be explained in terms of the theories proposed by Karve (1953) and Chekki (1966, 1968) which could be summarized as the pressure coming from parents and grandparents who wish to keep an existing alliance going in order to substantiate the loss of a daughter (sister) through getting her daughter into one's kin's family; to maintain group cohesiveness; and due to a deep-routed traditional customs regarding the familial harmony.

Both the maternal uncle's position and the amount of brideprice ("*Voli*" or "*Sullaponnu*") are relevant consideration when it comes to marriages. People say that if a girl marries her maternal uncle's son, the brideprice will be nominal. Otherwise, a person who is not her cross-cousin, wishing to marry the girl, has to pay a heavy brideprice as a compensation to her maternal uncle. Most of the Yerukala marriages in this regard are decided upon already during their childhood though the consummation of the marriages will take place after the two principals have attained puberty. As a rule, the primary marriages are arranged by the respective parents through negotiations and are conducted with grand rituals. Hence they are purely legal and secular. After marriage the bride moves to her husband's parents' house to live with them. As a consequence, we can find the movement of bands or groups with closed kith and kin during migrant life of Yerukalas. Uxorilocal marriages appear only very seldom.

Secondary Marriage

All secondary marriages should ideally be with a person from one's own phratry though not necessary one's own clan. They are in no way considered to be inferior to primary marriages. Yet they usually take place under certain extraordinary conditions when the first wife has remained sterile or died, has eloped or been suffering from a serious or chronic illness. Thus, a secondary marriage is a simple replacement of a primary wife by a woman of the same category, *i.e.* someone married to a classificatory brother.

Yerukalas value and practice polygyny and there is no limit for a male Yerukala to marry any number of females depending upon his status and ability to pay the brideprice. Then the senior wife has a degree of authority over the junior. In a sample of 474 unions 24 (5%) were polygynous and accordingly Yerukala society as such cannot be considered as a polygynous one since the frequency is less than 20 per cent. The secondary marriages workout around 10 per cent indicating its least an importance compared with those of Raj Gonds (von Fürer-Haimendorf, 1979). They also involve only a very simple ceremony. The primary marriage ties are continued in the event of secondary marriage without any difference.

Widow remarriages are found to be very rare, however, and take place according to a custom called "*Kudike*" or "*Seerakattinchadam*", *i.e.* offering a new *sari* to a widow in the presence of "*Kula Panchayat*" the assembly of the descent group. The percentage of widow remarriages is in quite agreement with general expectations, that is, when there will be surplus of women in reproductive age of a rapidly increasing population, men tend to marry girls younger than themselves and also the women may gradually be absorbed through polygyny as well as widower remarriages (Eaton and Mayer, 1953).

Summary and Conclusions

The social structure of Yerukala society is a complex clan system encompassed by an order of exogamous phratries four of which make up each of the four endogamous divisions of Yerukalas. The phratries (*Kavadi*, *Sathpadi*, *Manapadi*, and *Mendragutti* or *Kothadi*) are indicating various services performed to the major South Indian God, Lord Venkataramana Swami, and by this connection exhibit status inequality. The first two are said to be dominant and original while the latter two are scattered over the country and said to have resulted from inter-marriages with non-Yerukalas. No sound data exist in support of this mythical concept. Being an agnatic descent category, the phratry constitutes the principle of both descent and fraternal solidarity but never appears as a ritual or a totemic unit. Each phratry is again split up into several clans locally known as '*intiperlu*' (surnames) which precede the personal names of Yerukalas.

Irrespective of Yerukala divisions, the tribe is said to be divided into two broad mating groups—"*Pothu*" (Male) and "*Penti*" (Female), each in turn constituting all the families of the *Kavadi* and *Sathpadi* phratries respectively.

Alliance is seen taking place more frequently between these two phratries and that too between particular clans, *i.e.* the giving and receiving of daughters in a specified way. The primary marriage is not only a legal and secular union but also perpetuates the affinal ties even after death. The secondary marriage is not considered to be inferior to the primary one but takes place under unusual circumstances. Both the marriages will be decided after negotiations.

The incidence of consanguinity in marriage is found to be moderate (about 43%) according to the bilateral cross-cousin and uncle-niece marriages that are practiced. In view of the variation of consanguinity among the four divisions of Yerukalas, there appears to be difference in the usual kinship terminology compared to Dravidian type of Dumont (1957). Thus, the social structure and mating patterns among the four divisions of Yerukalas, in principle, show similarities with those of Andhra tribal populations—Raj, Gond, Koya, Kolam and Pardhan.

Acknowledgements

The author is greatful to his teachers Prof. M. Suryanarayana and Prof. T. Ramachandraiah, S.V. University, Tirupati for their help and suggestions.

REFERENCES

Burkhart, G. 1978. "Marriage Alliance and the Local Circle among some Udayars of South India," (pp. 171-210). In Sylvia Vatuk (ed.), *American Studies in the Anthropology*. New Delhi: Manohar. Chapter 7.

Census of India 1971. Series 2—*Andhra Pradesh* Part VI-A Town Directory, Andhra Pradesh: Director of Census Operations.

Chekki, D.A. 1966. *Kinship and Modernization.* Unpublished Ph.D. Thesis, Karnataka University, Dharwad, India.

____. 1968. "Inter-Kin Marriage: A Theoretical Framework," *Man in India*, 48: 337-348.

Dumont, L. 1957. "Hierarchy and Marriage Alliance in South Indian Kinship," *Occasional Papers of the Royal Anthropological Institute* No.12.

Eaton, J.W and A.J. Mayer. 1953. "The Social Biology of Very High Fertility among the Hutterites. The Demography of a Unique Population," *Human Biology*, 25: 206-264.

Fürer-Haimendorf, C. von. 1979. *The Gonds of Andhra Pradesh.* New Delhi: Vikas Publishing House Pvt. Ltd., Chapter 6.

Karve, I. 1953. *Kinship Organization in India.* (1st Edition) Poona. Deccan College.

____. 1961. *Hindu Society—An Interpretation.* Poona: Deccan College.

____. 1965. *Kinship Organization in India* (2nd Edition). Bombay: Asia Publishing House.

SIXTEEN

BEYOND THE TRIBAL SOCIETY: To be or Not to be a Tribe in India

S.N. RATHA

I

A four-fold division, termed as the *varnashrama,* characterized the ancient Indian society. The *varnas* were Brahmana, Ksatriya, Vaisya and Sudra. Initially and ideally, these divisions were not based upon birth but upon the quality and calling of the individual (*guna* and *karma*: Geeta IV.12). Down the corridors of time, the *varna* scheme was consolidated into endogamous sections of functionally interdependent groups in the society, such that inter-marriage between the different *varnas* lowered the status of the offsprings and led to the formation new endogamous divisions called *jati*. Further inter-marriages between *varnas* and the *jatis* and between the *jatis* led to the formation of new *jatis* (Manu X). In Manu's scheme, all such social formations, beyond the four *varnas*, include what in contemporary times have come to be known as castes, *Scheduled Castes* and *Scheduled Tribes* in Indian English. By the time the Indian society was exposed to the Europeans, it was constituted of innumerable *jatis*. The Portuguese called them 'casta'. Possibly they had not intimately come across with that section of the Indian population whom the English called "tribe".

II

In the test *Census of India* of 1872 and later the regular decennial *Census* initiated in 1881, the Indian population was divided into two "social types", tribes and castes, by which time the term "tribe" was already in vogue in Europe to designate non-European communities of Africa, Asia, Australia and the Americas. The term essentially did connote inferior, less civilized status and as having not yet evolved from a simpler primal state, a concept recurrent in the 19th century and early 20th century Anthropological literature parading evolutionism. The tribal society is supposed to represent the second stage in the evolution of society from primitive bands to nation states (Service, 1962: 110-42). Even Bailey's conceptualization of tribe-caste continuum (1961: 7-19) is an indirect acceptance of the evolutionary position in the specific context of the Indian society. However, if Manu's authority on social formations in India is accepted, the tribes are to be taken as genetic extensions of the *varnas*. Thus the Indian tribal societies are not the antecedent stages of civilization but its product, a socio-cultural response to a socio-cultural stimulus.

III

The terms, caste and tribe became handy for the colonial administrators to "divide and rule" India. Beginning in 1918, nine Orders/Notifications were issued in different times till 1936 listing the "Hill Tribes" and "Backward Tribes". Notwithstanding such categorization, the record of land rights (R.O.R.) in India continued to use the term *jati* to indicate all Indian social types. All communities—castes, tribes, even the Muslims and Christians—are recorded as "jati". The constitution Pandits of post British India stuck to the use of the term tribe to set aside a section of India's population to be scheduled under Article 342 of the Constitution, by the President. Article 365 (25) described "Scheduled Tribes…" (the compound term first appeared here) as "…such tribes or tribal communities as are deemed under Article 342 to be scheduled for the purpose of this Constitution". Article 342 prescribes the procedure to be followed in the matter of specification of *Scheduled Tribes*. The indicators used by the Government of India classify communities under "Scheduled Tribes" are "primitive traits, distinctive culture, geographical location, shy of external contact and backwardness". These criteria do not figure in the Constitution but have come to be accepted following the definitions coming down from the 1931 *Census* coined by Hutton, a Cambridge trained anthropologist, the report of the first *Backward Classes Commission* 1955 (Chairman Kaka Kalelkar), the *Advisory Committee on Revision of Scheduled Caste and Scheduled Tribe List* 1965 (Lokur Committee), and the *Joint Committee of the Parliament on the Scheduled Castes and Scheduled Tribes Order (Amendment) Bill,* 1967 and *Chanda Committee* 1969.

IV

From a run through some textbook definitions what emerges as an ideal tribe or tribal formation is that it is a social group of a simple uncomplicated kind consisting of a collection of families of common origin or derivation or descent and custom, possessing a distinctive language or dialect and culture, a name and a definite territory, engaged in joint activities for some common purpose.

Some have also used negative descriptors, such as, absence of any occupational specialization (Risley, 1901: 22), lack of state organization, absence of classes and literacy (Steward, 1954: 44), non-involvement in cash economy, little supra-village political organization, non-adherence to any great religion (Moerman, 1974: 54), limited cultural elaboration and non-existence of central regulative political organization (Sahlins, 1968) to identify tribes.

Tribal societies are said to be inadequately organized to bear an elaborate cultural development, where force is held in severalty and people living in a perpetual state of fear from violence (a situation described as "warre" by Sahlins borrowing the term and the concept from Hobbes), where separate institutions do not exist to control economic, social and religious activities, where all institutions revolve around the wisdom of peace making, where all rituals, economic transactions and kinship are expressions of reciprocity, friendliness, avoidance of unfriendly situations, and where "gain" is measured in terms of social advantages rather than material benefits (Sahlins, 1968).

Through the use of these indicators singly, severally, or in some combination, one can point at some human aggregates as tribes, still Fried does not find the necessity of a "tribal stage".

> "To appear in the transit from a single settlement with embedded political organization to state structured society" and goes on to add "that most tribes seem to be secondary phenomenon in a very specific sense: they well be the product of processes stimulated by the appearance of relatively highly organized societies amidst other societies which are organized much more simply." Thus "tribalism can be viewed as a reaction to the formation of a complex political structure rather than a necessary preliminary stage in its evolution" (*ibid*: 170).

He does not find the theoretical need for a tribal stage in the evolution of political organization and considers "tribalism" as a evolutionary *cul-de-sac*, "part of a spasmodic cycle that in and itself lacks the institutional raw material capable of leading to more complex forms of polity" (*ibid*: 173).

Tribal groups are not social organizations, Fried asserts, "whose integrity recedes into a remote past"; and "that there are clues indicating that the tribalism displayed is reaction to more recent events and conditions"; and "that tribalism can be made to play a major political role in a real present is not a modern discovery. Long before recent European colonialism, not to say neocolonialism, the Chinese, and the expanding state societies had grasped the essentials of divide and rule" (*ibid*: 173).

V

India is exposed to multiple and varied historical forces over several millennia. It is not hard to find social formations conforming to the indicators used in circumscribing tribal societies. So whatever be the administrative compulsions, surfacing of the tribal communities as distinct social types in India begins with the European colonialism.

The *Government of India* issued nine orders listing various communities in various states under the specified Schedule since 6-9-1950. With the introduction of *Tribal Subplan* (*TSP*) strategy for integrated-development of the *Scheduled Tribes* in 1975, some tribes or parts thereof have been identified as *Primitive Tribal Groups* (*PTG*). These groups are identified for their pre-agricultural level of technology, low level of literacy, small, stagnant or diminishing population, remote and isolated habitat, distinct cultural and ethnic individuality and specialized avocation, if any. The Government of India fixed these criteria through an administrative order (G.O.I., 1990: 146 and 153). Now, such groups number 75, and more are likely to be added.

Thus in India, "... tribe is an administrative and political concept" (Singh, 1994). *All* communities, irrespective of their socio-economic status, have been declared as tribes in Kinnaur, Jaunasar-Bawar, Pangwal and Ladakh (except one community). In common parlance, a tribe is one that is not a caste, *i.e.*, an individual is a member of some society by virtue of not being a member of other specific societies. "In South East Asia..." observes Moerman (1974: 54), "...a society is member of a tribal set by virtue of not being a member of the civilized set".

In a publication brought out by the *Government of India* in 1998 for "official use only" 608 communities are listed as *Scheduled Tribes* in an alphabetical order (G.O.I., 1998: 30-45). It appears to be an ever-growing list, and many more communities are likely to be added. The Constitution (Article 46) imposes the responsibility of improving the quality of life of the

Scheduled Tribes on the Union and the State Governments. Therefore, identifying communities fit enough to be "scheduled", has come to become a permanent administrative exercise; and tribal development has become a major, increasingly more important component of the nation's *Five-Year Plans.*

Special privileges are bestowed on the scheduled communities in the form of reservation in educational institutions, state legislatures, and the Union Parliament, scholarships, employment and promotions in government and public undertakings. Areas of tribal concentration are set aside (V and VI *Schedule* to the Constitution) as *Scheduled Areas* for special administrative and infrastructure inputs. These advantages motivate more and more communities to claim scheduled status. Thus the Constitution initiated a trend in creating a vested interest in the scheduled status. The reservations, initially supposed to be withdrawn after ten years, continue till today, being extended at the expiry of every ten years. Such extensions through amendments to the Constitution have almost become a permanent feature of the Constitution in spite of the caution issued by the *Commissioner of Scheduled Castes and Scheduled Tribes* several years back (X Report-1960-61, Part-1, p. 342). He wrote,

> "It is high time to ensure that backwardness does not reach a stage of becoming vested interest with some beneficiaries who are enjoying and monopolizing to themselves the special privileges granted to the backward classes under the excuse of safeguards provided for them in the Constitution."

No Indian language had a word in its vocabulary synonymous with the English word 'tribe'. Now several terms, often with different meanings, are in use. For example, in Oriya, it is "Adivasi" (early inhabitants); in Assamese it is "Janajati" (the term defies translation into English); in Telugu it is "Girijana" (hill people); and in Hindi it is "Adimjati" (early jati). Of late another controversial term has surfaced—"the indigenous people". Now every Indian claims the indigenous status.

VI

Anthropologists in India also do not project a unified view on the concept of the tribal society. While some, like T. B. Naik, hold tribal society completely different from caste society (Bailey, 1961: 9), others like G. S. Ghurye do not find any difference between the two; Bailey takes a stand between these two extremes (*ibid*: 11). Thus in India, there is a great deal of confusion in conceptualizing tribal society. To add to this confusion some tribal communities claim *varna* status—some as Brahman, some Ksatriya, some Vaisya and some Sudra (Singh, 1994: 7); and some castes claim tribal status.

In a nation-wide study of the communities undertaken by the *Anthropological Survey* it is noted that 11.80 per cent among the tribal communities claim their place in the *varna* system. 8.30 per cent claim Ksatriya status, 0.90 per cent Brahman status and 7.50 per cent Sudra status. For example, the Gaddi and the Pangwala of Himachal Pradesh and the Kagaty of Sikkim and West Bengal claim Brahman status whereas the Jaunsari tribes claim Vaisya status (*ibid*: 7). The same study reports that 171 (26.90%) of tribal communities perceive their status as "high", 298 (46.90%) as "middle" and 161 (25.30%) as "low". Among the non-tribal communities, 11.20 per cent perceive the tribal social status as "high", 39.20 as "middle" and 49.40 per cent as "low".

At the moment, a community named Durua in Koraput, having all the qualities of a *Primitive Tribal Group*, is yet to be scheduled (Rath, 2004). Several members of a non-Scheduled community, named Rona are surreptitiously changing their community nomenclature to Kotia, a scheduled community, and an innovative indigenous method of gaining the Scheduled Tribe status.

Those whose tribal identity is already established are innovating methods to establish distinct identities.

> "In their quest for a distinct identity", writes Roy Burman, "the tribal peoples created scripts for and literature in their languages. Today there are at least 10,000 publications including text-books. Intellectuals among them have brought out analytical history of their social processes, languages and literature. They raise their voices against display of their culture objects in museums without relating the same to their social, cultural, economic, historical and ecological contexts. There is a growing tendency to claim their religions as distinct spiritual calls. 5 per cent of the tribal population returned their religion by the name of their respective tribes or by names adopted by their respective tribes in 1981 census. In 1991, the corresponding figure was about 10 per cent" (Roy Burman, 1995: 10).

Some tribal communities are seen to be on warpath to safeguard the privacy of their habitats, for exclusive access, control and management of their resources, to maintain the traditional roles and role models in their socio-economic set-up in their interactions with the government and other agencies asserting their power at all levels. The recent governmental step of extending the provisions of the *Panchayati Raj* to tribal area is looked upon as historic landmark in the fulfilment of tribal aspirations. There are advantages attached to tribal status in India.

VII

So what looms large beyond the tribal societies in India is that there are communities in search of new social identities, to find a place in the "Schedule" eyeing for the special privileges guaranteed by the Constitution. Though the "word tribe lacked sociological vigour from its very inception" and that it is "the single most egregious case of meaninglessness in anthropological vocabulary", and "figures prominently on the list of putative technical terms ranked in order of degree of ambiguity" as alleged by Fried (1967: 154) and though the relevance of the concepts of tribe and the tribal society to anthropology and its practitioners is considerably denuded, the term *Scheduled Tribe* is unlikely to become obsolete in Indian English vocabulary and administrative jargon, or non-functional in Indian socio-political dynamics in any predictable future.

REFERENCES

Bailey, F.G. 1961. " 'Tribe' and 'Caste' In India," *Contributions to Indian Sociology*, V: 9-19.

Fried, Morton. H. 1967. *The Evolution of Political Society: An Essay in Political Anthropology.* New York: Random House (Chapter: The Concept of Tribe, pp.154-184).

Ghurye, G.S. 1943. *The Aborigines-"so-called"-and their Future.* Poona: Gokhale Institute of Politics and Economics, Publication No. 11.

Government of India. 1998. *Scheduled Tribes, Scheduled Areas and Tribal Areas in India*, Ministry of Social Justice and Empowerment, Tribal Development Division, New Delhi.

Moerman, Michael. 1974. "Accomplishing Ethnicity," (pp. 54-68) in Roy Turner (ed.), *Ethno Methodology*. Penguin.

Naik, T.B. "Editorial," in the *Bulletin of the Tribal Research Institute*, Chindwara, Madhya Pradesh, Volume 1, No. 3 (Referred to in Bailey 1961: 9).

Naroll, R. 1964. "On Ethnic Unit Classification," *Current Anthropology*, 5: 283-91.

Ramsukhdas, Swami. 1994. *Srimad Bhagavadgita* (With Sanskrit text, Transliteration and English Translation) Gorakhpur: Gita Press.

Risley, H.H. 1901. *People of India*. Bombay: Thacker & Co.

Roy Burman, B.K. 1995. Tribal Situation and Approach to Tribal Problems in India: A Preliminary Appraisal, Discussion Paper, Rajiv Gandhi Institute of Contemporary Studies, New Delhi.

Sahlins, D. Marshall. 1968. *Tribesman.* Prentice Hall.

Service, Elman R. 1962. *Primitive Social Organization: An Evolutionary Perspective.* New York: Random House.

Singh, K.S. 1994. *The Scheduled Tribes.* People of India, National Series I, Oxford University Press and Anthropological Survey of India.

Smith, Brian K. 1991. *The Laws of Manu with an Introduction and Notes.* Penguin Books.

Steward, Julian H. 1955. *Theory of Culture Change: The Methodology of Multilineal Evolution.* Urbana: Illinois University Press.

SEVENTEEN

TRIBAL SOCIETY IN INDIA AND THE WORLD: Meeting the Undead Dead

GEORG PFEFFER

Society is now one polished horde
formed of two mighty tribes,
the Bores and Bored.

(Lord Byron: *Don Juan,* Song XII, Stanza 95)

Tribal Society: Dead or Alive?

Tribal society is, as defined by Sahlins (1968) many years ago, an anarchic, unbound social something, without the distinction of specific domains, such as religion and politics, and based upon the familial mode of production. *We* lack, what is self-understood for tribal people, *i.e.* omnipresent descent groups and categories, collective marriage patterns and prescriptive rituals. *They* lack kings, councillors and committees, Brahmins and bishops, shops and shows. A tribal unit, say a residential or a descent group, as such will be herding sheep or hoeing hillocks collectively, just as, at least theoretically, the village or the lineage as such joins in sacrifice or takes offence, if any single member is offended, the collective acting to retaliate aggression. Opinion leaders may be, or may not be, leadership being a precarious position, not an administrative exercise in office and sovereignty.

Today, the central government of the state, though often far from being actually in control, demands the monopoly of power. In the strict sense, the kin-based formations of the tribal phase in human history, nowadays engulfed by claims and offices of legal-bureaucratic formalities, became superfluous since officers have moved into their upper storey of the social setup. Those European peoples who had put an end to the decentralised formations in Asia, America, Africa and Australia have later, through their anthropologists, exhumed the remains and tried to understand what they destroyed. Such a post-mortem, based upon the vital relicts of our times, will also be the object of this article.

After Sahlins, others have also noticed fuzzy boundaries when in search of unequivocal social entities, just as, like Byron, they had to register segments of sorts. Segments of what? His "tribes" and his "society" were certainly *not* the aggregate of a people in Byron's times, not the substance. In fact, he was writing about the privileged lot of the nobility, the insiders, not anyone. His "society" had nothing in common with dictionary explanations and similarly, the anthropological "tribe" offers no problems for authors of lexica, or *Notes and Queries*, but rather many for anthropological debates and for ethnographers like the authors of this volume who, after years of fieldwork, have scruples in setting their host society apart or not apart.

Today, debating tribal society in Western anthropology is a risky business. Though fears of being lynched are quite exaggerated, a public execution is on the cards, as the current trend condemns the term and those who work with it in theory, or, worse still, in ethnographic practice. Since, in case they ever did exist, tribes are said to be no longer, dealing with tribal society has been called an exercise in romanticism, obscurantism, neo-colonialism, illusionism, divide-and-rule-ism or any other form of yesterday-ism in contrast to updated social consciousness, modern or post-modern, and the relentless ethical demands[1] by an discipline in the age of globalisation and world or gendered systems, not to mention the ongoing impetus of developing the worlds of the have-nots or advancing the militant backlash of the deprived, the injured and insulted. Debates of descent categories and marriage preferences, grand give-away ceremonies and blueprints of communal rituals are said to obscure and obstruct class and gender consciousness as well as good governance, village aid and confidence building measures, the rise of the gross national product and the fall of the rate of corruption. If human rights, civil society, and secular science are our goals, the exoticism of studying tribal value-ideas is out.

Dominant discourse condemns what was once the professional brief, self-understood since Malinowski, *i.e.* engaging in extended ethnographic research in "little communities" on a "face-to-face" basis, when neither the ethnographer nor the ethnographees can find room to withdraw. Fieldwork used to be of the uni-centred kind, with fieldworkers being stuck for years in camps and villages of steppes or forests. Multi-centred ethnography is now the order of the day, *i.e.* participant observation in TV-stations with regular switches to hospitals or dinner parties and college football tournaments. All of this, of course, must be conducted in a self-reflexive disposition and the ethnographic outcome must not suppress the intricate woes and worries of the writer of culture. In fact, former fieldworkers too travelled through cities and engaged themselves in hospitals, just as all suffered from multiple worries but they failed to publicise these or the multiple exchanges with urban businessmen and officials.

When, four decades ago, my German teachers were shocked by the fact that I conducted fieldwork among urban latrine-cleaners (Pfeffer, 1970) or, in another project, among the leading intellectuals of an Indian province Pfeffer (1976), they vainly tried to convince me of the dogma that the tribal world was the only legitimate field of research for ethnographers, the sole subject of the discipline. I insisted that *anthropos* in social costume was not confined to the so-called *Naturvölker* ("nature peoples"). In a startling reversal, now the tribal affairs, my preoccupation over the last 25 years, have been addressed to the academic garbage bin while fieldwork flourishes more than ever before, as long as it is conducted in the semi-detached suburbia, the dancing classes of Open Universities, or the Christmas parties of Muslim immigrants to Europe. Not the social structure as such is the question—it must be our own—but the problematic details of it, even though the problems of some are not the problems of others. Paying heed to the self-reflexive perspective I should panic, or simply ignore this lasting egocentric indulgence. If Geertz is to be believed, many of us are "harassed by grave inner uncertainties amounting to almost a sort of epistemological hypochondria, concerning how one can know that anything one says about other forms of life is as a matter of fact so" (1988: 71). In fact, tempers and temperatures are on the rise, if, now-a-days, an ethnographer dares to leave the familiar world of shopping malls and mass media, union meetings and political parties, to settle in an obscure tribal village in search of unfamiliar ways to set the world and society as a whole into order.

Given the current out-casting of tribal studies, a flight into the realm of etymology will be a first and timid measure of defence, hopefully a leap towards more protected shores in flight from the guardians of political correctness, the bishops of methodological deconstruction and the yeomen of development, but then one never knows. By returning to the origins of the t-word, one may find an initial dry spot in the morass of epistemological disputes, since the Latin word *tribus*, of which the "tribe" in English and in many other languages is derived, had nothing to do with obscurization, discrimination, resistance and essentialization within discourse of the hegemonic or demotic kind. Whatever bias there may be in the term of today, it has been added in recently and is *not* an intrinsic value of the expression. The word is innocent! *Tribus* was a neutral quantitative term, applied by the inhabitants of the area around ancient Rome to anyone out of the given three ethnic thirds of the people, *i.e.* the Sabines, Etruscans, or Latins. The word alluded to the given segmentation, but not necessarily to the "segmentary society" of *African Political Systems*. A simple tri-partition of that whole, which we equate with the people of pre-imperial Latium, gave birth to the term under dispute. Later of course, the tribe was, in dominant opinion, associated with an inferior social status, just as the current trend disqualifies studies in tribal society. A formation of the tribal kind is even said to be an invention of the ethnographic writer, not an ontological entity. The tribe is generically different from categories of modern mass society, as far as boundary drawing, decision-making, or legitimacy and many other aspects are concerned, so as the simplest solution, its very existence is flatly denied.

However, this strategy of blotting out the unwanted is not an absolutely universal trend in current anthropology. If the segmentation of the discipline is viewed in earnest, the present volume is authored by representatives of—and addressed to—two major segments of the anthropological tribe, one being the many colleagues in India, probably more than a thousand in number, and the second comprising the American or other Commonwealth authors, called Westerners here, like their followers on the European continent whose native schools[2] have lost their significance since the 1960s. Representatives of these two major segments participated in the December 2004 Sambalpur Conference—in the middle of an Indian "tribal area"—and, between them, certain differences in matters of socialization soon became obvious.

Geertz's epistemological hypochondria has probably never reached India. It has certainly not infected those Indian colleagues who, as they say, "study the tribes", though in Delhi, of course, not to speak of the community of Indian anthropologists abroad, terminological correctness and a ceaseless application to Western trends and dogmas is self-understood. In fact, this particular segmentation in the profession has nothing to do with given, or natural, or primordial, or national, or any other essential differences and floor-crossing has been observed once in a while.

The other moiety mentioned, the Westerners, will also be defined by something that has *not* reached them. That something is the tribal world of India. It is known to very few Western colleagues only, whether the latter specialize on South Asia or not. In fact, those who have gained a reputation as Indianists would usually be knowledgeable either in the field of the written as well as the practiced versions of Hindu religion, including caste, or in the intricate domain of the complex political economy, or in both, but both are of limited utility in anthropological researches among the Ho[3] or the Sora[4], so the latter have never been given a room in the Western academia. In fact, usually the very existence of a specific societal type differing from caste society is denied by the experts on India.

However, again rare exceptions substantiate the rule and a number of these Westerners involved in fieldwork in the context of the *Scheduled Tribes* category participated in the Conference raising their voices as in previous publications. In fact, my rather impolite hypothesis would imply that the so-called "crisis of representation" has not even been noticed in the many departments between Lucknow and Tirupati, Dibrugarh and Baroda, just as names like Khurukh and Kharia, or Khasi and Koya, each referring to several hundred thousand tribal people, mean nothing to most Western Indianists, even though many millions of our Indian contemporaries have absolutely no problems to identify themselves with any one of such tribal units and, more important, with the specific values implied by such an identification. All are Indians, of course, and only a few years ago, Mr. Sangma, who is proud to belong to the Garo tribe, was the Speaker of the *Lok Sabha*, the Parliament of the Indian Union. Being Indian citizens, however, does not prevent these people from seeing themselves as members of a certain tribe, clan or local descent group, *i.e.* categories not present in the West and, since about twenty years, coloured by undertones of suspicion in major publications of Western anthropology. Lacking such a set of categories at home, authors seriously object to taking note of them abroad. They do not eat what they do not know, or want to know.

All Indians, however, are familiar with caste and subdivisions of caste and have no problems in allowing some Indians to operate with somewhat similar, if also very different, categories of the tribal peoples. Why and how should we take cognisance of such diverse developments? The following will shortly introduce the historians' accounts, to be followed by the proponents of "ethnohistory", *i.e.* the branch of anthropology that flourishes without the cumbersome craft of fieldwork and offers moral reasons for such rules of avoidance.

Post-Colonialism: Attacking the Unnamed General

The historiography of the people of India used to be confined to events and personalities deemed to be sufficiently exalted for this purpose by the historians of each period. Since the nineteen-eighties, however, Ranajit Guha (*e.g.* 1987) and his team have presented *Subaltern Studies*, *i.e.* highly competent researches in the history, approaching ethnography, of those subaltern Indians who had been be ignored by the establishment of the discipline. It was self-understood for the project that the tribes, also named *Adivasi* (*i.e.* aboriginals) in Indian jargon, belonged to these social segments of the population so that their history was introduced and discussed without the incriminatory inverted commas bracketing the term (*e.g.* Hardiman, 1984, 1987; Dasgupta, 1985).

By contrast, an altogether different approach is presented in so-called postcolonial studies, as may be exemplified by a recent work of Pels and Salemink on *Colonial Subjects* (1999). Their effort is a critique of *any* kind of ethnography. Regarding the tribes in India, a particular contribution of Pels (1999) ignores all references to anthropological theory or modern ethnography when treating the category as a colonial construction and offering an elaborate polemic against any work on tribal social structure. To my knowledge, Pels himself has never attempted to conduct ethnographic research in India, *i.e.* avoided acquiring a multiple linguistic competence and long-term stays in mud huts, just as he rejects all eminent authors dealing with caste in South Asian sociology, *e.g.* seminal contributions of authors like Marriott (*e.g.* 1976), or Dumont (*e.g.* 1980), not to speak of modern monographs on Indian Tribes such as those of Gell (1992) or Vitebsky (1993).

Being the editor of the leading European journal *Social Anthropology/ Anthropologie Sociale*, Pels, through his editorial policy[5], wields considerable influence upon the discipline. The recent polemic against tribal studies does not take the trouble to offer any name or exact reference with regard to living authors that are being attacked. *Anonymous* is at fault, an unnamed but very general set of, by implication, important colleagues who are accused of a "colonial *complicity* of *academic* anthropologists" (Pels and Salemink 1999: 6, their emphasis), *i.e.* of basing the discipline upon foundations of the colonial epoch. Such a strategy of critique does, of course, offer advantages, since nobody is likely to identify her or himself with the foul fellows. Given the normal course of events, the brave bashing of the unnamed should remain without a negative reaction.

The post-colonial critique of Pels and Salemink (1999) proceeds via several detours which my summary will not elaborate. The authors simply reject the segregation of professional and non-professional fieldworkers, and anthropology's confinement to the former, since as "a result, important moments in the development of anthropology are ignored" (Pels and Salemink, 1999: 1). Such segregation had "only recently become hegemonic", *i.e.* "in the second quarter of... [the twentieth] century" (*ibid.* 2/3), thus ignoring "its situatedness in a history of global inequality" (*ibid.* 3). In other words, the fact that Malinowski, Boas and the others criticised the policies of "Western" supremacy is held against them, though it is not quite clear, what their politically correct stand was to have been. They should, in any case, not have remained as "the 'detached' *observers*...to distract from their position in the field of local colonial interests" thus organizing the "intellectual containment of the practical anxieties of colonial rule" suffered by the "colonial subjects of anthropology...the 'tribes', or 'ethnic groups' targeted by both colonial states and anthropologists as future citizens" (*ibid.* 3). In short: "Throughout its history, the writing of ethnographies and anthropological reflections required authors to distance themselves from the relationships within which their experience of human difference was formed" (*ibid.* 4). As a positive alternative, the authors want us to take "account of the practical relationships between observers and observed and their subsequent transformation by the representations of ethnography" (*ibid.*). Thus until here the argument advances by the following steps:

1. Professional and non-professional anthropologists (*i.e.* colonial bigots) should not be distinguished,
2. Non-professional accounts can be treated as if they were those of professionals, both being determined by colonial interests, and
3. Only by distancing themselves from the colonial responsibility, anthropologists could form an experience of human difference, whereas this would not have been possible, if they had taken into account the practical relationships between observers and observed.

In fact, anthropologists are said to have tried "to *extricate* themselves from the colonial patronage system" (*ibid.* 6, emphasis given), though vainly so, since "there are clear continuities between the rhetoric of academic ethnography and the 'manners and customs' genres that preceded it" (*ibid.* 7). Thus follows the central conclusion: "(a) cademic anthropologists tend to transform their relation to the people studied...into a definition of the 'essence' of their object" (*ibid.* 8).

In other words, contemporary ethnography is no different from the early colonial stuff and, furthermore, academic anthropologists are said to "study people" in colonial style rather than *systems* of value-ideas, norms and behaviour. If, however, these anthropologists stress their professionalism, they are again caught on the wrong foot, since they are "reducing the relationship between observer and observed to an abstract method" (*ibid.*). Ordinarily, the colonial location sets the tone. For example, "the interpretation of 'caste' in India went through a major reinvention because the colonial regime increasingly relied on racialist forms of ethnological classifications" and "a correspondence between ideas about ignorance of paternity in the metropole, and ethnocidal state-formation in Australia, produced a blossoming of the former in terms of the 'virgin birth' controversy" (*ibid.* 15).

In short, Pels and Salemink, following Dirks, 1992, seriously want to link modern caste theories with a foundation of colonial racism, and on top of it link the "virgin birth controversy" (*e.g.* Leach, 1966/2000) with the ethnocide in Australia. In a racist intellectual environment, they note, "colonial administrations often tribalized and ethnicized a field of fluid ethnic interrelations" (*ibid.* 26), and these "distinctions were often the source of the ethnographic traditions into which the professional ethnographers arrived in the 'field'; in fact, they often made up the definition of the 'field' itself" (*ibid.* 27). Now we know: Tribal distinctions must again be seen as the work of the colonialists being later willingly adopted by academic anthropology. Similarly, "holist representation can be identified in most colonial ethnographies, and the rhetoric of ethnographic holism was not invented by professionals....All fieldworkers have to assume that social wholes can be understood and described by concentrating on certain key elements of society:...methodical constructs like kinship genealogy or social structure...are all synecdoches, parts of social relationships that are taken to be representatives of the society as a whole" (*ibid.* 34).

This last onslaught upon ethnography in general, based upon Clifford's earlier remarks (1983: 129-30), introduces a concept called "kinship genealogy" which I have never met with in anthropological writing, as a "representative of the society as a whole", though it does not say where this is being proposed by whom. However, Pels and Salemink themselves do not seem to know what they are writing about and do not seem to be particularly interested in knowing, such ignorance being the best evidence of their ethical purity. The overall jest of the polemics is clear: Academic anthropology should not attempt to reject compliance with colonial bigots since both the former and the latter depend upon the same relationships of power, the only relationship worth studying. Under these preconditions Pels *et al.* are offering *a double* perspective of the proper occupation for contemporary academic anthropology, either the analysis of real people (not synecdoches), or that of historic individuals who have proved to be responsible for the invention of some anthropological jargon.

Pels' subsequent essay is dealing with *The Rise and Fall of the Indian Aborigines*, elaborating on the life of the civil servant Brain Houghton Hodgson

(1800-1894) who is supposed to have invented the category of Indian aborigines as well as the special colonial policy towards those falling under this name (Pels, 1999). We learn many details of his biography, *e.g.* his personal health problems and his professional concern with linguistic studies, all combined under a single general question, the question of power and influence. If Pels writes about relationships, he means relationships of power.

Technically, his historical finding is quite wrong. Before Hodgson was born, Augustus Cleveland had already, as a result of the trouble created by Maler and Santhal tribesmen for the British administration, introduced such concepts and policies in the Rajmahal Hills during the last decade of the 18th century, but these technicalities are certainly not my relevant point. I simply fail to understand why Pels offers bio-graphical details of an Old India Hand as the anthropological craft, while, at the same time condemning field research and other attempts to overcome ethnocentrism. Though academic father-killing has been a regular past-time on the continent of Freud, slaying non-academic great-granduncles must carry different motives. In effect, our Dutch colleague does *not* hide his intention to equate contemporary ethnography—in tribal India or anywhere else—with colonial measures of "pacification", but he does not explicitly name such contemporary ethnography, *i.e.* authors with proper academic credentials, thereby forestalling any possibility of a reasoned controversy. Furthermore, in the regular "post-colonial" manner, he is keen to avoid any sort of holism and his criticism is directed *ad personam* (*i.e.* Hodgson) rather than against the colonial system as such. His real target is, of course, contemporary ethnography, but since he would have to *know* what he is criticizing, he prefers to turn the time back for a hundred years and write on more or less influential European colonialists in more or less scandalous power relationships in order to argue by analogy. Pels certainly does *not* want to understand non-European ideas of values, of ordering society, or of making a living, and he flatly denies the existence of an "ideal model for behaviour" (Pels and Salemink, 1999: 5) comprising indigenous categories that may be compared to norms and practices so that unavoidable contradictions and dynamics become evident. Ethnography, very much in colonial style, means "studying people" for Pels, so he presents colonial individuals and attacks contemporary—but anonymous—anthropologists.

In the same volume and the same spirit, Nicholas B. Dirks once again denounces an individual British administrator who had written on tribal society more than a hundred years ago. This man Thurston is supposed to have "made a great deal of …colonial reports that the Meriah 'tribe' of Central India practiced human sacrifice" which later "became a primary footnote for James

Frazer in...*The Golden Bough*" (Dirks, 1999: 170). Rather than discussing Dirks' argument of the now familiar kind, I would only like to register that to my knowledge no anthropologist—except Dirks—has ever heard of, or written about, a "Meriah 'tribe' ", whether the word tribe is written in penalizing inverted commas or not. Furthermore, Frazer does not quote Thurston, but the opposite is the case. Thurston (1907: 510) is quoting Frazer[6]. As mentioned by the author of *The Golden Bough* (Frazer, 1922: 571) he had, in fact, utilized Macpherson (1865) as his source, the Scottish officer who, as ample archival material can demonstrate, had personally rescued a number of would-be victims of human sacrifice. Furthermore, the complex logic of the sacrifice (*see* Hardenberg in this volume) continues to be applied today, though the victims have been buffaloes, not humans, since Macpherson's intervention. Anyone interested in other systems of ideas, compared to those of the own culture, *i.e.* any proponent of serious ethnography, could study the logic of this ritual today. This, however, would imply a step beyond the ethnocentrism of the inverted ancestor worship as advocated by the stalwarts of post-colonialism. To conclude: I am frankly flabbergasted to notice that Dirks, who insinuated that caste-was a colonial invention, has had the mind to invent factual data without further precautions. Not surprisingly, he tried to discredit ethnography without elementary information. Consequently, I would now like to discuss further approaches and goals of ethnography among people of a tribal heritage. This will be part of a more general effort of discerning their specific pattern of social relations.

Amazonian Ethnographers and Ethnography

South America, a context altogether different from things Indian, is well suited for initial examples of ethnographic diversity. In North-Western Amazonia two types of anthropological approaches have made news for the wider public, since two ethnographers of different continents and very different heritage have been working among the tribal Yanomami, or shifting cultivators who, over the last fifty years, have been visited by increasing numbers of government agents, adventurers, Christian missionaries and, last not least, anthropologists.

One of these two ethnographers is Jacques Lizot (1985) who has lived with the people for decades not years. His book is written like a novel. *Real* people come into action, people who have been Lizot's neighbours and friends. He relates their dramatic individual undertakings, even those of the violent or of the intimate kind, but tries to avoid interpretations. So-called "polyphone" representations fill the book, *i.e.* dialogues and monologues of various indigenous speakers collected by, and—at least so he says—not altered by the author. Boredom does not arise, because Yanomami individuals, not Lizot, convey in detail how they killed their enemies or captured their brides and the like. Voluntarily, so it seems, the author surrenders his authority to his long-term acquaintances. Rather different from the post-modern procedure, however, he does not talk about himself as the natural focus of ethnography, a policy which, for more than one reasons, may have been a wise move. To sum up: Lizot's *Tales of the Yanomami* let the reader know, how the author's friends and neighbours, let us call them Mr. and Ms. Yanomami, spend their time with conflicts and ambitions, intimacies and achievements, and frankly, I reject this course of ethnography for at least two reasons.

First, I dislike the idea to sell privacy to the public. If President Clinton writes his memoirs, it is (in more than one way) his own business, and if prominent Westerners must tolerate biographies, they knew the risk. Mr. and Ms. Yanomami, however, could not possibly conceive the impact of the global book market. The ethnographer betrays their trust—the trust of his friends (if they were his friends)—by publicizing their personal statements and performances within an altogether different context of the media for the sake of his career, his socio-political convictions or any other reason.

Secondly, disputes over the purpose of the anthropological endeavour cannot be avoided. Whereas a much advertised trend in Western anthropology of the last twenty years has made it a point to avoid any "closed" or "whole" or "systematic" accounts of a society, thus turning partiality, situationalism, and subjectivism into highest anthropological virtues, my rather old-fashioned approach is keen to decipher systems of thought through systems of classification and systems of social order as indicated by social categories, norms and practices and the contradictions between these analytical levels. I do, of course, admire the way Geertz can write, or convey intricacies and ambiguities, or failures of actors and actions when the system is at work, but a careful look at his essays also reveals his references to ethnographic basics, *i.e.* collections of categories, even if these are part of constructions, or constructions of informants. Similarly Geertz, when writing his real fiction, does this with an aim to broaden and enrich our communication, or "to penetrate into the unfamiliar universe of symbolic action" (1973: 24), *i.e.* improve cognition of *other* forms of modelling the world, or an entry into another kind of commonsense, or at least recognize that such another commonsense exists.

Frankly, I advocate *such* forms of othering. If writers like Lizot are fond of selling private matters in publications they simply reveal a certain familiar type of Western values such as sensationalism, individualism, non-authoritarian lifestyles and idiosyncratic protest against conventions[7]. In a rather all too apparent manner they seem to offer agency to informants, while in fact nobody can be fooled about the real authority managing the book project. Lizot's reports offer tales without systems of Yanomami categories, so these tales must appear as elaborate reports of deviations from our own sense of propriety. Polyphonic accounts, I think, at best offer the informants' style of narration. They do not, and they cannot, offer cultural analysis or the tremendous depth and differentiation of many tribal cosmologies. In short, by the apparent, but not real, shift of responsibilities, the anthropologist puts the blame on persons who cannot know what they are involved in and cannot defend themselves. The anthropologist on the other hand can, by such bestsellers, avoid wrestling with the thornier problems and contradictions in the field of meaning.

Lizot is only one of the Yanomami ethnographers. Better known is Napoleon Chagnon who, since the 1960s, has written several books on the people he calls 'fierce'. By comparison, he stands for the other extreme of ethnography. His monographs are of the conventional kind and one book has perhaps been the most widely used introduction to any tribal culture of the world. The chapters discuss ecology and economy, social organization, violence and feuds (or what he calls warfare) and they employ the style of language and the type of explanation that can be understood by any newcomer to the subject in any remote corner of a western country.

Leaving aside the simplicity of such constructs, my major problems with Chagnon arise from his conversion to sociobiology[8]. When studying "kinship" he is out to register genetic links between countless individuals, rather than the particular Yanomami vision of their world of kin (1983: 131-145). In fact, he goes after the many acts of physical procreation because he believes the Yanomami are driven to violence and feuding by intrinsic forces of "mate selection" within a certain "breeding population". In case they do genetically well in matters of "mate selection" they can aggrandize their "inclusive fitness". If I understand him correctly, increased "inclusive fitness" of an individual again leads to improved opportunities of "mate selection" and *vice versa*, just as the Yanomami principles of social organization, or those any humans for that matter, do not differ from the principles of social organization among birds and bees.

Individuals and individual decision-making, just as the wide range of possible socio-cultural values do not exist. Social norms and ratios of norm-conformity, or role conflicts and contradictions are secondary, not to speak of systems of religious thought. Human relations appear as being based upon somatic traits and, at the same time, as being unavoidably subjected to rules we know from competitive sports, or from the world of business. In a shorthand version, each Yanomami is driven by some biological forces to increase his or her genes in the way others in other parts of the world increase production or sales figures of given commodities. Once again a familiar logic, that of market forces, saves us from conceiving indigenous categories or concerns in Yanomami terms. We learn *nothing* about native ventures to find explanatory orders of existence, or of efforts to create a parallel world of meaning that could elucidate the immanent world. From the logical point of view, Chagnon's gene-maximization policy can either be a human universal and would then lack any explanatory value for the particular case of culture, or, if such universalism is rejected, Chagnon would associate certain particular somatic qualities with the Yanomami. Thereby, he would transgress against anthropology's first commandment postulating the physical homogeneity of humankind.

Thus for one and the same people we come across two ethnographic approaches which are both embedded in a familiar, a Western socio-cultural logic: Lizot presents the people as egocentric adventurers and anti-authoritarian hedonists of sorts like the young academic Europeans of the nineteen-seventies, while Chagnon shows us how gene-entrepreneurs fight under market conditions to increase the output. My criticism, I must emphasize, is offered quite apart from the other controversies concerning these two authors.

The question of alternatives is, of course, unavoidable. In fact, we can find several excellent ethnographies about other peoples of North-western Amazonia of which I mention Christine and Stephen Hugh-Jones' books on the Barasana in that region. Stephen offers a volume with detailed interpretive accounts of the major initiation rite and Christine elucidates Barasana mythological orientation and social structure. Both have made many intimate friends in years of fieldwork but certainly do not elaborate on the latters' private lives. They rather analyse the *system* of ideas which is a very tough job, since the categories of these Amazonians involve fruit and music and an extended order of space and time that is absolutely unfamiliar to Western thinking. Learning about alternative socio-cultural orders is anthropology's finest result.

Christine introduces readers to an *open* social system without the notion of "a discrete society" (1979: XVI). In fact, the benevolent ancestors are supposed to have, in the shape of Anaconda snakes, swum from the Milk River, the Amazon, up the numerous tributaries to their present locations. Mythical history thus conceives the superhumans as reversing empirical life, or the direction of the multiple rivers which offer the sources of livelihood. The identity of these Amazonians is similar to many others who all understand themselves as exogamous units, being expected to marry outsiders, in this case non-Barasana speaking a different language. Ideally a child grows up in a longhouse where several different "mothers" speak several different languages while the child ends up employing the, once again different, tongue of his "fathers".

Barasana are not differentiated by wealth, but a given hierarchy privileges the "chiefly" phratry of a settlement over that of dancers and singers who have a higher status than warriors or the lower ranked shamans and the lowest of them all, the so-called servants. The chiefly phratry forms marriage alliances with distant peoples, while the "servants" marry close-by under disreputable circumstances. Others take the intermediary route. The particular pattern of hierarchy is clothed in the language of relative seniority and is all pervasive. The phratries include several levels of similar but minor descent categories and the alliances differentiate bilateral, patrilateral and matrilateral cross-cousins or, in fact, parallel cousins of the two types as a ranked system of marital unions. No large or small aspect of Barasana existence is excluded from this hierarchy. It is *open*, avoiding segregation in any direction, while, at the same time, the logic of time and space is not universalist, or Western, or biological but confined to Amazonian ideas. The logical constructions of rituals and exchanges are highly sophisticated, and they are the heritage of the collective, not the work of particular individuals. Ethnography of the Hugh-Jones' type is tough in matters of field conditions and tougher still regarding efforts to find one's feet on ground, or obtain some understanding of how *anthropos* brings order into the world.

The Contrast: Gatherer-Hunters

Economically, the Barasana live on the fish of their rivers and the manioc they grow in their gardens. Away from the streams, however, in the interfluvial areas of the rainforest, other people live called Maku. They know how to cultivate manioc but in fact rely heavily on forest products (Chr. Hugh-Jones, 1979: 15) collecting and hunting the eatables, at times exchanging meat, curare and labour with the Barasana for cultivated products (Silverwood-Cope, 1972). The Maku conduct a semi-settled existence, frequently following hunting treks. Apparently "Maku mediate between the servant sibs...and the forest animals themselves in their 'animal houses'" (Chr. Hugh-Jones, 1979: 243). By their neighbours they are seen as rather intelligent animals, not as other Amazonian peoples who, living on the riversides, qualify as marriage partners. In other words, Barasana discriminate the gatherer-hunters as a different species and Maku seem to follow completely different moral rules.

Anthropology too has, since long, differentiated tribal people like the Barasana from gatherer-hunters like the Maku, initially on the basis of food production, but since the work of James Woodburn (1982) and others, it is clear that the worldview is equally relevant. The productive activity, *i.e.* the domestication of plants and animals, is not enough to define tribal society. The Buid of Mindoro on the Philippines, for example, do cultivate the sago palm in a very simplistic manner, but they also follow a gatherer-hunter morality, *i.e.* they evade conflicts and all acts of aggression, as we learn from Gibson's fine monograph (1986). Woodburn, perhaps like many of the older and little-known German ethnologists, separates the categories of "immediate return" gatherer-hunters from those of "delayed return" in productive activities, the latter bearing basic cultural features of tribal societies.

Returns are delayed, if either the means of production or the techniques applied to gather and hunt, or the methods of processing and storing the harvest are of a more refined kind. In yet another important act of classification Woodburn dissociates Australian aborigines from gatherer-hunters, even though their foraging used to offer immediate returns. However, men of aboriginal Australia, particularly elder men, used their control over women and younger men to obtain considerable economic advantages. They used to "invest" in wives and follow long-term strategies of gains in this respect, just as they were certainly not of the pacifist kind. The very complexity of Australian worldviews and social structures disallowed a status marked by the undifferentiated bands, rules, transcendent worlds, and economies of the gatherer-hunters.

North American Indigenous Classification

Once we follow Woodburn's classification, we will, of course, never entertain the idea of classifying the sophisticated chiefdoms on the American North-west Coast or the Prairies as gatherer-hunters, even if the tribal inhabitants of these regions may have failed to raise corn or other plants and confined their stock of domestic animals to dogs. The example of the Crow Indians may be mentioned for a moment and their sophisticated ritual and cosmology, or their complex system of phratries and clans, or their exciting life as members of what ethnographers have called "clubs". When the German Prince Maximilian of Wied-Neuwied met them on the upper Missouri in the 1830s, they were involved in eight different clubs (Lowie, 1935: 173), and Austrian-born Robert Lowie, perhaps inspired by the report, still met with two such "clubs", the Foxes and the Lumpwoods, when doing fieldwork 90 years ago. These organized youth associations were mutually aggressive fraternities who, in all their rivalry, nonetheless, followed strict rules of honour by way of self-discipline. Similarly, so-called bond-friendships kept together for life either two male or two female Crow (Lowie, 1935: 50) in the same manner that we presently meet everywhere in tribal India.

The Crow are mentioned here because during Lowie's lifetime, or until about 1950, almost all of Western anthropology was dedicated to the study of tribal society. Great personalities, such as the American scholars Morgan, Boas, or Kroeber, were involved in important research on systems of classification, and many European luminaries of later generations, like Lévi-Strauss, have obtained their theoretical insights only on the basis of the tough ethnographic work and the non-dogmatic and imaginative analyses of these forefathers. But Lowie's Crow, or the many other tribes we can meet today in these masterly monographs, were no longer autonomous when the ethnographers crossed their way. They represented what remained of great indigenous cultures after the onslaught of European armies and European epidemics. Lowie's informants were old people who, in their childhood, had still experienced glimpses of the old independent existence. Should they, therefore, have been ignored by Lowie and others? Should we have brushed away their existence because they were no longer tribal? I think, such a disqualification would have greatly impoverished our conceptions of *anthropos*[9] , but then I probably take a minority position.

Today, a good number of colleagues see themselves as "ethnohistorians" and many of them review the early encounters between Europeans and American tribes in the 17th and 18th century, or when the latter still were tribes. Thus Abler (1992) offers an account of Iroquois warfare with many references to inefficient co-ordination efforts of the Indians and factional disputes, just as he goes into the details of Iroquois killings, tortures and cannibalism. *War in the Tribal Zone* (1992), the title of the book, "explains" how tribes everywhere yielded to superior state power, and in the Iroquois case, Abler's argument is based on the logic of the fur trade combined with the alleged Iroquois greed for Western trade goods. Similar politico-economic "explanations" are offered by other contributions in that volume, and, perhaps, "ethnohistorians" in general, as if humans all over the world were inspired by a single and familiar motive only, the priority to accumulate material wealth. Going through this work, I wondered why we knew so little about Delaware warfare, Delaware factionalism, or cruel excesses of Delaware behaviour, since these people of a similar environment were equally victims of European expansionism.

Glimpses of a possible answer came from a short article of Jay Miller (1974). He mentions that Iroquois and Delaware were linked together by a concept that sounds strange to Western ears. Reports see the "whole Delaware 'nation' as *women* in contradistinction to the Iroquois 'nation' as *men*." (Miller, 1974: 507; his italics). Miller discusses two alternative anthropological interpretations of such classification: first, a minority position links the Delaware status with an alleged, but never documented, military defeat at the hands of the Iroquois. As "women", the Delaware could not fight, sell land, or sign treaties on their own (*ibid.*). They also sent wampum[10] to their "men" and used a metaphorical skirt, earrings, and a corn pounder. For Morgan, an Iroquois *honoris causa*[11], wampum was tribute, and the Delaware had been "degraded" (1851/1973: 338). By 1755, however, the Delaware petitioned the Iroquois to recognize them as men so that they could defend themselves. Apparently the Iroquois conveyed this status in specifically anatomical terms, but only in 1794 the Delaware were formally declared to be fully men (Miller 1974:508).

Secondly, however, the majority position in anthropology conceives a reciprocal agreement between the two sides. Any association of women with inferiority, ignominy, or subjugation only betrays the European bias of the sources (*ibid.*). As "women", the Delaware could remain aloof of the Western colonists. One source suggests that Iroquois wanted the others to fill the exalted status of women in the roles of peacemakers and as a sanctuary. The Delaware in turn became to be known as the "sister's children" of their Iroquois "mother's brothers". The former were equipped with medicines to anoint other "nations", just as they were entrusted with the belt of peace and the chain of friendship. "The Delaware chose the status of women because it assured their safety while the Iroquois and others waged wars....It was only after the Iroquois betrayed the covenant and fell upon the Delaware that the latter threw off their dress and revenged themselves. It is clear that the latter recognized themselves as a nation of women" (*ibid.* 509).

Again, I mention Miller's interpretation only because he offers alternatives to commonsensical "explanations" which, in the case of Westerners, would regularly allude to economics and politics. Only Western commonsense saw women—all over the world—as degraded, but I think any such assumption must be based upon the indigenous order of values, our subject of research, *before* we come to consider economic advantages. To offer a well-known contemporary example, the Palestinians would probably be much better of, had they found an agreement with the new state of Israel in 1948, but the goal "to be better off" is not the priority of all value systems.

Marginal Tribal Societies in Muslim Middle-Eastern States

Remaining in the Arab present, one is bound to witness huge and complex urban agglomerations as well as an autonomous tribal zone side by side and interspersed. Since those who offer a descriptive view would normally write in the city, the tribal world is declared to be "marginal", even though the values found in such "marginal societies" remain at the core of Arab self-consciousness. The mountain plateau of northern Yemen, for example, has been, since millennia, on the edge of empires. It has even been, at times, in the heart of such ancient states within one of the few general regions where human statehood is said to have been developed. Today, the tribes dominating the region, and each one a specific territory, date back their history to pre-Islamic times. They are a people of warriors, but in their midst they protect unarmed clients and also scholars or descendents of the Prophet who are "set aside from disputes" (1993: 30), as the ethnographer Paul Dresch[12] has elaborated. These clients and saints, like the officers of the government, would never infringe upon the tribal autonomy, the prime value. Today, due to the oil boom, many tribesmen are involved in national and transnational business ventures, as was a certain individual named Osama-bin-Laden some years ago. However, within their territory the adult males remain armed to the teeth with all sorts of weapons, the most modern among them for personal use only. Their history, as well as the atemporal patterns by which their society can be seen as a meaningful whole, has been elucidated in Dresch's fascinating ethnography. The author begins with the central categories in order to examine their meanings from all sides and angles and in all shades and ambiguities—of which there are many.

The two major tribes of the region, those of Hashid and Bakil, combine a population of "upwards of 500,000" (Dresch, 1993: 24). They are segmented into the standard non-exogamous patrilineal categories at highly irregular lower levels so that the account is a far cry from any attempt to trap tribesmen within the schematic application of segmentary oppositions. The score of possible confrontations has an ethical basis that is often discussed and refined by the tribesmen in self-conscious attempts to arrest what must be of a fleeting nature, since the persons' honour of is always involved. The quality of honour is referred to as *sharaf*, which implies distinction and distinctness (*ibid.* 39), or the paradoxical social value of being set apart from fellow humans. This personal aloofness is always at risk in public. It is openly at stake or exposed to a possible incursion from outside, the latter being termed as *ayb*. In this rather male oriented world, *ayb* may occur due to a tribesman's own demeaning action, *i.e.* killing a woman or anyone of inferior standing, or it may be inflicted upon him by somebody who is disgracing or insulting him. Thus "an *ayb* is a blameworthy action whether done or suffered" (*ibid.*).

Dresch's major point characterizes *ayb* as very much part of the public domain and as such, to be "rather foreign to our own representations of the person with their stress on presumed internal states.... What rankles afterwards is the insult, the attack on [a man's] public standing, not the wound to his self-respect" (*ibid.* 40). *Ayb* damages the *sharaf*, or honour, as presented to others and therefore as bound up with hyperbole. Tribal existence is presented as a drama the actors of which impersonate heroic conduct and credit the same to others just as they assimilate the ancestral *sharaf* to present concerns in a "distinctive view of history" (*ibid.* 41). The specific vocabulary is, in fact, employed at the first sign that honour may be slighted. The ethnographer's quality of analysis lies in his recognition that the "dramatic can emerge from the downright mundane with scant warning. What the outside might wish to distinguish as real and imaginary therefore cannot be separated without losing the significance of much that tribesmen do" (*ibid.* 42).

A tribesman should be "light-blooded". His self-image is probably quite the opposite of that of a Zen Buddhist. "Mercurial" is the term coined by Dresch (*ibid.* 42), *i.e.* "quick to respond to affronts and to take up arms in defence of honour, fearless and fierce like leopards". All of this refers to a public disposition irrespective of the actual frequency of violent behaviour. Sobriety of mind is not imperative. Two men may squabble over a strayed goat "and settle down to sniping at each other from house to house" (*ibid.* 43). The rhetoric assumes that *sharaf* has been passed on through the generations as a kind of ancestral substance and grandsons have it in common with their fathers and grandfathers, though they also look to their individual *sharaf* and share that of their father probably against that of their cousins.

Dresch calls this "the starting point for most social accountancy" (*ibid.* 44). But according to *namus* or the sexual honour of the womenfolk, a man's honour also depends upon his mother and he must "control" in order to "defend" his sister's and daughter's honour. Not that they are in imminent danger, but the imagery of defence must be retained. By this logic, giving a woman into marriage means giving her away as a hostage with implied subordination. The well-known "father's brother's daughter marriage" (also known as "self-marriage") must thus be seen as a general inclination of families to face inwards. Safety lies in autonomy. Dresch's significant comparative observation takes us to the "elementary structures of kinship": While many societies carve out identities of persons and collectives through establishing and maintaining relations between these parties, *i.e.* by being wholly dependent upon these relations, the "cutting off relations" is the prime necessity of the Yemeni tribesmen. Safety and normalcy is expected in the very lack of connections with others. Permanent commitments are dangerous since men can find themselves in hostile entanglements that "can be viciously bloody or only farcical. It is hard to predict which" (*ibid.* 47).

The lengthy example of Yemeni ethics may perhaps be relevant here for two reasons: First, tribal men and women are proud to see themselves as such, as members of their *qabila*. Self-pity is not part of their life. Secondly, the particular pattern of Muslim tribal society is old and widespread. Between, in the east, the Pakhtun on the Indus and the Berber in the High Atlas at the edge of north-western Africa, the pattern is similar though with regional variations. David M. Hart (2001) relates that about ten per cent of the population in these countries belong to the tribal society and have been "marginal tribes" since thousands of years, *i.e.* aware of and attracted by an urban administrative centre, but, as we read in the work of Ibn Khaldun, characterized by quite different values and, for that reason, torn between acts of aggression and accommodation that may be responsible for the instability of the political systems in the region. In case of the Muslim tribes, obviously political considerations must be applied, because they seem to dominate the minds of the people themselves.

Choices

Many other ethnographic examples of contemporary tribal societies allover the world could, of course, be introduced to an Indian anthropological public. Those of eastern Indonesia, for example, in which bride-givers and bride-takers are linked to one another over generations, but must never reverse the direction, because givers are superior to takers by way of economic, political, and ritual advantages. Elsewhere, as among the Ilongot on the Philippines, Renato Rosaldo (1980) found tribal people who had a fantastic collective memory, in present times being well aware of, and responding to, aggressions of the 19th century, a quality lacking in other tribal systems. But the social organization of the same Ilongot is almost unstructured, as if the eminent historical, or vertical dimension of collective thought was balanced by an unimpressive contemporary or horizontal order of the self.

Ethnic boundaries of societies in Highland New Guinea are, of course, notorious for their non-existence. Marilyn Strathern could demonstrate, how Westerners saw "persons as parts cut from a whole, imagined as relations…, for the anthropologist, society", while on the other hand,

> "A Melanesian death required the active severance of persons and relations—living persons rearranging their relationships among themselves when the deceased could no longer embody them....they anticipated and were made of acts similar to those which subsequently partitioned them. Parts were never dislocated...". (M. Strathern, 1992: 99).

The person as such was "socially complete [and]...made incomplete in its engagement and exchange with others." In other words, Highlanders conceive *dividuals* in the manner known from Marriott's work on Indian caste (Marriott, 1976). By exchanges, the person partially engages herself or himself with parts of others. Such relations must be constructed in life and de-constructed by others after death for society to be tied together and retained.

With this last example, another reference to the variability of human classification, I return to the "crisis of representation" and suggested solutions to this problem. Strathern (1992: 76) wants social research to differentiate three levels of the issue:

- On one we may ask, whether the contemporary people of the globe are, as post-modern authors want us to conceive, really made-up of multiple individual fragments rather than specific cultural *units*, and my response would point to a good number of tribal societies—rather than gatherer-hunters or highly administrated states—as being modelled as such cultural units, or valued systems, rather than technical arrangements to be altered at any time.
- On the other level, post-modernists apply a particular analytical tactic, that of de-construction, or the ethnographer's undoing of whatever systems she or he may have found, in order to explain away as illusionary any concept of value above the individual. Such a strategy, I believe, is the academic heritage of European efforts to undo tribal societies by administrative, religious, or physical policies of extinction. Amazonians, Australians, or Ilongot have long been exposed to pervasive conquerors who wanted them to assimilate to those in power or become cultural Europeans, *i.e.* unrelated, self-conscious individuals in the face of one almighty central power rather than being bound in self-understood communal systems of multiple layers, vague boundaries and ambiguous confrontations.
- Marilyn Strathern mentions yet a third level of the fragmentation complex: Anthropologists may find, as she has in New Guinea,

> indigenous images of relations marked by dissolution and reconstruction. These are of Highland post-modernists, so to say, who, being even more radical, would not just single out individual from individual but, below this level, separate the relational parts of a person—those setting the person in *relation* and thus into society—and re-assembling the person.

This third dimension is a matter of ethnographic particulars. As Berger's, Hardenberg's and Otten's contributions to this volume show, *other* particular ideological methods—not those of *dividualism* but those conceiving societal wholes as implemented by the Gadaba, the Dongria, or the Mali—may be found to *re-present* a certain order without reference to the Western type of empiricism, fragmentation and analysis. As Paula Rubel and Abraham Rosman have shown in their work on exchange among the American Indians of the Northwest Coast and in New Guinea the indigenous structural logic is to be the goal of our researches, even if much of anthropology has been "of late denying the existence of cultural boundaries", being set against the very idea of structure "for the time being" (Sahlins, 1999: 414).

To conclude, the above may illustrate the general methodological dichotomy of the approaches: Most Western anthropologists may be quite unaware of the fact that about a hundred million Indians are members of larger or smaller tribal societies on the subcontinent, just as Indian colleagues, concentrating their efforts upon understanding these tribal systems, are unaware of the fact that many Western anthropologists have simply disqualified such efforts since tribes and specifically tribal social values (or caste values, for that matter) are not supposed to exist. They globalize their own social environment in the sense that—under the guise of endless particularities—societal economy, morphology and ideology are to be of a uniform kind, *i.e.* determined by Western individualism. This new brand of intellectual hegemony has declared tribal society to be dead and accordingly, any contact with the undead dead must be polluting.

NOTES

1. An example of the battle against any hint of an "essentialist" approach and a fearless defence of human rights in a UNESCO publication is bravely presented by Herzfeld (2001).
2. The French and the Dutch used to offer alternatives to the English speaking departments.

3. For the political economy of the Ho *see* Yorke (1976).
4. For the religion of the Sora *see* Vitebsky (1993).
5. Amazingly, a recent article on Marcel Mauss could pass the editors even though the author's elaborate discussion had confounded the contemporary gatherer-hunters of Sri Lanka known as "Vedda" with the sacred Hindu texts of the second millennium B.C. known as 'Veda' (*see* Rousseleau, 2003: 198). I mention this only to pinpoint the standard of the editorial policy resulting from the general policy to discredit ethnographic research as such.
6. As is well known, the Golden Bough was first published in 1890 receiving "at least twenty-five reviews....Virtually every major newspaper and periodical in Britain gave the book a substantial notice....Then in late 1890 and early 1891 the serious journals weighed in with long, generally favourable review-essays." (Ackerman, 1987: 98).
7. Lizot, of course, follows Clastres' (1977) anarchism.
8. His extended contributions in this vein can be found in Chagnon and Irons (1978).
9. It is self-understood that the history of European conquest should simultaneously be elucidated by historians.
10. These were certain chains of pearls as units of gift exchange passed on also to commemorate contractual obligations.
11. *See* White (1959: 5) in Morgan, L.H. 1959; *The Indian Journals 1859-62* (Edited with an introduction by L.A. White) Ann Arbor, University of Michigan Press.
12. Dresch, Paul 1993. *Tribes, Government, and History in Yemen.* Oxford: Clarendon p. 30.

REFERENCES

Abler, Thomas S. 1992. "Beavers and Muskets: Iroquois Military Fortunes in the Face of European Colonization," (pp. 151-174) In Ferguson, R. Brian and Neil L. Whitehead (eds.): *War in the Tribal Zone*. Santa Fe: School of American Research Press.

Ackerman; Robert 1987. *J.G. Frazer. His Life and Work.* Cambridge: Cambridge University Press.

Chagnon, N. and W. Irons 1978 (eds.). *Sociobiology and Human Social Organization.* Scituate, Mass: Duxbury Press.

Chagnon, Napoleon 1983. *Yanomamö. The Fierce People.* New York. Holt: Rinehart and Winston, 3rd edition.

Clastres, Pierre 1977. *Archéologie de la violence: La guerre dans les sociétés primitives.* L'Aube: La Tour d'Aigues.

Clifford, James 1983; "On Ethnographic Authority," *Representations*, 2: 118-46.

Dasgupta, Swapan 1985. "Adivasi Politics in Midnapur, c. 1760-1924." (pp. 101-135) In Ranajit Guha (ed.), *Subaltern Studies IV. Writings on South Asian History and Society.* New Delhi: Oxford University Press.

Dirks, Nicholas B. 1992. "Castes of Mind". *Representations* 37 (winter): 56-78.

Dirks, Nicholas B. 1999. "The Crimes of Colonialism: Anthropology and the Textualization of India." pp. 153-179 In: Peter Pels and Oscar Salemink (eds.): *Colonial Subjects*. Ann Arbour: The University of Michigan Press.

Dresch, Paul 1993. *Tribes, Government, and History in Yemen*. Oxford, Clarendon.

Dumont, Louis. 1980. *Homo Hierarchicus. The Castes System and Its Implications*. Compl. Revised Edition. Chicago. The University of Chicago Press.

Ferguson, R. Brian and Neil L. Whitehead 1992 (eds.). *War in the Tribal Zone*. Santa Fe. School of American Research Press.

Frazer, James G. 1922. *The Golden Bough. A Study in Magic and Religion*. London. Macmillan.

Geertz, Clifford. 1973. *The Interpretation of Cultures. Selected Essays*. London. Fontana.

____. 1988; *Works and Lives. The Anthropologist as Author*. Stanford: Stanford University Press.

Gell, Simeran M.S. 1992. *The Ghotul in Muria Society*. Chur, Harwood Academic Publishers.

Gibson, Thomas. 1986. *Sacrifice and Sharing in the Philippine Highlands. Religion and Society among the Buid of Mindoro*. London: Athlone.

Guha Ranajit. 1987. "Chandra's Death," (pp. 135-165) In Ranajit Guha (ed.), *Subaltern Studies V. Writings on South Asian History and Society*. New Delhi: Oxford University Press.

Hardiman, David. 1984. "Adivasi Assertion in South Gujarat: The Devi Movement of 1922-3." (pp. 196-230). In Guha, Ranajit (ed.), *Subaltern Studies III. Writings on South Asian History and Society*. New Delhi: Oxford University Press.

____. 1987. "The Bhils and Shahukars of Eastern Gujarat." pp. 1-54. In Ranajit Guha (ed.) *Subaltern Studies V. Writings on South Asian History and Society*. New Delhi: Oxford University Press.

Herzfeld, Michael. 2001. *Anthropology. Theoretical Practice in Culture and Society*. Oxford: Blackwell.

Hugh-Jones, Christine. 1979. *From the Milk River. Spatial and Temporal Processes in Northwest Amazonia*. Cambridge: Cambridge University Press.

Hugh-Jones, Stephen. 1979. *The Palm and the Pleiades. Initiation and Cosmology in Northwest Amazonia*. Cambridge: Cambridge University Press.

Leach, Edmund. 1966/2000. "Virgin Birth," (pp. 102-119). In Hugh-Jones, Stephen and James Laidlaw (eds.), *The Essential Edmund Leach*. New Haven: Yale University Press.

Lizot, Jacques. 1985. *Tales of the Yanomami. Daily Life in the Venezuelan Forest*. Cambridge: Canto.

Lowie, Robert. 1935. *The Crow Indians*. New York: Rinehart and Co.

Macpherson, W. (ed.) 1865. *Memorials of the Service in India from the Correspondence of the Late Major Samuel Charles Macpherson. C.B., Political Agent at Gwalior during the Mutiny and formerly employed in the suppression of human sacrifice in Orissa edited by his brother*. London: John Murray.

Marriott, McKim. 1976. "Hindu Transactions: Diversity Without Dualism". In Bruce Kapferer (ed.): *Transaction and Meaning. Directions in the Anthropology of Exchange and Symbolic Behaviour*. Philadelphia, Institute of Human Issues.

Miller, Jay. 1974. "The Delaware as Women. A Symbolic Solution," *American Ethnologist*, 1 (3): 50714.

Pels, Peter. 1999. "The Rise and Fall of the Indian Aborigines. Orientalism, Anglicism, and the Emergence of an Ethnology of India, 1833-1869," (pp. 82-116) in Peter Pels and Oscar Salenink (ed.), *Colonial Subjects. Essays on the Political History of Anthropology.* Ann Arbor: The University of Michigan Press.

Pels, Peter and Oscar Salemink. 1999. "Introduction: Locating Colonial Subjects of Anthropology." pp. 1-52. In Pels, Peter and Oscar Salemink (eds.), op.cit.

Pfeffer, Georg. 1970. *Pariagruppen des Pandschab.* Munich: Renner.

____. 1976. *Puris Sasana Dörfer. Basis einer regionalen Elite.* Unpubl. Post-doctoral Thesis. Ruprecht Karl University of Heidelberg.

Rosaldo Renato. 1980. *Ilongot Headhunting 1883-1974. A Study of Society and History.* Stanford: Stanford University Press.

Sahlins, Marshall D. 1968. *Tribesmen.* Englewood Cliffs.

____. 1999. "Two or Three Things that I Know About Culture." *Journal of the Royal Anthropological Institute* 5 (3): 399-421.

Silverwood-Cope, P. 1972. *A Contribution to the Ethnography of the Columbian Makú.* Unpubl. Ph.D. Thesis, University of Cambridge.

Strathern, Marilyn 1992. "Parts and wholes: Refiguring relationships in a post-plural world." pp. 75-104. In Adam Kuper (ed.): *Conceptionalizing Society.* London: Routledge.

Thurston, Edgar. 1907. *Ethnographic Notes in Southern India,* Part II. Reprinted 1975 by Cosmo Publications.

Vitebsky, Piers. 1993. *Dialogues with the Dead. The Discussion of Mortality among the Sora of Eastern India.* Cambridge: Cambridge University Press.

White, Leslie A. 1959. "Introduction," in L.H. Morgan: *The Indian Journals 1859-62* (edited with an introduction by L.A. White) Ann Arbor: University of Michigan Press.

Woodburn, James. 1982.; Egalitarian Societies. *Man* (NS) 17: 431-51.

Yorke, Michael P. 1976. *Decisions and Analysis. Political Structure and Discourse Among the Ho tribals of India.* Ph.D. Thesis submitted to the School of Oriental and African Studies: University of London.

NOTES ON CONTRIBUTORS

Behera, Deepak Kumar is Professor and Head of the Department of Anthropology, Sambalpur University. He obtained his Master's degree (Gold Medallist) and Ph.D. from Sambalpur University, where he has been teaching Anthropology since 1985. He was a Fulbright Visiting Professor at the Dept. of Human Development, California State University, Long Beach during the fall semester, 2007. He has more than 80 research publications in reputed journals and edited volumes. Prof. Behera has authored/edited a total number of eighteen volumes. Of those eight are jointly with Prof. Georg Pfeffer of Institute of Ethnology of Free University of Berlin (Germany). He has successfully completed a dozen of research projects funded by national bodies like UGC, ICSSR, Ministry of Welfare, National Literacy Mission Authorities, Winrock International, Shastri Foundation Fellowship etc. Dr. Behera has participated in more than a dozen international conferences held in Mexico, Germany, Belgium, Sweden, Israel, Denmark, USA, UK, South Africa, China, Japan, Italy, Norway, Brasil, Singapore and has lectured at different universities and research institutes there. He was the editor of the journal—*Journal of Social Sciences* from 1997 to 2002. Prof. Behera is a member of the Executive Board of International Union of Anthropological and Ethnological Sciences (IUAES) for the period 1998-2008. He is the Chairperson of the IUAES Commission on Anthropology of Children, Youth and Childhood. Professor Behera has been recently elected as a member of the Permanent Council of IUAES. He was also the Officer-at-Large of the International Sociological Association Research Committee-53-Sociology of Childhood for the session 1998-2005. He is a member of the International Advisory Board of the Journal—*Sociological Analysis* (North Carolina, USA) and also a member of the Editorial Board of Global Gutter Press (Cambridge, UK). He has successfully guided 12 Ph.D. and more than thirty M.Phil scholars. Prof. Behera is the Director of the Institute of Evaluation, Research, Documentation and Training. His current interests in research are tribal and childhood studies.

Mailing Address: Head, Department of Anthropology
Sambalpur University
Sambalpur-768 019
Orissa
INDIA
Email: <behera.dk@gmail.com>

Berger, Peter studied Social and Cultural Anthropology at the Free University of Berlin where he obtained his Ph.D. and worked as lecturer and research assistant. He is currently lecturer of Indian Religions and the Anthropology of Religion at the University of Groningen, the Netherlands. His extended research has been conducted in tribal highland Orissa (India) and focused on the topics of social structure, ritual/sacrifice and food. A new interest are the Atharvaveda Brahmans of Orissa.

Mailing Address: Faculty of Theology and Religious Studies, RUG
Oude Boteringestraat 38
9712 GK Groningen
THE NETHERLANDS
Email: <P.Berger@rug.nl>

Das, N.K. (b. 1949) holds Master's Degree in Social Anthropology (Raipur) and Ph.D. in Anthropology (Gauhati University). As the senior social anthropologist in the Anthropological Survey of India, he has conducted intensive village studies and also guided research teams. He also acted as National Coordinators of projects on "Stratification among the Tribes", "People of India", "Study of the Syncretism in India" and "People of India: Cultural Diversity—Indigenous Knowledge Systems". Dr. Das has coordinated several international seminars and participated in them in India and abroad. Dr. Das has published over one hundred research papers in reputed national and international journals. His major books include *Ethnic Identity, Ethnicity, and Social Stratification* (1989); *Kinship, Politics and Law in Naga Society* (1993); *Anthropology of Weaker Sections* (1993), *Pre-Agricultural Communities of India* (1993), *Nagaland, People of India* (1994); *Culture,*

Religion and Critical Studies in Syncretism (2003); *and Identity, Cultural Pluralism and State in South Asia* (2008), *Tribes, Cultural Adaptations and Belief Systems* (2008) *and Stratification among tribes of India* (In Press). Dr. Das is Chief-Editor of the *Journal of Social Anthropology,* and Managing Editor of the *Journal Human Science,* The Journal of the Anthropological Survey of India.

Mailing Address: Dr. N.K. Das
Anthropological Survey of India
56, Russa Road (East)
First Lane , Tollygunge
Kolkata-700033
West Bengal
INDIA
Email: <nkdas49@gmail.com>

Demmer, Ulrich (born 1956) obtained his Ph.D. in Anthropology at the South Asia Institute, University of Heidelberg in 1993 and his post-doctoral Habilitation in 2001 in the University of Munich with his thesis bearing the title *Ritual and the Rhetorical Tradition of the Jēnu Kurrumba (South India).* At present he is conducting a research project on "Visual Culture" at the Department of Anthropology, University of Munich. His current interests in research are South Asia, ritual theories, oral traditions and social memory, anthropology of praxis, rhetorical theory of culture. Dr. Demmer was also associated with the Orissa Research Programme of the German Research Foundation and conducted fieldwork in the tribal belt of Southern Orissa.

Mailing Address: Institut fuer Voelkerkunde und Afrikanistik
Universitaet Munchen
Oettingenstr.67
80538 Munich
GERMANY
Email: <Ulrich.Demmer@t-online.de>

Erasmus, Piet is professor in Anthropology at the University of the Free State, Bloemfontein, South Africa. In addition to his teaching and research obligations, he also serves as the Programme Director for Culture Studies and BA Studies; is responsible for the Faculty of Humanity's Community Service; is the Interim Cluster Coordinator for the multidisciplinary research cluster

"Transformation in Highly Diverse Societies" and is the head of the Unit for Khoekhoe and San Studies. Some of his key areas of interest are identity discourse, cultural and ethnic revitalisation, and land issues. He has conducted fieldwork on all of these topics and has published various articles in accredited journals, research reports, chapters in books, as well as some books too.

Mailing Address: Department of Anthropology
University of the Free State
P. O. Box 339, Bloemfontein 9300
REPUBLIC OF SOUTH AFRICA
Email: <erasmusp.hum@ufs.ac.za>

Gangadharam, V. is professor of Social Anthropology in the Department of Anthropology, Sri Venkateswara University, Tirupati, Andhra Pradesh. He studied Social Cultural Anthropology for post-graduate degree from SriVenkateswara University. He joined the department as lecturer in 1985. His Ph.D. reseach is conducted among the Chenchu a food gathering and hunting tribe of Andhra Pradesh. He was awarded Ph.D. Degree for his work on Fertility Behaviour among the Chenchus by Sri Venkateswara University. He also worked as Research Associate at Indian Institute of Management, Ahmadebad from 1981 to 1985. His Research interests include Traditional Resource Management Systems, indigenous knowledge, medical anthropology and poverty. He has conducted field studies among the Chenchu, the Konda Reddy, the Koya, the Savara and other tribes of Andhra Pradesh. Currently he is working on an Impact Study of Special Economic Zones, and Pre-evaluation study of Female Condoms in Andhra Pradesh. He has published two books and several Research Articles in Reputed Journals. He is a member of Indian Anthropological Association, New Delhi. He has conducted eight research projects on various subjects like Irrigation projects, Non-Timber Forest Produce, Indigenous Water Harvesting, Tank Irrigation, Rituals of Rain and Irrigation etc. He has conducted a National Seminar on Ethno Hydrology and Hydro Mythology and Socially Sanctioned Ritual Prostitution.

Mailing Address: Department of Anthropology
Sri Venkateswara University
Tirupati – 517 502
Andhra Pradesh
INDIA
Email: <ganges_v@yahoo.com>

Gregory, Chris is a Reader in Social Anthropology in the Department of Archaeology and Anthropology at the Australian National University. He taught Economics at the University of Papua New Guinea from 1973 to 1975 where he developed an interest in anthropology and obtained a Ph.D. from Cambridge University. This was published in 1982 as *Gifts and Commodities*. From 1979 to 1982 he held research fellowships at Clare Hall, Cambridge, and in the Anthropology Department at the London School of Economics. He began fieldwork in Bastar District, India, in 1982 and has been a regular visitor to the area since then. Initial work focused on the rural marketing system but latter research has focused on the political economy and culture of rice as expressed in the Lachmi Jagar epic women sing and ritually enact. He has published a number of books and articles on this fieldwork as well as on more general questions of economy and kinship. He is on the editorial board of a *Social Analysis and Contributions to Indian Sociology* and has held visiting professorships in Berlin, Kyoto and Manchester.

Mailing Address: School of Archaeology and Anthropology
Faculty of Arts
Australian National University
Canberra, ACT
AUSTRALIA
Email: <chris.gregory@anu.edu.au>

Hardenberg, Roland is presently Associate Professor at the Institute of Ethnology and Cultural Anthropology at the University of Tuebingen, Germany. He received his Ph.D. from the Free University of Berlin with a thesis dealing with the renewal (*nabakalebara*) of the deities of the Jagannatha temple in the Hindu pilgrimage town of Puri. His post-doctoral thesis entitled "*Children of the Orissa Goddess: Society, Sacrifice and Marriage in the Highlands of Orissa*", was accepted as post-doctoral state degree by the University of Muenster, Germany. Recently, he has begun a new research project dealing with funeral sites and practices in post-socialist Kyrgyzstan.

Mailing Address: Institute of Ethnology and Cultural Anthropology
University of Tuebingen
Schloss
72070
GERMANY
Email: <hardenberg@gmx.de>

Narahari, Samudrala is a Professor in Anthropology at Andhra University, Visakhapatnam, Andhra Pradesh, India since1998. He joined the Department in 1984 as Assistant Professor and later promoted as Associate Professor in the same Deptt. in 1990. He obtained his Master Degree (M.Sc.) in Anthropology from Sri Venkateswara University, Tirupati , Andhra Pradesh, India in 1977 and got awarded Doctor of Philosophy (Ph.D.) from the same university in 1983 for his work on a nomadic tribe "The Yerukala" covering Socio-Cultural and Biological aspects. He has conducted fieldwork during his Masters Degree Programme on a nomadic tribe, *viz.*, The Nakkalas or Kurivikkaran in the fringe districts of Tamil Nadu and Andhra Pradesh States, India. He also studied some of the nomadic tribes like the Chenchu, the Challa Yanadi of Andhra Pradesh during his Post-Doctoral Programme at S.V. University, Tirupati from 1983-1985, *i.e.* till joining as faculty member in Andhra University, Visakhapatnam. He is interested to study Social Structure and Mating Patterns in several tribal groups since 1977. He has done Post Graduate Diploma in Statistics in 1978 from S.V. University, Tirupati. He is being conducting extensive and intensive fieldwork on several Primitive Tribal groups in North-Coastal Andhra Pradesh. He published as many as 75 research papers in both International and National reputed journals. He has also visited USA sponsored by Andhra University during April/June, 2005 to learn techniques in Molecular Anthropology, *i.e.*, DNA. He has participated in about 30 Conferences (both national and international) and presented several papers in social and biological anthropological aspects on nomadic, semi-nomadic and primitive tribal groups of Andhra Pradesh. He has been teaching ethnography, demography and population genetics at Post-Graduate, M.Phil. and Ph.D. levels. He has completed a Major Research Project on " 'Habits and Reproduction' in Primitive Tribal groups from North-Coastal Andhra Pradesh," sponsored by University Grants Commission, New Delhi (Rs. 7.50 lakhs) during 2005-2007. Recently he has got another Major Research Project on Metabolic Syndrome in Pediatric populations of different cultures which is also sponsored by the U.G.C., New Delhi and to be commenced from April, 2008.

Mailing Address: Department of Anthropology
Andhra University
Visakhapatnam-530 003
Andhra Pradesh
INDIA
Email: <narahari_samudrala@yahoo.co.in>

Otten, Tina is lecturer for Social Anthropology at Ruhr University, Bochum (Faculty of Social Sciences, School for Social Psychology and Social Anthropology) since 2007. Her fields of interest include medical anthropology, myth, ritual and gender issues. She obtained her Ph.D. from the Institute of Ethnology at the Free University of Berlin. The title of her Ph.D. is "Heilung durch Rituale. Vom Umgang mit Krankheit bei den Rona im Hochland Orissas, Indien" (Healing through rituals: concepts of health and illness among the Rona of Highland Orissa, India). In addition to her research on medical concepts she has conducted research on oral epics and fertility rituals in India, especially on the ritual cycle of *Bali Jatra.* Both research projects were funded by German Research Council (DFG) from 1999 till 2006.

Mailing Address: Dr. Tina Otten
Ruhr University Bochum
Faculty of Social Sciences
Social Psychology and Social Anthropology
GB 04/146
Universitätsstraße 150
44780 Bochum
GERMANY
Email: tina.otten@gmx.de

Pfeffer, Georg is professor of social anthropology in the Institute of Ethnology at the Free University of Berlin since 1985. He studied ethnology, sociology and history of religions at Freiburg University, Germany, where he obtained his doctoral degree in 1970 with a thesis on *Paria groups of the Panjab*. His post-doctoral thesis of Habilitation at the University of Heidelberg bore the title: *Puri's Sasana Villages: Basis of a Regional Elite*. In 1971 he was appointed Assistant Professor at the South Asia Institute of University of Heidelberg where he was promoted to the position of an Associate Professor in 1979. He has conducted fieldwork for several years in various parts of India and Pakistan. Since 1980 Prof. Pfeffer has undertaken numerous extended excursions to the Middle India Tribes. In addition to his teaching and research obligations in Berlin, he is an active member of several national and international academic societies and on the editorial board of the German *Zeitschrift Fur Ethnologie*. Prof. Pfeffer has published a number of articles in reputed international journals. He has brought out seven edited volumes on tribal studies jointly with Prof. D.K. Behera of Sambalpur University, India. Religious cults and kinship structures of the Scheduled Tribes in the Koraput and Phulbani districts of Orissa (India) are Prof. Pfeffer's key areas of interest.

Mailing Address: Institute of Ethnology
Free University of Berlin
Landoltweg 9-11
14195 Berlin
GERMANY
Email: <gpfeffer@gmx.com.

Ratha, S.N. (b.1936) got his Ph.D. degree from Gauhati University. He served Gauhati University from 1963 to 1976 as a Lecturer/Reader. He joined as Professor in Department of Anthropology, Sambalpur University and continued there till his retirement. He was the Vice-President of Ethnographic Folk Culture Society and Institute of Social Research and Applied Anthropology, Calcutta. He is the life member of Indian Science Congress Association, Indian Sociological Association, Indian Anthropological Association, Anthropological Society of North-East India, North-East Council for Social Science Research, Institute of Applied Anthropology and Social Research, Ethnographic and Folk Culture Society of India, Orissa Environmental Consciousness Society, Indian Anthropological Society and Associate of Current Anthropology and member of Editorial Board of the journal *Man and Life*. He has successfully completed a number of projects funded by National Institute of Urban Affairs, New Delhi (NUA) and ICSSR. He has successfully guided 16 Ph.D. dissertations. He has authored two books and edited two books. He has published more than 60 research papers in different edited volumes and journals on topics like caste, community and village studies, marriage and kinship, applied and development anthropology and paleo-anthropology. He has presented papers and chaired various sessions in different national and international conferences. He was the Chairman P.G. Council, Dean of Faculty of Arts and Director of Employment Bureau, member of Senate, Syndicate, and Advisory Council of Sambalpur University. He is the member of Advisory Board of Tribal and Harijan Research-cum-Training Institute, Orissa, State Advisory Board of Prison Administration, Board of Governors, REC, Rourkela, Board of Management, UCE, Burla and Advisory Council, Academy of Tribal Dialects and Culture, Bhubaneswar. At the national level he is the member of National Committee to Assess the Impact of Industrialization in Tribal Areas, Advisory Board, Department of Special Assistance in Anthropology, Ranchi, Advisory Committee to Review the Progress of Bench Mark Survey of Socio-economic Conditions of Bihar and Orissa, Advisory Committee, Anthropological Survey of India, Educational, Research and Innovations Committee (National Council of Educational

Research and Training). His areas of interest are caste studies, village studies, tribal studies and development studies.

Mailing Address: B 101 Solanki's Gulmohar
Brahmanwada
Begumpet
Hyderabad-500 016
INDIA
Email: <snratha@redifmail.com>

Rubel, Paula G. is Professor Emerita at Barnard College and Columbia University where she taught from 1965 to 1998. She specialized in Cultural Anthropology at Columbia University where she obtained her doctoral degree in 1963. Her dissertation *The Kalmyk Mongols: A Study in Continuity and Change* was published as Vol. 64, Indiana University Publications, Uralic and Altaic Series. She was appointed as an Assistant Professor at Barnard College, Columbia University in 1966, promoted to Associate Professor in 1970 and Full Professor in 1974. She conducted fieldwork with Abraham Rosman in Iran and Afghanistan in 1971, mainland Papua New Guinea in 1975 and New Ireland in 1987. She has been the recipient of many grants from the National Institutes of Health, the National Science Foundation and the Social Science Foundation and fellowships including a Guggenhim Fellowship. She is an active member of national as well as international organizations and is a Fellow of the Royal Anthropological Institute. She has co-authored *Feasting with Mine Enemy: Rank and Exchange among Northwest Coast Societies, Your Own Pigs You May Not Eat: A Comparative Study of New Guinea Societies, The Tapestry of Culture and Translating Cultures: Perspectives on Translation and Anthropology*, eds. as well as many scholarly articles with Abraham Rosman.

Mailing Address: 560 Riverside Drive, 18P
New York, N.Y. 10027
USA
Email: <pgr4@columbia.edu>

Rosman, Abraham is Professor Emeritus at Barnard College and Columbia University where he taught from 1962 until 1998. His doctorate was obtained from Yale University in 1962 and was based on fieldwork among the Kanuri of Bornu Province, in Northern Nigeria. He taught at Vassar College, Antioch

College and Yale University before coming to Columbia University in 1962. He became an Associate Professor in 1966, and a Full Professor in 1970. Together with Paula G. Rubel, he carried out field research in Iran, Afghanistan, Papua New Guinea and New Ireland. He has received grants from the Ford Foundation, the National Science Foundation, and The Social Science Research Council, and a Fellowship from the Guggenheim Foundation. Along with articles in various journals, he co-authored with Paula G. Rubel *Feasting with Mine Enemy: Rank and Exchange among Northwest Coast Societies*, a comparative analysis of the potlatch in six societies. Their article on the potlatch in the *American Anthropologist* was selected among the best articles in that journal from 1970 to 1990. They co-authored *Your Own Pigs You May Not Eat*: A Comparative Study of New Guinea Societies, and edited together Translating Cultures: Perspectives on Translation and Anthropology. They have also co-authored a popular introductory text book entitled *The Tapestry of Culture* which is going into its ninth edition.

Mailing Address: 560 Riverside Drive, 18P
New York, N.Y. 10027
USA
Email: <pgr4@columbia.edu>

Skoda, Uwe is an Assistant Professor, South Asian Studies, at the Aarhus University, Denmark. He currently works on transformations of kingship and the state in Middle India. He was a Fellow of the DFG Research Program "Cultural Encounters and the Discourses of Scholarship" at the Rostock University, Germany. He studied social anthropology, political science and history at the Free University of Berlin, Germany, at the Humboldt University of Berlin, Germany and the Brunel University of West London, UK. In 2003 he obtained his doctoral degree with a thesis on *The Aghria: A Peasant Caste on a Tribal Frontier* (Delhi: Manohar Publishers, 2005). Currently he is conducting a post-doctoral research on the transformation of kingship in Middle India in an historico-anthropological perspective. After being a member of the Orissa Research Project (ORP) funded by the German Research Council (DFG) from 2000 to 2004, he joined the Institute of Ethnology, Free University of Berlin, as a Lecturer in Anthropology from 2004 to 2006. Apart from his extensive field research in Middle/Central India, he is also an editor of the web-based South Asia Information Network *suedasien.info*. Studies in kinship and kingship, Indian politics as well as visual anthropology are his major research interests.

Mailing Address: Dr. Uwe Skoda
Assistant Professor
South Asian Studies
Aarhus University
DENMARK
Email: <skoda@gmx.com>

Suryanarayan, M. did his post-graduation and Ph.D. from Andhra University. He worked for his Ph.D. on a primitive tribal community (Saoras). He has published six books and more than 50 research articles. In the capacity of Senior Research Fellow in Anthropological Survey of India, he conducted an in-depth study on the marine fisher folk of Andhra Pradesh. He also worked as Research Assistant in Telugu Academy between 1971 and 1972. He joined the Deptt. of Anthropology, Sri Venkateswara University, Tirupati as a Lecturer in July 1972. He was a Professor when he retired from the Department. He is a member of the Advisory Board of *Journal of Social Sciences.* His current interest in research is sociology of gerontology.

Mailing Address: Deptt. of Anthropology
S.V. University
Tirupati-517 502
Andhra Pradesh
INDIA
Email: <profsurya@msn.com>

INDEX